Wild Things

Wild Things:
Nature and the Social Imagination

Edited by

William Beinart, Karen Middleton
and Simon Pooley

The White Horse Press

The White Horse Press, 10 High Street, Knapwell, Cambridge, CB23 4NR, UK

Set in 10 point Adobe Garamond Pro
Printed by Lightning Source

British Library Cataloguing in Publication Data
A catalogue record for this book is available from the British Library

ISBN   978-1-874267-75-1 (HB)
ISBN   978-1-874267-93-5 (PB)

Contents

List of Illustrations

List of Illustrations

List of Illustrations

Preface and Acknowledgements

This collection has evolved from a one-day conference on Wild Things: 'Nature' and the Social Imagination, held at St Antony's College, Oxford on 16 September 2011, under the auspices of the European Society for Environmental History (ESEH) and the European Association for Environmental History (UK). Twenty-eight researchers, grouped into six panels, presented recent work on cultural histories of the natural world. In selecting papers for this volume we have focused on contributions that appeared to us to make substantive and original contributions to environmental history in diverse fields. All address cultural aspects of environmental history, focusing on different social imaginations about nature. The chapters are also of interest for their geographical range, from Britain and Europe to North America and Africa – all areas in which environmental history is well developed as a field.

We would like to thank the contributors for their patience and especially Sarah Johnson of White Horse Press for her commitment to the collection, her encouragement and her work in guiding it towards publication.

Introduction

Wild Things: Nature and the Social Imagination

William Beinart, Karen Middleton and Simon Pooley

Nature, Culture and the Social Imagination

The natural world has been central not only to human survival and subsistence but to human culture. The folk narratives and stories fundamental to many societies featured elements of nature and non-human actors. Natural environments played key roles in the extraordinarily diverse everyday cultural lives that have evolved around finding food and shelter. In the religious sphere animals have acted as symbols and metaphors for the divine, as well as objects of worship and a means for communication with gods through sacrifice. Particular places, such as forests, groves and mountains, have long been imbued with sacred status. Landscapes and animals have been important subjects of art and literature across most human societies. The natural environment has informed national identity, from Rome's wolf-mother to the British oak. Our collection touches on such cultural representations of nature.

This book addresses a relatively narrow realm of cultural expression – the way that modern people have imagined and experienced nature over the last couple of centuries. Yet, these examples alert us to the potential for such forms of expression and imagination. They assist us to recognise the extraordinarily diverse ways in which human imaginations work around elements of the natural world.

Environmental history as a sub-discipline since the 1970s has focused on western conceptualisations of nature – arguably this was initially its strongest strand.[1] Historians working within this framework analysed the multiple meanings of nature and emphasised the significance of landscape, environment and wilderness in western thought. These studies showed that western societies – or at least the intellectuals and scientists on whom they largely focus – did not simply turn

---

1. Peter Coates, *Nature: Western Attitudes since Ancient Times* (Cambridge: Polity Press, 1998) for an overview. Key texts were Clarence Glacken, *Traces on the Rhodian Shore: Nature and Culture in Western Thought from Ancient Times to the End of the Eighteenth Century* (Berkeley: University of California Press, 1967); Roderick Nash, *Wilderness and the American Mind* (New Haven: Yale University Press, 1973); Donald Worster, *Nature's Economy: A History of Ecological Ideas* (New York: Cambridge University Press, 1977); Max Oelschlaeger, *The Idea of Wilderness: From Prehistory to the Age of Ecology* (New Haven: Yale University Press, 1991).

William Beinart, Karen Middleton and Simon Pooley

away from nature, nor separate ideas of nature and culture, in their long quest to understand and control their environments.

True, for the last couple of centuries, an increasing percentage of western people have lived in urban industrial contexts, mesmerised by people-centred religions and ideologies and gradually more distant from daily interaction with nature, wild places and animals (especially wild animals). The natural world was, for many engaged in economic production, whether in forests, fisheries or factories, a set of resources to dominate and exploit. Yet environmental historians record that culture did not entirely merge into an obsession with the human condition isolated from nature. There were frequent counterflows. Nature was a central concern, in the sciences and arts, for both enlightenment and Victorian thinkers, at the very time when the industrial revolution was transforming their societies.

Jardine, Secord and Spary do, however, detect a fundamental shift in scientific thinking since the Victorian era. With respect to early modern Britain, they argue for 'the importance of the roles assigned to natural history in the commonwealth of learning: as a universal discipline, prior to political, social and moral order'.[2] They see a long slow change so that 'today [1996] natural history seems marginal to our concerns, appearing primarily as an amateur, popular local study'. The cutting edge of scientific thinking increasingly lay elsewhere, they suggest, in the laboratory or in theories of the invisible world, rather than the visible observable world. Understanding the germ and the gene displaced older concerns of natural history while at the same time explanations of the human order have become fundamentally social and economic. The key turning point, for them, was the late nineteenth century.

Yet perhaps environmental historians have shown that even in the realm of science, nature was not so decisively cut out. Environmental sciences, such as forestry, ecology, ethology, climatology and marine biology, all came to maturity at different periods in the twentieth century.[3] Industry and empire prompted conservationist sciences, ideas and practices.[4] Western environmentalism was partly rooted in such sciences and a direct response to agrarian capitalism and the commodification of nature. By the late twentieth century, contemplating relations between humans and their environment became a central preoccupation, manifest in such areas as climate science, in the multidisciplinary concerns of environmentalists and in a resurgence of interest in indigenous or local knowledge. The natural world consistently found not only scholars, but protagonists, in twentieth century human societies. In sum, Radkau observes, the environmental history of the industrial age would be unjus-

---

2.   N. Jardine, J.A. Secord and E.C. Spary (eds.) *Cultures of Natural History* (Cambridge: Cambridge University Press, 1996), p. 3.

3.   Peter J. Bowler, *The Fontana History of the Environmental Sciences* (London: Fontana Press, 1992).

4.   Richard Grove, *Green Imperialism: Colonial Expansion, Tropical Island Edens and the Origins of Environmentalism, 1600–1860* (Cambridge: Cambridge University Press, 1995); William Beinart and Lotte Hughes, *Environment and Empire* (Oxford: Oxford University Press, 2007).

tifiably predictable if we read it simply as a victory for those who exploited natural resources over those who sought to live with them and protect them.[5]

Beyond the scientific sphere, environmental history as a field has been a small component of such intellectual reassertions. As noted, one strong strand has focused largely on the history of ideas. This often included elements of the history of science because science was so central in interpretations of nature. There is now a reasonably dense literature on the history of western intellectual ideas and, increasingly, of western and colonial ideas about non-western environments.[6] Landscape in western art is a deeply researched field, as is natural history and botanical painting.[7] Our collection grows from this literature, travels some less frequented routes and explores elements of popular culture as well as scientific and intellectual histories. While there are many exceptions, especially in the extra-European world, environmental history thus far has probably been more concerned with intellectual history and with the history of the natural sciences than with the popular imagination.

Industrialisation stimulated not only modern conservationism, and new ways of seeing natural environments, but also new technologies for representing nature. This collection includes essays on popular illustrated literature, photography, film and tourism – all-important vehicles for social imaginations of nature. Audiences for images of nature expanded with literacy, both in print and visual media. Arguably, the popular culture of modern environmentalism was deeply influenced by this increasingly global visual imagination.[8]

Nature and non-human actors have played diverse roles in popular imaginations. In respect of wild animals, especially predators, fear was often a primary response. As Simon Pooley illustrates in his chapter, crocodiles in South Africa provoked both fear and loathing and similar sentiments sometimes helped to seal the fate of wolves, coyotes, bears and other species in many parts of the world. More often, perhaps, nature served symbolically for more benign forces. Raymond Williams posited that in the British imagination, the countryside represented 'a natural way of life: of peace, innocence, and simple virtue'.[9] In an industrial world, nostalgia for the past centred on the village and the country as a natural, organic realm in contrast to urban industrial society perceived to be in crisis. It was figured

---

5. Joachim Radkau, *Nature and Power: A Global History of the Environment* (Cambridge: Cambridge University Press, 2008), p. 35.

6. Grove, *Green Imperialism*; David Arnold, *The Problem of Nature: Environment, Culture and European Expansion* (Oxford: Blackwell, 1996).

7. Simon Schama, *Landscape and Memory* (London: Fontana, 1996); Malcolm Andrews, *Landscape and Western Art* (Oxford: Oxford University Press, 1999); David Freedberg, *The Eye of the Lynx: Galileo, His Friends and the Beginning of Modern Natural History* (Chicago: University of Chicago Press, 2003).

8. William Beinart and Katie McKeown, 'Wildlife Media and Representations of Africa, 1950s to the 1970s', *Environmental History* 14/3 (2009): 429–452.

9. Raymond Williams, *The Country and the City* (St Albans: Paladin, 1975), p. 9.

William Beinart, Karen Middleton and Simon Pooley

as a world of independent and honourable men as well as an attractive environment. For American environmentalists also, from Henry David Thoreau to Aldo Leopold, nature was a benign force, a world of moral order, an antidote to commodification.

Wild Things, the Wild and Wilderness

Whereas European social imaginations of nature concentrated more on cultivated landscapes made by humans, or 'nature as landscape', American conservationist intellectuals of the later nineteenth and early twentieth century celebrated the idea of wilderness.[10] In some senses, their benign nature was the antithesis of an agrarian world; in it non-human species were dominant and people should intrude only as visitors or caretakers.[11] It was a world to be protected from humans. Theirs was a celebratory understanding of wilderness which has arguably helped to underpin a significant strand in western ideas.

Yet recent analyses in environmental history have been far more critical of the way that wilderness has been deployed as a concept in modern environmentalism. In African Studies particularly, the idea of wilderness has been construed negatively as helping to promote what Adams and McShane called the *Myth of Wild Africa*.[12] Ideas of wilderness, in the United States and Africa, are seen to deny occupation by indigenous people, diminish their role in shaping past environments and justify strategies of conservation that exclude them and marginalise their environmental concerns and needs.[13] Such analyses aim to deconstruct wilderness in the context of a mounting critique of conservationist interventions. Influential books such as Roderick Neumann's *Imposing Wilderness* (2002) argue that the so-called natural habitats which conservationists campaign to preserve by reservation have in fact been used, managed and shaped by people over long periods of time. In 2011 the BBC screened an important three-part series called *Unnatural Histories*, which traces the history of human agency in shaping iconic protected areas, such as Serengeti and Yellowstone. Critiques of the idea of wilderness are clearly moving from the groves of academic debate to the mainstream media that is usually much more

---

10. Coates, *Nature*.

11. Nash, *Wilderness and the American Mind*; Donald Worster, *A Passion for Nature: The Life of John Muir* (New York: Oxford University Press, 2008).

12. J.S. Adams and T.D. McShane, *The Myth of Wild Africa: Conservation Without Illusion* (Berkeley: University of California Press, 1997).

13. William Cronon, 'The Trouble with Wilderness or, Getting Back to the Wrong Nature', *Environmental History* 1/1 (1996); Roderick P. Neumann, *Imposing Wilderness: Struggles Over Livelihood and Nature Preservation in Africa* (Berkeley: University of California Press, 2002); Dan Brockington, *Fortress Conservation: The Preservation of the Mkomazi Game Reserve, Tanzania* (Oxford: James Currey, 2002); Jan Bender Shetler, *Imagining Serengeti: a History of Landscape Memory in Serengeti from the Earliest Times to the Present* (Athens OH: Ohio University Press, 2007); Ramachandra Guha, *Environmentalism: A Global History* (London: Longman, 2000).

Introduction

sympathetic to depicting unpeopled wilderness. Much of David Attenborough's filming, for example, has omitted people in nature. This is largely the case even in his sumptuously filmed new series called *Africa* (2013). But in the last episode, the team made an explicit attempt to include local people in debates about conservation.

This line of thinking has produced a more accurate history of wildernesses and been a valuable corrective to any notion of empty lands. It has contributed to some recognition of the rights of indigenous and local people to land that they once occupied. Yet the negative construction of the notion of wilderness – a result of particular arguments in political ecology – perhaps leaves us bereft of an important idea, and one that still has value. Environmental historians such as Nash, who were both analysts and protagonists of wilderness, recognised from the start that it was necessarily a managed area. There is an argument to be made for the value of concepts of wilderness, of wild places and wild things as more positive, exciting and universal notions.[14] These ideas and images are in common usage and we can explore their complex history; this is an important purpose of our collection. Such routes of travel, as well as some of the older critiques, are evident in some of the papers in this collection. Wilderness was often invoked in an ambivalent sense, as a carrier of awe and power but also of inspiration. In his chapter on images of German forests in popular literature, Johannes Zechner shows them perceived both as forbidding and as central to some versions of national identity. Tyler Cornelius explores the Columbia river as a carrier of elemental forces, a threat to human civilisation and order, but also as an exciting and treasured landscape.

The wildness perceived to lie in humans – often associated with animal characteristics – carries a similar ambiguous freight. The Troggs' song, *Wild Thing*, from which we borrowed the title of this collection, has only a few lines, which are suggestive rather than explicit.[15] Yet they seemed to conjure, in the febrile imagination of some young men in the 1960s, the excitement of natural, perhaps animal, rather than feminine or demure, qualities in a young woman. The metaphor of wildness extends the idea of elemental forces in nature to humans and captures their excitement as part of human sexuality – it is the 'animal' quality in human physiognomy and behaviour that can give a frisson to human interaction. Maurice Sendak's *Where the Wild Things Are* illustrates some of the same strands.[16] It follows the imaginative leap of a child, via a wolf costume, into a world beyond the human order, where wild things roam. The child is able to transpose himself into this sphere of excitement, establish himself as its king, and enter into an exciting anarchy. (He is, however, happy to sacrifice this world to return for his supper.) Here the imagination runs beyond nature as experienced, to nature as fantasised,

---

14. Beinart and McKeown, 'Wildlife Media'.
15. The Troggs, *Wild Thing* (1966), written by Chip Taylor.
16. Maurice Sendak, *Where the Wild Things Are* (New York: Harper and Row, 1963).

William Beinart, Karen Middleton and Simon Pooley

but it is still a positive fantasy based partly around wildness – as a condition to visit if not to inhabit.

Perhaps if we accept that wilderness and wild things no longer exist in an absolute sense, without any human history, if we accept that conservationists have produced in part new, rather than simply preserved, old wildernesses, we can free ourselves from some of the negative views of wilderness as exclusion. Those not schooled in the debates about the environmental history of Africa and the United States sometimes unselfconsciously do so. At the St Antony's conference Dick Mayon-White used the term wilderness to describe projects along the Thames river in England, where development and settlement was being controlled, indigenous species were being restored and public access protected. He did not, of course, mean that wolves and bears were being reintroduced. His usage of the word was contested during the discussion, because it was so controlled and partial a version of wilderness. Yet he thought of the idea in an unproblematically positive way, as a relative concept and as a public good. The fishermen would lose out, as also those seeking to moor boats, but arguably this was a gain for society as a whole. If we accept that wildernesses are in part a product of human intervention and shaped anthropogenically in some way – and that modern conceptions of wilderness are necessarily shaped by social imaginations – more complex meanings can be explored. As noted, some of the essays in the collection make a small contribution to doing so. We contend the inescapability of wild things and wilderness in the human imagination; these are concepts that always carry political meanings, but they need not simply be about dispossession.

Visual History

The first group of papers are excursions into visual elements of environmental history. As noted, visual representations of nature proliferated with new technology. They clearly became accessible to a rapidly expanding range of people, especially in western societies, and they enabled animals and landscapes to be imagined in different ways. It is tempting to make an argument for their particular power as vehicles of knowledge about nature and animals – and hence their capacity to influence public perceptions of nature.

In her chapter Karen Jones develops the historiography of hunting and photography by analysing their intertwined relations in the late nineteenth century United States. Since Susan Sontag's famous analogy between shooting with the gun and the camera, literature has connected these two forms of human interaction with wildlife.[17] The implication is generally that similar relations of power and agency

---

17. Susan Sontag, *On Photography* (Harmondsworth: Penguin, 1979); James R. Ryan, *Picturing Empire: Photography and the Visualization of the British Empire* (London: Reaktion, 1997); Gregg Mitman, *Reel Nature: America's Romance with Wildlife on Film* (Cambridge, Mass.: Harvard University Press,

were at work. In colonial contexts, for example, wildlife and indigenous people are both seen as objects and victims of this agency. But there is still limited material on the relationship between guns and cameras in specific contexts. Jones follows sportsmen who hunted and took photographs in the American West. She focuses especially on the nomenclature of photography on the game trail. She uses Donna Haraway's idea about the 'politics of reproduction' to analyse how photographs were staged, for example framing the animal adversary with the stalwart hunter hero.[18] Images also celebrated the technology used in environmental transformation. The language of shooting, loading and capture underlined an intriguing coincidence between the gun and the camera as active technologies wielded by the nineteenth-century sportsman. But Jones also departs from the analogy, exploring the way in which photography gradually became associated with animal appreciation and conservation; some hunters gave up the kill entirely in favour of a non-consumptive use of wildlife. Ultimately 'hunting with the camera' had a different impact. Such a trajectory was by no means confined to North America.[19] Jones both gives specific historical context and content to the analogy of gun and camera and notes its limits.

Beinart and Schafer connect visual culture in the west with Africa. They explore representations of African landscape, wildlife and related social contexts in Hollywood feature films. They take issue with authors who suggest that the Africa depicted in film is simply a figment of a rather lurid western imagination about the continent and an object of political-economic imperatives including the right to possess its land and riches. Leading Hollywood and British directors such as Zoltan Korda, John Huston and John Ford made a series of box office successes on Africa, from *The Macomber Affair* in 1947 to *Mogambo* in 1953. Certainly film is a medium which trades in illusion. The features used well-established Hollywood techniques, envisaging Africa largely through American and British eyes and giving major roles to dominant white men. Yet Beinart and Schafer argue that, somewhat surprisingly, Hollywood filmmakers became fascinated by Africa not only as an imaginary subject, but also as a location. They contributed to and mirrored grow-ing global interest in African landscapes and wildlife. The chapter also argues that the films reflected changing social practices amongst settlers, especially those who made their living from wildlife as hunters and game-capturers. They explore how activities around the safari and wildlife came to be central themes and why Hol-

1999); Mahesh Rangarajan, *India's Wildlife History. An Introduction* (Delhi: Permanent Black, 2001).

18. Donna Haraway, 'Teddy Bear Patriarchy: Taxidermy in the Garden of Eden, 1908–1936', *Social Text* 11 (1984): 19–64.

19. David Bunn, 'An Unnatural State: Tourism, Water and Wildlife Photography in the Early Kruger National Park', in William Beinart and Joann McGregor (eds.) *Social History and African Environ-ments* (Oxford: James Currey, 2003), pp. 199–218.

William Beinart, Karen Middleton and Simon Pooley

lywood and British directors went to huge effort and expense in order to capture authentic landscapes and wildlife sequences on screen.

Beinart and Schafer also question the dominant social constructivist discussion of visual depictions to produce a more dynamic reading of cinematic images, highlighting the interplay between film-makers and the powerful landscapes they illustrate, as well as recent developments in the world of hunting and conservation. By and large, individual named animals did not become 'actors' in the films, in the way of some Hollywood classics, but interactions between humans and animals sometimes did become part of the narrative and the plot.[20] African environments closely shaped the visual realm, the style and the subject matter of the films. These productions were most certainly acts of imagination and appealed to a strand in the post-war western imagination that was interested in exotic places and adventure. But script-writers and directors were not veering wildly from everyday experiences and landscapes; these products of the industry of illusion were made partly on location and aimed partly at 'landscape realism'.

Amy Halliday analyses a more recent exercise in photography of animals by a South African photographer, Daniel Naudé.[21] Wildlife photography has grown into a huge enterprise in the last century, with complex aesthetic and commercial connections.[22] It has helped to sell magazines and tourist destinations as well as to justify national parks and mobilise popular support and funding for conservation campaigns. Naudé develops a different focus: lavish photographic portraits of livestock, sometimes with their owners. Halliday argues that he draws on nineteenth century art celebrating the beauty of animals; there are also echoes of wildlife photography.

Halliday traces the significance of livestock in South African society and suggests that Naudé's photography attempts to place livestock and landscape at the heart of contemporary South African identity. Moreover, he concentrates on some breeds specific to South Africa, such as Afrikaner and Nguni cattle. Although his portfolio includes many striking images of black South Africans, Naude's portraiture is particularly significant in reconnecting with, reimagining and questioning Afrikaner identity on the land, at a time when Afrikaners have lost political power and are seeking new ways of conceiving themselves in post-apartheid South Africa. Halliday illuminates the links in Naudé's portraiture between human identity and animal histories. The portraits are often racially specific, but his photographs, taken together, also suggest elements of a common heritage and memory around livestock.

---

20. Compare Jonathan Burt, *Animals in Film* (London: Reaktion Books, 2000).

21. The reproduction of these photographs has been made possible with a grant from the Rhodes Chair of Race Relations Fund.

22. This was the subject of papers at the conference by Ellen Rogers ('Myth Making: Commodification of Nature through African Wildlife Imagery') and Joe Zammit-Lucia ('Visual Culture and Our Understanding of the "Environment"').

Introduction

Deliberate revisualisation and intentional reconstruction are also explicit themes in the chapter by Tyler Cornelius exploring the visual realm in relation to the emergence of internal tourism in the United States. While hunting and wildlife photography, as Jones illustrates, became entwined with early phases of tourism, the pursuit of scenic beauty represented a related but different impulse. In 1916 workers finished the construction of the Columbia River Highway, one of the earliest paved roads in the Pacific Northwest of the United States. It was designed to offer motorised visitors beautiful views of the spectacular Columbia gorge – literally paving the way for nature-oriented automobile tourism in the region. After its completion, the highway quickly became the most common way residents experienced the river. But in shortening the temporal distance between city and river, the road also reduced the cultural distance – re-scripting how most middle-class urbanites envisioned their relationship to the river and the surrounding hinterlands. Cornelius emphasises the wildness and timelessness of the scenery as well as the modernity of those who looked upon it. In this way the Columbia River Highway offered its visitors specific ideas about what to see and how to see it.

Cornelius argues that this vision of landscape and experience of aesthetic pleasure through new modes of tourism became part of American modernity. His analysis resonates with writing by David Bunn on the way in which early tourists learnt how to see wildlife in Africa in a new way – extolling its beauty rather than its economic value.[23] Visits to national parks, Bunn also suggests, were not simply an escape from modernity through a flight to perceived wilderness, but a component space in modern life as a temporary antidote to urban anxiety. Cornelius, however, concurs with some key works in American environmental history in noting the marginalisation of indigenous people in this new aesthetic – except as peripherally part of a frontier heritage. There is common ground between the technological reconstruction of landscape for visual consumption that Cornelius describes and the rise of camera-based visual culture that Karen Jones documents for the Rocky Mountains. But Cornelius emphasises the excitement of engineering routes into wild nature and the access provided to urban Americans. He suggests that the closing of the frontier did not necessarily entail – as Worster illustrates in *Dust Bowl* – environmental degradation or shutting off nature in the social imagination.[24]

Collectively these papers propose the potential power of visual images of nature. To Aldo Leopold 'the sight of geese was more important than television'.[25] He was expressing a heartfelt commitment, late in life, when this new medium burst into western households, to a land ethic and reverence for the natural world.

23. Bunn, 'An Unnatural State'.

24. Donald Worster, *Dust Bowl: the Southern Plains in the 1930s* (New York: Oxford University Press, 1979); Worster records alternative outcomes in other books.

25. John Sheail, *An Environmental History of Twentieth-Century Britain* (Basingstoke: Palgrave, 2002), p. 265.

William Beinart, Karen Middleton and Simon Pooley

To him direct experience of wilderness remained central to understanding and appreciating nature; television must have seemed the antithesis of these values. Yet television soon found natural history, or vice-versa, and also played a role in bringing geese into mass public consciousness. *The Incredible Flight of the Snow Geese* made by Des and Jen Bartlett for Anglia television's Survival series won an Emmy for best documentary of 1972–3 and reached audiences of perhaps 100 million. The Bartletts did not think that television was a barrier to viewing nature and imagined their audience 'thrilled as we have done to the sight and sound of thousands of geese tumbling out of the sky to the safety of a wildlife refuge'.[26] Arguably the camera, once it was disassociated from the gun, became a key medium for environmentalism.

Animal Histories

Although animals have always been integral to human conceptions of nature, Harriet Ritvo argued in 2004 that historians hesitated to take the histories of animals seriously. As animals are a particularly significant subject in this collection, we will discuss briefly some key lines of analysis that have emerged. At the time she published her book on *The Animal Estate* (1987), Ritvo thought that most historians responded to 'the mention of an animal-related research topic [with] ... surprise and amusement'.[27] Ritvo perhaps overlooked a large popular literature and influential precedents such as Keith Thomas's monograph on changing attitudes to nature.[28] However, there is no doubt that the subsequent rise of Animal Studies has introduced important new perspectives and highly committed scholarship. There is now a growing volume of detailed studies of animals in literary and cultural studies such as Morse and Danahay's *Victorian Animal Dreams*, Rothfel's *Representing Animals* and Baker's *Picturing the Beast*.[29] Philosophical and critical studies, such as Cary Wolfe's *Zoontologies*, touch on the concept and nature of animals.[30] Reaktion Press has published a popular book series called *Animal* with over 50 volumes. In 2011, an issue of *Environmental History* featured a special forum on 'Fifty years

26. Des and Jen Bartlett, *The Flight of the Snow Geese* (London: Collins and Harvill, 1975), p. 13.

27. Harriet Ritvo, 'Animal Planet', *Environmental History* 9/2 (2004): 205; Harriet Ritvo, *The Animal Estate: The English and Other Creatures in the Victorian Age* (London: Penguin, 1990, first published 1987).

28. Keith Thomas, *Man and the Natural World: Changing Attitudes in England, 1500–1800* (London: Penguin, 1984).

29. Steve Baker, *Picturing the Beast: Animals, Identity and Representation* (Champaign, IL: University of Illinois Press, 2002); Nigel Rothfels (ed.) *Representing Animals.* (Bloomington, IN: Indiana University Press, 2003); Deborah Morse and Martin Danahay (eds.) *Victorian Animal Dreams: Representations of Animals in Victorian Literature and Culture* (Aldershot: Ashgate, 2007).

30. Cary Wolfe, *Animal Rites: American Culture, the Discourse of Species, and Posthumanism Theory* (Chicago: University of Chicago Press, 2007).

of wildlife in America'.[31] Writing on animals has formed an important dimension of the Australian programme of the ecological humanities.[32] Themes have ranged from meat-eating, through explorations of the reciprocal relationships of communities of species including humans, to neglected uncharismatic species and the biopolitics of extinction.

Wendy Wheeler and Linda Williams observe the centrality of ethics in their introduction to a special issue on 'The Animals Turn'.[33] They argue that this shifting ethical perspective throws up new questions about the meaning of 'mind' and implies the need for a wider understanding of human care and consciousness embracing both the animals' part in human consciousness and the strange otherness of the consciousness of animals. In certain respects the concerns of animal studies scholars are animated by impulses analogous to those of environmental historians – conceptualising an intellectual underpinning for a moral agenda that aims at changing human relationships with the natural world. In both cases, as well, issues arise about the agency in history of non-human actors. The new morality of Animals Studies to some degree asserts this, perhaps with insufficient attention to other non-human environmental influences. As Wheeler and Williams note, 'the development of a new field of study is very often just as much about a creative meaning-generation, obliging us to think in new ways (to evolve one might say), as it is simply or only about the objects of study themselves'.

It has become quite common among contributors to recent humanist literature on animals to quote French social anthropologist Claude Lévi-Strauss's fifty year-old formulation, that animals are good to think with. (His aphorism, if he did invent it, is now applied to many different agents.) The revisionist approach to animal history is aimed at 'shifting emphasis from the human perspective toward that of other animals, exploring modes of animal resistance to human behaviors, and considering the ways the presence of animals refracts human notions like agency and species'.[34] In an echo of some broader contentions about nature in western history, it is argued that, in western moral philosophy since Classical times, humans have been set apart from – and above – all other animals. This separation has been justified on grounds of moral superiority and reinforced by the Cartesian separation between mind and body, associated with thinking and feeling, respectively. This in turn led to the idea that animals don't have history. As Francis Gooding puts it, in conventional work the human, a creature with what he terms 'thoughtful

31. *Environmental History* 16/3 (July 2011).

32. http://environmentalhumanities.org/

33. Wendy Wheeler and Linda Williams, 'The Animals Turn', *New Formations* 76 (2012): 5–7.

34. Sarah McFarland and Ryan Hediger (eds.) *Animals and Agency* (Leiden: Brill, 2009).

agency', is perceived to exist in historical time, whereas the natural world has no such thoughtful agency and therefore exists in unhistorical time.[35]

Much of the new animal history challenges this view. Just as extra-European and social historians broadened agency in economic, social, political, cultural and intellectual contexts from monarchs, presidents, emperors, generals and colonial officials to workers, peasants, colonised people, women, homosexuals, crowds and ethnic minorities, so too Animal Studies argues against non-human species being passive, unthinking presences in the active and thoughtful lives of humans. However, it is easier to place animals in the context of changing patterns of human behaviour – for example the transition from hunting to conservation, or from cruelty to sympathy – than to show how animal agency shaped these histories or how animals interacted with one another.

Environmental historians have, by and large, hesitated to confront issues of animal agency so directly. Alfred Crosby incorporated animals into his explanatory framework, but as part of a broader argument about environmental causation, rather than as protagonist of specific examples of animal agency.[36] William Beinart illustrated how the responses of jackals to the rise of sheep farming in South Africa could be traced historically and how jackals shaped human reactions.[37] Sandra Swart's *Riding High* (2011) explicitly sets out to write the history of a domesticated animal.[38] John McNeill's *Mosquito Empires* (2010) and Karen Brown's *Mad Dogs and Meerkats* (2011) are recent examples of a growing literature on the history of animals as vectors of disease and how this has shaped human history in important ways.[39] Perhaps Virginia Anderson's *Creatures of Empire* (2004) – an account of domestic animals in seventeenth-century colonial North America – makes the most explicit claim to go beyond the unintentional agency implied in Crosby. She attempts to demonstrate in detail that the lives of Indians and colonists were fashioned in part by the activities of animals and that these interactions influenced broader patterns of colonisation.[40]

35. Francis Gooding, 'Of Dodos and Dutchmen: Reflections on the Nature of History', *Critical Quarterly* 47/4 (2005): 33.

36. Alfred Crosby, *Ecological Imperialism: The Biological Expansion of Europe 900–1900* (New York: Cambridge University Press, 1986).

37. William Beinart, *The Rise of Conservation in South Africa: Settlers, Livestock, and the Environment 1770–1950* (Oxford: Oxford University Press, 2003).

38. Sandra Swart, *Riding High: Horses, Humans and History in South Africa* (Johannesburg: Wits University Press, 2011).

39. W.H. McNeill, *Plagues and Peoples* (New York: Anchor, 1977); Crosby, *Ecological Imperialism*; J.R. McNeill, *Mosquito Empires: Ecology and War in the Greater Caribbean, 1620–1914* (New York: Cambridge University Press, 2010); Karen Brown, *Mad Dogs and Meerkats: A History of Resurgent Rabies in Southern Africa* (Athens OH: Ohio University Press, 2011).

40. Virginia DeJohn Anderson, *Creatures of Empire: How Domestic Animals Transformed Early America* (New York: Oxford University Press, 2004).

Introduction

When it comes to animal histories, then, environmental historians find themselves in an interesting position. Some, it is true, have restricted themselves to the destructive capacities of human beings on the natural world. But many, in trying to extend the concerns of social history to the non-human world, are introducing new arguments about causation. They have generally been more cautious about non-human agency. Even so, they have arguably diminished – at least implicitly – the importance of human agency within and over nature. They have tried to enlarge the social imagination to embrace more than human society, to write more inclusive histories of the social-ecological systems which we inhabit on planet earth. A core challenge of writing animal histories is to acknowledge, with Harriet Ritvo, that human influence is so widespread that few animals can be described as completely wild. She suggests that we need to recognise the limits of animal agency, but make space for narratives and contexts where wild and domesticated animals have influenced the course of history.[41]

The chapters in this collection make relatively muted claims about animal agency, but find new routes along which to explore animals in social imaginations. In his chapter on Bristol Zoological Gardens, Andrew Flack examines the origins and development of the British trade in exotic animals. His chapter also bridges the visual and animal strands in this book. Focusing on the period from the foundation of the zoo in 1835, and the opening of its Gardens the following year, to the dawn of the 'ecological era' (c.1970), he records the forcible extraction of animals from habitats spanning the globe and their translocation to the prosperous Bristol suburb of Clifton.

Creatures were sought for a variety of reasons, reflecting the commercial and scientific interests of the Society, as well as the curiosity (and later, conscience) of the zoo's visiting public. Flack notes a tension between the scientific aim of creating a representative collection, in which all animal species were present and equally valued, and considerations of entertainment, which tended to favour crowd-pulling species such as big cats or polar bears. Priorities changed through time from favouring young, 'cuddly' versions of iconic creatures to particularly unusual or exotic attractions. He also considers animals that were never displayed, some of which were converted into food for the collection's carnivores. The focus in literature on zoos has tended to be the great cats, the seals, the penguins and other animals that were quintessential highpoints of zoo visits. Rothfels also recounts how 'the feeding of the lions at Berlin Zoo was at one time a spectacular event in which the lions were brought to a frenzy of excitement before being thrown large chunks of meat publicly hacked off a carcass by a keeper'.[42] By tracking also invisible animals,

---

41. Harriet Ritvo, 'Beasts in the Jungle (or Wherever)', in Ritvo, *Noble Cows & Hybrid Zebras: Essays on Animals & History* (Charlottesville: University of Virginia Press, 2010), pp.203–12.

42. Nigel Rothfels, *Savages and Beasts: The Birth of the Modern Zoo* (Baltimore: Johns Hopkins University Press, 2002), pp. 207, 211.

William Beinart, Karen Middleton and Simon Pooley

Flack provides new insights into the hidden as well as exhibited side of zoos. He concludes by addressing the new narratives of freedom and conservation that have been increasingly used to justify public zoos.

Daniel Allen's chapter on otter hunting and conservation in the United Kingdom focuses mainly on human attitudes to wild creatures, or at least animals outside captivity. He starts by noting a key conundrum. Otters were persecuted during the first half of the twentieth century and wiped out of most rivers; they were perceived as fish-killers and valued as a source of sport. But even at the time, some represented them as victims threatened with extinction and their role was transformed in popular literature. They became widely admired for their beauty, mysterious ways and capacity to survive. By the late twentieth century, populations were recovering and expanding their territory so successfully that there were calls for a cull to reduce their impact on local fish stocks. Conservationists oppose this, and the public are shocked by the suggestion that one of the nation's favourite mammals should be killed. The long history of otter hunting in Britain has largely been forgotten following its legal cessation in 1978. This chapter provides a cultural history of the hunted otter, offering much-needed context to debates on conservation and allowing a touch of animal agency.

We cannot, however, assume that there is an immutable change. Contemporary calls for a cull to restore fish stocks highlight the continued divergence in views about even so popular an animal. They are also a reminder that otters survive in a very managed environment where human interests and conflicts will shape where they gambol. Allen approaches the otter as a cultural object around which people formed arguments, practices and identities. Otter hunters, anti-blood-sports campaigners, popular writers and ecologists all offered different versions of human–otter relations, revealing how they styled themselves in relation to this particular animal.

In his chapter 'No Tears for the Crocodiles' Simon Pooley shifts attention to water creatures that have not attracted such sympathy. In 1956–58 South Africans joined an unprecedented chorus demanding the slaughter of all Nile crocodiles in Zululand. Pooley provides an instructive study of how the 'crocodile menace' was produced and imagined. In part it resulted from environmental interventions and changing human activities around Lake St Lucia. In part it mushroomed from prejudice and ignorance about this species that was exploited by a variety of interests ranging from commercial hunters to anglers, farmers and nationalist politicians. The debate was intensified by conflict over the future of Lake St Lucia (now a UNESCO World Heritage Site) and its shores. Some saw it as primarily a recreational space, others as a natural resource, while conservationists wished it to be a place to preserve untouched nature and wild, dangerous fauna.

Pooley draws on a wide range of source materials – including natural history texts, fiction, newspapers, autobiographies, technical reports and films – in order to argue that powerful social imaginings of crocodiles both enabled their persecution and obscured the actual motivations for the planned cull. Ensuring their survival in the region required addressing popular and expert prejudice through research into their actual biology and habits. It also required finding a way of accommodating both the needs of a potentially dangerous but ecologically important predator, and the needs and aspirations of human inhabitants and visitors to the Lake. This chapter represents a significant addition to the meagre historical literature on human–crocodile interactions, and addresses a major (species) gap in the broader history of wildlife conservation in Africa.

Trees, Nature and Identity

Forests and trees have long been central to the everyday practice and social imagination of human communities, providing material resources for livelihoods and intellectual resources for the elaboration of meaning. Their management, use and conceptualisation have figured centrally in natural history, environmental history and classic histories of the English countryside such as Oliver Rackham's *Ancient Woodland* (1980).[43] The subject of regulation, as Clarence Glacken demonstrated in his history of western ideas about nature, forests and access to woodland, has long and repeatedly given rise to contestation both within local communities and between local communities and higher authority.[44] Such struggles have been documented for many contexts from pre-colonial Indian kingdoms, through French and British colonies to modern nation-states. [45]

Forest histories often explore conflict, especially in colonial contexts, where tensions developed between conservationist governments and indigenous people who felt they had the right to use the forests. India, where close on twenty per cent of the surface area was reserved in some way as forest land, has generated a particularly valuable social history of forests; Guha's *The Unquiet Woods* (1990) and subsequent research welded environmental history and subaltern studies. There are parallels with the history of wilderness and wildlife in that much of this genre is critical of colonial conservationism for bludgeoning indigenous rights and knowledge.[46]

---

43. Oliver Rackham, *Ancient Wooldland: Its History, Vegetation and Uses in England* (London: Edward Arnold, 1980).

44. Glacken, *Traces on the Rhodian Shore*.

45. Ramachandra Guha, *The Unquiet Woods: Ecological Change and Peasant Resistance in the Himalaya* (Delhi: Oxford University Press, 1990); Ann Grodzins Gold and Ram Gujar Bhoju, *In the Time of Trees and Sorrow: Nature, Power, and Memory in Rajasthan* (Durham NC: Duke University Press, 2002); Raymond Bryant, *The Political Ecology of Forestry in Burma, 1824–1994* (London: Hurst,1997); Alain Bertrand *et al.* (eds.) *L'État et la gestion locale durable des forêts en Afrique francophone et à Madagascar* (Paris: Harmattan, 2006); Tamara Whited, *Forests and Peasant Politics in Modern France* (New Haven: Yale University Press, 2000).

46. Didier Babin (ed.) *Beyond Tropical Deforestation* (Paris: UNESCO, 2004).

16

William Beinart, Karen Middleton and Simon Pooley

Forest history has been treated both as a metaphor for, and a key to, broader environmental change. Richard Grove argued in *Green Imperialism* (1995) that the experience of deforestation in early colonial contexts stimulated some of the earliest western discourse on environmental degradation and climate change.[47] Fairhead and Leach's *Misreading the African Landscape* became a paradigmatic discussion of colonial misunderstanding of African deforestation and environmental change more generally.[48] Forest history has been the site for debates over ordered monocultures of often-exotic species versus the preservation of untidy biodiversity-rich habitats of native species.[49] In forests, as much as in the visual realm, nature and identity are often closely intertwined. Trees and forests figure centrally in the construction of social identities and in the imagination of national histories, from the ancient forests of Germany to Canada and India.[50] Simon Schama's *Landscape and Memory* (1995) gives a starring role to trees and forests. [51]

Why have trees (and tree products) been such central objects of human thought and action? For Auricchio *et al.* it is by virtue of their ubiquity across cultures, their usefulness in every aspect of life, their often superhuman sizes and their uncommon longevity.[52] Noting that their defining traits sometimes seem paradoxical (passive materials and active forces, useful types and beloved individuals, elements of nature put to social use), they suggest that trees stand at the intersection of some of our most fundamental epistemological categories. Anthropologist Maurice Bloch muses that, like animals, trees are good to think with. He argues that the symbolic power of trees comes from the fact that they share life with humans yet are different from them. Communality between arboreal and human forms is more problematic than between humans and nonhuman animals because trees are somehow felt by humans to be less alive.[53]

Contributions to the history of forests and trees in this volume develop ideas about landscape, memory and identity. Johannes Zechner argues that, around 1800, influential German-speaking intellectuals increasingly ascribed political

47. Grove, *Green Imperialism*; Gregory A. Barton, *Empire Forestry and the Origins of Environmentalism* (Cambridge: Cambridge University Press, 2002).

48. James Fairhead and Melissa Leach, *Misreading the African Landscape: Society and Ecology in a Forest-Savanna Mosaic* (Cambridge: Cambridge University Press, 1996).

49. Rackham, *Ancient Woodlands*; Barton, *Empire Forestry*; S. Ravi Rajan, *Modernising Nature: Forestry and Imperial Eco-development 1800–1950* (Oxford: Oxford University Press, 2006).

50. G. Cederlöf and K. Sivaramakrishnan (eds.) *Ecological Nationalisms: Nature, Livelihoods, and Identities in South Asia* (Delhi: Permanent Black, 2005).

51. Schama, *Landscape and Memory*.

52. L. Auricchio, E. Heckendorn Cook and G. Pacini (eds.) *Invaluable Trees, Cultures of Nature, 1660–1830* (Oxford: Voltaire Foundation, 2012).

53. Maurice Bloch, 'Why trees, too, are good to think with: towards an anthropology of the meaning of life', in Laura Rival (ed.) *The Social Life of Trees: Anthropological Perspectives on Tree Symbolism* (Oxford: Berg, 1998), pp. 39–55.

Introduction

meanings to the silvicultural sphere. 'German Forest' and 'German Oak' grew to epitomise the imagined nature of the nation – symbols against societal and spatial fragmentation. Following the poetic evocation of '*Waldeinsamkeit*' by Ludwig Tieck and Joseph von Eichendorff, the Grimm brothers' fairy tales glorified the woods as a Germanic treasure of the past. Subsequently, patriotic publicists like Friedrich Ludwig Jahn or Ernst Moritz Arndt propagated them as a native symbol of sovereignty and continuity. Zechner examines this shift from the poetry of the forest, to its incorporation in political symbolism in the nineteenth century.

Reading Zechner's study we are led to contemplate two broader questions. The first concerns the relationship between the negative, dark and eerie and the positive, merry and green aspects of forest symbolism. Some writers stress the otherness of forests in human perspective. Thus, in much the same way as Paul Shepard and others explore *How Animals Made Us Human*,[54] so too Robert Pogue Harrison analyses forests as 'the shadow of civilization', 'the boundary or edge against which we build our selves and our society'.[55] The evolution of ideas about the 'German forest' is interesting in this respect since, during the very period studied by Zechner, forests became both more central symbols of German identity and places of dangerous otherness in popular literature.

Karen Middleton's chapter focuses on environmental discourse and practice in the Indian Ocean island of Madagascar. Like Zechner she analyses trees and nationalism, but in the context of state-building in a former French colony that gained independence in 1960. Under the First Republic, the new government attempted to promote a tree festival called the 'Cult of the Tree'. At first inspection this initiative seems to substantiate the thesis that is often asserted about the survival of colonial forestry and conservationist discourses after political independence. Probed more deeply, however, the tree cult as practiced under President Tsiranana proves subversive of colonial tradition on several counts. It was adopted and reinvented by a President keen to instil a sense of unity and nationhood in a divided population while also addressing issues around food security. Above all, it was forged in a context of distinctively global concerns with rapidly rising populations in the 1960s. Middleton stresses the creativity and innovation that characterised Madagascar's environmental discourse and practice at this time. She argues that Africanists should be cautious about emphasising the persistence of a colonial legacy in forestry – and rather explore new and complex postcolonial forms of environmental policy and practice, including the development of ecological nationalism.

Middleton shows how various narratives about deforestation as well as projects of reforestation in southern Madagascar keyed in with political concerns about nationhood. The idiom of denuded or dessicated land served to express

---

54. Paul Shepard, *The Others: How Animals Made Us Human* (Washington DC: Island Press, 1996).

55. Robert Pogue Harrison, *Forests, the Shadow of Civilization* (Chicago: University of Chicago Press, 1992), pp. 10, 16.

William Beinart, Karen Middleton and Simon Pooley

fears about the condition of the national polity as much as of the environment, and tree planting was proposed as a restorative, healing balm in the face of social discord. As Fernandez notes, 'trees, by certain associative processes, can excite the moral imagination concerning the health or disease of corporate bodies, bodies corporeal and bodies politic as it were, and are thus powerful or power-associated imaginative devices'.[56]

Themes of nature and national identity also figure in Lauren Derby's excursion into revolutionary dirt in Haiti, the troubled Caribbean state. Exploring the historical significance of mud cake production, Derby shows how this curious food product, which renders soil among one of Haiti's most important export commodities after labour, incorporates multiple allusions to key events in Haitian history, most notably the early nineteenth-century Haitian revolution. Noting that the recipe calls for soil culled from Haitian revolutionary battle-grounds and key sites of emergent nationhood, Derby proposes that the Haitian mud patty, far from being a food substitute or a sign of abjection, is a form of gustatory nationalism. Popular nationalism, she argues, is here embodied in material culture and the environment.

Yet the relationship between mud cakes, popular nationalism and Haitian identity is also problematic because there is lack of consensus even among Haitians as to whether mud is a natural or proper thing for people to eat. Such differing opinions about what constitutes a proper human being may be partly attributable to long-standing class differentials within Haitian society, which cut across a common history. They may also reflect conflicting representations of Haiti's revolution. Celebrated by some as 'Black Jacobins' upholding the principles of equality, liberty and fraternity, another literature developed in the nineteenth century portrayed black Haitians as rather less than full human beings, not averse to cannibalism, infant sacrifice, voodoo and other forms of ritualistic barbarism. Derby explores the mud cake as a symbolic phenomenon within several contexts which date from slavery, including the cultural significance of clay as a means of ritual adornment and for constructs of femininity – since mud cakes are first and foremost a women's product and food. A tension between animality and humanity is still evident in contemporary ideas about mud cakes. They are sometimes aligned with what is positively valued in Haitian society, sometimes with the negative.

Human beings and their existential possibilities are also core questions for the scientific endeavours described by Sven Mesinovic in his chapter on the underwater laboratories that were built in 1969 by West Germany and the United States. These were multi-dimensional projects that drew on contemporary developments in science and reflected current political concerns. Mesinovic carefully peels away their various objectives: research on marine wildlife; research into the adaptabil-

---

56. James W. Fernandez, 'Trees of Knowledge of Self and Other in Culture: On Models for the Moral Imagination', in Laura Rival (ed.) *The Social Life of Trees: Anthropological Perspectives on Tree Symbolism* (Oxford: Berg, 1998), pp. 85, 92–3.

ity of human beings to unfamiliar environments; political and territorial claims in international waters; and research into artificial worlds. The latter was linked functionally to space exploration and driven partly by 1960s fears of expanding human populations that triggered a perceived need to find new living space for the world's teeming multitudes.

Mesinovic also shows how the underwater laboratories and outer space were informed by, and in turn informed, the science of ecology. Analysing the Tektite (US) and Helgoland (German) projects as embodiments of environmental concepts, he describes a shift in focus from the individual to the habitat as body and space became politicised in new ways. Mesinovic argues that this was part of broader shift that overturned the hierarchical chain of being and rendered humans and the natural world more equal. It seems paradoxical that science in this and similar experiments was so closely allied to the pursuit of imagined modes of existence. They were applying scientific techniques to the idea that *Homo sapiens* might be able to transcend their terrestrial existence and adapt to life under seas – an idea that has long fed the human imagination from tales about mermaids to the novels of Jules Verne.

The underwater, artificial worlds described by Mesinovic involve a less antagonistic relationship between men-in-the-sea and the world of terrestrial human beings than that figured in Jules Verne. They also offer a more benign vision of technology than immediate post-war, end-of-the-world novels such as Nevil Shute's *On The Beach* (1957) and John Wyndham's *The Day of the Triffids* (1951). But they share the same mid-century concern with human survival in, and potential adaptability to, 'unnatural' landscapes, against a Cold War setting. Similar themes reappear in *The Spy Who Loved Me* (1977), the James Bond film in which shipping tycoon, scientist and anarchist Karl Stromberg, who leads a self-contained submarine existence similar to that of 'Nemo' [Nobody], the protagonist of Verne's novel, plans to destroy Moscow and New York, trigger nuclear war and establish a new civilisation underseas. These ostensibly rational scientific projects of underwater laboratories and outer space underline Ingold's observation that 'as objectively self-aware and self-interpreting animals, humans can describe their environment, and report on their actions within it, as though they had themselves stepped outside it, posing as mere spectators.'[57]

Conclusion

Our chapters suggest that the diversity of social imaginations about nature has not diminished in industrial or urban society. New technologies, especially visual

---

57. Tim Ingold, 'Culture and the Perception of the Environment', in Elisabeth Croll and David Parkin (eds.) *Bush Base: Forest Farm. Culture, Environment and Development* (London and New York: Routledge, 1992), p. 52.

20

William Beinart, Karen Middleton and Simon Pooley

technologies, have multiplied the ways in which humans can see and interpret the natural world – even if they sometimes also distance people from direct experience of nature. In certain respects the growth of environmental sciences and late twentieth century environmentalism, including environmental history itself, have hugely expanded knowledge and fed new ideas into the social imagination of nature. Our chapters are focused on popular as much as scientific imaginations and this is clearly a field that requires more research. We are arguing that ideas about wilderness and wild things should be salvaged as exciting concepts. Wildness can both form part of the human condition, and of modernity, and protect something of a world that stands a little apart from all-consuming human dominance. In sum, it is important that we do discover how humans have imagined nature, and think about new ways of doing so, as a route to creating space for other species and a natural world.

REFERENCES

Adams, J.S. and T.D. McShane. 1997. *The Myth of Wild Africa: Conservation Without Illusion.* Berkeley: University of California Press.

Anderson, Virginia DeJohn. 2004. *Creatures of Empire: How Domestic Animals Transformed Early America.* Oxford: Oxford University Press.

Andrews, Malcolm. 1999. *Landscape and Western Art.* Oxford: Oxford University Press.

Arnold, David. 1996. *The Problem of Nature: Environment, Culture and European Expansion.* Oxford: Blackwell

Auricchio, Laura, Elizabeth Heckendorn Cook and Giulia Pacini. 2012. 'Introduction: Invaluable trees', in L. Auricchio, E. Heckendorn Cook and G. Pacini (eds.) *Invaluable Trees, Cultures of Nature, 1660–1830.* Oxford: Voltaire Foundation. pp. 1–26.

Baker, Steve. 2001. *Picturing the Beast: Animals, Identity and Representation.* Champaign: University of Illinois Press.

Babin, Didier (ed.) 2004. *Beyond Tropical Deforestation.* Paris: UNESCO.

Bartlett, Des and Jen. 1975. *The Flight of the Snow Geese.* London: Collins and Harvill.

Barton, Gregory A. 2002. *Empire Forestry and the Origins of Environmentalism.* Cambridge: Cambridge University Press.

Beinart, William. 2003. *The Rise of Conservation in South Africa: Settlers, Livestock and the Environment 1779–1950.* Oxford: Oxford University Press.

Beinart, William and Joann McGregor (eds.) 2003, *Social History and African Environments.* Oxford: James Currey.

Beinart, William and Katie McKeown. 2009. 'Wildlife Media and Representations of Africa, 1950s to the 1970s'. *Environmental History* 14/3: 429–452.

Bertrand, Alain *et al.* (eds.) 2006. *L'État et la gestion locale durable des forêts en Afrique francophone et à Madagascar.* Paris: Harmattan.

Bloch, Maurice. 1998. 'Why trees, too, are good to think with: towards an anthropology of the meaning of life', in Laura Rival (ed.) *The Social Life of Trees: anthropological perspectives on tree symbolism*. Oxford: Berg. pp. 39–55.

Bowler, Peter J. 1992. *The Fontana History of the Environmental Sciences* London: Fontana Press.

Brockington, Dan. 2002. *Fortress Conservation: The Preservation of the Mkomazi Game Reserve, Tanzania*. Oxford: James Currey.

Brown, Karen. 2011. *Mad Dogs and Meerkats: A History of Resurgent Rabies in Southern Africa*. Athens OH: Ohio University Press.

Bryant, Raymond. 1997. *The Political Ecology of Forestry in Burma, 1824–1994*. London: Hurst.

Bunn, David. 2003. 'An Unnatural State: Tourism, Water and Wildlife Photography in the Early Kruger National Park', in William Beinart and Joann McGregor (eds.) *Social History and African Environments*. Oxford: James Currey. pp. 199–218.

Burt, Jonathan. 2000. *Animals in Film*. London: Reaktion Books.

Coates, Peter. 1998. *Nature: Western Attitudes since Ancient Times*. Cambridge: Polity Press.

Cederlöf, Gunnel and K. Sivaramakrishnan (eds.) 2005. *Ecological Nationalisms: Nature, Livelihoods, and Identities in South Asia*. Delhi: Permanent Black.

Cronon, William. 1996. 'The Trouble with Wilderness or, Getting Back to the Wrong Nature'. *Environmental History* 1/1: 7–55.

Fairhead, James and Melissa Leach. 1996. *Misreading the African Landscape. Society and ecology in a forest-savanna mosaic*. Cambridge: Cambridge University Press.

Fernandez, James W. 1998. 'TRees of Knowledge of Self and Other in Culture: On Models for the Moral Imagination', in Laura Rival (ed.) *The Social Life of Trees: anthropological perspectives on tree symbolism*. Oxford: Berg. pp. 81–110.

Freedberg, David. 2003. *The Eye of the Lynx: Galileo, His Friends and the Beginning of Modern Natural History*. Chicago: University of Chicago Press.

Glacken, Clarence. 1967. *Traces on the Rhodian Shore: Nature and Culture in Western Thought from Ancient Times to the End of the Eighteenth Century*. Berkeley: University of California Press.

Gooding, Francis. 2005. 'Of Dodos and Dutchmen: Reflections on the Nature of History'. *Critical Quarterly* 47/4: 32–47.

Gold, Ann Grodzins and Ram Gujar Bhoju. 2002. *In the time of Trees and Sorrow: Nature, Power, and Memory in Rajasthan*. Durham, N.C: Duke University Press.

Grove, Richard. *Green Imperialism: Colonial Expansion, Tropical Island Edens and the Origins of Environmentalism, 1600–1860*. Cambridge: Cambridge University Press.

Guha, Ramachandra. 1990. *The Unquiet Woods: Ecological Change and Peasant Resistance in the Himalaya*. Delhi: Oxford University Press.

Guha, Ramachandra. 2000. *Environmentalism: A Global History*. London: Longman.

Haraway, Donna. 1984. 'Teddy Bear Patriarchy: Taxidermy in the Garden of Eden, 1908–1936'. *Social Text* 11: 19–64.

Harrison, Robert Pogue. 1992. *Forests, the Shadow of Civilization.* Chicago: University of Chicago Press.

Ingold, Tim. 1992. 'Culture and the Perception of the Environment', in D. Parkin and E. Croll (eds.) *Bush Base: Forest Farm: culture, environment and development.* London: Routledge. pp. 39–56.

Jardine, N., J.A. Secord and E.C. Spary (eds.) 1996. *Cultures of Natural History.* Cambridge: Cambridge University Press.

McFarland, Sarah and Ryan Hediger. 2009. 'Approaching the agency of other animals: an introduction', in S. McFarland and R. Hediger (eds.) *Animals and Agency.* Ebook Library. Leiden; Boston: Brill. pp. 1–20.

Mitman, Gregg. 1999. *Reel Nature: America's Romance with Wildlife on Film.* Cambridge, Mass.: Harvard University Press.

McNeill, J.R. 2010. *Mosquito Empires: Ecology and War in the Greater Caribbean, 1620–1914.* New York: Cambridge University Press.

McNeill, W.H. 1977. *Plagues and Peoples.* New York: Anchor.

Morse, Deborah and Martin Danahay (eds.) 2007. *Victorian Animal Dreams: Representations of Animals in Victorian Literature and Culture.* Aldershot: Ashgate.

Nash, Roderick. 1973. *Wilderness and the American Mind.* New Haven: Yale University Press.

Neumann, Roderick P. 2002. *Imposing Wilderness: Struggles over Livelihood and Nature Preservation in Africa.* Berkeley: University of California Press

Oelschlaeger, Max. 1991. *The Idea of Wilderness: From Prehistory to the Age of Ecology* New Haven: Yale University Press.

Rackham, Oliver. 1980. *Ancient Woodland: Its History, Vegetation and Uses in England.* London: Edward Arnold.

Radkau, Joachim. 2008. *Nature and Power: A Global History of the Environment.* Cambridge: Cambridge University Press.

Rajan, S. Ravi. 2006, *Modernising Nature: Forestry and Imperial Eco-development 1800–1950.* Oxford: Oxford University Press.

Rangarajan, Mahesh. 2001. *India's Wildlife History. An Introduction.* Delhi: Permanent Black in association with The Ranthambhore Foundation.

Ritvo, Harriet. 1989. *The Animal Estate: The English and Other Creatures in the Victorian Age.* Cambridge MA: Harvard University Press.

Ritvo, Harriet. 2004. 'Animal Planet'. *Environmental History* 9/2: 204–20.

Ritvo, Harriet. 2010. *Noble Cows and Hybrid Zebras: Essays on Animals and History.* Chalottesville: University of Virginia Press.

Rival, Laura (ed.) 1998. *The Social Life of Trees. Anthropological Perspectives on Tree Symbolism.* Oxford: Berg.

Rothfels, Nigel. 2002. *Savages and Beasts: The Birth of the Modern Zoo.* Baltimore Md; London: Johns Hopkins University Press.

Rothfels, Nigel (ed.) 2003. *Representing Animals.* Bloomington: Indiana University Press.

Ryan, James R. 1997. *Picturing Empire: Photography and the Visualization of the British Empire.* London: Reaktion.

Schama, Simon. 1995. *Landscape and Memory.* London: HarperCollins.

Sendak, Maurice. 1963. *Where the Wild Things Are.* New York: Harper and Row.

Sheail, John. 2002. *An Environmental History of Twentieth-Century Britain.* Basingstoke: Palgrave.

Shepard, Paul. 1996. *The Others: How Animals Made Us Human.* Washington DC: Island Press/Shearwater Books.

Shetler, Jan Bender. 2007. *Imagining Serengeti: a History of Landscape Memory in Serengeti from the Earliest Times to the Present.* Athens OH: Ohio University Press.

Sontag, Susan. 1979. *On Photography.* Harmondsworth: Penguin

Swart, Sandra. 2011. *Riding High: Horses, Humans and History in South Africa.* Johannesburg: Wits University Press.

Thomas, Keith. 1983. *Man and the Natural World: Changing Attitudes in England, 1500–1800.* London: Allen Lane.

The Troggs. 1966. *Wild Thing.* Written by Chip Taylor.

Wheeler, Wendy and Linda Williams. 2012. 'The Animals Turn'. *New Formations.* **76**: 5–7.

Whited, Tamara. 2000. *Forests and Peasant Politics in Modern France.* New Haven: Yale University Press.

Williams, Raymond. 1995. *The Country and the City.* St Albans: Paladin.

Wolfe, Cary (ed.) 2003. *Zoontologies: the Question of the Animal.* Minneapolis: University of Minnesota Press.

Worster, Donald. 1977. *Nature's Economy: A History of Ecological Ideas.* New York: Cambridge University Press.

Worster, Donald. 1979. *Dust Bowl: the Southern Plains in the 1930s.* New York: Oxford University Press.

Worster, Donald. 2008. *A Passion for Nature: The Life of John Muir.* New York: Oxford University Press.

Chapter 1

'Hunting with the Camera': Photography, Animals and the Technology of the Chase in the Rocky Mountains

Karen Jones

This chapter considers the intertwined relations between hunting, gun cultures and photography in the nineteenth century by looking at the experiences of sportsmen in the American West. Of particular interest here is the way in which the camera lens informs our understanding of hunting and its codes of environmental engagement, as well as pointing to the complicated exchange between technology, the material landscape and the social imagination. The 'politics of reproduction', to use Donna Haraway's phrase, makes the visual culture of nature a challenging terrain for the environmental historian to 'read' and one not without its paradoxes.[1] Leaving aside the politicised discourse that has commonly framed discussion on hunting, the relationship between the game trail, the gun and conservation proves a complex one. As various scholars have elucidated, hunters have occupied a raft of environmental positions, including appreciators and abusers, imperial architects and masculine adventurers, keen natural historians and 'penitent butchers'.[2] By placing a camera in the picture, this chapter sheds light on the variegated territory of the hunt and its imprint on a specific geography. I focus on the point of contact between the material and the imagined landscape, of encounter, staging and storytelling, colonial image capture and the relationship between environmental transformation and technologies of leisure. Deconstructing the photography of 'wild things' presents us with an intriguing conundrum. On one hand, the language of shooting, loading and capture suggests an affinity between the gun and the camera as active agents of empire and conquest. At the same time, the photographic gaze promoted a view of the game trail founded on appreciation and an ethos of preservation (in image and environmental activity). For some, the allure of 'hunting with the camera' became so powerful it obscured the need for the gun entirely.

---

1. Donna Haraway, 'Teddy Bear Patriarchy: Taxidermy in the Garden of Eden, 1908–1936', *Social Text* 11 (1984): 19–64, 25.

2. The idea of the 'penitent butcher' was raised first in the British press surrounding the establishment of the Society for the Preservation of the Wild Fauna of the Empire (1903), an organ largely comprised of aristocratic sportsmen. See Richard Fitter and Peter Scott, *The Penitent Butchers: The Fauna Preservation Society 1903–1978* (London: Collins, 1978).

'Hunting with the Camera'

Cameras, Guns and the Technology of Storytelling

The camera represented just one of many media that the nineteenth-century sport hunter used to record the experience of the game trail. Literature, art, theatre and taxidermy also featured in the arsenal of representation in a culture that prized reminiscence as a critical part of the hunting bargain. Documentation was an important marker for the sportsman adventurer, one that incorporated ideas of permanent record and preservation with rubrics of collection, scientific catalogue and historical inventory. The American West was not alone in being configured as a storied landscape, but it was marked by a particularly vibrant cultural 'after-life' of the hunt. As sporting writer 'Heclawa', author of *In the Heart of the Bitter-root Mountains* (1895) noted: 'the author is fully conscious of the fact that he is adding another to the vast number of books on hunting and kindred subjects with which the book-stores are already flooded'.[3] The trans-media culture of the hunt served the purposes of autobiography (of historical record, masculine proving and identity politics) and was complicit in creating a collective mythology, or bio-geography, of the American West as a place of adventure and of nature: a hunter's paradise roamed by formidable animals and vigorous hunter heroes. Narratives of strenuous adventuring in the wilderness attested to the power of material environments to inspire our social imagination, and left a rich storied past for excavation. At the same time, beneath the story was a broader process of assimilation, competing claims on natural resources, and political markers of race, gender and class: all of which were viewed through the camera lens.

If the story allowed for the narration of the hunt as a quest, incorporating axioms of movement, rapture, edification, challenge and victory, then photography promised a fresh application: the graphic capture of the hunt. Developed by William Henry Fox Talbot in 1839, the camera was a product of the nineteenth century and one well placed to speak to the period's fascination with historical register, technological fetishism, natural history and imperial expansion. In the American West, photography was used to illuminate processes of settlement and belonging, to record 'exotic' landscapes and peoples and to create a narrative of frontier as-similation. As Megan Williams points out, 'its instantaneous ability to transform the present into the past makes the photograph the quintessential mirror of the "new" American experience and of our desire for an immediately useable past'.[4] The image allowed for the capture of both history and geography. Susan Sontag explains thus: 'Faced with the awesome spread and alien-ness of a newly settled continent, people wielded cameras as a way of taking possession of the places they visited.'[5]

---

3. Heclawa, *In the Heart of the Bitter-Root Mountains: The Story of the Carbin Hunting Party* (New York: G.P. Putnam's, 1895) p. v.

4. Megan R. Williams, *Through the Negative: The Photographic Image and the Written Word in Nine-teenth Century America* (New York: Routledge, 2003) p. 3.

5. Susan Sontag, *On Photography* (New York: Penguin, 1977) p. 8.

Karen Jones

From the outset, the camera acquired an association not only with depiction but also with reproduction. Oliver Wendell Holmes pointed to the juxtaposition of mortality and immortality in image culture when he wrote how the 'shadows' of the photograph remained where 'their originals fade away'.[6] Much philosophising took place as to the capacity of the camera to change the way humans viewed landscapes both social and natural. In the realm of hunting more specifically, the camera promised a 'portrait chronicle': a way of recording the sporting encounter, capturing the animal as image and presenting an added trophy souvenir to boot.[7] L.W. Brownell thus saw the camera as an essential part of the sportsman's tool-kit. In *Photography for the Sportsman Naturalist* (1904), he relished the prospect of being taken 'back in memory, away from the haunts of men, to the woods'.[8] The journal and the sketchpad had served as customary mediums of memorial and now the hunter included a modish addition that promised the alluring prospect of technical accuracy, biotic realism and the re-living of the moment. For Brownell at least, this signalled a new 'epoch' in the storied landscape of the game trail and, in turn, of the social imagination of nature: 'Heretofore, in our nature works and sportsman's books we have had to be content with drawings, always inaccurate, often ludicrous, and sometimes even grotesque in their untruthfulness to nature.'[9]

Evidence of the developing interest of the hunting fraternity in photography could be found in sporting literature such as the popular magazine *Forest and Stream* as well a slew of manuals including Brownell's *Photography for the Sportsman Naturalist*. Amateur photography became an important part of the hunting modus, with sportsmen using camera equipment and reflecting on its use. Scottish hunter Andrew Williamson packed a camera on his 1878 trip to the Rocky Mountains for purposes of 'amusement' at the time and to capture the experience for later reflection.[10] Others entrusted the job of recording to professional photographers, who accompanied hunting parties after the fashion of local guides (some, in fact, combined both jobs). Men such as Laton Huffman and Frank Jay Haynes ran a brisk trade as visual actuaries for visiting sportsmen in the 1880s across the plains. A fecund example of the synchronous infrastructures of economics, recreation and empire in the American West, Haynes used a converted railroad car as studio, which, fitted with displays and a darkroom, ran the rails of the Northern Pacific snapping proud tourists and their trophies. Huffman worked out of a studio at Miles City that was made from the timbers of an old buffalo steamer, depicting local life and

---

6. Oliver Wendell Holmes, 'The Stereoscope and the Stereograph', *Atlantic Monthly* 3 (1859): 738–48.

7. Williams, *Through the Negative*, p. 3.

8. L.W. Brownell, *Photography for the Sportsman Naturalist* (New York: Macmillan, 1904) pp. 25–6.

9. Ibid. p. 3.

10. Andrew Williamson, *Sport and Photography in the Rocky Mountains* (Edinburgh, David Douglas, 1880) p. 1.

'Hunting with the Camera'

hunting parties, and selling postcards, prints and collotypes by mail order to a national audience seeking what Roland Barthes called 'adventure by animation'.[11]

L.W. Brownell articulated the thoughts of many hunters when he talked about the essential compatibility of the gun and the camera as supportive instruments of the chase. Both demanded similar skills, the photographer in the wilds required to 'learn all there is to know about still hunting and then double every precaution'.[12] The discovery of quarry, the pursuit, and the capture figured equally in the mechanics of gun hunting and camera hunting. Both fostered an engagement with nature founded on woodcraft, stealth and knowledge of the habits of wildlife. They shared a powerful and associative vernacular in the language of aiming, loading and shooting. At base, gun and camera represented objects of utility, tools of the trail, but their functional appeal suggested much more at play. Carrying 'the machine in the garden' spoke of modernity, masculinity and science.[13] Hunters talked at length about the mechanisms and performance of guns and other equipment, gracing the wilderness trail with a technological fetishism. These devices served as media through which the hunter communicated with nature and his own cultural musings. Hunters gave names to their firearms, talked of their 'voice' in speaking to animal quarry and imprinted them with a kind of agency. Gun and camera involved the production of a trophy souvenir. According to Susan Sontag, the camera was just another iteration of the gun, a 'fantasy machine' and a 'death weapon'.[14]

Sometimes the association was stark, as in the case of those manufacturers who sold a range of novelty cameras on their weaponised credentials, the most famous of which was probably Etienne Jules Marey's gun camera (1882), a photographic 'rifle' based on the Gatling gun. An advertisement for London inventor Thomas Skaife's 'pistolgraph' (1859) read thus: 'in size and shape not unlike a pistol ... held in the hand, and manipulated by means of a trigger, like a pistol'.[15] Significantly, the gun camera never cultivated a market presence beyond novelty status – in fact, the British Photographical Society issued forth sharp criticism of Skaife's 'hideous and unscientific' contraption.[16] That said, gun cameras elucidated an important synergy between the words of image capture, firearms, and the close scrutiny of wildlife on the hunting trail.

---

11. Roland Barthes, *Camera Lucida: Reflections on Photography* (London: Vintage, 1993) p. 20.

12. Brownell, *Photography*, p. 108.

13. Leo Marx, *The Machine in the Garden: Technology and the Pastoral Ideal in America* (New York: Oxford University Press, 1964).

14. Sontag, *On Photography*, pp. 13–15.

15. Scovill's Manufacturing Co. 1886. *Scovill's Photo Series No.20, Dry Plate Making for Americans* (New York: n.p,) p. 22.

16. *British Journal of Photography*, 15 December 1860: 968; *British Journal of Photography*, 1 May 1860: 138.

Karen Jones

Figure 1. Etienne Marey's photographic gun.

Photograph: David Monniaux, Wikimedia Commons.

KILBURN GUN CAMERA,

For 4 x 5 Pictures.

Price, $27.00.

Gunstock Attachment only $5.00.

Figure 2. Kilburn's gun camera.

Scovill's Photo. Series No. 20, Dry Plate Making for Amateurs (New York: Scovill Mfg. Co, 1886) p. a22

'Hunting with the Camera'

Designing the camera as a pseudo-weapon spoke of pragmatism, target audience, the tactile 'feel' of the product and its gratifying ergonomics as well as technological gimmickry. Marey's gun camera enabled the 'shooting' of birds in flight through its ease of aim and ability to take twelve pictures a 'round', each one exposed in just 1/72nd of a second. Likewise, Massachusetts photographer B.W. Kilburn claimed his 'gun camera' (1883) was more effective and portable owing to its gun-like design: a four by five inch box atop a rifle stock.

Certainly, there were important caveats to the gun–camera nexus, notably in the fact that the camera proffered a bloodless hunt – the pistolgraph, for instance, pointed out its mandate as distinctly different from the gun: 'one being constructed to take life, the other likenesses' – and encouraged the development of a cinemato-graphic gaze on the four-legged (Eadweard Muybridge visited Marey's studio in France as part of his studies in motion capture).[17] Equally, technical restrictions limited the capacity of the camera to rival the Sharps and the Winchester for impact on the hunting trail. Although camera technology in the nineteenth century moved on apace (especially with developments in wet plates and glass negatives from mid-century), it was not until Eastman's Kodak No. 1 (1888) that a truly fast portable camera with film loading realised the potential of a 'snapshot'. At the same time, however, the practices, psychology and designs of the hunting photographer pointed to an affiliation between gun and camera that attested to embedded cultures of empire, technology and appropriation in the search for wild things.

Staging the Hunt: Production and Performance on the Game Trail

The photographic safari involved a lot of preparation for a successful shoot. Wil-liamson recalled how his friends had suggested he leave the camera at home when he announced his plan to travel to the Rockies, in order to avoid the trouble. He took it with him but spent three weeks emptying his cargo boxes and reassembling the equipment (which had been packed in felt-lined crates). The transport of cameras and related paraphernalia prior to the mobile Kodak models was not easy. Nor was the prospect of hauling all the equipment needed for the picturing of the animal across the rugged terrain of the Rocky Mountains. Huffman's self-made camera weighed fifty pounds, while the typical haul of photographic supplies weighed in at close to 120. Travelling with sportsman George Shields in 1880, Huffman turned 'frantic' as the mule carrying his supplies waded into a swollen river.[18] Williamson, meanwhile, was faced with the task of transporting his photographic equipment by donkey, cutting a new trail and draping his camera in blankets to protect it from

17. *Scovill's Photo Series*, p. 22.
18. George Shields, *Rustlings in the Rockies* (Chicago: Belford, Clarke and Co., 1883) pp. 82–6.

the chill wind as he captured an image of a nine point stag shot on a precipice overlooking the Piney Range.[19]

The way in which hunters chose to frame their photographic journeys was instructive. Despite a governing mantra of capturing the moment, the practicalities of the enterprise meant that every image was necessarily staged and studied in its execution – this was not yet a technology of the instantaneous. It took time to set up the shot and to develop the images (either, as wet plates, in darkroom tents, or, with dry plates, after packing out from the game trail). The medium itself tended towards the staging of nature in standardised frames of reference. As Victor Burgin notes, 'Compressed against the viewing screen into a single plane, chopped by the viewfinder into neat rectangles ... the naturalness of the world ostensibly open before the camera is a deceit.'[20] Within the camera sight, subject matter was constructed, posed and mediated according to technical limits.

Further framing devices came in the form of aesthetic arrangement and narrative device. A visual iteration of the hunting story, the social imagination of nature courtesy of the new possibilities of the camera, came in various forms. Two of these are discussed here: the photographic album and the single image. The most interesting aspect of the photographic album was its arrangement in the form of a quest. This was, in many ways, a representation of the dynamics of the game trail in realistic aesthetics. The camera aided the hunter in his desire to speak of journeying and pursuits both geographical and ontological. Jon McIntire's 'Photographic Album of a Rocky Mountain Hunting Trip' (1898) was typical in tracing the tracks of gaming from the railway depot to final trophy display.[21] The visual autobiography was expansive, telling of an encounter with a nature both material and idealised, of the charms of camp life, the motion of the expedition and the first kill. Piles of antlers and trophies grew ever larger with each rifle shot and camera pose. The montage of images presented a powerful narrative of a natural and social landscape of the hunt entwined: the hunter and his entourage, the contest with the animal and the beauty of western scenery, all refracted through a lens that was both documentary and heroic in style. Significantly, the album genre typically contained little text, as though the visuals of the chase spoke for themselves. In this way, photographic culture suggested a new way of framing the hunt, and indeed of the animal – one based around visual code and an attendant sense of biotic realism. As Laton Huffman asserted, photographs were seen 'in a class by themselves ... they tell their own story'.[22]

---

19. Williamson, *Sport*, pp. 1, 24.

20. Victor Burgin (ed.) *Thinking Photography* (London: Macmillan, 1982) p. 47.

21. Jon McIntire, 'Photographic Album of a Rocky Mountain Hunting Trip, 1898', WA photos 37, Beinecke Rare Book & Manuscripts Library, University of Yale, p. 37.

22. L.A. Huffman to George Bird Grinnell, undated c. May 1912, George Grinnell Papers 25/42, Yale University Library.

'Hunting with the Camera'

For all its visual power of conviction, though, the photograph album needed a degree of narrative contextualisation. In Williamson's (unpublished) photographic journal, the image was paramount, but it still included 'a few notes, explanatory of the photographs taken, and a short account of the excellent sport obtained'.[23] On a broader level, the collective artefacts in the social imagination of the hunt – literature, oral testimony, art and, most importantly, material experience – embellished the image and gave it contextual framing. Photography certainly introduced new ways of 'seeing' nature.[24] Yet, it also filtered its visions through other cultural forms. As Victor Burgin notes, 'Objects present to the camera are *already in use* in the production of meanings, and photography has no choice but to operate upon such meanings'.[25] Image and text worked in synchronicity to extend a tradition of the American West as a hunter's paradise, but the camera was not free to invent its meanings entirely.

Unless included within a sporting autobiography, the individual photograph stood alone, often literally so, on a mantelpiece. Here, the story was filled in by the oral testimony of the hunter hero. Also present were a series of genre archetypes: wild scenery, biotic abundance, strenuous adventuring, hyper-masculinity and contest with nature red in tooth and claw. The western theatre framed the picture as setting and also exuded a 'presence', a sense of grandeur, to match the gravitas of the action depicted (John Ford later used the iconic buttes of Monument Valley in a similar way in the Hollywood western of the 1930s and 1940s). Common to the canon was a presentation of the 'life' of the hunt, especially of the campfire and its iconic status as a meeting point and site of reflection. As sportsman William Pickett noted: 'In Mountain Life ... There is only one living room; that is around the camp fire'.[26] Packing boxes, supplies, tents and smouldering fire pits illustrated the architecture of the trail, the culture of the ordinary, and one which consciously conveyed a scene of wilderness authority, activity and frontier spirit.

Whereas the storied landscape of the hunt in literature lavished attention on the moment of kill – the visceral connect between hunter and animal – photography found that difficult. The limits of technology, of biotic realism over imaginative narrative, as well as the practical mechanics of timing camera and gun trajectory (not to mention the behaviour of a charging grizzly) rendered a 'snapshot' of the moment of contest and kill a tough prospect. Some deployed staging techniques, re-playing the contest using taxidermy animals, although such practices were usually reserved for the popular stereograph market, hungry for tales of western ferocity. B.W. Kilburn, inventor of the gun camera, produced a photograph in this

23. Williamson, *Sport*, p. 5.

24. See the essay by Beinart and Schafer in this collection.

25. Burgin, *Thinking*, p. 47.

26. William D. Pickett, 'Diary for 1876', pp. 18–9. From William D. Pickett Diary, SC1436, Montana Historical Society, Helena, Montana.

mould called 'Treed at Last' (1898), which featured a 'world turned upside down' in which the hunter cowered in a tree to escape an angry grizzly.[27] Such theatrics confirmed the relationship between the photograph and taxidermy in their focus on the animal body and also pointed to the importance of staging and storytelling in the visual 'afterlife' of hunting.

For the purposes of memorialisation, though, the trophy shot was the staple choice of the sportsman, almost to the point of cliché. Typically depicting a hunter posed with dead animals, the trophy photograph presented a triumphant human protagonist grasping a rifle and sometimes flanked by loyal dogs (the domestic allies of the hunt). Exuding a sense of manly authority, the hunter hero addressed the camera gaze directly. Also essential to the presentation was the trophy animal. Some photographs displayed a multitude of trophies – antlers stacked high, pelts drying in the sun, a wall of mounted heads – a powerful signifier of the cornucopian frontier as well as the provenance of the triumphant hunter. At other times, focus was on the individual quarry, the vanquished grizzly, bison or elk, presented as a faunal nemesis and masculine hero to match the sapient victor. The visual power of the composition lay in its proof of conquest, much like the taxidermy mounts which many sportsmen mounted in their homes to animate the 'great indoors' with trailside reminiscence. As Brownell pointed out in *Photography for the Sportsman Naturalist* (1904), the hunter 'can bring home with him not only trophies in the way of antlers and skins, but also pictures of the game he was seeking, taken in their native haunts'.[28]

In many ways, the trophy photograph presented a complicated (and some might say disturbing) message about environmental relations and the hunt. A sense of wilderness mystique abounded and yet, in the majority of cases, the spoils of the hunt were laid on the floor, dressed and hung from poles or depicted as disembodied heads or freshly stripped antlers. These fragments of animality 'told' the story of the hunt but also spoke of processes of environmental dislocation.

Photography thus offered a sanctification of the hunt and its carnal violence and yet traded in a vision of romantic adventuring that was almost entirely bloodless. It preserved the moment of the kill for time immortal, blurring the figurative boundary between life and death, the vibrant biotics of the hunting encounter and its necessary denouement. Important too, the pictorial version of the hunt represented a site of rapture, catharsis and reverence, and also of consumption and colonialism. As Susan Sontag notes, the camera contained the ability both to 'consecrate and desecrate'.[29] In her study of Civil War photography, Williams suggests a process at work whereby the comforting undulations of rolling hills served

---

27. B.W. Kilburn, 'Treed at Last', Photographic Study Collection RC2009.057, National Cowboy & Western Heritage Museum, Oklahoma.

28. Brownell, *Photography*, p. 25.

29. Sontag, *On Photography*, p. 65.

figuratively to remove the bloody carnage of the battlefield, allowing for history to enact remembrance and find redemption.[30] The trophy photograph, arguably, performed a similar sleight – deploying the monumental vibrancy of the frontier as well as broader associations of recreation, exploration and science effectively to sanitise, and indeed sanctify, the violent and unpleasant elements of the hunt. Hunters did not shy from violence, just presented it in a ritualised, glorious and, in its own way, theatrical style. For all its emphasis on documentary record, this too was a stage: a social imagination of the game trail presented in realist guise. Photographic images scarcely showed the butchering of animals (the mechanics of transforming the corpse into trophy were pretty messy), instead favouring the heroic record. Hunters held antlers aloft in triumph, stood over vanquished prey with guns at the ready and placed an imperial boot print on the animal body in a symbolic act of claiming. This genre convention, of course, was not unique to the American theatre, instead comprising part of a transnational canon of trophy display that marked diverse landscapes of Euro-American hunting encounter. Sometimes the photographic captions invoked humour, as in the case of a photograph of a rifle leaned against the corpse of a grizzly in Shields' *Cruisings in the Cascades* (1889) which was entitled: 'Death and the cause of it'.[31] Codes of imperial authority and jocular adventuring fused in a visual (and performative) demonstration of domination of the wilds. In the staging of nature, the hunter was author, co-producer and actor.

Reframing Nature: Conservation, Hunting and the Camera

By the latter years of the nineteenth century, the status of the American West as a hunter's paradise was under threat. Processes of westward expansion that saw the alienation of wildlife habitat and the harvesting of animal capital on an industrial scale created a scenario many had scarcely thought possible. The bison, which had numbered in their millions, blackening the plains and stopping the transcontinental railroad in its tracks when the herds crossed, numbered a sorrowful few hundred by the 1880s. As historian Francis Parkman remarked in the 1892 edition of *The Oregon* Trail: 'the wild West has been tamed and its savage charms have withered'.[32] For the sport hunting community, the foreseen end of hunting opportunities and the degradation of landscape raised alarm bells and engendered new approaches to the game trail. Driven by a mantra of fair chase and wise use, sportsmen formed organisations and emerged as an important lobby for the conservation of wildlife and national parks. The foremost was the Boone and Crockett Club (1887), co-founded by Theodore Roosevelt and George Grinnell among others. The sporting

---

30. Williams, *Through the Negative*, p. 6.

31. George Shields, *Cruisings in the Cascades.* (Chicago: Rand McNally, 1889) p. 66.

32. Francis Parkman, *The Oregon Trail.* (Boston: Little, Brown & Co. 1892), p. ix.

Karen Jones

community, of course, had been complicit in the slaughter (the trophy was, after all, another form of animal capital), although many would argue that the main culprits of wildlife destruction were the amassed forces of the market and modern industrialism. Within the sporting conservation community there was a sense of penitence – George Grinnell noted the need to restore 'some of the beautiful things to nature which our selfishness has destroyed' – and universal disdain for the 'game hogs' that mowed down animals en masse for dollar reward or idle fun.[33] The sporting naturalist fraternity represented a complex one: driven by altruism and the ethics of species preservation (not just game) for the nation at large but also trading a culture of enfranchisement that endorsed their rights to game and excluded others (often with class and racial overtones). As historian Karl Jacoby notes, the history of game preservation is one that complicates 'any easy moral tale about conservation'.[34] This fresh discourse on hunting in an age of scarcity also took the camera into account as part of a necessary reframing of the hunting encounter.

Sporting conservationists called for urgent and concerted action to stem the destruction of wildlife, in the shape of legislation, game bags and seasons, and the establishment of parks and reserves. The camera weighed into the bargain as a way of recording vanishing species, demonstrating the ethical inclinations of the 'true' sportsman and highlighting the wonders of natural history. From its role as a visual actuary of the hunting quest, the photographic gaze took a fresh turn: one that foregrounded activism and appreciation over the dynamics of the trophy. In a post-frontier world, new rules seemingly applied and even the most ardent sport hunters determined that hunting with a camera represented a good surrogate in order to address the crisis facing hunter's paradise. In the preface to *Camera Shots at Big Game* (1901), a canonical exposition on camera-hunting, Theodore Roosevelt proselytised on the necessity of game conservation and the importance of the camera as a visual document of natural history. He castigated the wanton butchery of the professional market hunter and wrote: 'More and more, as it becomes necessary to preserve the game, let us hope that the camera will largely supplant the rifle.'[35] *Forest and Stream* debated the merits of the camera at length, notably in a series of editorials from George Grinnell in which his viewpoint on the subject changed from seeing the camera as a useful addition to the gun to a position of primacy on the basis of its non-consumptive approach to 'capturing' animals. As Grinnell

---

33. George Grinnell, 'The Game is Not for Us Alone', clipping, n.d., *Rod and Gun News*, HM223: George Grinnell Papers, Box 35, folder 198: Series Subject files, West 1923–9, Yale University Library.

34. Karl Jacoby, *Crimes Against Nature: Squatters, Poachers, Thieves and the Hidden History of American Conservation* (University of California Press: Berkeley, 2001) p. 146.

35. Allen Grant Wallihan and Mary Augusta Wallihan, *Camera Shots at Big Game.* (New York: Doubleday, Page & Co. 1901) pp. 11–12.

vociferated: 'the wild world is not made the poorer by one life for his shot, nor nature's peace disturbed, nor her nicely adjusted balance jarred'.[36]

Significantly, Grinnell noted that the average sportsman would be unlikely embrace life without the hunt, but might well be convinced to trade one 'weapon' for another.[37] Such comment spoke once more to the synchronicity between gun and camera, as hunting writer James Swan points out: 'Up until a certain moment in the hunt, the emotional chemistry between man and nature, especially man and animals, is the same whether hunting with a 35mm Nikon camera, a powerful pair of Bushnell binoculars, or a Remington shotgun. Man and beast are engaged in a game of proximity.'[38] Some hunters, of course, failed to see how the camera could provide anything that approximated the excitement of armed pursuit – Edgar Randolph railed against the 'camera enthusiast, who possesses merely a platonic love of sport' – while others were persuaded on the basis of conservation crisis, ethical vantage and shared axioms of woodcraft, stalking and technological capture.[39] Sporting discourse, in fact, noted that hitting the game trail armed with a camera represented an ultimate test of masculine resilience and hunting skill. As naturalist William Hornaday contended: 'any duffer with a good check book, a professional guide, and a high-powered repeating rifle can kill big game, but it takes good woodcraft, skill and endurance of a high order ... to secure a really fine photograph'.[40] Roosevelt, meanwhile, explained that in the mantra of the sporting naturalist, the pleasure of the chase was multifaceted in nature:

> it is an excellent thing to have a nation proficient in marksmanship, and it is highly undesirable that the rifle should be wholly laid by. But the shot is, after all, only a small part of the free life in the wilderness. The chief attractions lie in the physical hardihood for which the life calls, the sense of limitless freedom which it brings, and the remoteness and wild charm of primitive nature. All of these we get exactly as much in hunting with the camera as in hunting with the rifle.[41]

Viewed through the frame of conservation, the virtues of hunting with the camera and the engagement with nature offered therein, won sporting converts.

---

36. George Grinnell, 'Hunting with a Camera', *Forest & Stream* May 5, 1892: 427; George Grinnell, 'Shooting Without a Gun', *Forest & Stream* October 6, 1892: 287.

37. Grinnell, 'Hunting with a Camera': 427.

38. James Swan, *The Sacred Art of Hunting*. (Minocqua, WI: Willow Creek Press, 1999) p. 120.

39. Edgar Randolph, *Inter-Ocean Hunting Tales* (New York: Forest & Stream, 1908) p. iii.

40. William Hornaday, *A Wild Animal Round Up* (New York: Charles Scribner's 1925) p. 331.

41. Theodore Roosevelt, *The Wilderness Hunter* (New York: G.P. Putnam's, 1893) p. 29.

36

Karen Jones

Take Only Pictures: 'Harmless' Hunters and the Non-Consumptive Capture of Wildlife

Two westerners whose activities pointed to the complex interface between hunting, conservation and the camera were Allen Grant and Mary Wallihan. Settling in Lay, Colorado in 1860, the couple ran a homestead and a post office, engaged in pursuits of hunting and natural history and developed an attendant interest in photography (Mary bartered her first camera from a group of hunters in exchange for buckskin gloves she had made). Publications of their work, *Hoofs, Claws and Antlers of the Rocky Mountains, by the Camera* (1894) and *Camera Shots at Big Game* (1901), paid heed to the cultural archaeology of hunting imagery in their raft of trophy shots and, indeed, their titles. Text narratives that accompanied the images described the quest for a 'good head' and the adrenaline of the stalk in typical sporting parlance. Meanwhile, the practicalities of camera hunting meant that a 'photographic bag' involved the shooting of animal subjects as a matter of course (in one instance, the Wallihans described in detail the despatch of a cougar, following a striking camera shot of it balanced atop a branch).[42]

While they represented a new phase of photographic engagement, the inherent tensions in wildlife photography were clearly evident in their pictures. To all intents and purposes they forwarded the non-consumptive use of nature, but also featured the traditional modalities of the hunt. C.G. Schillings, author of *With Flashlight and Rifle* (1906), undertook a photographic safari in German East Africa in the 1890s during which he used bait, hunted at night to attract animals and duly shot his animal subjects following their image capture.[43] By the 1930s, wildlife photography had matured sufficiently for exponent Cherry Kearton to critically reflect on his progenitors, who 'while pretending to forward the interests of natural history, frequently [take] as big a toll of animal life as the big game hunter proper'.[44] Accordingly, for historian James Ryan, the camera hunter and the gun hunter were complicit in a culture of empire where the natural world served as grand playground for masculine heroics, the photograph analogous to the bullet 'in the terms of domination, away from a celebration of brute force over the natural world to a more subtle though no less powerful mastery of nature through colonial mastery and stewardship'.[45] The landscape of nature photography was deeply politicised and one that boasted an ancestry irrevocably connected to the hunt.

42. Wallihan and Wallihan, *Camera Shots*; Allen Grant Wallihan and Mary Augusta Wallihan, *Hoofs, Claws and Antlers of the Rocky Mountains, by the Camera* (Denver: Frank Thayer, 1894) pp. 42, 31.
43. C.G. Schillings, *With Flashlight and Rifle A Record of Hunting Adventures and of Studies in Wild Life in Equatorial East Africa* (London: Frederic Whyte, 1906) p. xiv.
44. Cherry Kearton, *Wildlife Across the World* (London: Arrowsmith, 1923) p. 14.
45. James Ryan, *Picturing Empire: Photography and the Visualization of the British Empire.* (London: Reaktion, 1997) p. 136.

At the same time, however, the photographic medium promised an environmental bargain and a way of looking at the animal based on a radically different platform. As William Beinart and Katie McKeown have noted of the African theatre, literary and visual media prioritised the animal subject as a focal point and encouraged new ways of seeing wildlife in an environmental(ist) frame. Similar mechanisms operated for the pioneering camera hunters of the nineteenth-century American West, where the photographic pursuit centred on the (fleeting) capture of a live body and a study of the ways of wild things without the invasive entry of the firearm.[46] Significantly, alongside the conventional typologies of the chase, Allen and Mary Wallihan talked in earnest about the excitement of apprehending a deer unawares. Part of the magic of the encounter was the fact that after the 'shot' the deer moved off along the trail unperturbed. In addition to trophy plates, *Hoofs, Claws and Antlers* contained images nothing short of revolutionary for the time, in which the animal was not only sole subject of the photograph but appeared to 'speak' for itself and to assert ownership of its visual terrain. Captions reading 'what do we hear?', 'who are you?' and 'my audience' subtly re-orientated the photographic gaze to something approximating biocentric, the viewer placed in the geography and social imagination of the animal.[47] The overriding remit of the Wallihans' work, meanwhile, rested with the promotion of conservation through image culture – bringing wild things 'to life' in the public eye and building advocacy for the material cause of wildlife protection. Here, the preservation of the historical moment of the hunt for the benefit of sports was subsidiary to preserving 'the game in photography for the world at large'.

Some who chose to hunt with the camera recognised their vocation as decidedly heretical. Significantly, many of those were reformed hunters. Testimonials frequently issued strident attacks on the gun and its environmental imprint, while axioms of regret and redemption also proved common, as though autobiographical rendition served purposes of confession and catharsis. William Wright, hunter, taxidermist and author of *The Grizzly Bear* (1909), admitted that his scrutiny of animals had started out with one view in mind: to study their habits in order to advance the kill. Over time, though, his view altered to a position where 'interest in my opponent grew to overshadow my interest in the game'.[48] Sensory engagement with the animal seemingly inspired a new (and unarmed) approach to the natural

46. William Beinart and Katie McKeown, 'Wildlife Media and Representations of Africa, 1950s–1970s', *Environmental History* 14/3 (2009): 429–53.

47. Wallihan and Wallihan, *Hoofs, Claws and Antlers*, pp. 10–13, 16, 32, 48, 43; Wallihan and Wallihan *Camera Shots*, p. 11. See also Matthew Brower, *Developing Animals: Wildlife and Early American Photography.* (Minneapolis: University of Minnesota Press, 2011) pp. 25–82; Gregg Mitman, *Reel Nature: America's Romance with Wildlife on Film.* (Seattle: University of Washington Press, 1999) pp. 5–25.

48. William Wright, *The Grizzly Bear.* (New York, Charles Scribner's, 1909) p. 11.

world. A.W. Dimock's *Wall Street and the Wilds* (1915) offered the usual storytelling codes of edification and frontier renewal, with an added sense of contrition
and a manifesto style:

> I like to forget the brutal bags of game I made in the long ago, but the thought of
> each camera shot brings pleasure. The life history of birds and animals as pictured
> by the camera contrast curiously with the game bag product of the fowling piece
> and the bloody trophies of the rifle ... One represents conservation and instruction,
> the other destruction alone.[49]

Dimock saw his writings as 'fugitive' in nature.[50]

Advocates of the 'harmless' hunt explained the ideological framework of
their pursuit in terms of wildlife conservation, humane ethics, personal redemption
and even the refractions of the camera lens itself. For Rowland Robinson, author of
Hunting Without a Gun (1905), the possibilities of unarmed hunting (hiking) made
for a decidedly richer environmental experience than the 'savage blood thirst that
we dignify by calling it love of sport'. Gone was the pressure to find a 'bag' (the goal
so beloved of hunting stories and trophy albums) and instead there was occasion
to 'drift about' in the woods 'in search of nothing'.[51] For those taking a camera to
the woods, a further transaction was possible, one that preserved the mechanics
of the quest and the cult of strenuous masculinity but left the faunal complement
undisturbed. As Dimock pointed out: 'Leatherstocking himself couldn't have crept
up on those antelope more silently than did I.'[52] Meanwhile, it was the particular
dynamic of the photographic gaze that brought Dimock to ethical epiphany: 'the
use of the camera had developed humanity in me until I couldn't bear to wantonly
kill the beautiful creatures'.[53] The camera seemingly represented a radical technology, able to inspire a transformative view of nature founded on biotic encounter,
or what cultural theorist Laura Mulvey calls scopophilia, the love of looking. As
the *New York Times* explained in an editorial dedicated to camera hunting: 'Once
one becomes a devotee of this form of bloodless hunting with its mainly pictorial
rewards, he often loses interest in the sanguinary sport and takes up photography
in the forest in earnest.'[54]

Michigan-based camera hunter George Shiras, who referred to himself as a
'pioneer in this new sport', ably highlighted the complicated relationship between

---

49. A.W. Dimock, *Wall Street and the Wilds*. (New York: Outing Publishers, 1915) p. 452.

50. Ibid. p. 453.

51. Rowland Robinson, *Hunting without a Gun* (New York: Forest & Stream, 1905), pp. 1–3.

52. Dimock, *Wall Street*, pp. 444–6.

53. Ibid. p. 428.

54. Laura Mulvey, 'Visual Pleasure and Narrative Cinema', *Screen* 16/3 (1975): 6–18; 'Hunting with
     the Camera', *New York Times*, 18 June 1916.

hunting, conservation and the various technologies of the chase.[55] A skilled hunter, Shiras developed an interest in natural history from time spent at Whitefish Lake, Michigan. His forays into the world of photography certainly bore the hallmark of a hunting lineage, notably in use of hunting lures and blinds to capture animals in images. Shiras was a member of the Boone and Crockett Club, and a harsh critic of 'misguided humanitarians who demand continuous protection for all things'.[56] As his camera work evolved, however, Shiras made the transition into a 'harmless' hunter, a development that he saw as a direct result of interaction with material nature and a necessary recourse in a modern industrial nation. Most significantly, Shiras' example pointed to the importance of these new visual images in bridging a gap between the imperial world of nineteenth century hunting culture and the wildlife photography (and filmmaking) industry of the twentieth century. Starkly evident in the portfolio of Shiras (and, indeed, in the pioneers including Schillings) was attention to the image, to the innovative use of technology and to the focus on wild *life* in its natural setting. The 'Midnight Series', a series of nocturnal dioramas in which deer were the directors and the actors in the photograph (courtesy of flash cameras connected to trip wires) won awards at the Paris Exposition (1900) and the grand prize at the St. Louis World's Fair (1904). Shiras showcased his work in *National Geographic* (July 1906), the first time the magazine had featured animal photography within its pages. A testament to the emergence of a very different kind of trophy (one founded on visual consumption and on the live animal), one commentator in Paris noted 'How happy I would be to place these splendid pieces in my hunting castle.'[57]

Conclusion: Hunting, Photography and the Social Imagination of Nature

The image culture of the camera told the story of a landscape encountered, claimed, consumed and idealised. As part of a broader transmedia storytelling, photography conspired in the invention of a frontier tradition of grand landscapes, charismatic animals and vigorous heroes. Hunting played a key role in this story as a vector by which various communities engaged with the material world on a practical and an ideological level. Specifically, the visual 'afterlife' of the hunt as crafted by photography constructed a fecund geography of hunter's paradise that drew inspiration from the material environment and the social imagination. As a medium of communication and memorial, the camera served the purposes of both personal

---

55. George Shiras, *Hunting Wild Life with Camera and Flashlight* (Washington, D.C.: National Geographic, 1936) p. vii.

56. Ibid. p. xx.

57. Ibid. p. viii.

and national biography. As Williams notes, 'The experience *of* the photograph is equated with *living* the scene it depicts.'[58]

Photographic depictions of the hunt offered a striking, vibrant and ultimately complicated picture of wild things. The advertising for Kilburn's gun camera, for example, noted its 'conformity with the laws of Mr Bergh's Society for the Prevention of Cruelty to Animals' and its similarity to 'an ordinary shotgun … [W]hen a bird rises it must be brought to the shoulder, a dead aim taken at the feathered object, and the trigger pulled'.[59] On one hand, the camera and the gun emerged as devices of co-production and were complicit in the cultural economy of the hunt. Both operated as tools of empire, part of a Euro-American nexus that apprehended the world through an authoritative lens of exploration, settlement, scientific catalogue and historical document. Photography locked the hunter in a visual capture with the object of his quest and conveyed a powerful message of masculine authority over wild things. Read more heretically, however, the photographic gaze scrutinised a different environment, one that privileged the live animal over the dead one and pointed to a fundamentally different relationship between object and user, user and environment. In the final analysis, the abiding message of the game trail speaks of an interconnection between material and imagined landscapes, of the power of wild things to enliven our experience and of the convoluted relationships between society and the technologies we use to capture the natural world.

REFERENCES

Barthes, Roland. 1993. *Camera Lucida: Reflections on Photography*. London: Vintage.

Brower, Matthew. 2011. *Developing Animals: Wildlife and Early American Photography*. Minneapolis: University of Minnesota Press.

Brownell, L. W. 1904. *Photography for the Sportsman Naturalist*. New York: Macmillan.

Burgin, Victor (ed.) 1982. *Thinking Photography*. London: Macmillan.

Dimock, A.W. 1915. *Wall Street and the Wilds*. New York: Outing Publishers.

Dunlap, Thomas. 1988. *Ecology and the American Mind, 1850–1990*. New Jersey: Princeton University Press.

Dunlap, Thomas. 1988. 'Sport Hunting and Conservation', *Environmental Review* 12/1: 51–9.

Fitter, Richard and Peter Scott. 1978. *The Penitent Butchers: The Fauna Preservation Society 1903–1978*. London: Collins.

Gillespie, Greg. 2007. *Hunting for Empire: Narratives of Sport in Rupert's Land, 1840–1870*. Vancouver: UBC Press.

Grinnell, George. May 5, 1892. 'Hunting with a Camera', *Forest & Stream*.

---

58. Martha Sandweiss, *Print the Legend: Photography and the American West*. (New Haven: Yale University Press, 2002) p. 6; Williams, p. 11.

59. *Scovill's Photo Series*, p. 22.

Grinnell, George. October 6, 1892. 'Shooting Without a Gun', *Forest & Stream*.

Haraway, Donna. 1984. 'Teddy Bear Patriarchy: Taxidermy in the Garden of Eden, New York City, 1908–1936', *Social Text* 11: 19–64.

Heclawa. 1895. *In the Heart of the Bitter-Root Mountains: The Story of the Carbin Hunting Party*. New York: G.P. Putnam's.

Herman, Daniel. 2003. *Hunting and the American Imagination*. Washington, D.C.: Smithsonian Institution Press.

Holmes, Oliver Wendell. 1859. 'The Stereoscope and the Stereograph', *Atlantic Monthly* 3: 738–48.

Hornaday, William. 1925. *A Wild Animal Round Up*. New York: Charles Scribner's.

'Hunting with the Camera', *New York Times*, 18 June 1916.

Jacoby, Karl. 2001. *Crimes Against Nature: Squatters, Poachers, Thieves and the Hidden History of American Conservation*. University of California Press: Berkeley.

Kearton, Cherry. 1923. *Wildlife Across the World*. London: Arrowsmith.

Loo, Tina. 2002. 'Of Moose and Men: Hunting for Masculinities in British Columbia, 1880–1939', *Western Historical Quarterly* 32: 296–319.

Marx, Leo. 1964. *The Machine in the Garden: Technology and the Pastoral Ideal in America*. New York: Oxford University Press.

Mackenzie, John M. 1988. *The Empire of Nature: Hunting, Conservation and British Imperialism*. Manchester: Manchester University Press.

Merritt, John I. 1985. *Baronets and Buffalo: The British Sportsman in the American West, 1833–1881*. Missoula, Montana: Mountain Press Publishing Co.

Mitman, Gregg. 1999. *Reel Nature: America's Romance with Wildlife on Film*. Seattle: University of Washington Press.

Mulvey, Laura. 1975. 'Visual Pleasure and Narrative Cinema', *Screen* 16/3: 6–18.

Parkman, Francis. 1892. *The Oregon Trail*. Boston: Little, Brown & Co.

Randolph, Edgar. 1908. *Inter-Ocean Hunting Tales*. New York: Forest & Stream, 1908.

Reiger, John. 2001. *American Sportsmen and the Origins of Conservation*. Corvallis: Oregon State University Press.

Ritvo, Harriet. 1987. *The Animal Estate: The English and Other Creatures in the Victorian Age*. Cambridge, MA: Harvard University Press.

Robinson, Rowland. 1905. *Hunting without a Gun*. New York: Forest & Stream.

Roosevelt, Theodore. 1893. *The Wilderness Hunter*. New York: G.P. Putnam's.

Rotundo, Anthony. 1993. *American Manhood: Transformations on Masculinity from the Revolution to the Modern Era*. New York: Basic Books.

Ryan, James. 1997. *Picturing Empire: Photography and the Visualization of the British Empire*. London: Reaktion.

Sandweiss, Martha. 2002. *Print the Legend: Photography and the American West*. New Haven: Yale University Press.

42

Karen Jones

Schillings, C.G. 1906. *With Flashlight and Rifle A Record of Hunting Adventures and of Studies in Wild Life in Equatorial East Africa.* London: Frederic Whyte.

Scovill's Manufacturing Co. 1886. *Scovill's Photo Series No.20, Dry Plate Making for* Americans. New York: n.p.

Shields, George. 1883. *Rustlings in the Rockies.* Chicago: Belford, Clarke and Co.

Shields, George. 1889. *Cruisings in the Cascades.* Chicago: Rand McNally.

Shiras, George. 1936. *Hunting Wild Life with Camera and Flashlight.* Washington, D.C.: National Geographic.

Slotkin, Richard. 1973. *Regeneration Through Violence: The Myth of the American Frontier, 1600–1800.* Middletown: Wesleyan University Press.

Slotkin, Richard. 1985. *The Fatal Environment: The Myth of the Frontier in the Age of Industrialization, 1800–1890.* New York: Atheneum.

Smith, Henry Nash. 1950. *Virgin Land: The American West as Symbol and Myth.* Cambridge, MA: Harvard University Press.

Sontag, Susan. 1977. *On Photography.* New York: Penguin.

Swan, James. 1999. *The Sacred Art of Hunting.* Minocqua, WI: Willow Creek Press.

Wallihan, Allen Grant and Mary Augusta Wallihan. 1894. *Hoofs, Claws and Antlers of the Rocky Mountains, by the Camera.* Denver: Frank Thayer.

Wallihan, Allen Grant and Mary Augusta Wallihan. 1901. *Camera Shots at Big Game.* New York: Doubleday, Page & Co.

Warren, Louis S. 1997. *The Hunter's Game: Poachers and Conservationists in Twentieth Century America.* New Haven: Yale University Press.

Williams, Megan R. 2003. *Through the Negative: The Photographic Image and the Written Word in Nineteenth Century America.* New York: Routledge.

Williamson, Andrew. 1880. *Sport and Photography in the Rocky Mountains.* Edinburgh: David Douglas.

Wonders, Karen. 2005. 'Hunting Narratives of the Age of Empire', *Environment and History* 11: 269–91.

Wright, William. 1909. *The Grizzly Bear.* New York, Charles Scribner's.

Archival Sources

Grinnell, George. 'The Game is Not for Us Alone', clipping, n.d. *Rod and Gun News*, HM223: George Grinnell Papers, Box 35, folder 198: Series Subject files, West 1923–9, Yale University Library.

Huffman, L.A. to George Bird Grinnell, undated c. May 1912, George Grinnell Papers 25/42, Yale University Library.

Kilburn, B.W. 'Treed at Last', Photographic Study Collection RC2009.057, National Cowboy & Western Heritage Museum, Oklahoma.

McIntire, Jon. 'Photographic Album of a Rocky Mountain hunting trip, 1898', WA photos 37, Beinecke Rare Book & Manuscripts Library, University of Yale.

'Hunting with the Camera'

Pickett, William D. 'Diary for 1876', 18–19. From William D. Pickett Diary, SC1436, Montana Historical Society, Helena, Montana.

Chapter Two

Hollywood in Africa 1947–62:
Imaginative Construction and Landscape Realism

William Beinart and Dominique Schafer

Introduction: Feature Film and Representations of Africa

Our aim in this chapter is to explore representations of African landscape, wildlife and related social contexts in feature films from c. 1947–1962. The scale of film-making in post-war Africa, particularly East Africa, is now being recognised. Our discussion largely covers the period from *The Macomber Affair* (1947) to *Hatari!* (1962); *Born Free* (1966) and its sequels represent a significant change in focus. Especially from 1950 to 1953, feature films set in East Africa were remarkably successful. Leading directors employing stellar Hollywood actors released a sequence of productions that were amongst the top box office earners of their time: *King Solomon's Mines* (2nd in 1950), *The African Queen* (7th in 1951), *The Snows of Kilimanjaro* (3rd in 1952) and *Mogambo* (11th in 1953).[1] A number of African-based British films also reached wide audiences, notably *Where No Vultures Fly* (1951), chosen for the Royal Command Performance and the top British money-maker of 1952.[2] In addition, some feature length documentaries, such as Lewis Cotlow and Armand Denis's *Savage Splendor* (1949), attracted large audiences. Billed as the first technicolour feature film made in Africa, it was released by RKO and surprisingly became its most profitable film of that year. Denis followed it with *Below the Sahara* in 1953 – a year which also saw the start of sustained television coverage in the United Kingdom of natural history and African wildlife.[3]

These films were not in our view classics. Most are uneven in their quality and include an uneasy portrayal of the late colonial period from the vantage point of heroic whites; they are interesting partly for this latter reason. We will not, however,

---

1. Michael J. Anderson, 'Hatari! And the Hollywood Safari Picture', *Senses of Cinema* **52** (2009). He takes the figures from http://www.boxofficereport.com/ybon/rental.shtml
2. Anthony Steel Obituary, The Powell and Pressburger Pages, Accessed online: http://www.powell-pressburger.org/Obits/Steel/Indie.html
3. Armand Denis, *On Safari: The Story of My Life* (London: Collins, 1963).

mainly be pursuing themes of empire, race and gender in this chapter. (For the same reason, we will also omit productions based on the Mau Mau rebellion in Kenya at this period.)[4] Our focus is on a more specific aspect of such feature films: all were made partly on location and all, to some degree, used wildlife and landscape in their narratives. They have been collectively called safari pictures and – while this title is not entirely appropriate– we will explore how hunting and wildlife came to be central themes. These films were one of the major vehicles through which many people in the West encountered Africa. How do we make sense of their concerns and what did they feed into the general store of images on Africa during this late colonial period?

   Much of the academic literature on representations of Africa, particularly in connection with wildlife and landscape, is driven by a critique of the 'myth of wild Africa'.[5] In this discussion, authors such as Adams and McShane take issue with an Africa constructed as wild, or as empty of people, or as a figment of a rather lurid western imagination about the continent, including the right to possess its land and riches and a tendency to perpetuate racial hierarchies. Andre Bazin has been quoted as describing earlier 'safari pictures', such as *Trader Horn* (1931) – another box-office success – as a 'shameless search after the spectacular and the sensational', propagating a 'myth of an Africa inhabited by savages and wild beasts'.[6] Kevin Dunn emphasises less the critique of wild Africa and more the 'otherness and the dynamics of power' with Africans framed essentially through a white lens.[7] Derek Bouse, exploring wildlife documentaries more generally, adds an illuminating discussion of how nature is 'manipulated, intensified, dramatized, and fictionalized' in film.[8] He not only examines the techniques and conventions used, but also discusses the tendency to show a 'primal, untouched Eden, existing in a realm of "mythic time"'.[9]

   These discussions reflect a more general, deeply set and powerful strand in African Studies that seeks to identify, explain and reject problematic western stereotypes. Wildness and racism have become, with considerable justification, central themes in the analysis of misrepresentations of Africans and Africa. Roy Grinker *et al.* suggest that 'Africa was a "blank" space in Europe's collective imagination which

4.   David M. Anderson, 'Mau Mau at the Movies: Contemporary Representations of an Anti-Colonial War', *South African Historical Journal* **48** (2003): 71–89.

5.   J.S. Adams and T.D. McShane, *The Myth of Wild Africa: Conservation Without Illusion* (Berkeley: University of California Press, 1997).

6.   Anderson, '*Hatari!*', quoting A. Bazin, 'The Virtues and Limitations of Montage', in *What is Cinema? Vol 1*, trans. by Hugh Gray (Berkeley: University of California Press, 2005), p. 15.

7.   K. Dunn, 'Lights … Camera … Africa: Images of Africa and Africans in Western Popular Films of the 1930s', *African Studies Review* **39**/1 (1996): 149–175.

8.   Derek Bouse, *Wildlife Films* (Philadelphia: University of Pennsylvania Press, 2000), p. 8.

9.   Bouse, *Wildlife Films*, p. 15, quoting Barbara Novak.

William Beinart and Dominique Schafer

could be populated with all sorts of invented creatures.'[10] Following a similar logic Ruth Mayer starts her book on *Artificial Africas* – which touches on Tarzan films amongst other topics – by asserting 'this is not a book about Africa. It is a book about speculations, projections, fantasies and fears.'[11] We come away from such literature with a sense that film – a medium that trades in illusion – has contributed particularly to disturbing representations and imaginary Africas.

Our view of these films differs in some respects. Clearly they were products of western imaginations, but they were not simply that. In an article on documentary natural history film in Africa during the post-war period, Beinart and McKeown suggest that it is valuable to look beyond the construction of wild Africa and to understand how these images were linked to scientific advances, how they aimed to educate audiences, why they had power and how the images stared back. [12] This argument is less convincing in relation to feature films which are often both more fantastical and more racist and do not generally aim at 'true to nature' depictions. Yet many of the directors were concerned to display African landscapes in extended sequences. Some landscape and wildlife sequences were shot by the same cameramen who produced documentaries, or with the same techniques. To a surprising degree these feature films also reflected social process in late colonial Africa. In certain respects they could be called realist. We do not suggest that realism is synonymous with reality or truth– it is a set of visual depictions and narrative strategies that of-fers an artistic interpretation of environments and social practices. Social realism is associated with particular movements in cinema that explicitly use the medium as a vehicle for social commentary – often from a leftish or popular perspective. It is linked with gritty emotions, representations of working class life, crime and social division or the down-at-heel corners of urban society. The idea of social realism does not sit easily with the safari films. We propose, instead, the idea of landscape realism.

In the most sustained analysis of these safari films, Michael Anderson discusses them from a rather different vantage point. He is less concerned about representations of Africa and more with the relationship between fictional and documentary elements in the films. Danger in the face of natural hazards is an element in the narrative of most of these African pictures. Feature films tend to capture this by including documentary footage of wild animals, sometimes induced to be aggressive, and then cutting away to separately filmed scenes with the actors.

10. Roy Richard Grinker, Christopher B. Steiner and Stephen C. Lubkemann (eds.) *Perspectives on Africa: a Reader in Culture, History, and Representation* (Chichester: Wiley-Blackwell, 2010), p. 23, discussing Christopher L. Miller, *Blank Darkness: Africanist discourse in French* (Chicago: University of Chicago Press, 1985) on the longer term of French views of Africa. Thanks to David Pratten for the reference.

11. Ruth Mayer, *Artificial Africas: Colonial Images in the Times of Globalization* (New Hampshire: University Press of New England, 2002), p. 1.

12. W. Beinart and K. McKeown, 'Wildlife Media and Representations of Africa, 1950s to the 1970s', *Environmental History* **14**/3 (2009): 429–452.

Spliced together, the juxtaposition was intended to convey to audiences that the stars were in danger. In some cases, stand-ins were used with animals in the same frame. The effects were created by a form of montage. Clearly this was convincing to audiences at the time, especially because the sequences made sense as part of a narrative. Anderson praises *Hatari!* (1962, meaning danger in Swahili) because its director Howard Hawks did sometimes insert its stars, notably John Wayne, in the same frame as the animals – and thus fashioned an expanded documentary, non-fictional space within a fictional narrative. He argues that *Hatari!* was the first to achieve this filmic effect: 'ultimately, *Hatari!* realizes the desire of all Hollywood safari pictures: to show real bodies in real African spaces in real danger'.[13]

We are less convinced about *Hatari!* Firstly, it is in many senses an unrelieved film of possession – focusing on game capture by Americans in vehicles. Secondly, some earlier films also contained wildlife, or other natural hazards, in the same frame as actors. And thirdly, compared to *Born Free* (1966), the integration of wildlife and actors is limited; the latter film also expresses a far more challenging set of ideas about the relationship between people and wild animals. Nevertheless, Anderson helps to open up some important issues about location filming, documentary inserts and landscape or environmental realism in these African feature films.

We agree with Anderson that the boundary between documentary and non-documentary elements could be porous, but differ in seeing this manifested in a number of earlier films. We suggest that, to a surprising degree, the images and some of the narratives in these earlier films rest heavily on both location filming and historical, rather than purely imagined, social contexts. David Anderson makes a similar point about the rapidity with which the movie industry responded to Mau Mau and tried to comment in different ways on contemporary politics and social forces.[14] The films are certainly fictional and embellish, manipulate, exoticise and renature African landscapes in the pursuit of narrative excitement. They render Africa into a cinematographic terrain that was contained within Hollywood and Ealing's mainstream conventions.[15] But ultimately, some of the interest of these films resides specifically in their evocation of African landscapes and social contexts.

The mainstream could also be quite a wide cinematic channel. Some of the directors who made films in Africa were political dissidents or mavericks.[16] Zoltan Korda, who directed *The Macomber Affair* (1947), had liberal, anti-imperial

13. Anderson, '*Hatari!*' As this is an online journal, page numbers are not given.

14. Anderson, 'Mau Mau at the Movies': 71.

15. *Where No Vultures Fly* was partly made in Ealing, the oldest British film studio, which was at the peak of its success in the late 1940s and early 1950s.

16. Robert A. Rosenstone, *Visions of the Past: The Challenges of Film to Our Idea of History* (Cambridge, Mass.: Harvard University Press, 1995); Robert Brent Toplin, *History by Hollywood: the Use and Abuse of the American Past* (Champaign, IL: University of Illinois Press, 1996).

William Beinart and Dominique Schafer

leanings and went on to make the more politically challenging *Cry The Beloved Country* (1952).[17] Korda filmed parts of Alan Paton's novel in South Africa using black American and local actors; it helped to launch Sidney Poitier's career. Henry King, who directed *The Snows of Kilimanjaro* (1952), went on to address racial prejudice in *Love is a Many-Splendored Thing* (1955). King often worked with Gregory Peck, a graduate in English literature, who took the lead male role both in *The Macomber Affair* and *Snows of Kilimanjaro*. Peck was a Democrat, whose career peaked with the powerful civil rights film *To Kill a Mockingbird* (1962). John Huston (*The African Queen*), John Ford (*Mogambo*) and Howard Hawks (*Hatari!*) were all unconventional in their politics and in the 1950s all opposed in different ways the McCarthyite witch-hunts in Hollywood. Ford developed close relationships with the Navaho communities around Monument Valley, Utah, and provided them with employment and acting opportunities. In the late 1940s, he considered making a film about Afrikaners, based on a Stuart Cloete novel, 'but the difficulty in making the racist Boers sympathetic killed the story fairly quickly'.[18] *Where No Vultures Fly* explicitly contested imperial hunting. Thus some of the key feature films under discussion were made by innovative directors with unconventional political leanings.

Locations and Landscape Realism

This article explores the intersection between visual representation on film, and the world that is being represented. Film could be made anywhere and films about Africa were sometimes made largely or entirely outside the continent. It would have been feasible and much cheaper to make most of these films in studios or to utilise more convenient locations in the United States. Nor did this necessarily diminish the product. Zoltan Korda made two African films, *Sanders of the River* (1935) and *The Four Feathers* (1939), partly on location when he was working for his brother, Alexander, in London.[19] But he made *Sahara* (1943) a 'grim, gritty war film about desert survival', starring Humphrey Bogart, in a southern Californian desert.[20] Given wartime constraints, Ford filmed his evocative adaption of *How Green Was My Valley* (1941), about Wales, on a carefully constructed set at Twentieth Century Fox's Malibu ranch in the United States.[21] *Casablanca* (1942) was shot entirely in

---

17. Charles Druzin, *Korda: Britain's Only Movie Mogul* (London: Sidgwick and Jackson, 2002), pp. 202–3; Martin Stockham, *The Korda Collection: Alexander Korda's Film Classics* (London: Channel 4, Box Tree, 1992), pp. 26–7.

18. Scott Eyman, *Print the Legend: the Life and Times of John Ford* (New York: Simon and Schuster, 1999), p. 364.

19. Stockham, *Korda Collection*.

20. A.M. Sperber and E. Lax, *Bogart* (London: Phoenix, 1997), p. 442ff.

21. Eyman, *John Ford*, p. 235.

studios except for stock footage of Paris and some airport scenes. Yet it successfully suggested an exotic Moroccan urban environment and became a classic.

Many films at this time were hybrid productions in the sense that they combined studio and location shots. Korda's *The Macomber Affair* (1947) used a Hollywood studio and a six-week trip to the Mexican bush for scenes with the main actors.[22] However, it also included sequences specifically filmed in Africa by a second camera unit rather than stock film of African wildlife. The African scenes in King's *The Snows of Kilimanjaro* (1951) were largely filmed in a studio on the Fox lot. Ava Gardner recalled, 'all of stage 8, in fact, was turned into a massive African hunting camp courtesy of a three-hundred-fifty-by-forty-foot cyclorama painting of snowy Mt. Kilimanjaro itself. And some of the props they used, like an elephant-foot stool, came direct from Zanuck's office.'[23] But some footage was filmed in Kenya, including the scenes with a hyena.

Despite these cost-saving devices, directors Korda and King were concerned to create an authentic atmosphere of the safari camp. It is not always easy in *Macomber* to distinguish between studio, Mexico and African location. The African shots include not only wildlife but vehicles and people. Korda took care to include the same type of vehicles in both locations and the cutting between African background and Mexican scenes with the main actors is skilled. The film shot in Africa is often more grainy and less sharp than that shot in Mexico and California. The film was shot in black and white, which made it is easier to disguise the shifts in scene. But the terrain of the locations is not dissimilar and viewers have to keep a sharp eye on acacia trees to spot when the camera was in Kenya.

Yet commitment to location shooting was growing in Hollywood. Ford increasingly made films with dramatic scenery and first used Monument Valley, scene of nine of his Westerns, in *Stagecoach* (1939).[24] He returned to this valley for a sequence of films before going to Africa for *Mogambo* (1953). Ford made 'natural exteriors' an important element in his 'visual rhetoric'.[25] Authentic landscape was seen to lend power and a new dynamism to Westerns. In *Red River* (1949) Hawks deployed thousands of cattle and horses in many scenes to give the atmosphere of a long-distance cattle run. He included a stampede that was replicated with African wild animals by Compton Bennett and Andrew Marton in *King Solomon's Mines* (1950). The idea may have been taken from Harry Watt's Australian documentary-style feature film, *The Overlanders* (1946). Watt, who was schooled in the British

---

22. John Griggs, *The Films of Gregory Peck* (London: Columbus Books, 1984), pp. 56–62.

23. Ava Gardner, *Ava: My Story* (New York: Bantam Books, 1990), p. 167. Darryl F. Zanuck was founder of Twentieth Century Fox.

24. Peter Bogdanovich, *John Ford* (London: Studio Vista, 1967); Eyman, *John Ford*.

25. T. Gallagher, *John Ford: The Man and his Films* (Berkeley: University of California Press, 1986).

William Beinart and Dominique Schafer

documentary movement and co-directed the famous *Night Train* (1936), filmed much of *Where No Vultures Fly* in Kenya.

Cotlow and Denis's *Savage Splendor* (1949) was entirely filmed in Africa, using a travelogue style of presentation. They claimed to have covered 22,000 miles over ten months, visiting West and Central as well as East Africa. Unlike Korda in *Macomber*, they used colour, as did all the subsequent films discussed here. Although colour cinematography was well-established by this time, the equipment was still cumbersome and expensive. But it enhanced the potential of location shooting of landscape. A number of key themes and scenes in *Savage Splendor* were subsequently developed in later feature films and Denis worked as a cameraman and advisor on *King Solomon's Mines*. Denis was establishing a style that celebrated wildlife, the African savannah, the use of acacias as a framing device, and major landmarks such as Kilimanjaro. He clearly took the crew to some of the scenes that he had filmed in *Savage Splendor* and the final 'Watusi' dance sequence in *King Solomon's Mines* imitated a shorter version in the earlier film.

King Solomon's Mines to some degree shared the travelogue format of *Savage Splendor*. Both used authentic locations but were not specific about those locations. Bennett and Marton covered a great deal of ground in Africa, from Murchison

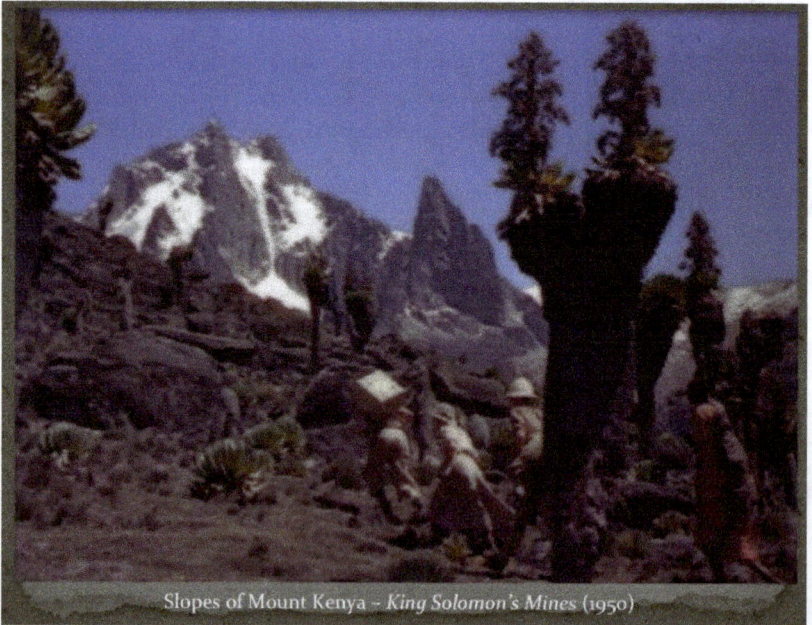

Slopes of Mount Kenya – *King Solomon's Mines* (1950)

Figure 1. Still from King Solomon's Mines, *Mount Kenya.*

Falls in Uganda, to Stanleyville in Congo and various locations in Kenya. (They also filmed in California and New Mexico). The film takes the viewer through very diverse landscapes (from waterfalls and tropical forests to deserts, rolling plains and snowy peaks) in order to create the impression of a long quest. Allan Quartermain, played by Stewart Granger, agrees to go on an expedition with Mrs Curtis and her brother, in search of her missing husband. Each landscape has a challenge for Quartermain to overcome. But although great efforts were made by the directors to film authentic locations, and the scenes at Murchison falls and on Mount Kenya are especially striking, the sequence in the film made no geographical sense as a route. It is an imaginary trip through real landscapes. In this sense, the directors were both evoking a generic Africa, and carefully visualising particular scenes that were recognisable to some of their audience.

Directors and producers not only took great pains to find African locations, but in the cases of Huston (*The African Queen*) and Ford (*Mogambo*) chose places far off the beaten track for key scenes. Aside from a shared interest in authentic landscapes, the motives of studios and directors were mixed, and not all the same. Huston, Ford and Hawks *(Hatari!)* were in varying degrees keen to experience adventure or hunting in East Africa. Huston took advantage of an extended period on location to hunt more assiduously than any other director. Peter Viertel, who was on location as a script-writer for *The African Queen,* wrote a book *White Hunter, Black Heart* (1953) based on his experiences that Clint Eastwood (1990) later made into a film. In the book, John Wilson (Huston) phones Verill (Viertel) 'How would you like to go to Africa? Help me. Keep me company. There's a little work to be done on the script, and then you can stay on and we'll hunt.'[26] As Viertel wrote in his afterword:

> Huston was not enamored of *The African Queen.* He liked the novel and was anxious to make another film with Spiegel, but the fact that he would be able to travel to Africa was, I soon discovered, almost equally important to him … [I]t became apparent that, aside from making a movie, Huston was anxious to try his hand at big-game hunting, in those days a sport indulged in only by millionaires and macho writers the likes of Hemingway and Ruark.[27]

Viertel left in the middle of filming, partly due to Huston's obsessive desire to kill an elephant, and his lack of focus on the film. Based in Uganda and the DRC, Huston went shooting every morning to 'get game for the pot'.[28] Katherine Hepburn, the lead woman actor, initially criticised him, but he converted her to this pastime. Humphrey Bogart, the male lead, drily observed, 'Katie what's happened to you?

---

26. P. Viertel, *White Hunter, Black Heart* (London: Penguin, 1953), p. 5.

27. Ibid. p. 412.

28. Robert Emmet Long, *John Huston Interviews* (Jackson: University of Mississippi Press, 2001), p. 156.

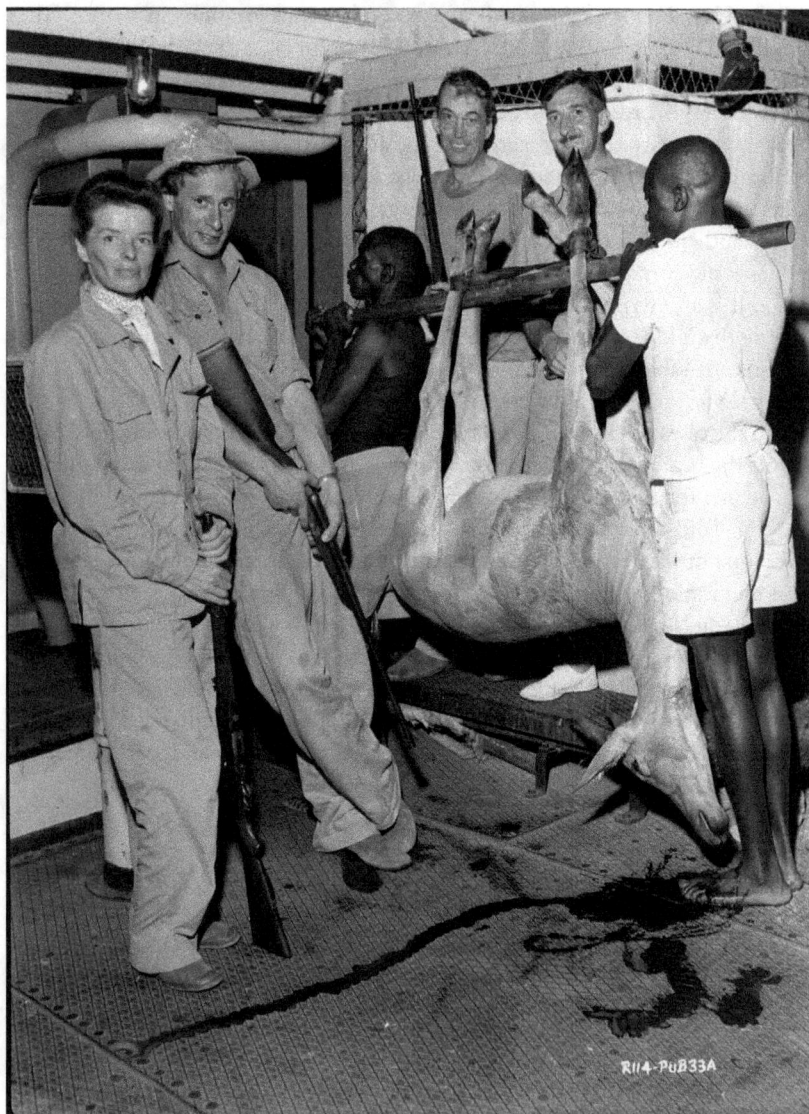

Figure 2. Katharine Hepburn after a kudu hunt.

Source: Wisconsin Center for Film and Theater Research, Image ID: 101654.

You're a decent human being … that son of a bitch has gotten to you.'[29] Hepburn was unembarrassed; 'back at the houseboat we ate the kudu. It was a great treat. And I had been "hunting in Africa".'[30] In her vivid illustrated memoir of the filming, subtitled *How I Went to Africa with Bogart, Bacall and Huston and Almost Lost My Mind*, Hepburn recalls her enthusiasm for the experience, as well as her trials with dysentery. She managed to avoid bilharzia because all the scenes where the actors had to be immersed in water were shot in a tank in London. Bogart himself was uneasy about slaughtering wild animals.[31] By contrast, Stewart Granger, star of *King Solomon's Mines*, bought three high quality hunting rifles in London before he departed.[32] He was bowled over by the wildlife on arrival and peppered his recollections of filming in Africa with accounts of animals and hunting.

In addition to the directors' own lust for adventure, there was a perception that audiences, that were seeing more documentary images, expected authentic landscapes. Moreover, sterling devalued sharply after the Second World War, and particularly in 1949, so that it was cheaper for Hollywood studios to make films in British colonies. American production companies were also finding it difficult to repatriate profits, so filming outside the US was one way of using funds that could be materialised in saleable celluloid. *Mogambo*, in particular, was pursued by MGM not least for financial reasons. Although it is surely not his best, *Mogambo* had the highest domestic first-year gross of any of John Ford's films ($5.2m). The Kenyan, Tanzanian and Ugandan colonial governments by and large promoted the film industry as a means of raising revenue and tourist interest.

Hemingway, Landscape and Social Contexts

As we have noted, parts of *The Macomber Affair* were filmed in Kenya in 1946, launching this sequence of safari pictures. We will suggest that this and some subsequent films not only used African landscapes but reflected some significant social processes in East Africa. *The Macomber Affair* was based on a Hemingway short story. Hemingway had visited East Africa for nearly two months in 1933–4 for an upmarket hunting safari.[33] In his study of Hemingway's experiences in Africa, Christopher Ondaatje suggests – perhaps with overstatement – that Africa always occupied a significant place in Hemingway's imagination, despite his relatively brief sojourns there; he visited only once again in 1953–4. On both occasions, he chose Philip Percival, who had been on the Roosevelt safari, and chaperoned many

---

29. K. Hepburn, *The Making of the African Queen: How I Went to Africa with Bogart, Bacall and Huston and Almost Lost My Mind* (London: Century Hutchinson, 1987), p. 124.

30. Ibid. p. 99.

31. Lauren Bacall, *By Myself* (London: Jonathan Cape, 1979), p. 184.

32. Stewart Granger, *Sparks Fly Upwards* (London: Granada, 1981), p. 168.

33. C. Ondaatje, *Hemingway in Africa: The Last Safari* (Toronto: HarperCollins, 2003), p. 21.

William Beinart and Dominique Schafer

wealthy clients, as his guide. Percival was president of the East African Professional Hunters Association for over thirty years – a trade association for 'sportsmen who contracted their services as safari guides, organizers and entertainers to their millionaire clients'.[34]

Figure 3. Hemingway in Africa.

Source: Wikimedia Commons: http://commons.wikimedia.org/wiki/File:Ernest_ Hemingway_on_safari,_1934.jpg

In addition to two short stories, *The Short Happy Life of Francis Macomber* and *The Snows of Kilimanjaro* (both first published in *Cosmopolitan* magazine in 1936), Hemingway wrote a longer work on Africa, *Green Hills of Africa* (1935), in which he aimed 'to write an absolutely true book to see whether the shape of a country and the pattern of a month's action can, if truly presented, compete with a work of imagination'.[35] It is clearly the most autobiographical of his African works, and comes close to a documentary style, although he is deliberately opaque about

---

34. E. I. Steinhart, 'Hunters, Poachers and Gamekeepers: Towards a Social History of Hunting in Colonial Kenya', *Journal of African History* **30**/2 (1989): 254.

35. Ondaatje, *Hemingway*, p. 125; Ernest Hemingway, *Green Hills of Africa* (London: Arrow Books, 2004), foreword.

locations. Hemingway was an experienced writer of journalism and reportage. *Green Hills* is not a report, nor a diary or a history, but an attempt to reconstruct the experience, soon after he returned to the US, expressing all the intensity that he clearly felt. To some degree it was an experiment with form. He wrote about landscape, the minutiae of hunting and shooting, the animals and the safari team – notably 'Pop', or Percival – and some of the black assistants.

The short story *Macomber* is a fictional rendition of the same experience, but – we suggest – aims to locate the story precisely within the safari camp and the social relations of the elite hunt that Hemingway experienced. The story features Francis Macomber, a wealthy American socialite and businessman, who takes his wife Margot on safari in Africa. The marriage is troubled and she is a strong and astringent personality; Macomber hopes that the trip will help to mend their relationship. The central drama takes place around a lion hunt. Before they set out, Macomber is full of bravado – and indeed a central point is to distinguish bravery from bravado. When Macomber only injures the lion, the party goes into the bush to kill it. But he lacks the courage to face the charging animal and runs away, leaving the professional hunter Wilson, and his African assistants, to deliver the coup de grace. The code of professional hunters in theory disallowed leaving injured animals. As further evidence of his spinelessness, Macomber later picks on one of the African servants. Margot relentlessly taunts Macomber for cowardice and praises Wilson's courage and manliness. The story enables Hemingway to explore the ideas he was learning about hunting and its codes, as well as more generic ideas of manliness and gender.

Macomber has an epiphany of kinds, when he performs better in a buffalo hunt. Wilson acknowledges Macomber's loss of fear as a rite of passage – a moment in which he finds his manhood and is finally happy. But as a wounded buffalo turns to charge, Margot, in their vehicle, has a rush of blood to the head and shoots. Her bullet hits her husband in the back. Although the film version made some changes, it followed the story reasonably closely until the final scenes. The striking feature of the film version of *Macomber* is the professional white hunter's easy dominance of all of spheres of the safari operation – animals, clients, women, African workers, knowledge, language and nature. In the short story, he was less faultless. Hemingway cast Wilson as less than handsome and he was often referred to as red-faced; Macomber, by contrast, was portrayed as rather smooth. In the film, the casting is almost inverted, with the tall, dark Peck playing a suave and good-looking hunter while Macomber (played by Robert Preston) is shorter and squatter – physically as well as mentally a lesser man. Incongruously, the film script retained occasional use of 'red-faced' in reference to Peck (Wilson). Peck was offset against Macomber, who was by turns arrogant and pitiable. In Hemingway's terms, the African landscape and the hunting safari briefly made a man of Macomber. But the resolution was his death – he died happy after only a short spell as a true man.

William Beinart and Dominique Schafer

The African landscape played a central role in the story and the film.[36] Hemingway was not happy with the cinematic rendition of either of his stories. He signed the rights for *Snows of Kilimanjaro* for financial reasons ($75,000) to Darryl Zanuck, another big game hunter who identified with Hemingway's stories. Hemingway later called *Snows of Kilimanjaro*, the *Snows of Zanuck,* and told Ava Gardner that 'the only two good things in it were you and the hyena'.[37] Nevertheless, Korda's *Macomber*, especially, showed some complexity of motive, and made an attempt to capture Hemingway's 'truth' about African environments and hunting safaris.

Safari as Concept and Reality in Films

Safari was a practice and concept that changed over time.[38] Adopted into English around 1890, the word was initially associated with the slave trade, exploration and commercial ivory hunting. As colonial control in Africa expanded, 'adventure was redefined, erasing privation, hardship and threat, and replacing them with comfort and luxury'.[39] Safari became more associated with sports hunting and then – as in Hemingway's second trip – a more general tourist experience designed to view nature rather than shoot animals. By the time he was 55, Hemingway expressed as much interest in live birds as he had before in dead kudu. Some safaris were visual experiences broadcast to a much larger number of people through film and photography.[40]

Safari companies specialised in 'outfitting' expeditions, supplying everything from vehicles and tents to hunters and African auxiliaries. By the 1940s, guides and hunters knew where to find animals and could thrill clients with a sense of danger while generally keeping them sufficiently safe to avoid major mishap. Camps became increasingly luxurious with 'modern amenities such as daily newspapers, double walled tents, mosquito netting, chemical toilets, air mattresses and mess tables'.[41] Light planes were used to transport visitors in medical and other emergencies; *Macomber* starts at an airfield and *Snows of Kilimanjaro* ends with a plane rescue.

---

36. Suzanne Del Gizzo, 'Going Home: Hemingway, Primitivism and Identity', *Modern Fiction Studies* **49**/3 (2003): 506.

37. Gardner, *My Story*, p. 168.

38. Amy Staples, 'Safari Adventure: Forgotten Cinematic Journeys in Africa', *Film History* **18** (2006); Edward I. Steinhart, *Black Poachers, White Hunters: A Social History of Hunting in Colonial Kenya* (Oxford: James Currey Publishers, 2006).

39. M. Cejas, 'Tourism "Back in Time": Performing the "Essence of Safari" in Africa', *Intercultural Communications Studies* **16**/3 (2007): 121.

40. Pascal James Imperato and Eleanor M. Imperato, *They Married Adventure: The Wandering Lives of Martin and Osa Johnson* (New Brunswick NJ: Rutgers Univ. Press, 1992).

41. Cejas, 'Tourism': 125.

Hollywood in Africa 1947–62

Ker and Downey established themselves as one of the leading safari companies after the Second World War.[42] Both partners had taken hunting parties down to the Mara triangle in the 1930s, before it became Maasai Mara national park, where hunting was fairly unrestricted. Both had prestigious client lists but they were not highly capitalised. After the Second World War protected areas and national parks were hesitantly expanded by the colonial government in Kenya. At the same time, regular passenger air services from Europe became more widely established. Opportunities were changing and so were tastes. Ker and Downey became increasingly committed conservationists, favouring photographic over hunting trips.

Film was deeply embedded in this transition because film-makers used the same safari companies that serviced hunters and photographers. They needed experienced hunters to set up camps, to find and handle animals and to stand in for actors in scenes perceived as dangerous. Servicing film became an important part of Ker and Downey's business and *Macomber* was the first major film that they outfitted.[43] They travelled to Maasai Mara with the relatively small second camera crew (compared with later films), but even so had to beg and scrape to find sufficient equipment. They also secured permission from the Kenyan government to breach hunting regulations so that they could kill a lion and hunt a buffalo from a vehicle. By contrast, Mervyn Cowie, the Kenyan conservationist on whom the hero of *Where No Vultures Fly* was modelled, refused to allow any animals to be killed in filming.[44]

Ker and Downey found the lion that featured in *Macomber*, set up the wildlife shots and provided special effects and extras when needed. Film work could be lucrative, although it did not suit all the safari companies and Donald Ker found *Macomber* very testing.

> Everything had to be done according to the script ... We had to work to coax ... lion and buffalo into country with the required setting and background and when once there could not be photographed till the light was perfect and the clouds had to be of the right formation. When all this was according to the director's satisfaction the lion had to be made to charge, and it is not always easy to make a lion charge when you want him to, but he often charges when you don't want him to.[45]

Ker was, however, content to diversify from hunting. At the end of 1947, he led a major expedition by the Academy of Natural Sciences of Philadelphia through Kenya, Uganda, Gabon, Cameroon and into the Sahara. He also worked with the Edgar Monsanto Queeny expeditions in the early 1950s, which made ethnographic and

---

42. Jan Hemsing, *Ker and Downey Safaris: The Inside Story* (Nairobi: Ker and Downey Safari Ltd, 1989).

43. Ibid. p. 41ff.

44. Mervyn Cowie, *Fly Vulture* (London: Harrap, 1961), p. 165.

45. Hemsing, *Ker and Downey*, p. 46.

William Beinart and Dominique Schafer

wildlife film. The success of *Macomber* brought Ker and Downey a string of commissions. Some of their hunters were involved in *Where No Vultures Fly* and *Snows of Kilimanjaro* and the company was still playing this role for *Out of Africa* (1986).

Professional hunters and safari firms influenced films in other ways. Stewart Granger stayed with Philip Percival – model for the hunter in *Macomber* – at his farm near Machakos at the start of filming for *King Solomon's Mines*.[46] Percival made suggestions about costume and firearms – including a leopard skin band for Granger's broad-brimmed hat. This had first appeared in *Macomber* and was frequently copied in 1950s productions. *King Solomon's Mines* in turn helped to reshape safaris. Outfitted by a new company, Safariland, it was one of the most expensive films made at the time, with a budget of US $3.5 million. Most expenditure was on location and equipment. 60,000 pounds of equipment was shipped to Mombasa, including seven specially constructed trucks and a snow plough (for the footage on Mount Kenya). Film was flown from Hollywood to Africa and back in custom designed, refrigerated cans to keep it at a constant, cool temperature.

Mogambo was on a similar scale. Ava Gardner recalled, 'not only did it take eight genuine white hunters to get us in gear, but once we settled our encampment was 300 tents strong'.[47] There were also daily flights 'in sturdy old DC3s' to supply goods and take out newly shot film 'carefully packed in dry ice'.[48] Some of the actors stayed in Nairobi, flying to the locations on the Kigera river and elsewhere when needed. Gardner praised MGM for 'thinking of everything … the film's expense account even had a notation of 5,000 African francs, (14 dollars in change in those days) written off as "gratuities to witch doctors for favourable omens"'.[49] The Mau Mau rebellion had begun and extra policing was also required.

Film, along with other forces, changed the nature of the safari and to a degree, the film-makers, living in camp, shot what was around them. The visual representation and spatial dimensions of a number of scenes reflected distinctive aspects of the tented safari camps which were their daily reality. But the camps (both in reality and on film) were unfenced and open to animals moving across the landscape, or snakes and insects crawling out of the bush. At least in smaller camps, it was a world of porous boundaries, where there was no very clear distinction between indoors and outdoors. Safari camps were a haven of safety in the wild, but also gave a sense of imminent danger because animals could penetrate. Some of the films exploit this porosity, for example when a cheetah comes into a tent in *King Solomon's Mines* and a hyena in *Snows*.

---

46. Granger, *Sparks Fly Upwards*, pp. 173–4.
47. Gardner, *My Story*, p. 179.
48. Brian Herne, *White Hunters: the Golden Age of African Safaris* (New York: Henry Holt, 1999), p. 191.
49. Gardner, *My Story*, p. 179.

Hollywood in Africa 1947–62

Carr Hartley and Wildlife Capture

Most of the feature films include short sequences of African wildlife in documentary style, showing its beauty or its danger. In *The Macomber Affair* these scenes – such as giraffes running – are cut to separate shots of the stars (in Mexico) in a vehicle. The latter provide one of the few moments where the actors visibly share a moment of joy, although it was in this case entirely acted. In general, as Michael Anderson notes, the earlier Hollywood films separated the wild animal sequences from those involving actors. But in *King Solomon's Mines*, antelope and zebra were induced to stampede around a low barrier of rocks behind which the actors (or their stand-ins) sheltered. The film actually shows animals sweeping past this obstacle with people and wildlife in the same frame. And there was also quite widespread use of semi-domesticated wild animals which were habituated to people and which appeared in the same frame as actors or their substitutes.

A number of Kenyan white settlers adopted wild animal orphans of various species and kept them as pets on their farms. Carr Hartley, who owned a farm near Rumuruti in Laikipia (formerly northern Maasai territory), provided a full range of habituated animals for use by the film companies.[50] He was born in 1910 in Kenya and developed a deep knowledge of wildlife through early experience as an elephant and buffalo control officer. He was also involved briefly in hunting safari expeditions and – over a longer period – in leading motor tours of East Africa. His property, which expanded to about 30,000 acres, was rich in wildlife which crossed the boundaries of private and public space. Especially after the Second World War, Hartley responded to an increasing demand by zoos, circuses, and individuals for African wild animals. He, his sons and his African assistants developed innovative methods of capturing many species before the advent of immobilisation darts. They used a fleet of motor vehicles and depended on speed, lassos, ropes and careful coordination with experienced teams.

Their animals, captured from all over East Africa, had to be weaned onto a new diet that could keep them alive. By the late 1940s, Carr Hartley housed a wide variety of species in large paddocks around the farmstead – everything from lions and cheetahs to giraffes, baby elephants, rhino and hippos. Some species, such as elephants, were allowed to move freely but became habituated to their on-farm diets of sweet porridge. Hartley and his wife were fascinated by animals and kept some as semi-domesticated pets. He was soon found by film-makers who required biddable wild animals for their scenes. Of the big cats, cheetahs were the easiest to habituate and were widely used in India for hunting. Some had been exported from Kenya

---

50. Interviews, Roy Carr-Hartley, Nairobi, 2009 and Brian Carr-Hartley, Amanzimtoti, South Africa, 2010. Some of these paragraphs are based on the Carr-Hartley family archives in Amanzimtoti.

William Beinart and Dominique Schafer

to India.[51] The Hartleys' semi-domesticated cheetahs appeared with actors in *King Solomon's Mines, Mogambo, Odongo* (1956) and *Hatari!* It was Hartley's pet hyena, Willie, that Hemingway thought had stolen the show in *Snows of Kilimanjaro*.

As in the case of the hunting safari, animal capture and captive wild animals became themes for feature films. This interest preceded Hartley's operation, notably in films made with Frank Buck in the 1930s – one of which was called *Bring 'em Back Alive*. Armand Denis had been involved in Buck's film *Wild Cargo* made in Asia in 1934; he did not enjoy the experience.[52] But Denis and Cotlow, when filming *Savage Splendor*, found the Hartley operation at Rumuruti far more to their liking. They operated partly from the ranch and the film included extended sequences of animal capture with Carr Hartley's teams. Denis claims in his book to have developed a system for capturing rhinos safely during the making of the film. In fact, Hartley had already done so and his teams became expert in the difficult task of black rhino capture and translocation. Carr Hartley also habituated rhinos and many visitors to the Rumuruti ranch were photographed sitting on these animals in the 1950s and 1960s. Michaela Denis, wife of Armand, entitled one of her books *Ride a Rhino*.[53]

The huge entourage that was *King Solomon's Mines* camped in their hundreds at Rumuruti – for them it was but one stop in an extended African safari. Stewart Granger wrote enthusiastically of his experiences there and of his plan with Hartley to film an authentic rhino charge. When MGM demurred, he shot a rhino for a trophy instead.[54] Ford started filming *Mogambo* there. Clark Gable played an American adventurer with a game capture operation. An extended early sequence showed him and Ava Gardner interacting with a range of wild animals, in and out of cages, and they were also photographed with the rhinos.[55] One of the later *Tarzan* films, starring Gordon Scott, was made partly on the farm; the family remember that the muscular Scott was distinctly unheroic in his capacity to weather African conditions. *Odongo* (1956), starring Rhonda Fleming, was essentially a feature film structured around the Hartley farm, rather than game capture beyond it. It was followed by a television series, shown over two years in the UK, and also shot on the farm, called *Jungle Boy*, in which the teenage Michael Carr Hartley played the central role alongside the animals. During this period in the late 1950s, there were film crews almost permanently on the Rumuruti ranch, despite its distance from Nairobi on dirt roads. (There was an airstrip.) Film needed the animals and directors found the farm an attractive place to work. In turn, animal capture and

51. John Pinfold, 'Cheetah Racing Remembered: an Exploration through the Sources', *African Research and Documentation* **111** (2009).

52. Armand Denis, *On Safari*, p. 55ff; 236ff.

53. Michaela Denis, *Ride a Rhino* (London: Sphere Books Ltd. 1967), first published1959.

54. Granger, *Sparks Fly Upwards*, p. 180.

55. Carr-Hartley family archive.

interactions with captured animals became embedded as a significant storyline in feature films and reflected social processes and landscapes that the film-makers were encountering in East Africa.

Howard Hawks's *Hatari!* took large scale animal capture, rather than safari hunting, as its central theme. It is not clear how far it was modelled on the Hartley enterprise. It was mainly shot on location on a farm near Arusha in Tanzania where there was a similar capture business operated by a South African. Carr Hartley bought this farm shortly afterwards and established it as a second base for his business in the 1960s. Some sequences for *Hatari!* were filmed on a farm recently purchased in Tanzania by Hardy Kruger, the German actor, who also participated in the film. As in the case of *The Macomber Affair* and *Mogambo*, the film was a barely fictional attempt at filmic representation of a set of established social practices in relation to animal capture.

Rhino charging the car - *Hatari!* (1962)

Figure 4. Rhino charge – a still from Hatari!

Hatari! was nevertheless a challenge for film-makers because it attempted to show extended animal capture episodes. It was difficult to mobilise different species of wild animals in the best cinematographic conditions. When animal stampedes were filmed, classically in *The Overlanders*, *Red River* and *King Solomon's Mines*, a static camera could be used and the visual excitement was created by the rush of animals hurtling past – a force of nature. To film animal capture authentically, the cameramen had to keep up with the action over rough terrain – they relied

William Beinart and Dominique Schafer

on a vehicle with 'hundreds of shock absorbers'.[56] The hunters employed for the film made extensive use of light planes to mobilise animals for action shots and to coordinate the movement of the chasing vehicles. One of the hunters who oversaw operations recalled 'there were occasions when the rhino refused to be pushed, and turned round and took it out on one of the cars ... it was really quite exciting'.[57] This was in fact captured on camera and appeared in the film. Attempts to induce an elephant to stampede into a safari camp failed.

The theme of game capture occupied a place in between the hunting narratives and conservation films. It seems at times to be portrayed as morally superior to hunting. In *Odongo*, for example, the African child actor cannot bear seeing wildlife hunted and killed but loves to have them around him. The semi-domesticated animals on the Carr Hartley farm are portrayed as living in relatively benign conditions. The idea that spending a life time in captivity or undergoing traumatic relocations to overseas zoos and circuses might be a fate worse than death is hardly debated in *Mogambo, Odongo*, or *Hatari!* Carr Hartley did, however, publicly justify his operations. By the 1950s he deployed conservationist arguments for their translocation to reserves and zoos, suggesting that many wild animals would not otherwise survive. *Africa, Texas Style* (1965), directed by Ivan Tors, also presented a sympathetic view of wildlife capture. In this case, when the villain of the film tried to free the paddocked animals, they were shown to return to their shelters and human minders.[58] Film-makers, and it seems audiences, were evidently captivated by these portrayals of human–wildlife relationships.[59]

Wild animal orphanages were another feature of Kenyan conservation in the 1950s and 1960s. The scale of hunting and trapping, both licensed and unlicensed, combined with droughts, the expansion of settlements and the disturbance of habitat was decimating wildlife and resulted in significant numbers of motherless animals. Some orphaned animals were taken to the Hartleys. Daphne Sheldrick, at Tsavo National Park, found herself with a couple of young elephants abandoned during a dry year in 1954. She started taking in orphaned animals and experimenting with diets in captivity.[60] She called a domesticated buffalo weaver-bird, Gregory Peck. The idea of a more institutional animal sanctuary was raised in various contexts in the 1950s and eventually one was established at the Nairobi National Park in 1963.

The charm of baby animals, particularly elephants, was celebrated in a number of contemporary publications, and was also exploited in feature film. One of the subplots of *Hatari!* involved Elsa Martinelli's relationship with a baby elephant

56. Hemsing, *Ker and Downey*, p. 73.

57. Hemsing, *Ker and Downey*, p. 74.

58. Sue Hart, *Life with Daktari: Two Vets in East Africa* (London: The Companion Book Club, 1969), ch. 10.

59. Beinart and McKeown, 'Wildlife Media'.

60. Daphne Sheldrick, *Orphans of Tsavo* (London: Collins and Harvill, 1966).

she rescued after its mother was killed by poachers. Soon she is caring for three orphan elephants, which become like pets, frolicking with her in the water and demanding her attention. This theme adds a humorous and photogenic element to the film. These scenes are always accompanied by a jazzy circus style tune, entitled 'Baby Elephant Walk', composed especially for *Hatari!* by Henry Mancini (of *Pink Panther* fame). The music became one of Mancini's most popular works and was later used as musical shorthand for 'kookiness of any stripe'.[61] There were many popular Africa-linked hits at the time, especially those adapted by Bert Kampfaert. In 1962, the Orlons released a dance song called 'Wah Wahtusi'. The reference may have been to the dance sequence in *King Solomon's Mines.* Chubby Checker also recorded a version, stimulating a dance craze in the United States called The Watusi.

Conservation

Although conservation was less significant for Hollywood than hunting, capture and baby elephants, it was picked up in Watt's Ealing-produced *Where No Vultures Fly* (1951). Wildlife conservation was not pioneered in Kenya but by the 1930s a small lobby of officials and settlers became alarmed by the impact of hunting, expanding settlement and pastoral farming. Mervyn Cowie, a Kenyan born settler, Oxford graduate and conservation champion, was appointed chair of the National Parks Administration and founded Nairobi National Park in 1946. A few years later, Tsavo, Kenya's largest park, was gazetted. Wardens also worked outside of parks to licence and control hunting by whites and blacks. David Sheldrick, at Tsavo, and George Adamson, who worked in the vast Northern Frontier District, both encouraged African hunters and poachers to turn their skills to game ranging. Steinhart argues that in Tsavo, the majority of African staff were Kamba and Waata ex-poachers; Sheldrick's campaign 'altered the traditions of hunting and game-keeping in important ways'.[62] This strategy is retold in *Where No Vultures Fly* (1951).

Based on Cowie's campaign, this British film came to be regarded as a landmark conservationist feature film.[63] Its protagonist, Tom Payton (played by Anthony Steel), takes a rather purist view of conservation and tries to prohibit all forms of hunting in his park. Eventually he is persuaded to allow controlled hunting and game capture, in return for funds which he could use to train and hire game rangers. His relations with the local people were tense, as they justified hunting (or in his view poaching) for subsistence. The director, Harry Watt, was clearly trying to give some space to this argument. A key character is the British cynic, Man-

---

61. '*Hatari!*' Allmusic.com, http://www.allmusic.com/cg/amg.dll?p=amg&sql=10:38120rja-c48x

62. Edward I. Steinhart, 'Hunters, Poachers and Gamekeepers: Towards a Social History of Hunting in Colonial Kenya', *Journal of African History* **30**/2 (1989): 263.

63. Cowie, *Fly Vulture*; Steinhart, *Black Poachers.*

William Beinart and Dominique Schafer

nering, who is later found to be in league with the poachers and purchasing ivory for his own profit. Watt showed the diversity of interests around wildlife, offered a complicated view of white morality and presented debates about conservation. However, although Africans played key roles as the poachers and, in the end, game rangers, they are given little individual agency. The film lionises Payton who uses his knowledge of Africa to overcome all tribulations and emerge successful in his quest.

Despite some similarities with Hollywood productions in representations of race and the colonial social order, *Where No Vultures Fly* evinces significantly different concerns. Watt was committed to conservation. One of the major reasons he wanted to make the film was to bring international attention to the cause, and to influence colonial governments. He respected Cowie's terms that 'no animals can be killed in any National Parks to make the picture'. In his memoir, *Fly Vulture*, Cowie explains how Watt went to endless trouble to make use of animal carcasses that had been culled in other parts of Kenya, and transported them miles to make them look as if they had been killed at Amboseli where some of the sequences were filmed.[64] *West of Zanzibar* (1956), which focused on the ivory trade, was a sequel of kinds to *Where No Vultures Fly* with a strong anti-poaching message. The film again starred Steel as Tom Payton. It is a more stereotyped production, with a heroic white conservationist, naive Africans and demonised Arab traders.

In Conclusion

Certainly there are some predictable elements in the narrative strategies and social hierarchies of these films, which reflect some of the Hollywood, and colonial, commonplaces at the time. A dominant man tends to hold power, knowledge and loyalty. There are quests of kinds and challenges of nature overcome. The films may seem to be part of western imagination mythologising Africa. But we have argued that the relationship between representation on film and the world that is being represented is more complex. Michael Anderson notes the documentary ambitions of *Hatari!* – particularly in respect of the presence of animals in the same frame as actors. We suggest a deeper landscape realism in these productions. Writers and directors were interested in capturing African landscapes and alert to changing social practices, especially amongst East African settlers and vistors. They did not need to tax their imaginations too far in discovering intriguing themes with potential for film narratives: hunting, safaris, wildlife capture, orphaned animals and conservation. Men like Armand Denis, who had extensive experience in documentary filming in Africa, provided ideas and guidance. This phase of film-making in East Africa was also triggered partly by Hemingway's attempt to write 'truth' about Africa. Most important for our discussion, while many sequences, especially in *Macomber* and *Snows of Kilimanjaro*, were filmed in studios, all the films used

---

64. Cowie, *Fly Vulture*, p. 165.

Hollywood in Africa 1947–62

African locations. In most, the stars were brought to Africa to work in authentic landscapes and even, to a degree, with African animals. Hollywood (and Ealing) did not invent a mythic Africa. African environments and landscapes gave visual and narrative power to the films and in this way, amongst others, also became part of the global visual imagination.

References

Adams, J.S. and T.D. McShane. 1997. *The Myth of Wild Africa: Conservation Without Illusion*. Berkeley: University of California Press.

Anderson, David M. 2003. 'Mau Mau at the Movies: Contemporary Representations of an Anti-Colonial War', *South African Historical Journal* **48**: 71–89.

Anderson, Michael J. 2009. '*Hatari!* And the Hollywood Safari Picture', *Senses of Cinema* **52**.

Bacall, Lauren. 1979. *By Myself*. London: Jonathan Cape.

Beinart, W. and K. McKeown. 2009. 'Wildlife Media and Representations of Africa, 1950s to the 1970s', *Environmental History* **14**/3: 429–452.

Bogdanovich, Peter. 1967. *John Ford*. London: Studio Vista.

Bouse, Derek. 2000. *Wildlife Films*. Philadelphia: University of Pennsylvania Press.

Cejas, M. 2007. 'Tourism "Back in Time": Performing the "Essence of Safari" in Africa', *Intercultural Communications Studies* **16**/3.

Cowie, Mervyn. 1961. *Fly Vulture*. London: Harrap.

Del Gizzo, Suzanne. 2003. 'Going Home: Hemingway, Primitivism and Identity', *Modern Fiction Studies* **49**/3.

Denis, Armand. 1963. *On Safari: The Story of My Life*. London: Collins.

Denis, Michaela. 1967. *Ride a Rhino*. London: Sphere Books Ltd.

Dunn, K. 1996. 'Lights ... Camera ... Africa: Images of Africa and Africans in Western Popular Films of the 1930s', *African Studies Review* **39**/1: 149–175.

Druzin, Charles. 2002. *Korda: Britain's Only Movie Mogul*. London: Sidgwick and Jackson.

Eyman, Scott. 1999. *Print the Legend: the Life and Times of John Ford*. New York: Simon and Schuster.

Gallagher, T. 1986. *John Ford: The Man and his Films*. Berkeley: University of California Press.

Gardner, Ava. 1990. *Ava: My Story*. New York: Bantam Books.

Griggs, John. 1984. *The Films of Gregory Peck*. London: Columbus Books.

Granger, Stewart. 1981. *Sparks Fly Upwards*. London: Granada.

Grinker, Roy Richard, Christopher B. Steiner and Stephen C. Lubkemann (eds.) 2010. *Perspectives on Africa: a Reader in Culture, History, and Representation*. Chichester: Wiley-Blackwell.

Hart, Sue. 1969. *Life with Daktari: Two Vets in East Africa*. London: The Companion Book Club.

William Beinart and Dominique Schafer

Hemingway, E. 2004. *Green Hills of Africa*. London: Arrow Books. First published 1935.

Hemsing, Jan. 1989. *Ker and Downey Safaris: The Inside Story*. Nairobi: Ker and Downey Safari Ltd.

Hepburn, K. 1987. *The Making of the African Queen: How I Went to Africa with Bogart, Bacall and Huston and Almost Lost My Mind*. London: Century Hutchinson.

Herne, Brian. 1999. *White Hunters: the Golden Age of African Safaris*. New York: Henry Holt.

Imperato, Pascal James and Eleanor M. Imperato. 1992. *They Married Adventure: The Wandering Lives of Martin and Osa Johnson*. New Brunswick NJ: Rutgers Univ. Press.

Long, Robert Emmet. 2001. *John Huston Interviews*. Jackson: University of Mississippi Press.

Mayer, Ruth. 2002. *Artificial Africas: Colonial Images in the Times of Globalization*. New Hampshire: University Press of New England.

Ondaatje, C. 2003. *Hemingway in Africa: The Last Safari*. Toronto: HarperCollins.

Pinfold, John. 2009. 'Cheetah Racing Remembered: an Exploration through the Sources', *African Research and Documentation* **111**.

Rosenstone, Robert A. 1995. *Visions of the Past: The Challenges of Film to Our Idea of History*. Cambridge, Mass.: Harvard University Press).

Sheldrick, Daphne. 1966. *Orphans of Tsavo*. London: Collins and Harvill.

Sperber, A.M. and E. Lax. 1997. *Bogart*. London: Phoenix.

Staples, Amy. 2006. 'Safari Adventure: Forgotten Cinematic Journeys in Africa', *Film History* **18**.

Steinhart, Edward. I. 1989. 'Hunters, Poachers and Gamekeepers: Towards a Social History of Hunting in Colonial Kenya', *Journal of African History* **30**/2.

Steinhart, Edward. I. 2006. *Black Poachers, White Hunters: A Social History of Hunting in Colonial Kenya*. Oxford: James Currey Publishers.

Stockham, Martin. 1992. *The Korda Collection: Alexander Korda's Film Classics*. London: Channel 4, Box Tree.

Toplin, Robert Brent. 1996. *History by Hollywood: The Use and Abuse of the American Past*. Champaign, IL: University of Illinois Press.

Chapter 3

Livestock, Identity and the Social Imagination in South Africa

Amy Halliday

Regina Nelani cradles the soft, woolly body of a lamb in her fake-fur-sheathed arms (Figure 1). A tenant farmer who depends on her small flock of sheep for her

Figure 1. Regina Nelani.

Barkly East, Eastern Cape, 27 July 2010. C-print ©Daniel Naudé. Courtesy of Stevenson, Cape Town and Johannesburg.

livelihood, Regina gets up every few hours during the night to nurse this orphaned lamb – its mother killed by jackals – from a Black Label beer bottle fitted with a plastic teat.[1] An unknown light source pierces the dark interior of the hut like a Baroque painting, illuminating the plump body stretched across Regina's lap between her strong, anchoring hands. The pyramidal composition of the figures reads as a classical *pietà*, registering a complex set of emotions and associations that go beyond the animal as agricultural commodity.

Meanwhile, in the portrait *David Tieties with his three-day-old donkey. Verneuk Pan, Northern Cape, 6 April 2009* (Figure 2), the shadows cast by the relentless Karoo

Figure 2. David Tieties with his three-day-old donkey.

Verneukpan, Northern Cape, 6 April 2009. C-print ©Daniel Naudé. Courtesy of Stevenson, Cape Town and Johannesburg.

---

1.   Information supplied during an interview with the artist conducted on 27 July 2011.

sun stretch diagonally across the picture plane, hinting at the desolate expanse of the flat salt pans of Verneukpan on either side.

From the feet of David Tieties, the melded shadow of man and animal seems to beckon their forms beyond the edges of the frame; urging them on, or marking where they have been. The sense of thick time and considerable distance cast by the shadows' visual push-and-pull invokes something of the character of David's life: David is one of the Great Karoo's so-called – and self-attributed – 'Karretjiemense' (donkey-cart people), itinerant sheep-shearers who travel between farms, sometimes setting up temporary shelters on verges (from materials carried on their carts), but often sleeping in their carts and wholly dependent for transport on their donkeys.

The Karoo – the semi-arid and arid heartland of South Africa – overlaps parts of today's Eastern, Western and Northern Cape provinces, as well as the Free State. It is prime land for extensive sheep, cattle, goat and game farms, but its seemingly immutable surfaces belie a deep history of conflict between settlers and indigenous peoples, as well as between settler groups (the Karoo featured prominently in the Anglo-Boer war). The Karretjiemense trace their ancestry to the Khoisan, who were largely dispossessed of land and livestock and coercively integrated into the agricultural labour force by the Boers – the descendants of early Dutch (as well as French Huguenot and German) settlers – in the eighteenth century. The peripatetic lifestyle of the Karretjiemense emerged as a self-determined response to commercial agricultural expansion from the mid-nineteenth century: carts provided mobility, a prop for roadside shelter and a locus for domestic life, with donkeys thus key to multiple social and economic purposes. The acquisition of a donkey by a young man would enable his independence, and the ability to set up a new family unit.[2] Sheep-shearing was generally a migrant, seasonal job, for which the Karretjiemense gained a small proportion of contracts alongside Africans from the Transkei and Ciskei, as well as semi-migrant whites in the Northern Cape (until the early twentieth century). However, due to increasingly concentrated land ownership from the mid-twentieth century, and the economic stagnation of many of the small Karoo towns and villages which once provided other forms of unskilled employment, there are now vastly more Karretjie people than sheep-shearing contracts.

The continued structural violence of colonialism and apartheid plays out on the *platteland* (the 'flat lands'), where large sheep farms are still white-owned and farm labourers have no share in the agricultural economy.[3] Despite being

---

2.   Sarah Adriana Steyn, 'Childhood: An Anthropological Study of Itinerancy and Domestic Fluid-ity amongst the Karretjie People of the South African Karoo' (unpublished dissertation, 2009), p. 87. Available: http://uir.unisa.ac.za/bitstream/handle/10500/4065/MA.dissertation._steyn_a.pdf?sequence=1

3.   This is particularly true of the Northern Cape, where most Karretjiemense live, as one third of the country's privately owned commercial farmland is situated in this province, which boasts only 2% of the population. See Cherryl Walker, 'Looking Forward, Looking Back: Beyond the Narrative of

'opportunistically "discovered" as citizens of the country by the main political parties in the run-up to the 1994 election', and occasionally drawn into projects of Khoisan identity politics and land claims, the Karretjiemense continue to be amongst the poorest, most disenfranchised communities in South Africa.[4] They lack access to infrastructure, resources and secure employment, and are dispersed across immense swathes of land, making them largely invisible in terms of official poverty assessments and interventions (as is often the case with rural poverty). The portrait of David Tieties captures something of the vulnerability of his position: David's slight frame seems almost dwarfed by the gangly donkey foal he clasps; furry knees falling against trouser-clad, delicate hoofs dangling above cheap train-ers. This knock-kneed donkey will, in about two months' time, be strong enough to pull David's cart and David's marginal identity will continue to be defined as that of a *karretjieman*.

Despite most South Africans now living in cities, an entanglement with animals is still the everyday experience of many, particularly in rural areas: from established (mostly white) commercial farmers to newly-settled claimants of land redistribution programmes, from subsistence hunters to rangeland herders.[5] Many black city dwellers also retain links with homesteads and communal tenure arrange-ments in former 'homelands', some maintaining variations of traditional cultural practices such as *lobola* (the payment of cattle to a bride's family), or the ritual slaughter of livestock as intermediaries with the ancestors at significant moments of celebration, change or crisis.[6] However, images documenting the diverse iterations of the agricultural economy in South African history – and its ongoing role in shap-ing social relations today – are scarce in a visual market dominated by the familiar trope of safari imaging, which constantly reasserts the country as quintessentially 'wild'. And yet 'taming' the wild – the progressive improvement and cultivation of natural resources – was central to the ideological project of settler colonialism.[7]

Young South African photographer Daniel Naudé, who captured these compelling portraits of Regina Nelani and David Tieties, has responded to this gap

Loss and Restoration in the History of Land', in M. Godby (ed.) *The Lie of the Land: Representa-tions of the South African Landscape* (Cape Town: exhibition catalogue, 2010) pp. 12–27. p. 21.

4. Michael de Jongh, 'No Fixed Abode: The Poorest of the Poor and Elusive Identities in Rural South Africa', *Journal of Southern African Studies* 28/2 (2002): 441–460.

5. Based on statistics published on the Unicef website: http://www.unicef.org/infobycountry/southafrica_statistics.html

6. See the discussion of the multiple and ongoing social and economic utility of cattle in Lovemore Musemva and Abyssinia Mushunje, 'Marketing challenges and opportunities faced by the Nguni cattle project beneficiaries in the Eastern Cape Province of South Africa', in Ajuruchukwu Obi, *Institutional Constraints to Small Farmer Development in Southern Africa* (Wageningen: Wageningen Academic Publishers, 2011) pp. 121–135.

7. Kay Anderson, 'A Walk on the Wild Side: A Critical Geography of Domestication', *Progress in Human Geography* 21 (1997): 463–485.

in the international image economy through two extended photographic essays. The first series, *African Animals and Scenery,* is a homage to the natural history folio of the same name by early nineteenth century artist and explorer Samuel Daniell who set out from the Cape into the unmapped interior of South Africa during the first British occupation.[8] The second, *Animal Farm,* is an extension of Naudé's interest in questions of breeding, land ownership and what constitutes 'indigeneity', and includes a number of rare double portraits of human and animal subjects. Naudé is predominantly known for his lavish portraits of cows, goats, horses, donkeys and indigenous dogs, set within the variegated landscapes of the Karoo, Transkei and old Transvaal regions of South Africa; areas with deeply embedded environmental and political histories of domestication, exploitation and conflict.[9]

Taking his photographs with a medium-format camera with a top viewfinder, the photographer seldom uses a tripod, but spends hours silently stalking skittish Africanis dogs or languorous bovine subjects, often kneeling or lying on the ground in wait for the perfect shot, an alignment of land and livestock that resonates with him. One journalist has referred to him as a 'hunter with a Hasselblad'.[10] And certainly the hunting metaphor is apposite, for trophy hunting – initially with guns and, more recently, with cameras – has long been a framing device for perceiving the South African landscape and its animals.[11] For Naudé, livestock emerge as curiously

---

8. For more on Samuel Daniell, see Thomas Sutton, *The Daniells: Artists and Travellers* (London: Bodley Head, 1954).

9. The Transkei refers to the area of the Eastern Cape established, along with the Ciskei, as an 'independent' homeland for the Xhosa during apartheid, during which black South Africans were divided according to ethnicity and granted shares of the land vastly demographically disproportionate to that granted to whites. The main area of the Transkei stretches from the Umtamvuna River in the north to the Great Kei River in the south, and is bounded by the Indian Ocean, Drakensburg mountains and Lesotho to east and west. It remains an important centre of the rural agricultural economy. The Transvaal is an area associated with the land north of the Vaal River. After a series of interrelated wars and forced migrations (known as the Mfecane) between indigenous people in the regions led to the ascent of the Ndebele in the area in the first half of the nineteenth century, the Boers founded the South African Republic (called the Transvaal) as an independent republic in 1856. It was annexed by the English in 1877 and again after the Anglo-Boer war in 1902 before becoming the Transvaal Province of the Union of South Africa in 1910. Within what was once the Transvaal province is the 'Bushveld' region of grassland (sub-tropical woodland) that covers much of today's Limpopo Province and some of the North West Province. It is prime cattle and game farming territory. The significance of the Veld in the construction of Afrikaner identity is explored in Jeremy Foster, *Washed with Sun: Landscape and the Making of White South Africa* (Pittsburgh: University of Pittsburgh Press, 2008).

10. Janine Stephen, 'Hunter with a Hasselblad', *Business Day* 20 March 2009: 14. For an in-depth discussion of the historical interweaving of discourses of hunting and photography invoked by this newspaper article, see Karen Jones, '"Hunting with the Camera": Photography, Animals and the Technology of the Chase in the Rocky Mountains' in the present volume.

11. John MacKenzie traces the seventeenth-century hunting trophies of the Dutch at the Cape Town Castle as an antecedent of museum specimen exhibition and ways of viewing the natural environment, increasingly reinforced by colonial hunting practices. 'The South African Museum, Cape

Amy Halliday

liminal bodies, poised between nature and culture: the embodiment of wildness tamed, but so often overlooked in the country's visual traditions. Michael Godby unpacks this tension in a discussion of the ambiguous position of agriculture and animal husbandry in South African landscape art: are farmlands and livestock part of a natural order or a foreign intervention into it? Godby suggests, by looking at the seamless inclusion of livestock (and the absence of fences, gates and roads) in various landscapes by white artists in the twentieth century, that 'ownership is made to appear more natural the more fully the property is integrated into the landscape'.[12] As a result, livestock bodies help to naturalise (white) claims to land and its 'improvement'. By making recourse to individual socio-economic relationships between humans and livestock, laying bare the link between livestock, land and ownership and interrogating the anxieties around breeds and breeding, Naudé's images start to unpick these visual traditions, effectively 'denaturing' livestock.

Naudé's intervention into dominant modes of imaging the natural world in South Africa – from colonial natural history to today's tourist-attracting photographic safaris – is timely, for South African historiography has witnessed a recent turn to environmental concerns. However, a lacuna still remains in the rigorous interrogation of the country's past and present: the central role of livestock accumulation and the forms of knowledge that accrued around it, ranging from veterinary developments to vernacular or indigenous knowledge, from breed standards to environmental regulation and state intervention. Accounts of early capitalism in South Africa, for example, retain a largely 'Randcentric' focus on the mineral revolution and the social and political relations of labour, despite evidence of a simultaneous (and related) 'intensification in pastoral production, which exceeded that of diamonds nationally'.[13] William Beinart is one of the few scholars who has addressed this issue, most notably in *The Rise of Conservation in South Africa: Settlers, Livestock, and the Environment 1770–1950* (2008). Naudé, I argue, eloquently uses photography to reveal how livestock, land and knowledge form a neglected nexus of power and identity. By drawing attention to correspondences and slippages between issues of human and animal breeding, indigeneity and ethnicity, Naudé poses durable questions about how environmental histories continue to shape social relations in South Africa.

Town' in *Museums and Empire: Natural History, Human Cultures and Colonial Identities* (Manchester and New York: Manchester University Press, 2009) p. 78.

12. Michael Godby, 'Introduction: Interface, Contestations, Interventions, Inventions, Interrogations', in M. Godby (ed.) *The Lie of the Land: Representations of the South African Landscape* (Cape Town: exhibition catalogue, 2010) pp. 60–135. p.94.

13. William Beinart, *The Rise of Conservation in South Africa: Settlers, Livestock, and the Environment 1770–1950* (Oxford: Oxford University Press, 2008) p.16.

Livestock Portraiture and the Image of Good Breeding in England and South Africa

Naudé's photographs (Figures 3–5) – with their large scale, saturated colour, insistence on profile views and compressed depth of field (which heightens an anatomical awareness of each animal's sculptural presence and conformation) – draw on pictorial conventions from eighteenth century natural history illustration and animal portraiture. It is difficult to look at Naudé's honorific images of livestock, pictured from a slightly low angle so as to increase their stature – and hung on the walls of homes and galleries – without calling to mind the painting of George Stubbs. Stubbs, whose naturalistic animal portraits were simultaneously works of fine art

Figure 3. Merino sheep.

Graaff-Reinet, Eastern Cape, 15 May 2010. C-print ©Daniel Naudé. Courtesy of Stevenson, Cape Town and Johannesburg.

Figure 4. Black Nguni bull.

Stella, North West Province, 2 March 2010. C-print ©Daniel Naudé. Courtesy of Stevenson, Cape Town and Johannesburg.

and empirically rendered representations with strong links to natural history, is perhaps the most famous exponent of the tradition of animal portraiture.[14] Animal portraiture as a genre, beyond an extension of (or inclusion in) landscape painting or human portraiture, emerged in England in the mid to late eighteenth century.[15]

---

14. For more on Stubbs's union of the anatomical and aesthetic elements of animal portraiture, see Judy Egerton, *George Stubbs, Painter* (New Haven and London: Yale University Press, 2007) pp.16–35.

15. It should be noted, however, that the Dutch Golden Age produced honorific images of cattle, imbued with nationalistic sentiment (for example, Paulus Potter's much-admired *Young Bull* of 1647), but these did not constitute an independent genre. Alex Potts, 'Natural Order and the Call of the Wild: The Politics of Animal Picturing', *Oxford Art Journal* 13/1 (1990): 12–33. 13.

Figure 5. Appaloosa horse in foal.

Curry's Post, KwaZulu-Natal, 23 October 2009. C-print ©Daniel Naudé. Courtesy of Stevenson, Cape Town and Johannesburg.

Stubbs's subjects range from wild animals – often exotic captives of empire that he observed in the royal zoological gardens – to prize livestock, from the grandeur of horses and hounds in hunting scenes to the domestic scale of faithful pet dogs.[16] His commissioners included scientists, who championed him for his empirical eye, and aristocratic landowners, many of whom were 'breeders and owners of "fine animals" as well as owners of "fine art"'.[17] As a result, the images spoke volumes

---

16. This theme would subsequently be elaborated in allegorical terms by Edward Landseer. See Diane Donald, 'Landseer's Dogs', in *Picturing Animals in Britain: 1750–1850* (New Haven and London: Yale University Press, 2007) pp.126–158.

17. Potts, 'Natural Order': 13.

about human pedigree and connoisseurship through the refined characteristics and stature of specific animals and through the art collections which acted as a form both of commemoration and of conspicuous consumption.

As Harriet Ritvo traces in the *Animal Estate: The English and Other Creatures in the Victorian Age* (1987), images of elite cattle in England were metonymically associated with agricultural improvement and patriotism, as increased yields in meat and dairy were needed to cater to a rapidly expanding population and were thus in the national interest. Moreover, livestock portraiture:

> embodied the values of the wealthy, often aristocratic landowners who produced exemplary livestock ... The rhetoric of connoisseurship that accompanied their production and display emphasised these distinctive characteristics, not only within the community of elite stock breeders, but also to the multitudes who paid to admire either individual animals on tour or prize stock assembled at shows.[18]

By the close of the eighteenth and throughout the nineteenth century in Britain, exhibitions of 'exceptional livestock' were annual fixtures on the social calendar. Dominated by the aristocracy, these livestock shows celebrated animals – and, by extension, breeders – of exceptional pedigree, such that spectacle, status and the science of husbandry overlapped.[19] Moreover, agricultural societies were formed to 'popularise and instruct the common husbandmen in the latest agricultural principles and practices'. From the mid-nineteenth century, breeding associations with defined studbooks would further entrench the overlap of animal pedigree with anxieties around human status, class and 'purity'.[20]

The Victorian polymath Francis Galton took this overlap one step further. In the context of urban overcrowding, a rise in criminality, and the widespread perception of social degeneration, Galton became convinced that the lessons of animal domestication and selective breeding could and should be applied to humans in order to improve the national 'stock' of human capital. In his research, Galton was constantly frustrated by the lack of sufficient human data over successive generations to construct an overarching theory of heredity. But, in visiting livestock exhibitions and perusing studbooks, he realised that these sources offered untapped opportunities for rigorously testing his ideas.[21] Most notably, by the late nineteenth century, livestock shows usually involved photographic portraits of prize stock. And thus, in 1898, Galton wrote a letter to the journal *Nature*, entitled 'Photographic Measurement of Horses and Other Animals'. In it, Galton stated:

18. Harriet Ritvo, *The Animal Estate: The English and Other Creatures in the Victorian Age* (Cambridge, Massachusetts: Harvard University Press, 1987) p.46.

19. Cynthia Huff, 'Victorian Exhibitionism and Eugenics: The Case of Francis Galton and the 1899 Crystal Palace Dog Show', *Victorian Review* 28/2 (2002): 1–20. 4.

20. Ritvo, *Animal Estate*, pp. 46–58.

21. Huff, *Victorian Exhibitionism*.

Valuable horses are habitually photographed by professionals and amateurs, and beautiful portraits of them appear in newspapers ... [and] in shows of pedigree stock it is frequently required that the prize-winners should be photographed, it being of obvious importance that the appearance of the progenitors of the animals should be known before selections are made for pairing ... If photographs of horses and other pedigree stock could be rendered available for strict scientific studies in heredity, the material is copious, and as it would in time extend through many generations, should far exceed in value anything that is now procurable for those purposes.[22]

Like their antecedents in oil on canvas, both the public and professional value and utility of pedigree photography was already established. Thus Galton proposed a further dimension be considered, by which 'an ordinary photograph would be transformed from a mere picture into a record of real scientific value'.[23] Galton outlined several basic instructions to be carried out regarding the positioning of the animal and the marking out of the space so as to correctly measure the animal's physical dimensions from the resulting photograph, accommodating the distance and angle between the subject and the camera. Informed by his work in human anthropometry, used to measure and assess various human groups by connecting physical measurements with various internal capacities, Galton's instructions for livestock photography ensured the uniformity and accuracy of the images and the validity of subsequent measurements taken from them with callipers.[24] In the statistical and photographic data he obtained from livestock and dog shows, Galton would, over time, develop his theory of Eugenics.

In South Africa, a 'Society for the encouragement of the agricultural arts and sciences' had been established in the late eighteenth century by Cape Governor George Yonge during the first British occupation (on the advice of visiting agriculturalist William Duckitt, who arrived in the Cape with some pedigree cattle and the newest in farming implements from England).[25] It was later revived by Lord Charles Somerset, governor from 1814 to 1826. Lord Somerset set an example by importing European horses, sheep, cattle and hunting dogs (and setting up a hunt) and encouraging the latest methods in the cultivation of land and livestock. English settlers – who were soon distributed over extensive areas of land (in the Cape, on the eastern frontier and later in Natal) – established various local agricultural societies and shows. English agricultural societies were strengthened in the Cape subsequent

---

22. Francis Galton, 'Photographic Measurement of Horses and Other Animals', *Nature* 57 (1898): 230–2. 230–1.

23. Ibid.: 231.

24. Ibid.: 232.

25. Although the Dutch governor Simon van der Stel promoted fairs and markets, these did not actively promote animal husbandry or include an agricultural show element. For a brief history of agricultural societies in South Africa, see Thelma Gutsche, *A Very Smart Medal: The Story of the Witwatersrand Agricultural Society* (Cape Town: Howard Timmins, 1970) pp.13–14.

to the Great Trek, in which great numbers of Boers left the British-controlled colony to found independent republics inland: English farmers were able to buy land in key districts, fostering a large export economy based on wool, angora and ostrich plumage (catering to Europe's millinery fashions).

The Afrikanerbond, largely based on the farmers' associations of the Boers, acted as the mouthpiece of Afrikaners (particularly in the Cape colony) from the late nineteenth century up to the Union in 1910. However, across the vast distances of the Boer republics of the South African Republic (often informally referred to as the Transvaal) and Orange Free State, it was difficult for agricultural societies to flourish in the small *dorps* scattered among the wider farming population. The mineral revolution proved a great stimulus to agricultural production in the interior. Oxen were needed for expanded draught power in arable production and transport and markets expanded for meat and other consumer goods. A mutually-inflecting increase in population size and agricultural yield catalysed livestock improvement experiments in South African in a similar fashion to those in England.[26] The expansion of the veterinary service would likewise contribute to this development. Afrikaner interest in agricultural societies and shows, previously the preserve largely of English settlers and a minority of 'progressive' Afrikaners, became more widespread and, by the early twentieth century, the great Rand Show in Johannesburg (founded by the Witwaterand Agricultural Society) had become 'a genuine marketplace for ideas and products' for Boer and Englishman alike.[27]

Agricultural shows were not only popular with the public, they were also reported in both general and specialist publications. In England, the *Illustrated London News*, for example, would regularly publish multiple engravings of prize-winning animals, such that these images were widely circulated in town and country. Livestock painters travelled all over the land to these shows, drawing animals in their pens and undertaking commissions for stock-owners and breeders. As Elspeth Moncrief has examined in her study *Farm Animal Portraits*, in the Victorian era, 'the culture of the show ring was probably the single biggest impetus to livestock portraiture', a visual tradition which may have spread to the colonies along with the British pedigree livestock that was coveted by, and exported to, Australia and South Africa particularly.[28] Moncrief traces the rise of livestock portraiture to the selective breeding experiments of Robert Bakewell (1725–1795), which constitute

---

26. See also Andrew Ainslie's discussion of the impact of the discovery of diamonds on agricultural production in the Eastern Cape, *Cattle Ownership and Production in the Communal Areas of the Eastern Cape, South Africa* (Cape Town: University of the Western Cape. PLAAS Research Report no. 10, 2002) p. 21.

27. Gutsche discusses the educational role of the Witwatersrand Agricultural Society in the Rand Agricultural Show in 1970: *A Very Smart Medal*, p. 115.

28. Elizabeth Moncrief, *Farm Animal Portraits* (Woodbridge, Suffolk: Antique Collectors' Club Ltd,1996) pp.104–6.

'one of the earliest forms of genetic engineering. He awakened the country to the concept that certain characteristics could be selected in individual livestock and perpetuated and fixed in their progeny.'[29] For Moncrief, Bakewell's principles were the foundation of the development of pedigree livestock and, in turn, the rise of farm animal portraiture, initially in painting and engraving, but later in photography.[30] In South Africa, the country's oldest magazine, *Farmer's Weekly*, established in 1911 by Englishman John Rodrick – who would become the country's most famous pedigree livestock auctioneer – was significant for its pioneering role in agricultural journalism and in the fostering of a national (settler) agricultural identity. Most editions included photographs of prize-winning and pedigree livestock, as well as the latest in agricultural technology, and the magazine was circulated widely, distributed by road and rail throughout the country. In the 1970s, the magazine would claim to be the first to harness the potential of full colour printing for publishing photographs of champion animals at important shows, a feature that remains amongst the most popular in the magazine today.[31]

A Breed Apart: The Socio-Political Construction of Afrikaner and Nguni Cattle

Naudé's contemporary images of livestock – each image focused on the physical conformation of individual animals and anchored in the ascription of breed in the title – are deeply embedded in these visual and historical discourses of pedigree and purity, which acquired specific valences within the South African context. These issues are most palpable in Naudé's double portraits of human and animal subjects. Two images of (human) Afrikaners open up a particularly productive dialogue at the intersection of livestock breeding and portraiture: that of Dirk, an attendant and technician at the anatomy school of the famous veterinary college at Onderstepoort, Pretoria (Figure 6) and that of Ben Fyfer, a cattle farmer from Louwna in the North West Province (Figure 7). In the former, Dirk's thin limbs, ensconced in the long socks and khaki shorts that stand as stereotypical Afrikaner garb, are enclosed by the articulated skeleton of an Afrikaner bull, a visual doubling of the specimen's armature. In the latter, a bull-necked farmer sits sturdily at his desk. His own hirsute face is suspended in visual parenthesis between two others: the mounted trophy head of one of his prize stud Nguni cattle and a fondly painted portrait of the same bull by his daughter.[32]

---

29. Ibid. p. 15.

30. Ibid. p. 167.

31. George Nicholas, 'And the Decades Roll By ...', Centenary edition of the *Farmer's Weekly*, 2011.

32. Background information provided by the artist in an informal interview conducted Wednesday 29 August 2011.

Figure 6. Dirk next to an Afrikaner bull skeleton.

Onderstepoort, Pretoria, 27 October 2010. C-print ©Daniel Naudé. Courtesy of Stevenson, Cape Town and Johannesburg.

The multiple framing and media of photography, taxidermy, painting and anatomical reconstruction are brought to bear on one another, suggesting an integral connection between animal and human portrait subjects. Each human subject is engaged in a livelihood which involves constant recourse to animal bodies: veterinary science and farming. The lived relationship of human–animal interaction is materially reinscribed in the images through the human subjects' compositional framing by these animal bodies. Moreover, the animal bodies are, in the captions, expressly identified as 'Afrikaner' or 'Nguni', terms more familiarly used to refer to

Figure 7. Ben Fyfer, an Nguni cattle farmer, at his desk.

Louwna, North West Province, 2 March 2010. C-print ©Daniel Naudé. Courtesy of Stevenson, Cape Town and Johannesburg.

cultural or linguistic human identities in South Africa: The term 'Afrikaner' refers to white South Africans descended from early settlers, while 'Nguni' was the general anthropological term used for the African people of the East Coast (both terms also denote relationships to language). Through an act of semantic metonymy, the hybrid breed of cattle selectively bred (and 'improved') by many Afrikaner livestock farmers came to be known as such, while 'Nguni' became a category for old African breeds of cattle. But what is at stake in the taxonomy of breeds?

Amy Halliday

A 1917 cartoon from the Johannesburg newspaper, *The Star,* may offer some insights (Figure 8). As Saul Dubow has examined in his book *Scientific Racism in Modern South Africa* (1995), Francis Galton's eugenic theories had a diverse and contradictory uptake in South Africa (playing only an inferential role in the elaboration of segregationist theory) and racial difference tended to be understood more in Social Darwinist terms until the 1930s.[33] Nevertheless, Union rhetoric echoed Galton's language of hereditary distance and proximity: on the one hand, the coming together of close kin, such as the European-descended English and Afrikaners, promoted a hybrid vigour, strengthening the national stock. On the other hand, intermixing between supposedly distinct 'races' was commonly believed to result in decreased fertility, as well as moral and physical degeneration. In Galton's England, eugenics expressed a deep-seated belief in Anglo-Saxon supremacy, even as it spoke to widespread anxieties in the Victorian middle class around social 'degeneration' (particularly the rise of criminality, indolence and 'feeble-mindedness') in a context of rapid industrialisation and urbanisation. Similarly, in South Africa:

> The transforming power of the late nineteenth-century mineral revolution and the experience of industrialisation raised the issue of the political relationship between white and black in an acute form. The problems associated with the creation of a modern industrial society compounded classic eugenic and Malthusian anxieties about the differential birth-rate of the 'residuum' with new fears about race degeneration. Thus, the perception of an increasing urban black population gave a sharp twist to white fears of the corruptive potential presented by racial mixing.[34]

An attempt at the consolidation of white settler identity, subsequent to the South African (Anglo-Boer) war, was one of the most definitive responses to these anxieties. This consolidation, though never fully realised, operated on a popular level through eugenic discourse around the 'horror of "race fusion" or "miscegenation"'.[35] Simultaneously, the rise of breed standards and increasing state intervention in the agricultural and veterinary industries in South Africa meant that the bodies of livestock became a site of inscription surrounding race 'purity', environmental fitness, and degenerative interbreeding.

The cartoon responds to the annual Rand Show – an agricultural spectacle founded by the Witwatersrand Agricultural Society in the late nineteenth century. The Rand Show was a primary arena for the popular dissemination of the latest ideas and technologies in agriculture and animal husbandry, with a large section devoted to livestock shows. Saul Dubow, in *A Commonwealth of Knowledge: Science, Sensibility, and White South Africa 1820–2000* (2006), contends that knowledge-centred

---

33. See the chapter 'The Equivocal Message of Eugenics' in Saul Dubow, *Scientific Racism in Modern South Africa* (Cambridge: Cambridge University Press, 1995) pp.166–196.

34. Ibid. p.168.

35. Ibid. p.180.

Figure 8. 'Aristocracy at the Show – and Only Man is Vile'.

This cartoon by Edward Arnold Packer appeared in The Star newspaper shortly after the 1917 Rand Agricultural Show. Image courtesy of Museum Africa.

institutions and endeavours (from scientific associations to literary magazines) in the late nineteenth and early twentieth centuries helped to bridge the ethnic divide between Dutch/Afrikaans and English settlers (despite ongoing political rifts and rivalries), aiding in the construction of a more unified colonial identity, particularly amongst the rising mercantile and agrarian middle classes. The pursuit of science – and the development of local institutions and publications no longer wholly dependent on England – also helped to cement an emerging racial order. White colonists became producers and consumers of knowledge about the land and its people – a set of expertise and practices 'closely bound up with claims to be rights-bearing citizens of a country that they were consciously making their own'.[36] And, as Kay Anderson has investigated in her study of the Royal Agricultural Show in Sydney, the agricultural show in the colonies was a major site for the visualisation

36. Saul Dubow, *A Commonwealth of Knowledge: Science, Sensibility, and White South Africa, 1820–2000* (Oxford: Oxford University Press, 2006) p. 4.

and stabilisation of the ontology of settler colonialism, centred on the triumph of 'improvement'.[37]

In the cartoon, the animal gaze has been turned on the human spectators, suggesting just how 'human' the concerns of animal bloodlines had become. This is particularly salient in a moment of South African history in which, despite ongoing rifts between English and Afrikaner, white power was being consolidated in the face of the so-called 'native question'. A monocled horse, clearly an Anglophone member of the progressive middle to upper agrarian class, appraises the spectator, whose cross-hatched cheeks suggest an ambiguous skin tone. The horse remarks to the adjacent thoroughbred ox: 'Great Scot! I'll bet there are a few missing links in his pedigree, what?' The ox retorts, 'It's just one of those "scrub" humans. Ignore it, my dear, ignore it'. The punchline revolves around one of the agricultural sector's most pervasive concerns at the time: that of the danger posed to pure, imported stock bloodlines, and to the quality of grazing land, by the 'overwhelming' numbers of apparently inferior indigenous cattle.[38] The cartoon reveals how human class and racial anxieties became interwoven with the agricultural project of abolishing 'scrub' animals and promoting 'pure' (European) breeds. It also evokes the discourses of natural history, glossed by Social Darwinism, in which so-called Bantu and Hottentot groups were associated with the lower evolutionary rungs of humanity, potentially as 'missing links' between man and animal.[39]

Nguni cattle, the most numerous subjects of Naudé's portraits, were particularly targeted as 'economically valueless "scrub" cattle'.[40] The heterogeneous coat patterns of the cattle – which are given lyrical names and form an integral part of Zulu oral culture – along with variable horn-shapes and conformation, were popularly read as evidence of indiscriminate bloodlines and dubious genetics, for you could never be sure what the next generation of cattle would look like.[41] Moreover, the size and lack of enclosure of the communal tenure herds led to concern about the spread of disease and overgrazing. Instead, imported stock was highly prized by white commercial farmers and official schemes advised Africans to switch to these 'improved' breeds, restrict the size of their herds and 'subscribe to strict state

---

37. Kay Anderson, 'White Natures: Sydney's Royal Agricultural Show in PostHumanist Perspective', *Transactions of the Institute of British Geographers* 28/4 (2003): 422–441.

38. See Ainslie, *Cattle Ownership*, pp. 6–8, 28–29.

39. See Saul Dubow, 'Physical Anthropology and the Quest for the "Missing Link"', in his *Scientific Racism*, pp. 20–65.

40. Jane Carruthers, 'The Knowledge that is in Names', *Environmental History* 12/2 (2007): 299–301. 300.

41. Wolfgang Bayer, Rauri Alcock and Peter Gilles, 'Going Backwards? – Moving Forward? – Nguni Cattle in Communal Kwazulu-Natal', *Rural Poverty Reduction through Research for Development and Transformation*. A Scientific Paper Presented at a Conference Held at the Agricultural and Horticultural Faculty, Humboldt–Universität, Berlin. October 5–7, 2004. pp. 1–7. Available: http://www.tropentag.de/2004/abstracts/full/326.pdf

veterinary interventions'.[42] This 'advice' was largely resisted, however, reflecting the strong cultural salience and invisible capital of Nguni cattle in communities in which they embody wealth and status, provide various utilities and are the object of ritual sacrifice. Nevertheless, by the 1930s and 1940s in African farming areas (later 'homelands') like the Transkei, state policies encouraging 'stock improvement' and 'land rehabilitation' included the introduction of European breeds, as well as the culling (usually through enforced sale) and castration of nondescript 'scrub' bulls (though these measures were often sporadically implemented and largely ineffective, given the reproduction rate of cattle).[43] While part of these official schemes represents the strength of conservationist attitudes of the time, they also contributed to the ongoing undermining of the socio-cultural base and economic independence of black South Africans.

Despite mandated preference for imported breeds, there was one notable indigenous cattle breed that escaped classification as 'scrub' livestock, and this was the Afrikaner or Afrikander: the animal with which Dirk is pictured in Naudé's portrait. This specimen – the articulated skeleton of an Afrikaner bull – was constructed many decades ago as a teaching model for the students of the Onderstepoort Veterinary Institute in Pretoria, South Africa. The original bull was donated by a local farmer. Unlike the majority of the anatomical collection, the specimen does not display a developmental anomaly or specific pathology, but represents what from the perspective of veterinary practitioners might be considered a 'standard' model. The lab technician would have spent hours slowly simmering the tissue from the bones, degreasing them, painstakingly reassembling them and finally setting the entire articulated specimen in a steel armature.

But the preserved and mounted skeleton is more than just a didactic tool. It is also a cultural monument commemorating the draught animal that pulled the ox-wagons of the Afrikaners who set out on the Great Trek. Taking place in South Africa from the 1830s to 1850s, the Great Trek was the mass emigration of Afrikaners from the British Cape Colony, in which the Afrikaners journeyed inland to establish independent republics.[44] From the late nineteenth century, as the ideology of Afrikaner nationalism began to foment, the interweaving of Afrikaner history and strong Calvinist traditions recast the Great Trek as the South African equivalent of a biblical exodus from British dominion to the Promised Land of the Boer republics.[45] As the Great Trek assumed a central position in the construction of Afrikaner identity, so the narrative and genealogical pedigrees of the Afrikaner

42. Carruthers, 'Knowledge': 300.
43. Ainslie, *Cattle Ownership*, pp. 28–30.
44. See the discussion 'The Afrikaner Great Trek, 1836–1854' in Leonard Thomson, *A History of South Africa* (3rd ed.) [2000] (New Haven and London: Yale University Press, 2001) p. 87–96.
45. As Saul Dubow explores in 'Afrikaner Nationalism, Apartheid and the Conceptualisation of Race', this was not necessarily the 'self-perception of the Boers at the time of the Trek', but rather part

Bull become intertwined: its genetic characteristics associated with the ability to endure hardship and emerge with its character unaltered.

Afrikaner nationalism – as well as broadly eugenic concerns around miscegenation, race purity and human 'breeding' in South Africa – reached a formative point in the interwar period.[46] And it was in this context that a telling article emerged in the *Journal of Heredity* (1933). Writing about the origin and development of the breed, Helmut Epstein declared that the Afrikaner breed of cattle was:

> not a mixed but a pure breed, evolved from indigenous cattle by severe and careful selection. A mixed breed would never have been capable of such a marvellous preservation of its pure and uniform character in every part of this country as the red Afrikander cattle were after the profound economic changes following the Great Trek, the Rinderpest of the nineties and the destructive consequences of the Anglo-Boer War.[47]

Here, the 'purity' of the breed is used to account for its survival over generations of environmental and political adversity, its unique conformation emerging as the result of these travails. Because it was 'evolved' from indigenous cattle, the breed was simultaneously produced as autochthonous and 'improved'; the article thereby associated Afrikaners with a lineage of both indigeneity (something that white South Africans – and particularly Afrikaners – were shaping for themselves in the socio-political sphere of the 1930s) and progressive cultivation of the land and its resources (a central tenet legitimating land seizure, set in contrast to the practices of African pastoralists and communal farmers).[48] The historical and genetic pedigree of Afrikaner cattle and the pedigree of the Afrikaner nation emerge in the article as thoroughly entangled. Moreover, an association for the protection and systematic breeding of the Afrikaner was set up in 1912, one of the first professional bodies to produce a standardised studbook. Today, the Afrikaner Breeding Society continues to extol the narrative of the Afrikaner as a 'hardy, no-nonsense breed' that survived despite near 'extermination ... [by] Rinderpest or ... during the South African War' due to the efforts of 'some breeders [who], to their credit, succeeded in keeping their Afrikaner stock pure'. [49]

Just prior to Epstein's article extolling the virtues of the Afrikaner, a small herd of Nguni cattle (though it should be noted that after the Rinderpest and

---

of the romantic – though no less powerful – mythology of the Boer experience, as developed by modern nationalist intellectuals. *The Journal of African History* 33/2 (1992): 209–237. 224.

46. Dubow, *Scientific Racism*.

47. Helmut Epstein, 'Descent and Origin of the Afrikander Cattle', *The Journal of Heredity* 24/12 (1933): 449–462. 450.

48. Andrew Ainslie discusses the ideological discourse of an 'irrational and inefficient' African sector, set in contrast to English and Afrikaner agricultural practices, in 'Introduction: Setting the Scene' in Ainslie, *Cattle Ownership*, pp.1–17.

49. [no author], 'The Society: History'. Available: http://www.afrikanerbees.com/Society-History.htm

East Coast Fever of the early twentieth century, there were very few 'pure' Nguni remaining on the East coast) was purchased from the interior of Maputaland in 1931 and transferred to the Onderstepoort Vetinary Research Institute. In 1950, the herd, with additional purchases from local Zulu communities in Nongoma, Ingwavuma, Ubombo and Hlabisa, was sent to Bartlow Combine Research Station (seven adjacent farms in the Hluhluwe district of the old Natal province), where outside genetic influence was eliminated from 1957 to 1981 and assortive mating used to select for type, conformation and weight. Already from the 1930s, milestone research by Onderstepoort Professor H.H. Curson and R.W. Thornton (1936) and by J.H.R. Bisschop (1937) revealed the positive potential of the breed, with attempted dissemination in a series of publications and talks at livestock shows and farmers' days.[50] Moreover, an important study by the Department of Agriculture in 1950 acknowledged:

> With the exception of the Afrikander breed, little or no attention has been paid to the improvement or study of the potentialities of the indigenous breed of cattle in South Africa ... The failure of the exotic breeds has brought about an appreciation of the importance of a harmonious relationship between the hereditary complex of a breed and the prevailing environmental conditions of a specific region. It is generally accepted today, that the most important aspect of any livestock improvement policy is to secure a type which, by virtue of its hereditary constitution, will thrive, and successfully reproduce and produce in a given area.[51]

And yet, so strong was the prevailing belief in the inferiority of 'scrub' Nguni cattle to both European breeds and the Afrikaner that it was only in 1983 that the Nguni was finally recognised as an official breed.[52] By this point, however, preferences in African farming areas had turned to higher-yielding breeds such as Brahmans, which have some of the same characteristics as Nguni cattle but are bigger, as well as Bonsmara (an Afrikaner-European cross).

Marguerite Poland, whose lavishly illustrated text *The Abundant Herds* (2003) is evidence of the upsurge in interest in Nguni cattle in post-1994 South Africa, laments the manner in which agriculture and animal husbandry in much of the twentieth century was framed by and filtered through the social imagination, constructing the Nguni as 'a breed apart':

> It is a sad indictment of South African society that the deeply rooted racial prejudices that have been the dominant theme in the history of this country should have

50. W.D. Gertenbach and A.A. Kars, 'Towards the conservation of the indigenous cattle of KwaZulu-Natal', *South African Journal of Animal Science* **29**/2 (1999): 55–63. 56.

51. F.N. Bonsma, J.H.R. Bisschop, W.G. Barnard, J.A. Van Rensburg, J.J. Duvenhage, H.P.D. Van Wyk and F. Watermeyer, *Nguni-Cattle: Report on Indigenous Cattle in South Africa*, Department of Agriculture Pamphlet 311 (Pretoria, The Government Printer, 1950) p. 1.

52. Marguerite Poland, David Hammond-Tooke and Lee Voigt, *The Abundant Herds: A Celebration of the Nguni Cattle of the Zulu People* (Cape Town: Fernwood Press, 2003) p. 106.

Amy Halliday

carried over into attitudes towards the livestock of the indigenous population. The very qualities of hardiness, fertility and adaptability that government and stockmen have tried so hard to introduce through imported breeds, existed – largely unrecognised – in the indigenous herds for hundreds of years, acquired through centuries of adaptation and natural selection.[53]

Since the 1980s, numerous longitudinal studies using data from the Bartlow Combine herd have reinforced the benefits of farming with indigenous Nguni cattle: they display a natural immunity to endemic disease and tick infestation, have an ability to reproduce quickly, even under harsh environmental conditions, and are more productive without manufactured supplementary feeds than other breeds, resulting in less carbon emissions and catering to a more ecologically-conscious international context (including the current 'vogue' for organic foods).[54] Moreover, since 1994, Nguni cattle have been mobilised as icons of indigenous knowledge and ethnic pride, duly feted – and farmed – by South Africans of all ethnic groups. They have also been integrated into a cultural heritage economy that seeks to revalue the country's rare 'indigenous' breeds and celebrate the precolonial stewardship of the land.[55]

However, the majority of the country's commercial and stud Nguni farms are today owned by white, predominantly Afrikaner, farmers such as Ben Fyfer, pictured in Naudé's image. While the reevaluation of the breed has reinvigorated the commercial sector, there appears to be less interest in Nguni cattle in small-scale and communal farming areas. Recent studies suggest that African stock-owners articulate preferences for bigger-framed imported and cross-bred stock and sometimes perceive Nguni cattle as 'something for the white farmers'.[56] In response both to the scientific evidence of the suitability of the breed to small-scale communal farming (as a low maintenance breed which adapts well to low-input farm systems) and to the change in eco-political context, post-apartheid land redistribution programmes have increasingly been paired with livestock loans of Nguni bulls (often along with in-calf heifers) to create new nucleus herds. Though these programmes have been largely unsuccessful, they nonetheless present a telling inversion of the livestock 'improvement' policies of the early twentieth century. As Andrew Ainslie points out in his analysis of the history and current state of cattle ownership and production in the Eastern Cape, it is:

the stuff of legends that, whilst the state spent a great deal of time and resources

---

53. Ibid. p. 108.

54. L. Musemwa, A. Mushunje, M. Chimonyo and C. Mapiye, 'Low Cattle Market Off-Take Rates in Communal Production Systems of South Africa: Causes and Mitigation Strategies', *Journal of Sustainable Development in Africa* 12/5 (2010): 209–226. 210.

55. Carruthers, 'Knowledge': 300.

56. Bayer *et al.* 'Going Backwards?' p. 6.

castrating and culling 'scrub' Nguni/Nkone bulls in rural areas, those Nguni bulls which survived this regime are now in the hands of commercial 'white' stud breeders and fetch up to R40 000 per head. Indeed the Eastern Cape Department of Agriculture and Land Affairs announced recently that it had 'facilitated the ordering of 20 breed bulls which were sold to [African] stock farmers at a low price in order to improve the breed of cattle in the province' (*Daily Dispatch*, 16 February, 1999).[57]

Taking Stock

Returning then, to Naudé's images of Ben Fyfer and Dirk, Regina Nelani and David Tieties, it is clear that these images offer more than just human portraits: they provide snapshots of a country in flux, where socio-political identity is deeply invested in livestock and land, and historical conflict, change and continuity encoded in breeds and breeding. The two (human) Afrikaners, Dirk and Ben, set alongside the bovine relics of the articulated Afrikaner skeleton and the Nguni trophy, offer a dialectic, perhaps, of Afrikaner identity and status in contemporary South Africa. If the prosperous Ben Fyfer, ensconced in his office, represents the ongoing structural legacies of settler colonialism and apartheid policy (with its land and agricultural subsidies) in which much material prosperity – including the harnessing of new indigenous icons – remains in the same hands, Dirk's ageing image paints the shadow side of the new dispensation; the dislocation of an Afrikaner minority that must articulate a new sense of self against a compromised history.[58] The portraits of Regina Nelani, her dignified bearing engaging the viewer straight on, and David Tieties, who looks slightly askance, offer additional tableaux of the South African rural landscape. Enfolding their animal charges, Regina and David reveal how livestock in South Africa adumbrate lived experience, contributing to individual human livelihoods and often (particularly in the case of dogs, horses and cattle) partaking in complex relationships of affection and reciprocity.

Naudé's project thus seeks to redress the paucity of attention paid to South Africa's domestic animals and rural life in both national historiography and international image economies. While much of the reimagining of nature currently registering in environmental history and contemporary art revolves around ideas of wild(er)ness, Naudé opens up the complexities of the 'natural' world to include livestock and the contested scrub and grasslands in which they range, recognising that the amount of land devoted to livestock far outstrips that apportioned to wildlife in South Africa. Moreover, as changes in the socio-economic environment lead to an increase in integrated game and livestock farming, the borders of wild

57. Ainslie, *Cattle Breeding*, p. 29.

58. Mads Vestergaard, 'Who's Got the Map? The Negotiation of Afrikaner Identities in Post-Apartheid South Africa', *Daedelus* **130**/1 (2001): 19–41.

Amy Halliday

and tame, nature and culture – the fault-lines upon which South African history and its landscapes have been shaped – become ever more fraught.

REFERENCES

Ainslie, Andrew (ed.) 2002. *Cattle Ownership and Production in the Communal Areas of the Eastern Cape, South Africa*. Cape Town: University of the Western Cape, PLAAS Research Report no. 10.

Anderson, Kay. 1997. 'A Walk on the Wild Side: A Critical Geography of Domestication'. *Progress in Human Geography* 21: 463–485.

Anderson, Kay. 2003. 'White Natures: Sydney's Royal Agricultural Show in Post-Humanist Perspective'. *Transactions of the Institute of British Geographers* 28/4: 422–441.

Bayer, Wolfgang, Rauri Alcock and Peter Gilles. 2004. 'Going Backwards? – Moving Forward? – Nguni Cattle in Communal Kwazulu-Natal', *Rural Poverty Reduction through Research for Development and Transformation*, A Scientific Paper Presented at a Conference Held at the Agricultural and Horticultural Faculty, Humboldt–Universität, Berlin. October 5–7, 2004. pp. 1–7. Available: http://www.tropentag.de/2004/abstracts/full/326.pdf

Beinart, William. 'Soil Erosion, Conservation and Ideas about Development: A Southern African Exploration: 1900–1960'. *Journal of Southern African Studies* 11/1: 52–83.

Beinart, William. 2008. *The Rise of Conservation in South Africa: Settlers, Livestock, and the Environment 1770–1950*. Oxford: Oxford University Press.

Bonsma, F.N., J.H.R. Bisschop, W.G. Barnard, J.A. Van Rensburg, J.J. Duvenhage, H.P.D. Van Wyk, and F. Watermeyer. 1950. *Nguni-Cattle: Report on Indigenous Cattle in South Africa*, Department of Agriculture Pamphlet 311. Pretoria: The Government Printer.

Carruthers, Jane. 2007. 'The Knowledge that is in Names'. *Environmental History* 12/2: 299–301.

Coetzee, J.M. 1998. *White Writing: On the Culture of Letters in South Africa*. New Haven and London: Yale University Press.

de Jongh, Michael. 2002. 'No Fixed Abode: The Poorest of the Poor and Elusive Identities in Rural South Africa'. *Journal of Southern African Studies* 28/2: 441–460.

Donald, Diana. 2007. *Picturing Animals in Britain: 1750–1850*. New Haven and London: Yale University Press.

Dubow, Saul. 1992. 'Afrikaner Nationalism, Apartheid and the Conceptualisation of Race'. *The Journal of African History* 33/2: 209–237.

Dubow, Saul. 2006. *A Commonwealth of Knowledge: Science, Sensibility, and White South Africa, 1820–2000*. Oxford: Oxford University Press.

Dubow, Saul. 1995. *Scientific Racism in Modern South Africa*. Cambridge: Cambridge University Press.

Epstein, Helmut. 1933. 'Descent and Origin of the Afrikander Cattle'. *Journal of Heredity* 24/12: 448–462.

Ewen, Stuart and Elizabeth Ewen. 2008. *Typecasting: On the Arts and Sciences of Human Inequality*. New York: Seven Stories Press.

Foster, Jeremy. 2008. *Washed with Sun: Landscape and the Making of White South Africa*. Pittsburgh: University of Pittsburgh Press.

Gertenbach, W.D. and A.A. Kars. 1999. 'Towards the conservation of the indigenous cattle of KwaZulu-Natal'. *South African Journal of Animal Science* 29/2: 55–63.

Galton, Francis. 1898. 'Photographic Measurement of Horses and Other Animals'. *Nature* 57: 230–2.

Godby, Michael. 'Introduction: Interface, Contestations, Interventions, Inventions, Inter-rogations', in M. Godby (ed.) *The Lie of the Land: Representations of the South African Landscape*. Cape Town: exhibition catalogue, 2010. pp. 60–135.

Gutsche, Thelma. 1970. *A Very Smart Medal: The Story of the Witwatersrand Agricultural Society*. Cape Town: Howard Timmins.

Huff, Cynthia. 2002. 'Victorian Exhibitionism and Eugenics: The Case of Francis Galton and the 1899 Crystal Palace Dog Show'. *Victorian Review* 28/2: 1–20.

Kars, A.A., G.J. Erasmus and J. van der Westhuizen. 1994. 'Factors influencing growth traits in the Nguni cattle stud at Bartlow Combine'. *South African Journal of Animal Science* 24/1: 18–21.

MacKenzie, John M. *Museums and Empire: Natural History, Human Cultures and Colonial Identities*. Manchester and New York, Manchester University Press, 2009.

Moncrief, Elizabeth. 1996. *Farm Animal Portraits*, Woodbridge: Antique Collectors' Club Ltd.

Musemwa, L., A. Mushunje, M. Chimonyo and C. Mapiye. 2010. 'Low Cattle Market Off-Take Rates in Communal Production Systems of South Africa: Causes and Mitigation Strategies'. *Journal of Sustainable Development in Africa* 12/5: 209–226.

Musemva, Lovemore and Abyssinia Mushunje. 2011. 'Marketing challenges and opportunities faced by the Nguni cattle project beneficiaries in the Eastern Cape Province of South Africa', in A. Obi (ed.) *Institutional Constraints to Small Farmer Development in Southern Africa*. Wageningen: Wageningen Academic Publishers. pp. 121–135.

Nicholas, George. 2011. 'And the Decades Roll By...', Centenary edition of the *Farmer's Weekly*.

Poland, Marguerite, David Hammond-Tooke and Lee Voigt. 2003. *The Abundant Herds: A Celebration of the Nguni Cattle of the Zulu People*. Cape Town: Fernwood Press.

Potts, Alex. 1990. 'Natural Order and the Call of the Wild: The Politics of Animal Pictur-ing'. *Oxford Art Journal* 13/1: 12–33.

Ritvo, Harriet. 1987. *The Animal Estate: The English and Other Creatures in the Victorian Age*. Cambridge, Massachusetts: Harvard University Press.

Schoeman, S.J. 1989. 'Recent research into the production potential of indigenous cattle with special reference to the Sanga'. *South African Journal of Animal Science* 19/2: 55–61.

Steyn, Sarah Adriana. 'Childhood: An Anthropological Study of Itinerancy and Domes-tic Fluidity amongst the Karretjie People of the South African Karoo', unpublished dissertation, 2009. Available: http://uir.unisa.ac.za/bitstream/handle/10500/4065/MA.dissertation._steyn_a.pdf?sequence=1

92

Amy Halliday

Sutton, Thomas. 1954. *The Daniells: Artists and Travellers*. London: Bodley Head.

Thomson, Leonard. 2001. *A History of South Africa* (3rd ed.) [2000]. New Haven and London: Yale University Press.

Vestergaard, Mads. 2001. 'Who's Got the Map? The Negotiation of Afrikaner Identities in Post-Apartheid South Africa'. *Daedalus* **130**/1: 19–41.

Yarwood, Richard and Nick Evans. 2002. 'Taking Stock of Farm Animals and Rurality', in C. Philo and C. Wilbert (eds.) *Animal Spaces, Beastly Places: New Geographies of Human–Animal Relations*. New York and London: Routledge. pp. 99–115.

Chapter 4

Building a Scenic Landscape: Nature and History on the Columbia River Highway, 1913–1916

Tyler A. Cornelius

In the upper Northwest corner of the United States runs the large, powerful and productive Columbia River. Draining a large expanse of the North American West, the river is one of the longest on the continent, bending and twisting its way through the vast interior Columbia Plain before turning sharply west, crossing the mountains and eventually emptying its contents into the Pacific. Near the end of its course, in an area known as the Columbia River Gorge, the Columbia moves between two starkly different ecosystems. It passes from the dry, sage-covered grasslands and irrigated farm fields of the east to the verdant, evergreen forests of the west. In the middle runs the Cascade Range, where the Columbia has cut a wide, broad canyon. Visitors are often struck by the dramatic beauty of their surroundings: the size and powerful flow of the river, the steep cliffs that line the canyon walls, and the cascading waterfalls that fall to the valley floor.

Today the Columbia River Gorge is one of the most popular natural attractions in the region, now protected by U.S. federal law as a National Scenic Area. But at the beginning of the twentieth century, this landscape was far less accessible and acclaimed. One of the last areas of the continental United States to be invaded and settled by Euro-Americans, the Pacific Northwest of the late nineteenth century remained a region on the precipice of significant economic, cultural and environmental change. In the early 1900s much of the region was comparatively undeveloped, still covered in old-growth forest, with vast tracts of land that had yet to be farmed, logged or put to productive use. It was in this context that several local residents set out on an ambitious development project, a plan to build the first modern road through the Columbia River Gorge. The Columbia River Highway was widely praised as an engineering marvel, one of the first paved roads in the region. Interestingly, the highway was planned and built when there were still relatively few automobiles in operation, and even fewer people who had considered using them to visit a place as difficult to reach as the Columbia River Gorge. Designed to be more than a transportation artery, the Columbia River Highway was built to bring tourists to nature, to deliver beautiful views of the spectacular Gorge landscape

Tyler A. Cornelius

and to bring visitors into the region – literally 'paving the way' for a new way of visiting scenic landmarks along the Columbia River.

In shortening the temporal distance to nearby cities, the highway also reduced the cultural distance – rescripting how most middle-class urbanites envisioned their relationship to the landscape and the surrounding hinterlands. As previously un-named spaces were transformed into discrete natural places, the 'nature' of the Columbia River Gorge's landscape was reimagined for more and diverse types of visitors. Moreover, these visitors began to see the landscape from different vantage points – from high above the river or deep within its canyons and, importantly, from the constructed artifice of a roadway. The Gorge's great waterfalls – previously only glimpsed in passing (or hidden altogether) – became points of interest, destinations along a specific route, attractions that could be named, photographed and then marketed. In exploring the planning, promotion and construction of this road, I will examine how the highway marked an important turning point in the history of the Columbia River Gorge and the region. I argue that the highway did not create the Gorge or its beautiful views, but it did organise the way that humans viewed the landscape and, in a way, create the object known as the 'Scenic Columbia River Gorge'. In this chapter I explore the history of the Columbia River Highway to explain how a road could change a landscape and how ideas associated with a road helped to change understandings of nature and history in the early twentieth century North American West.

Tourism in the Columbia River Gorge

At the turn of the century, the Pacific Northwest was not a centre of industry, agricultural production or population. Local residents sought to improve their region (and their fortunes) by promoting public projects that would attract industrial development, capital investment and increases in population. It was in this context that business interests in the nearby city of Portland, Oregon sought projects that might take advantage of the natural beauty the region offered.

While the road was new, the landscape it traversed was already well-known. Most who travelled through the Columbia River Gorge had done so by water – first by small boat and eventually by steamship. Despite a preponderance of boats and people, transportation on this part of the Columbia River remained an onerous and often dangerous endeavor up to the 1850s. It was then that several entrepreneurial residents completed rail portages around the Columbia's most problematic natural barriers – the massive rapids at Celilo and the Cascades. Rail portages around these falls improved transportation on the river considerably, made river travel on the Columbia a more palatable investment, but mostly hinted that an overland route through the area was still highly desirable. Throughout this period, violent clashes between Indian peoples and invading settlers along the river escalated to

Figure 1. Highway and Benson Bridge at Multnomah Falls.

George Weister. 1916. Samuel Lancaster surveyed the location of the highway with visual strategies in mind, framing particular views and placing the road near waterfalls and scenic vistas. Oregon Historical Society, OrHi 18964.

the point that the federal government eventually investigated an alternative to the water route. From 1872 to 1876 the U.S. government built the first wagon road to run through the area. Impractically steep, this road was a nightmare when it rained – which was much of the time. In 1882, few complained when the Oregon Railway and Navigation Company destroyed parts of the road in laying the first continuous railroad route through the area.[1] By the turn of the century, there were railroad routes on both sides of the river, yet the area remained relatively isolated from the growing city of Portland, Oregon. With limited roads in the region, the Gorge's railroad route remained the primary artery by which people and goods moved east and west through the region.

By the mid-1880s the Union Pacific Railroad was actively promoting the Columbia River Gorge as a scenic destination.[2] In addition, steamboat entrepreneurs planned cruises from Portland, with trips ranging from one day to two, depending on how far upriver visitors wanted to travel.[3] Historian Frances Fuller Victor wrote glowingly of her trip up the Columbia in her history of the region:

> We have enjoyed river, forest, mountains, and snowpeaks … sitting out upon the steamer's deck, of a summer morning, we are not much troubled with visions of storms: the scene is as peaceful as it is magnificent. Steaming ahead, straight into the heart of the mountains, where they rise to a height of four thousand feet, each moment affords a fresh delight to the wondering senses. The panorama of grandeur and beauty seems endless.[4]

These romantic sensibilities became common tourist descriptions of the landscapes and the North American West.

The increase of nature-based tourism in the Gorge, like the increase of tourism throughout the region, was tied to broad social and economic changes. As more of the middle class gained disposable income, they spent it on goods and services less essential to everyday life. Mass media and the advertising industry were creating the

---

1. Dwight A. Smith, *Columbia River Highway Historic District: Nomination of the Old Columbia River Highway in the Columbia Gorge to the National Register of Historic Places* (Salem: Oregon Department of Transportation, 1984) pp. 55–56; and Ronald J. Fahl, 'S.C. Lancaster and the Columbia River Highway: Engineer as Conservationist', *Oregon Historical Quarterly* 74 (June 1973): 107–8.

2. For an example see *Wealth and Resources of Oregon and Washington, The Pacific Northwest, A Complete Guide over the Local Lines of the Union Pacific Railway* (Portland: Passenger Department of the Oregon Railway and Navigation Company, 1889).

3. Steamboat tourism on the Columbia was part of the larger development of a middle-class tourist industry, one that was fully formed by the end of the nineteenth century. As early as the 1860s, a bevy of tourism promoters, guidebook writers and railroad companies began promoting the scenery of the U.S. West. See John F. Sears, *Sacred Places: American Tourist Attractions in the Nineteenth Century* (New York: Oxford University Press, 1989).

4. Francis Fuller Victor, *Atlantis Arisen, or Talks of a Tourist about Oregon and Washington* (Philadelphia: J. B. Lippincott, 1891) pp. 54–55.

foundations for a nascent consumer culture. When consumerism prompted a shift away from the values of work, thrift and delayed gratification, North Americans found solace in the sanctioned consumption of the outdoors, where they could pursue relaxation, therapeutic recreation and moral regeneration.[5] Railroad tourism, once limited to the elite because of its prohibitive costs, became increasingly accessible to the middle classes and Americans quickly adopted automobiles, a new form of recreational travel that lowered the cost of travel even more.

From 1900 to 1906 the number of automobiles in the United States grew from 8,000 to 100,000 and almost overnight a new form of tourism was born.[6] After 1908, when Henry Ford's assembly line invented the mass production of his automobiles, an increasing number of middle-class Americans could afford to take to the roads. With automobile tourism gaining in popularity, a number of groups formed to promote auto travel to Western U.S. landscapes. In 1906, a national campaign called 'See America First' sought to encourage wealthier Americans to forego a European sojourn in favor of a national driving tour of America's great scenic places. Travelling the West was an activity loaded with national meaning and often it was presented in explicitly symbolic terms. Marguerite Shaffer, in her book *See America First: Tourism and National Identity, 1880–1940*, revealed how proponents of a national driving tour often returned to an overarching theme of the value of Western scenery. Western landscapes connected ideas about natural abundance to the promise and potential of the nation.[7] One booster wrote that the landscape was

> a treasure house filled to overflowing with the rarest gems of towering snow-capped mountains; noble rivers, bearing in their broad bosoms the commerce of a nation; blue lakes smiling in the face of unclouded skies, gorgeous sunsets, whose ravishing beauty fills the soul with reverential awe, while over all and around all there is an atmosphere so pure that simply breathing it brings life to the lifeless, hope to the hopeless, and happiness to the miserable.[8]

Such rhetoric contrasted the West with the East in oppositional terms. As the East was industrial, urban, modern and possibly corrupt, the West was virtuous, natural, free and therapeutic. In this way, Shaffer argued, entrepreneurs could sell an idea that promised the best of both worlds – 'the virtues of nature combined with

5. Paul Sutter, *Driven Wild: How the Fight Against Automobiles Launched the Modern Wilderness Movement* (Seattle: University of Washington Press, 2004) pp. 21, 27; Gail Bederman, *Manliness and Civilization: A Cultural History of Gender and Race in the United States, 1880–1917* (Chicago: University of Chicago Press, 1995) pp. 12–13.

6. Sutter, *Driven Wild*, p. 24.

7. Marguerite Shaffer, *See America First: Tourism and National Identity, 1880–1940* (Washington D.C.: Smithsonian Institution Press, 2001), p. 38.

8. Fisher Harris, 'Europe v. America', *Western Monthly* (December 1908): 15, as quoted in Shaffer, p. 38.

the benefits of commerce'.[9] Despite the national trends, in the first decade of the twentieth century there were relatively few automobiles in the Pacific Northwest, likely because there were even fewer roads to accommodate them. Roads in rural areas of Oregon were really no more than 'dilapidated wagon paths'.[10] Filled with ruts in the summer, and clogged with mud in the winter, almost none of these roads were designed with automobile travel in mind. Roads in urban areas were only slightly more suitable, really only functioning in good weather. Often buried in snow or mud, the Pacific Northwest climate generally limited automobile travel to the drier months and even then automobile owners could usually only operate their vehicles at slow speeds.[11] Frequent bridge washouts were an additional problem to be overcome. C. Lester Horn, who worked on the construction of the Columbia River Highway, recalled:

> Though the automobile had become a common sight on the streets of the cities, highways beyond the city limits were limited and poor. From Portland, for instance, one could travel on paved highways hardly twenty-five miles in any direction; dirt roads suitable for auto use did not connect those cities with other important areas; during much of the year the motorist had to go well provided with towing equipment, and frequently call farmers from their fields or homes (sometimes a long distance from the spot in the forest where his car was mired).[12]

Spatially, automobiles did not serve to connect things – at least not on the geographic scale one might expect. Automobiles operated in smaller geographies, in relatively tiny, self-contained islands, where they could drive around in small areas. It was a rare automobile owner who broke out of these confined geographies, mostly because it took so much work to do so, especially in wet seasons.

Dreams of a Scenic Highway

In July 1915 there were fewer than 8,000 cars in the Portland area, and around 12,000 in the entire state – a ratio of roughly one car to 18 residents.[13] By 1922, there were 37,717 cars registered in Portland's Multnomah County alone, which amounted to a ratio of one car to every 6.3 persons. By 1928, automobile owner-

9. Shaffer, p. 39. On efforts promoting scenic automobile tourism see also Warren James Belasco, *Americans on the Road: From Autocamp to Motel, 1910–1945* (Cambrige: MIT Press, 1979), David Louter, *Windshield Wilderness: Cars, Roads, and Nature in Washington's National Parks* (Seattle: University of Washington Press, 2006) and Sutter, *Driven Wild.*

10. Smith, *Columbia River Highway*, p. 56.

11. Ibid.

12. C. Lester Horn, 'Oregon's Columbia River Highway', *Oregon Historical Quarterly* 74 (June 1973): 255.

13. E. Kimbark MacColl, *The Growth of a City: Power and Politics in Portland, Oregon, 1915–1950* (Portland: Georgian Press, 1979), p. 26.

ship had increased so that there was one car to every 3.44 persons.[14] Despite this relatively rapid increase in cars on the roadways, when highway proponents first set out to advocate for a paved highway in the Columbia River Gorge, most citizens did not find the idea particularly compelling.

The idea of building a road through the Gorge had trickled around the region at the turn of the century but the momentum that culminated in its construction originated with one man – the ubiquitous Sam Hill. He first gained fame as a Harvard-educated attorney who worked for James J. Hill's Northern Pacific Railroad, eventually marrying into the elder Hill's family in 1888. Rich and ambitious, Sam Hill was prone to undertaking colourful public-works projects and was known for his business acumen, skill in promotion and interest in economic development. Described as charismatic and personable, Sam Hill impressed others as hard-working and humble, an image he himself helped to cultivate by soliciting positive newspaper stories from his friends working at local newspapers. Fred Lockley, the author of many of the newspaper articles on the Columbia River Highway, described him as follows:

> If you saw him in his broad-brimmed gray hat with a red bandanna around his neck, wearing his well-worn corduroys, stopping his auto to shovel a sharp-cornered rock out of the road, you would think he was a road supervisor. He works on the roads as if he were on salary and afraid he would lose his job if he didn't put in full-time at hard work. I have ridden a good many thousand miles with him over the highways, over mountain trails and through the sagebrush and desert and he is always the same ... if he doesn't work or travel sixteen hours a day, he feels he has wasted the day.[15]

Active in the business community and in a number of fraternal organisations, Hill also happened to be an outspoken advocate for building new and better roads. A founding member of the Washington State Good Roads Association, he once noted that 'Good roads are more than my hobby; they are my religion'.[16] Drawn to roads because of his fascination with automobiles and his expertise in transportation networks, Hill also believed that improvements in the region's infrastructure were essential to helping lower transportation costs for rural farmers.

---

14. Oregon State Highway Commission, *Fifth Biennial Report of the State Highway Commission of the State of Oregon, 1921–22* (1923) p. 113; *Eighth Biennial Report of the State Highway Commission* (Salem: State Printing Department, 1929), p. 147.

15. Fred Lockley, as quoted in John E. Tuhy, *The Prince of Castle Nowhere* (Portland: Timber Press, 1983), p. 144.

16. For information on Samuel Hill's life and career in the Pacific Northwest, see Thelma Kimmel, *Who the Sam Hill Was Sam Hill?* (The Dalles, OR: Optimist Printers, 1972); Lois Davis Plotts, *Maryhill, Sam Hill and Me* (Camas, WA: Post Publications, 1979); and Tuhy, *The Prince of Castle Nowhere*. For information on his career promoting good roads see *Brief History of the Washington State Good Roads Association* (Seattle: Washington State Good Roads Association, 1939) and Paul Dorpat and Genevieve McCoy, *Building Washington: A History of Washington State Public Works* (Seattle: Tartu Publications, 1998) pp. 63–88. Quotation is from Tuhy, p. 129.

Professing an antipathy towards urban life and its perceived vices, Hill saw the construction of good roads as a way to slow migration to urban areas and shifting social relations. Hill wrote:

> I believe in man on the land. We cannot afford to have our producers leave the land and come to the city and become parasites. We want our girls to stay on the farm and become mothers of a virile race of men and not just go to the city and become manicurists, stenographers, and variety actresses. We want our boys to stay on the farm and not succumb to the lure of the Great White Way or become chauffeurs and clerks ... we cannot keep the ambitious boy or girl on the farm unless we make life attractive and comfortable.[17]

In this way Hill's support of roads corresponded with other widely held anxieties of the era, in particular changing gender roles and racial mixing – which were frequently figured in antipathy towards cities. Of course, there was an irony built into Hill's fears and desires. Better roads for markets also meant better roads for farm kids to escape upon, as the young and mobile often left the countryside for a life in the city.

When Hill met one of the most prominent road-construction engineers in 1906, he sensed an opportunity to add an important ally to his favorite cause. Born in Mississippi in 1864, Samuel Lancaster first worked as railroad construction engineer until 1886, when at the age of 22, he contracted typhoid and became paralysed from the waist down. After a long eighteen-month recovery, a period of time where he taught himself to walk again by using a crude wooden frame, Samuel Lancaster returned to his professional career as a city engineer for Jackson, Tennessee, where he oversaw the implementation of a system of hard-surfaced 'macadam' roads. The project, one of the first of its kind, brought him national recognition, and it was soon afterwards that he was asked to be a consulting engineer for the Bureau of Public Roads. It was in this capacity that Samuel Lancaster travelled to Los Angeles, where, in 1906, he met Sam Hill.[18]

Having secured a capable engineer to oversee the project, Hill set about building support for this publicly-funded proposal – especially in Portland's business community. While it was not unusual for business leaders to coalesce and organise around a local development project, the tenacity with which a small group of elite Portlanders pushed this particular endeavor is striking. Most of the most prominent civic organisations lent their support to building the highway. These groups included the Portland Chamber of Commerce, the Press Club and the Royal Rosarians – a fraternal group associated with Portland's Rose Festival. Boosters even convinced groups of men from Portland to participate in volunteer 'work parties', where men volunteered a day's labour to be a part of a 'historic'

---

17. Ibid. p. 135.
18. Tuhy, *The Prince*, pp. 132–133 and Fahl, 'S.C. Lancaster': 105.

Figure 2. Volunteer road workers from Portland.

Supporters of the scenic highway organised volunteer 'work' parties where interested Portlanders could travel to the construction site by train, work for a few hours, enjoy a boxed lunch and then return to Portland. Oregon Historical Society, OrHi 38744.

project. One participant recalled how the men would be taken on a hike over a few miles of road, eat in some beautiful spot, engage in a roundtable discussion of the project and then return to Portland by train.[19] Portland's Advertising Club created a number of advertisements, special reports, pamphlets and newspaper features that promoted the Highway to out-of-town tourists, and sent speakers out of state to gush about the roadside scenery.[20]

While Hill and others worked to build support within state and local government, a steady stream of newspaper articles in the two most prominent regional newspapers, the *Oregonian* and the *Oregon Daily Journal*, extolled the virtues and value of the project.[21] *Oregon Daily Journal* reporter Marshall N. Dana described a conversation he had with George Coleman, a 'star advertising man' who came to see the Columbia River Highway:

Coleman had been talking in explosions, epigrams, exclamations in endeavor to

---

19. Horn, 'Oregon's': 269.

20. Fahl, 'S.C. Lancaster': 120.

21. For an example, see Addison Bennett, 'Columbia Highway Progress is Rapid', *Oregonian*, 22 Feb. 1914, sec.1, p. 12 and editorials; *Oregon Journal*, 15 May 1914, p. 8, 19 July 1914, sec. 2, p. 4.

convey his appreciation. On the summit of Crown point he stood silent. 'Tell me what you think of the Columbia river highway as an advertising asset to Portland', I asked. 'Its value is incalculable', he answered, 'It will make Portland as famous as Niagara Falls has made America. Thousands of people will come here year after year with no other motive than to see the Columbia river highway. It will not be possible for anyone to see this great road and not go away talking about it. And what is said will be praise and the terms will be superlatives. It will not be possible for anyone to see this highway and not want his friends to see it. Your first visitors will go away urging their friends to come and see what is as far beyond description as heaven is above earth'.[22]

Western historian Frederick Jackson Turner, visiting from Harvard University, praised the highway in the newspapers. 'It is wonderful', he remarked, 'You have set a standard in highway construction that will be hard to follow. I have traveled over Europe but have seen nothing to compare with it.'[23] Other famous visitors included Theodore Roosevelt, General George W. Goethals (builder of the Panama Canal), Vice President Thomas R. Marshall and Presidential aspirant William G. McAdoo. Samuel Lancaster later bragged that they received nearly unanimous support in newspaper coverage.[24]

Yet the highway plan was not without its detractors. Early opposition to the plan centred on concerns about its cost. Many residents doubted that such a large sum of money should be spent on subsidising automobile touring, which was largely seen as the province of wealthy elites. At the time of the highway's construction, easy access to remote forests and scenic waterfalls was beyond the reach of most of the urban working-class in Portland and this fact alone structured their impressions of nature-based tourism. Labour leaders focused on who would benefit. Opposition to protecting nature was as much about challenging the moral authority of those who advocated for it, as it was about putting natural resources into production. This pattern of prioritising production over conservation was found throughout the West, and often it forced conservationists to argue that many of these public lands had little or no 'productive potential'.[25]

---

22. Marshall N. Dana, 'Beautiful Columbia River Highway Invaluable Advertising Asset to City', (Date, Publication unknown – but probably written in late 1914, around the time the first phase of highway construction was nearing completion) Oregon Historical Society, Vertical File, Roads – Columbia River Highway, Folder 2.

23. *Oregon Journal*, 23 Aug. 1914, sec. 4, p. 8.

24. Samuel C. Lancaster, *The Columbia: American's Great Highway through the Cascade Mountains to the Sea*, (Portland, Or.: Samuel Christopher Lancaster, 1915) p. 114.

25. For a detailed discussion of working-class attitudes about conservation in the region, see Lawrence M. Lipin, *Workers and the Wild: Conservation, Consumerism, and Labor in Oregon, 1910–1930* (Urbana and Chicago: University of Illinois Press, 2007) pp. 11, 39, 44–45. See also Lawrence M. Lipin, 'Cast Aside the Automobile Enthusiast: Class Conflict, Tax Policy, and the Preservation of Nature in Progressive-Era Oregon', *Oregon Historical Quarterly* 107 (Summer 2006): 176. I am indebted to him for pointing the way toward many of these primary sources.

Figure 3. Tourists at Crown Point.

George Weister. 1918. Oregon Historical Society, OrHi 19183.

Hill's efforts to promote a tourist economy contradicted working-class ideas about production and the proper use of natural resources. For many it was just a matter of where and how roads ought to be built and whose interests the roads might serve. Instead of a scenic highway, labour organisations favoured construction of roads that would bring producers closer together.[26] A better option, they thought, would be to keep natural resources in the public domain, to be developed and integrated into the economy, so that they could benefit all.[27] One labour paper pointed out that 'very little of the land adjoining the highway can ever be tilled. It is a scenic road pure and simple and should the abutting land ever be cleared and tilled, the scenery would be spoiled and the object in building the road defeated.'[28] Rural opponents framed the issue as one that benefited 'joy riders' over farming interests. By dismissing the plan to build the highway as the whim of a 'few pleasure seekers', they understood the act of gazing at scenery as the purview of the elites. 'The fight is between the farmer and the auto people', one Grange official stated,

---

26. Lipin, *Workers and the Wild*, p. 3.

27. Ibid. p. 46.

28. 'Wonderful Road, But', *Portland Labor Press*, 3 May 1915, p. 2.

'The former wants roads so they can get their produce to market, while the latter wants one road across the state so they can ride fast in an automobile'.[29]

To its advocates, the benefits of the highway were obvious – it would stimulate commerce *and* provide recreation in the form of scenic vistas. Yet, even after Hill's political efforts were successful, and the highway had received public financing, the *idea* of a highway still did not inspire the type of public support he had hoped for. Despite the lofty rhetoric, progressive-era Portland was suspicious of large public expenditures. To remedy the situation, Hill and Lancaster took their 'show on the road', presenting their road in a slideshow.

In preparing their presentation, the two men spent considerable time and resources attending to the images. The story they planned to tell was not polemical, but instead visual – one based in aesthetics. In their efforts to present the project in the most favorable light, Hill and Lancaster invested in 'stereoptican' slides – photographs on glass that could be projected by a large lantern. Images of the Columbia River Gorge were projected onto giant screens and the use of the slide technology gave a thoroughly modern sensibility to their 'technologically-advanced' proposal. By all accounts, the experience of seeing Hill and Lancaster's slideshow delighted local audiences. Slideshows were still novel and they recast this local landmark in an attractive fashion. Hill paid artists to hand-colour the glass-plated slides, so that bright green trees and blue rivers contrasted with the grey hues of the rock.

In the slides, the colours of the landscape jumped out at the viewer, as overly saturated hues of green and yellow accentuated the pristine qualities of the landscape around the roadway. Dark-green Douglas fir trees received one hue, while deciduous trees like willow and poplar received another. Shadows stretched across the greenery, giving contrast to its colours and putting focus upon the light in the sky. In the slides, the colours were too bold to be realistic, and too saturated to see in everyday life, but they were aesthetically beautiful and were striking when shown with an impressive new technology. In one slide depicting the view of Crown Point, a wide, majestic Columbia River flows into the distance and the beauty is pastoral, picturesque and romantic. In a later slide depicting the highway itself, the camera angle frames the shapes of Sheppard's Dell bridge; its clear sharp lines, the square and sharp corners of its pedestals, and the perfect arc of its foundation stand like a Greek temple in the wilderness. Like Thomas Cole's famous paintings *The Course of Empire* (1833–6), the nods to classical architecture encouraged new ways of interpreting the landscape.

Hill and Lancaster used the slideshow exhaustively to attract crowds and gain support for their project and later to promote the highway as a tourist destination. In Corvallis, Oregon the slides brought out 'frequent cheers' from the audience and newspaper accounts reported that audiences appreciated both the pictures and

29. Oregon State Federation of Labor, *Proceedings of the Ninth Convention* (The Dalles, Oregon, 1912) p. 13, as quoted in Lipin, p. 41.

the promises. By 1915, a reporter exaggerated that Hill and Lancaster must have presented the lecture and slideshow to '20,000 Portland school children, taking them in classes of twenty at a time'.[30] Following the completion of the highway in 1916, Lancaster travelled to the eastern U.S. to speak with civic groups, present his slides to various organisations, and promote the road to newspaper editors and publishers. He gave the slideshow to 1,800 people at the U.S. Chamber of Commerce alone and similar presentations to the national Rotary Club, Commercial Club, National Press Club and others. The next year he visited the Brooklyn Institute of Arts and Sciences, American Scenic and Historic Preservation Society, the National Geographic Society and the National Good Roads Association. His national pro-motional tour visited Philadelphia, New York, Boston, Toledo, Detroit, Chicago and St. Paul. The *Oregonian* covered his publicity tour and reported that his efforts would 'spread the facts regarding the highway's attractions before millions of people wherever English is spoken', adding that 'descriptive stories of the highway are now in the course of preparation for … *World's Work, National Geographic Magazine, Ford Times, Saturday Evening Post, Country Gentleman,* and a number of others.'

The intensity that they brought to their project is noteworthy. While the building of the Columbia River Highway was certainly an impressive technologi-cal feat, what is striking is the extent to which it was self-consciously *presented* as such in the slideshows. Particularly notable was the idea that modern construction methods, and modern representational strategies could provide access to pre-modern natural settings. In this way, those taken with the engineering could simultaneously appreciate both an aesthetic of modernity and an aesthetic of a romantic, almost timeless nature. Importantly, the juxtaposition of the two impulses, technological and romantic, encouraged this type of interpretation. The presence of the highway suggested that humans could control and master nature and the presence of the scenery gave them a reason for doing so. The two men were promoting the splendour of the views, but also the splendour of getting to the viewpoints.

As the workers carved out the proposed road route with picks, axes, shovels and sweat, they prepared the highway (and the nature around it) for the automobile tourists to come. The result was a winding ribbon of concrete that stamped the landscape with a symbol of man's technological mastery, while simultaneously rei-fying the surrounding area as primeval and wild. In this way, boosters rationalised development as preservation and road-planners and engineers embraced romantic ideas about the natural world, and what the natural world could do to alleviate the social problems of contemporary society.[31] Hill and Lancaster had placed the landscape into a story that was familiar to the region's first Euro-American explor-ers, second-generation settlers and even its newest arrivals. For people who wrote

---

30. See Tuhy, *The Prince,* pp. 131, 140; *Oregonian,* 21 March 1916, p. 13, and Fahl, 'S.C. Lancaster': 124.

31. See Paul Sutter, *Driven Wild* and David Louter, *Windshield Wilderness.*

glowingly of romantic nature, who appreciated and consumed landscape art and who associated the beauty of nature with the divine hand of God, travelling over a new and modern highway to gaze at beautiful scenery was just further evidence of the benefits that modern technology could offer. The two patterns of knowing the landscape merged together as one – a dominating modernity was balanced by a harmonious pastoral, each getting its meaning from the other.

It wouldn't be long before emblems of mechanised technology began to be seen as problematic. In the United States early conservation battles over Hetch-Hetchy and Niagara Falls showed the limits to which the 'natural' could co-exist with the 'technological'. But in the early decades of the twentieth century, proponents viewed the road as a device to facilitate appreciation for the natural world, which would then lead to preservation. Any inconsistencies between roads and wild nature would not arise for a decade or so after the highway's construction.

Building a New Space and Place

The details of the highway's construction reveal the centrality of this juxtaposition. In October 1913, highways were built using sheer manpower. Hundreds of workers wielded shovels and picks, axes and saws to clear a path through dense forest and over steep slopes. Horses and mules hauled rock and gravel and a special wagon blended the bituminous macadam mixture used in paving the surface of the road-way. To pave the Columbia River Highway, Hill and Lancaster brought in rock crushers, rollers and screens for the crushed rock. They shipped in heavy oil and heated the oil-based asphalt before spraying it onto the road's surface. This type of construction required the macadam to be layered six inches thick, rolled down to four inches as it cooled and then layered all over again.[32]

When surveying to determine the best route for the highway, the engineers began by noting the most pleasant locations – often views of the river from above and below. For several weeks, the team travelled throughout the area, photograph-ing and mapping where the highway might fit on the rocky slopes and wooded terrain. Particular care was given to frame the natural scenes they encountered and Lancaster focused on how visitors would see the river. He told a newspaper, 'On starting the surveys our first business was to find the beauty spots, or those points where the most beautiful things along the line might be seen to the best advantage, and if possible to locate the road in such a way as to reach them.'[33] K.P. Billner, one of the engineers who oversaw the construction of bridges, told a trade journal that

---

32. See the *First Annual Report*, pp. 46–47; *Oregonian*, 20 February 1914, p. 9, 10 July 1914, pp.1–2; *Oregon Journal*, 3 Jan. 1915, pict. supp., p. 1, as quoted in Fahl, 'S.C. Lancaster': 115. See also Tuhy, *The Prince*, p. 136.

33. *Oregon Journal*, 3 Jan. 1915, p. 2.

they aimed to be 'artistic' and in 'harmony with the surroundings'.[34] Lancaster was acting, as one historian has argued, as both an engineer and a conservationist.[35]

A number of design features reflected Hill and Lancaster's desire to make road and nature blend seamlessly together. Notably, Lancaster specified that local rock be used in an attempt to make the built structures match the basalt and granite found in the Gorge. Stylistic features that adorned stone bridges, masonry walls and windowed tunnels reflected a desire to beautify rather than distract. Lancaster had seen Italian dry masonry in his earlier trip to Europe and hired Italian-Americans familiar with the technique to craft walls and railings.[36] The construction of the Mitchell Point tunnel featured natural basalt columns, in contrast to the masonry columns found on the Axenstrasse in Switzerland. Lancaster publicised such features, and on more than one occasion publicly confessed his love of the outdoors.

> My love for the beautiful is inherited from my mother ... When I made a preliminary survey here and found myself standing waist-deep in the ferns, I remembered my mother's long ago warning, 'Oh Samuel, do be careful of my Boston fern!' And I then pledged myself that none of this wild beauty should be marred where it could be prevented. The highway was so built that not one tree was felled, not one fern was crushed, unnecessarily.[37]

East of Multnomah Falls, where there was little room for railroad tracks, let alone a highway, Lancaster designed an 860-foot concrete viaduct to skirt along the slope, 'in order not to disturb the mountain, and ruin the trees and flowering shrubs, which are so beautiful'.[38]

The physical dimensions of the road were dictated both by the nature of the landscape, and by the nature of the automobile which then travelled at speeds from ten to twelve miles per hour.[39] Strict attention was given to maintaining a minimal grade, and the engineers often bragged of the standardised dimensions of

---

34. K.P. Billner, 'Design Features of the Various Types of Reinforced Concrete Bridges Along the Columbia River Highway in Oregon', *Engineering and Contracting* 10 (February 1915): 121, as quoted in Robert W. Hadlow, *Historic Columbia River Highway Recording Project*. (Washington D. C.: Historic American Engineering Record, HABS/HAER Division, National Park Service, U.S. Dept. of the Interior, 1994) sec. 1, 4.

35. Note the title of Fahl's article, 'S.C. Lancaster and the Columbia River Highway: Engineer as Conservationist.'

36. Hadlow, *Historic Columbia*, sec. 1, 22–23 and Fahl, 'S.C. Lancaster': 125.

37. Samuel Lancaster, as told to Marguerite Norris Davis, *St. Nicholas Magazine*, March 1924, as quoted in Lancaster, *The Columbia, America's Great Highway through the Cascade Mountains to the Sea*, Appendix A.

38. Lancaster, 'The Columbia River Highway in the Oregon Country': 7, as quoted in Fahl, 'S.C. Lancaster': 126.

39. The speed of travel on the roadway has been surprisingly difficult to confirm, but these figures come from Edward M. Miller, 'That was an Eventful Day in Portland', Undated, Oregon Historical Society, Vertical File, Roads – Columbia River Highway, Folder 2.

Figure 4. Highway's approach to Mitchell Point.

Arthur M. Prentiss. 1916. Oregon Historical Society, OrHi 38745.

Figure 5. Tunnel at Mitchell Point.

John Arthur Elliott modeled the 390-foot Mitchell Point Tunnel on the tunnel overlooking Lake Uri (Lake Lucerne) on the Auxenstrasse, in Switzerland. While the Swiss tunnel's
window openings were constructed with masonry columns, Elliot hoped to best that design
with natural basalt supports and window alignments designed to accentuate natural light
– another example of how planners sought to produce features that would fit within the
natural landscape. Oregon Historical Society, 3587.

the road – 24 feet in width, with no grade heavier than five per cent.[40] In several
portions of the highway, curves with small radii alternated back and forth, making
nearly complete figure of eight patterns in order to avoid steeper grades. In other
places the road's path curved to move closer to trees and workers took care not to
disturb vegetation that might have been cleared in other locales. The result of all
these design features was an intimacy with the landscape that was more immediate
than many roads constructed subsequently.

By the time it was finished, the Columbia River Highway was widely known
as an engineering wonder – a winding, scenic road like no other in the country,
one eventually emulated by road engineers for highways in several National Parks,

40. Lancaster, *The Columbia*, p. 106.

Tyler A. Cornelius

including Glacier, Rocky Mountain and Yosemite. Designed exclusively for automobiles, the highway's nineteen bridges and four tunnels impressed nearly all who travelled to see it, and it drew national coverage in popular newspapers and magazines such as *Sunset, Scientific American* and the *New York Times*, as well as trade publications, including *Good Roads, Engineering News, American Forestry* and

Figure 6. The Rowena Loops.

The snaking, curving figure of eight pattern that came to be called 'The Rowena Loops' is an example of how the Columbia River Highway was built to accommodate early automobiles that travelled at slower speeds. The curves' tight radii and the highway's meandering path strive to maintain a gentle five per cent grade. Oregon Historical Society, OrHi 4218.

Building a Scenic Landscape

Contracting.[41] The small radii of curves, however, eventually made the highway obsolete for cars travelling at faster speeds.

As the route turned forest into road, the *human* world of the Gorge changed with it. More than just ushering in an era of tourism, the highway brought with it profound changes in how humans interacted with the natural landscape. Automobiles were having a profound affect upon both the spatial and social organisation of human communities. The onset of 'automobility', a term used to describe the many social, cultural, technological and ecological facets of an automobile-based transportation system, profoundly affected the cultural world of those who moved in and out of the Gorge's spaces. Visiting the Gorge now linked roads, cars, passengers, petroleum industries and a host of other objects, technologies and signs, many of which were previously absent or less significant.[42] As was true in so many other places, automobiles changed the organisation of the Gorge's towns and the surrounding cities. They shaped how, when and why people travelled and influenced the location of homes and services.

Wolfgang Schivelbusch, in his landmark study of railroads, noted how changes in motive power altered human interactions with time and space within a landscape.[43] Changes in motive technology, he argued, affected the temporal organisation of a landscape.[44] This contraction of time and space meant that railroad travelers formed different relationships with the landscape they travelled within. Visual perception was diminished by velocity, as railroad passengers missed details in the foreground and saw landscapes through the technologies that moved them. The result was a 'panoramization' of the landscape, which required the 'de-concentration or dispersal of attention' to adapt to the conditions of rail travel.

Early automobile travel provoked a different set of interactions between humans and landscapes, yet similar patterns emerge. Automobiles distanced passengers from the immediacy of the world around them and the amount of time it

41. For a sampling of national press coverage, see Henry L. Bowlby, 'The Columbia Highway in Oregon', *Engineering News* (1915): 62–64; Walter Prichard Eaton, 'Through Oregon on High', *New York Times*, 4 September 1921: 31; Randal R. Howard, 'Through the Columbia River Gorge by Auto', *Sunset Magazine*, August 1915: 303–6; Joe D. Thomison, 'The Columbia River Road', *Sunset Magazine*, 4 September 1921; George C. Warren, 'The Columbia River Highway', *Contracting*, May 1916: 1–43, 86–8; 'A Beautiful Link in Our Highway System', *Scientific American* 114 (1916): 1; 'The Columbia River Highway: A State Road that is a Model of Artistic Engineering', in *Scientific American Supplement*, 1 July 1916; 'The Columbia Highway in Oregon', *American Forestry* 22 (1916): 12–19; 'The Columbia River Highway in Oregon', *Good Roads*, 1 January 1916: 3–8.

42. For a brief discussion of 'automobility' and its effects, see Mike Featherstone, 'Automobilities: An Introduction', in *Theory, Culture & Society* 21/4–5 (2004): 1–24 and John Urry, 'The "System" of Automobility', in *Theory, Culture & Society* 21/4–5 (2004): 25–39.

43. Wolfgang Schivelbusch, *The Railway Journey: The Industrialization of Time and Space in the Nineteenth Century* (Berkeley: University of California Press, 1986) p. 23.

44. Ibid. p. 33.

Tyler A. Cornelius

took them between natural sites was dramatically reduced. Although drivers experienced natural spaces with more freedom than train passengers, a tourist circuit, or fixed route, emerged – one dictated by the distance a person could reasonably travel in a day. Residents from nearby Portland began to experience the Gorge as a series of stops – each one corresponding to a particular scenic vista, a picturesque waterfall, a roadhouse, gas station or hotel. Guidebooks, postcards and other tourist memorabilia adopted the new spatial organisation of the landscape and natural features that had previously been 'undiscovered' gained fame as they were featured as one in a series of attractions. In addition, more people moved in to live in the area and the Gorge's economic system began to change in response to this dramatic new human geography.

For many residents of the Pacific Northwest, the construction of the highway marked the moment when visiting the Columbia River Gorge became a much more convenient prospect. The area had gained an entirely new constituency. Portland and the Gorge had moved closer together, both in terms of the time it took to travel from one place to another and culturally, as evidenced by the larger number of visitors that now moved through the landscape with increased regularity. Portlanders, with their varied and multiple interests, took a greater interest in what type of space the Columbia River Gorge would be. In this way, the reduction of physical and temporal distance that accompanied highway construction remade the human geography of the landscape. Technological change was bringing new and different forms of social and political power to the hinterland.

After the completion of the highway, far more tourists experienced the Columbia Gorge by road rather than water and there were more of them. Visitors consumed the Columbia by visiting viewpoints along the route. Yet it remains important to note that the tourists who travelled the Columbia River Highway didn't necessarily think in one unified way. Individual reactions to the landscape were structured by the subjectivities of any given person. Tourists who visited the highway gave meaning to the experience through their own filters, on their own terms.[45] That said, one physical route constrained and channelled most tourists down a single path – one that conferred individual freedom within a certain set of constraints. Tourists largely experienced certain features in uniform ways. Highway road-stops became the vistas that were reproduced in newspapers, on postcards, and by aspiring photographers. In this way the highway helped create a market for views and then for memorabilia celebrating those views. On the Columbia River Highway, nature, views of nature, and the experience of viewing nature, were all impulses that could be linked, then packaged, advertised and sold. Such an experience produced a common story – a story that emphasised the landscape's scenic qualities over others, drawing attention to all that romantic nature had to offer.

---

45. Clifford D. Nelson, *The Guestbooks of Crown Point Chalet 1915–1927* (Published by the author, 2001).

Building a Scenic Landscape

Imagining History through Tourism – The Dedication of the Highway

The completion of the scenic highway gave Hill, Lancaster and local supporters the cause for both celebration and reflection. The road they created was a testament to human progress, a symbol of how Oregonians (and all Americans) could enjoy the redemptive qualities of scenic nature *and* the comforts of modern day life. To commemorate the occasion in 1916, the builders, boosters and local politicians organised a formal dedication at the highway's most prominent tourist destination – Multnomah Falls. A closer look at the dedication ceremony reveals how an emphasis on the scenic enabled visitors and local residents to re-imagine the area's past, present and future.

To celebrate the project's completion, highway boosters were prepared to pull out all the stops. The dedication planning committee was largely made up of the same rich and powerful patrons who had supported it from the beginning, including the mayor of Portland and the governor of Oregon. To promote the occasion, the dedication committee sent copies of Lancaster's now finished book to the governor of every state, arranged for articles to appear in major newspapers throughout the country and sent invitations to Congressmen and several foreign nations. Organisers spared no expense, building elaborate props and even placing large cannons high upon the river bluffs so that they could shoot off 48 rounds in celebration, one for each state in the union. The committee managed to arrange for the participation of U.S. President Woodrow Wilson, who agreed to dedicate the highway by pushing a button from afar.[46] Lancaster explained the plan, framing the highway dedication in national terms:

> In the White House, at exactly 8 p.m., President Wilson will press an electric button which will close a circuit reaching across the Continent. This will operate an electric magnet on Crown Point at 5 p.m., Pacific Coast time, and cause a weight to drop which will unfurl our flag to the breezes of the Pacific Ocean. By this means the President will extend his hand across the Continent, thus reaching into the future and unfurling the flag of freedom three hours ahead of Washington time.[47]

Having scored a major publicity coup with the participation of the President, ceremony boosters planned a dedication that would connect the construction of a highway to heroic tales of national expansion, and they made sure that those who attended would not be disappointed.

Accounts of 7 June 1916 described a hectic day in the Columbia River Gorge. Portland citizen Edward M. Miller recalled automobiles driving over the road from morning until night, as Portlanders made the most of the Labor Day holiday. He was particularly taken with the many types of cars that made the trip:

---

46 *Oregonian*, 21 Nov. 1915, sec. 1, p. 6, 28 Nov. 1915, p. 16, 28 May 1916, sec. 5, p. 2; *Oregon Journal*, 28 May 1916, sec. 3, p. 5.

47. Lancaster, *The Columbia*, p. 128.

114

Tyler A. Cornelius

Figure 7. Dedication of Columbia Highway. Benson Bridges at Multnomah Falls.
Oregon Historical Society, OrHi 11730.

There were big, powerful cars, medium-priced cars and tiny little cars; brand-new, glittering cars of the 1916 model; middle-aged cars and spavined old wrecks that coughed heavily at every grade; and there were truck loads of pretty girls from Portland business houses blowing holiday horns at those who sought to pass them.[48]

A special train from Portland brought additional visitors to the event and rose petals were scattered throughout the grounds.[49] The event began with a local tradition, a pageant that featured the Rose Queen, accompanied by a host of attendants, including King Joy, Miss Columbia, a throng of maids in waiting, crownbearers, trumpeteers, fairy-dancers and bearers of the winged 'Wheel of Progress' – a richly decorated automobile.

Figure 8. Royal Rosarians at the Columbia River Highway dedication.
Oregon Historical Society, OrHi 106233.

Half-way through, in the midst of the dedication ceremony, the crowd gasped when a group of men dressed in generic Native American attire interrupted the proceedings. The *Oregonian* described the scene wherein a fictional Chief Multnomah emerged:

---

48. Miller, 'That was an Eventful Day in Portland.'

49. Fahl, 'S.C. Lancaster': 123.

Tyler A. Cornelius

About the time that everyone thought the dedication was proceeding famously a wild war whoop was heard from the woods above the falls. Presently an Indian appeared on the bridge. He took in the sight below, then rushed madly down the trail and dashed onto the platform. He confronted the Queen. By eloquent gesture he proclaimed his ownership of the great falls and the country surrounding. 'What right have you here?' he demanded in the sign language of the Indian, taking in the Queen and all of her attendants with a majestic sweep of his arm. The Queen stepped from her throne and approached the old Indian. She extended her hand in friendship. The warrior dramatically refused. He threw his blanket over his shoulder, and, turning, for the first time saw the great number of white people present. With the painful knowledge that his days as ruler were over he threw down his bow and arrows and sulked away.[50]

Capping the entire spectacle was the Rose Queen's dedication of the highway. As the 'Wheel of Progress' escorted her down the highway, she sprinkled water from Multnomah Falls upon the roadway. The dedication concluded with the release of carrier pigeons, each bearing invitations to the residents of Los Angeles, Pasadena, San Francisco, Sacramento, Seattle, Vancouver and Victoria.[51] The spectacle then finished with a singing of the national anthem, followed by a rendition of 'America, the Beautiful'.

In celebrating the opening of their highway Portlanders engaged in a dramatic imagining of past, present and future, thereby inventing the stories they wanted to tell about the roadway, about the natural spaces in the Gorge, even about their city and country. In doing so they also connected an imagined pioneer history to the modernity of the present and to their vision of the region's future. Out of all the possible, multiple ways to celebrate the highway (the scenery of the Columbia, the modernity of the highway, the harmony between the two), the narrative that they chose was a progressive taming of the wild, a universal narrative that merged all stories into one, a meta-narrative infused with nationalist and colonial meaning. Evocations of pioneer hardships and disappearing Indians helped middle-class Portlanders celebrate their region within an established national context, even as the very real Native presence was first ignored, and then mocked, by a man dressed up in feathers and buckskin. The stark oppositions, between past and present, savagery and civilisation, 'Indian Chief' and Rose Queen, all helped to first simplify, and then obscure, the region's actual colonial history of violence and dispossession, allowing those who viewed the pageant to imagine the region's identity in relation to these powerful and evocative stories.

Like other racialised representations of Native American peoples, the invention of a Chief Multnomah helped to personify this imagined past. In playing Indian, those who dedicated the highway did more than just position themselves as the

---

50. 'Highway is Dedicated', *Oregonian*, 8 June 1916, pp. 1, 16.

51. Fahl, 'S.C. Lancaster': 140–141, n. 81.

benefactors in an epic conflict between savagery and civilisation. They understood *nature* as evidence of a manifest destiny, a divine truth that had already come to pass. The unveiling of the Columbia's scenic potential was not only a celebration of its past but its future, the culmination of that larger story that ended with the technological mastery of the machine in the garden. Fictionalised, generic Native characters, who remained part of nature, who retreated back to the forest after refusing the seemingly obvious benefits of modernity, helped Portlanders understand the significance of their new technological accomplishment. The people who moved through the Columbia River Gorge could now experience the best of all worlds – a modernity that promised to deliver the moral power of pristine nature to redeem and renew. In this way the landscape of the Columbia functioned as an ideological marker of Euro-American superiority, the backdrop for an epic march of history now made visible in the landscape. The landscape's scenic qualities – the lush vegetation, cascading waterfalls, large Douglas Fir trees and dramatic vistas – came to be understood in relation to these larger narratives and Portlanders who were keen to forget a history of dispossession could look at the natural world and infuse it with these new meanings.

In this way the dedication of the Columbia River Highway allowed both locals and tourists an opportunity to celebrate more than the completion of a roadway. The ceremony united Portland's business elite with a growing middle class eager to craft identity through consumption. It connected a piece of public infrastructure to a now timeless and romantic past, by celebrating an idealised history that was free of both violence and dispossession. It positioned nature as redemptive and the Columbia as the fealty of Portland's kingdom. In this way, the Columbia River Highway reinforced and legitimised this powerful story, constructing a landscape full of contrasts between the modern and the ancient, the technologically advanced and the timeless. With the completion of the roadway, the idea of nature had taken on new meanings in the amorphous, shifting undercurrents of the region's social imagination.

REFERENCES

Bederman, Gail. 1995. *Manliness and Civilization: a Cultural History of Gender and Race in the United States, 1880–1917.* Women in culture and society. Chicago: University of Chicago Press.

Booth, R. A. Barratt. 1922. *Fifth Biennial Report of the Oregon State Highway Commission Covering the Period December 1, 1920, to November 30, 1922 / Yeon, J. B.* Biennial report of the Oregon State Highway Commission; 5th; Salem, Ore.: State of Oregon.

Belasco, Warren James. 1979. *Americans on the Road: from Autocamp to Motel, 1910–1945.* Cambridge, Mass.: MIT Press.

118

Tyler A. Cornelius

Dorpat, Paul. 1998. *Building Washington: A History of Washington State Public Works / McCoy, Genevieve*. Seattle, Wash.: Tartu Publications.

Fahl, Ronald J. 1973. 'S.C. Lancaster and the Columbia River Highway: Engineer as Conservationist'. *Oregon Historical Quarterly* 74 (June): 101–144.

Featherstone, Mike. 2004. 'Automobilities: An Introduction'. *Theory, Culture, & Society* 21/4–5: 1–24.

Hadlow, Robert W. 1994. *Historic Columbia River Highway Recording Project*. Washington D. C.: Historic American Engineering Record, HABS/HAER Division, National Park Service, U.S. Dept. of the Interior.

Horn, C. Lester. 1973. 'Oregon's Columbia River Highway'. *Oregon Historical Quarterly* 74 (June): 249–71.

Kimmel, Thelma. 1972. *Who the Sam Hill Was Sam Hill?* The Dalles, Ore.: Optimist Printers.

Lancaster, Samuel Christopher. 1915. *The Columbia: America's Great Highway through the Cascade Mountains to the Sea*. Portland, Or.: Samuel Christopher Lancaster.

Lipin, Lawrence M. 2006. '"Cast Aside the Automobile Enthuasiast"'. *Oregon Historical Quarterly* 107/2: 166–195.

Lipin, Lawrence M. 2007. *Workers and the Wild: Conservation, Consumerism, and Labor in Oregon, 1910–30*. Urbana: University of Illinois Press.

Louter, David. 2006. *Windshield Wilderness: Cars, Roads, and Nature in Washington's National Parks*. Weyerhaeuser environmental books. Seattle: University of Washington Press.

MacColl, E. Kimbark. 1979. *The Growth of a City: Power and Politics in Portland, Oregon, 1915–1950*. Portland, Or.: Georgian Press.

Miller, Charles N, and Union Pacific Railway Company. 1889. *Wealth and Resources of Oregon and Washington, the Pacific Northwest: A Complete Guide Over the Local Lines of the Union Pacific Railway*. Portland, Or.: Passengr Dept. of the Union Pacific ry.

Nelson, Clifford D. 2001. *The Guestbooks of Crown Point Chalet (1915–1927): A Research Project*. Benicia, Calif.: C.D. Nelson.

Oregon State Federation of Labor. 1912. *Proceedings of the Ninth Convention*. The Dalles, Oregon.

Oregon State Highway Commission. 1929. *Eighth Biennial Report of the State Highway Commission*. Salem: State Printing Department.

Oregon State Highway Commission. 1923. *Fifth Biennial Report of the State Highway commission of the State of Oregon, 1921–22*. Salem: State Printing Department.

Plotts, Lois Davis. 1978. *Maryhill, Sam Hill and Me*. [S.l. : s.n.].

Schivelbusch, Wolfgang. 1986. *The Railway Journey: the Industrialization of Time and Space in the 19th Century*. Geschichte der Eisenbahnreise. Berkeley: University of California Press; Berg.

Sears, John F. 1989. *Sacred Places: American Tourist Attractions in the Nineteenth Century*. New York: Oxford University Press.

Shaffer, Marguerite S. 2001. *See America First: Tourism and National Identity, 1880–1940*. Washington: Smithsonian Institution Press.

Smith, Dwight A. 1984. *Columbia River Highway Historic District: Nomination of the Old Columbia River Highway in the Columbia Gorge to the National Register of Historic Places*. Salem: Oregon Department of Transportation.

Sutter, Paul. 2002. *Driven Wild: how the Fight against Automobiles Launched the Modern Wilderness Movement*. Weyerhaeuser environmental books. Seattle: University of Washington Press.

Tuhy, John E. 1983. *Sam Hill: the Prince of Castle Nowhere*. Portland, Or.: Timber Press.

Urry, John. 2004. 'The "System" of Automobility'. *Theory, Culture, & Society* 21/4–5: 25–39.

Victor, Frances Fuller and Cairns Collection of American Women Writers. 1891. *Atlantis Arisen; or, Talks of a Tourist about Oregon and Washington*. Philadelphia: J. B. Lippincott Company.

Washington State Good Roads Association. 1939. *Brief History of the Washington State Good Roads Association*. Seattle: Washington State Good Roads Association.

Chapter 5

The Hunted Otter in Britain, 1830–1939

Daniel Allen

In the twenty-first century, the otter is known as a symbol of survival; a species once persecuted, threatened with extinction now legally protected and seemingly thriving in the wild.[1] An increased impact on local fish stocks has also led to serious calls for a cull from sections of the fishery community.[2] Conservationists oppose this and the public are shocked by the mere suggestion of killing one of the nation's favourite mammals.

Memories of the hunted otter have been largely lost. With the cessation of otter hunting in 1978, the activity became unfamiliar, even unknown, to the majority of the British public. The lack of scholarly attention until this century suggests this was much the same for historians and geographers. In the case of the otter in Britain, much like other formerly hunted animals, most debates have therefore been taking place in a historical vacuum.[3] By focusing on past practices of killing (and responses to them) this chapter provides a cultural history of the hunted otter, offering much-needed context to future debates on otter conservation.[4]

Otter Hunting

For centuries the otter was killed in Britain for its fish eating ways. By the nineteenth century the animal was increasingly valued as a gallant sporting adversary and otter hunting achieved a particular fashion and vogue. Hunts with formalised organisational structures, rules, uniforms and territories sprung up on river valleys across the country. The fifteen hunts in existence in 1880 had grown to 22 by 1910.

---

1. According to the International Otter Survival Fund (IOSF) the estimated otter population in Britain is 10,000.

2. Jasper Copping and Graham Mole, 'Anglers Call for Cull of Otters over Fish Havoc', *The Daily Telegraph*, 7 June 2009.

3. Michael Tichelar, '"Putting Animals into Politics": The Labour Party and Hunting in the First Half of the Twentieth Century', *Rural History* 17/2 (2006): 213–34.

4. Daniel Allen, *Otter* (London: Reaktion Books, 2010). This chapter is an extended version of 'Otter Hunting for Sport', pp. 62–90. Permission to reproduce this material was kindly granted by Reaktion Books.

In the years to 1939 the number fluctuated between 19 and 26. Each generally had between 100 and 300 subscribers and on special occasions crowds of over 500 people were recorded.

The historical centres for otter hunting included Wales and the Welsh Borders, south-west and north-west England and southern Scotland. Otter hunting was by no means standardised or unchanging. Throughout Britain the institutional structures and territorial organisation of otter hunts varied greatly. Different people also had different reasons for finding and distinct modes of killing the otter. Until the 1860s all otter hunts were privately owned, many were rather small informal affairs and none exclusively hunted the otter. There were essentially three types of hunt. The first was the estate pack. These were small and tended to exist at localised levels hunting waters in and around the estate. A number of important families had hounds and hunt servants in their residence. The Fourth Earl of Aberdeen, George Hamilton-Gordon M.P., kept a small pack at Haddo House for example. The second type was the travelling pack. Although based at an estate, they would take their hounds, by invitation, to any part of the country with the prospect of sport. As a result they travelled great distances and hunted many rivers. Of the earliest travelling packs the most famous belonged to Mr James Lomax. Residing at Clayton Hall, Great Harwood, Lancashire, his home waters were the banks and estuaries of the Hodder, Lune, Ribble and Wyre. Although these waters covered

Figure 1. B.W. Macbeth, 'An Otter Hunt in Somersetshire: In at the death'.

Men, women and children of all classes could enjoy a day of otter hunting. Source: *Graphic,* 1896.

much of Lancashire and parts of Yorkshire and Cumberland, Lomax also ventured to Northumberland, Scotland, Wales and its borders. The third type of hunt was the dual pack. Many sportsmen in Wales and Devon kept hounds to hunt not just otters but whatever wild animal came to hand. Convenient quarry included deer, fox, hare, marten-cat, polecat, badger and otter.[5]

The season for the hunting otters was from April to October. This was not shaped around the breeding habits of the animal. The physical disposition of humans and hounds was the determining factor. As Walsh states in *British Rural Sports*: 'No other season but the summer will suit this sport, because the cold water of early spring, winter, or autumn, will chill and cramp hounds and men to a dangerous degree.'[6] During the summer months the otter held an unrivalled status in the hunting calendar. As the century progressed more and more sportsmen became solely devoted to hunting this animal. The sport attracted people from different social and economic backgrounds. In Northumberland otter hunting was predominantly a working man's pastime, enjoyed by farmers, innkeepers, tailors, shoemakers, joiners and blacksmiths. This was much the same in Carlisle. Here the local people enjoyed the sport so much that they set up the first subscription pack in 1864. As an official hunt club all members paid a subscription, the master and committee controlled the club and a paid huntsman was responsible for the hounds. For a small donation, non-subscribers were also openly welcomed. The Hawkstone OH (est. 1870) in Shropshire, on the other hand, was an aristocratic hunting club. Subscription fees remained high to keep it exclusive. The Crowhurst OH (est. 1903) was a largely middle class organisation with a female Master, Mrs Mildred Cheesman. This pack was styled as a cosmopolitan hunt within reach of London. Members of the Royal Family were even drawn to the sport. King George V and Queen Elizabeth II each headed the subscription list of the Eastern Counties OH (est. 1898) during their reigns.[7]

By the twentieth century the activity had reached a 'new phase of existence'.[8] In its popular modern form the majority of hunts were financed by subscriptions, meets and hunting calendars were fixed and formalised, packs of hounds had increased dramatically, hunting countries were becoming established and many packs were solely devoted to killing the otter. The chosen mode of killing had also become standardised. Throughout the nineteenth century there had been two options. The first was by the teeth and jaws of hounds. All otter hunters regarded this method to be legitimate and fair. The second mode of killing involved striking the otter with

5. Daniel Allen, 'The cultural and historical geographies of otter hunting in Britain, 1830–1939'. Ph.D. University of Nottingham, 2006. (AHRC Award No. 02/63215), pp. 39–83.

6. Dr John Henry Walsh, *British Rural Sports* (London: Routledge & Co. 1856) p. 169.

7. Allen, 'The cultural and historical geographies', pp. 39–83.

8. Ludovic Charles Richard Cameron, *Otters and Otter Hunting* (London: L. Upcott Gill, 1908) p. 35

a barbed spear, known as the otter grain. This was employed in addition to the first mode by some hunts, but was denounced as unfair and illegitimate by others. Although each of these modes led to the same outcome, different otter hunters had different ideas about the legitimacy of killing.

Legitimate Modes of Killing

Devotees of the spear regarded their mode of killing as sport. It just so happened that spears were the 'chief requites' for killing.[9] The spear was essentially a strong ashen pole, measuring between six to twelve feet in length, shod with a sharp iron head. Transfixing the otter was seen as the most sportsmanlike and fair method. Not only did it allow the otter to die fighting, it also prevented the hounds from getting mauled, yet familiarised them with the quarry and gave them a taste of blood. Perhaps most importantly, as 'a good worry' was considered to be an 'animated part of the hunt', this ritual was also relished as the concluding spectacle of death.[10] Spear packs generally took a utilitarian stance. This was largely informed by the public perception of otter as fish-killer. In order to deter riparian owners, pisciculturists and anglers from freely killing the animal, otter hunters had to publicise their intent to kill. The spear was an obvious symbol of this.

Spearing was also a ritualistic rite of passage. It required strength, agility, endurance, perseverance and precision. In 1835 a youthful William Pook Collier aged only fifteen, gained permission from his father to take control of his pack for just one day. After only two hours on the River Yarty, William had speared his first otter, weighing 24 lbs. To honour this achievement, the otter was stuffed, a celebratory dinner was held and the hunt's president officially initiated William as a member of the Culmstock Society of Otter Hunters.[11] This form of initiation was still prevalent in the late nineteenth century.[12]

By the twentieth century these skills were no longer valued. Non-spearing otter hunters had become increasingly accepted and embraced as model sportsmen. In the 1849 *Guide to Foxhounds, Staghounds, Harriers and Otter Hounds*, for instance, the huntsman who received highest praise, Mr Lomax, had shunned artificial aids since establishing his pack in 1829. The section dedicated to his pack read:

> No hounds or man in England understand the habits of the otter better than Mr Lomax and his hounds. He has killed the amphibious animal from Lancashire to

9. Walsh, *British Rural Sports*, p. 167.

10. Plunger, 'Reminiscences of Otter Hunting', *The Field* 9 August 1862: 137.

11. Geoffrey Pring, *Records of the Culmstock Otterhounds, c 1790–1957* (Exeter: The Quay Printing Works Ltd, 1958).

12. On 1 May 1869, Captain Edwards, Master of the Dewsland OH of Pembrokeshire, played a prominent role in spearing the otter. This was acknowledged as the best sport witnessed by everyone involved.

Lands End, and uses neither net, spear, nor any other warlike engines, save horn and hound, in pursuit of his game.[13]

This disapproval of 'warlike engines' was increasingly vocalised as the nineteenth century progressed. More often than not their absence was used to underline the high level of skill and sportsmanship that a huntsman held.

The hunting experience also became more important than the need to kill. William Turnbull, a member of the Bellingham OH (1850s–60) and John Gallon's OH (1830–73), emphasised this point in his 1896 publication *Recollections of an Otter-Hunter*. Counteractive strategies were often taken to ensure a good day's sport: 'We invariably tried to capture the otter, instead of killing him, and never destroyed a female, as a hunt could afterwards be arranged and friends invited.'[14] If females were 'never destroyed' they could, in theory, continue to breed and thus maintain an animal to be hunted. Similarly, if an otter was captured rather than killed, its presence was ensured for the next hunt. This meant that the laborious process of finding could instantly be exchanged for the excitement of the chase or even the conclusive scene of 'fair combat'. This was a sure-fire way of showcasing a pack, displaying skills such as tailing (grabbing the otter by its tail, often out of the water, and lifting it out of reach from the hounds) and impressing distinguished 'friends'. In his *Diary of Otter Hunting, from AD 1829 to 1871,* James Lomax also made it clear that the lives of otters were intentionally spared on a regular basis. Throughout his diary there are numerous entries noting how hounds were 'called off for fear of killing'.[15] Although Lomax rarely justifies these actions explicitly, his words, like Turnbull's, often reveal an ongoing consideration for future sport.

When new packs emerged they chose not to adopt the spear. Its use dwindled and its adherents disappeared as hunts disbanded and packs changed hands. The Wooler OH of Northumberland, for example, disbanded in the late 1860s. When Sir Rowland Hill's OH was taken over by his brother Geoffrey in 1869, he chose not to adopt the spear. The Cheriton OH decided to abandon the spear in 1874, soon followed by the Dartmoor OH in 1876. Mr Colliers OH was last to give to up in 1884, 'as his field did not care to see so gallant a beast suffer such an end'.[16] By the twentieth century most otter hunters spoke of the 'remote and barbarous days of the spear',[17] and broadly regarded spearing as one of the 'blood-thirsty methods

13. Gelert, *Fore's Guide to the Foxhounds and Staghounds of England; to which are added, the Otter-Hounds and Harriers of Several Counties* (London: Whittaker & Co., 1849) pp. 87–8.

14. William Turnbull, *Recollections of an Otter Hunter* (Farrow-on-Tyne: Brogdon and Wightman, 1896) p. 32.

15. James Lomax, *Diary of Otter Hunting* (Liverpool: Henry Young & Sons, 1892) p. 63.

16. Pring, *Records,* p. 35

17. Captain T.W. Sheppard, 'Decadence of Otter Hunting', *The Field* 20 October 1906: 658.

used by our forefathers'.[18] The end of spearing brought the standardisation of killing. With this, the type of dogs selected to hunt otters became more important, and the number of hounds used in a pack increased. In 1842, for example, Grantley Berkeley, the man who was described as the 'best of modern otter-slayers and the most experienced authority on the sport',[19] had a pack that consisted of four old foxhounds, three white terriers and several men armed with spears. As the century progressed packs grew and the prominent pedigrees consisted of either foxhounds, otterhounds, crossbred hounds, or a mixture of each. By 1910 all packs comprised between ten and 25 couples.

As the sport became increasingly popular, otter hunters increasingly took the moral high ground on killing. Articles in *The Field* repeatedly attacked 'lutracide', the killing of otters by means other than hunting with hounds. In January 1896 one correspondent wrote: 'I beg to be allowed to protest most strongly against the barbarous and unsportsmanlike destruction of two otters with powder and shot'.[20] In 1901 Rawdon B. Lee went further by aligning the hunted otter with the hunted fox: 'anyone who shoots or traps an otter thereabouts is looked upon in much the same light as is the miscreant who commits vulpecide in the Quorn or any other foxhunting country'.[21]

Otter Preservation

If otter hunters wanted to preserve the otter they had to convince fishery proprietors, riparian owners and angling associations that killing should be reserved for them only. They had to attempt to claim sole ownership of the animal. Otter hunters mobilised a number of strategies. The first step was firmly to establish the otter as a recognised beast of chase or sporting quarry. For this to be achieved it was vital that people were aware of the sport itself and the impact lutracide had on it. Robert Preston tried to publicise this in *The Field* on 21 April 1866. He wrote:

> Otters are slowly but surely decreasing, and though for a season or two they may appear to be more plentiful in some rivers, yet before this century has passed away they will follow the example of many of our other English quadrupeds, and the rivers will know them no more. Until that day comes, let every sportsman see as much fair otter hunting as he can, and try to avert the evil day by forbidding these rare and beautiful animals to be exterminated by over-officious angling associations, keepers, and water-bailiffs.[22]

---

18. David Jardine Bell-Irving, *Tally-Ho! Fifty Years of Sporting Reminiscences* (Dumfries: Courier and Herald Press, 1920) p. 120.

19. Anonymous, 'Otter-Hunting', *Illustrated London News* 27 May 1842, no pagination.

20. Sob Sigillo Piscatoris, 'Destruction of Otters', *The Field* 25 January 1896: 114

21. Rawdon B. Lee, 'Otters and Otter Hunting', *The Field* 30 March 1901: 424.

22. Robert Preston, 'Otter Hounds', *The Field* 21 April 1866: 327.

Daniel Allen

In this passage the otter is not condemned. Rather, the living creature is appreciated for being present, valued for its aesthetic qualities and celebrated for the fun its existence provides sportsmen. For this sportsman only those who respected these qualities should have a right to kill the animal. All others would be responsible for its 'extermination'. This emphasis of the hunting experience over the necessity to kill became a staple in modern otter hunting rhetoric. To make the argument more effective the idea of sportsmanship was brought into the equation. An example of this appeared in *The Field* on 9 May 1868. The correspondent wrote:

> I hope it is possible to get up an otter preservation society ... I trust that you will interest many country squires to spare a few fish for the poor fellow, and not knock him on the head if he happens to kill even a salmon. With the new style of breeding, by which I see there are millions of trout and salmon turned out annually, the few he wants will not be missed, and then we can add one more to our national sports. I wish some of the otter killers would try one day's otter hunting; they would then as soon think of killing a fox as an otter.[23]

In this passage otter preservation is tied to the growth of the sport. If 'otter killers' spared the animal, they could join a pack and enjoy otter hunting. What is perhaps more revealing is the call to 'add one more to our national sports' and the alignment of otters with foxes. Otter hunters of the 1860s were desperate to be accepted and respected within the broader sports fraternity. Fox hunting, with long-established codes of killing, was the archetypal model of field sports. Through the idea of sportsmanship it was generally accepted that foxes were only killed by foxhunters. By aligning the quarry the correspondent was trying to convince the reader that the two sports were set to the same high standard, and that otters should be treated in the same way.

Converting killing into preservation was a difficult task as otter hunters had to persuade those with vested interests in fish that the otter was important to them. By the twentieth century a new strategy was widely adopted. This involved dispelling myths about the otter's diet and presenting an updated natural history of the animal. L.C.R. Cameron played an important role in this process. In the 1908 publication *Otters and Otter-Hunting* he provided a detailed account of the quarry's eating habits:

> The food of the otter is of great interest to those who are asked to preserve him ... A bitch otter invariably feeds her young on frogs ... Their first experience of a fish diet is small eels, which there is no doubt otters prefer to all else ... Frogs and eels are the greatest enemies of fish spawn, and would, unchecked, deplete the best-stocked trout river in a comparatively brief space of time. But the otter does more than this, by keeping down the number of moorhens and dabchicks – also eaters of fish-spawn; thinning out water-voles that do so much to destroy the banks of navigable rivers; and consuming large numbers of crayfish, which destroy the larvae of the May-fly

---

23. J.D. 'Otter Preservation', *The Field* 9 May 1868: 368.

and other forms of fish food … The otter … will not take trout in preference to the so-called 'coarse fish', if he had the choice; and most coarse fish feed on trout spawn when they get the chance … In salmon rivers otters undoubtedly take salmon, but not where there are other and more easily-caught fish to be had.[24]

Although it is accepted that the otter eats fish, it is not presented as piscatorial pest. Instead the animal is shown to have an extremely varied diet. By outlining the animal's broader position in the food chain each of its preferences is said to be beneficial to fish-stocks and the riverside. This essentially styled the animal as a protector of fish: 'the otter is doing that which is without the power of man, to ensure the preservation of fish life and the supply of fish-food in our streams and ponds'.[25] In this new role the absence of otters did not mean the presence of fish. It was quite the contrary: 'if there were no fish there would be fewer otters, so it is certain that were there no otters there would be fewer fish'.[26] In these terms the animal became a valuable asset to those with vested interests in fish.

The final step for otter hunters was to claim exclusive rights for killing this asset. To do this they argued that the animal should be kept within reasonable bounds, but should 'not be ruthlessly destroyed by trap and gun'.[27] This was a real case of self-preservation. Set against the 'ruthless' modes of killing, hunting with hounds was presented as 'the best and most humane manner of preventing the undue increase of otters … while ensuring their preservation as one of the most interesting creatures in the British fauna'.[28] The increased appreciation the otter gained through its re-styled identity as fish-protector was transferred to hunting. The eating habits of the otter had been used to publicise the broader purpose of the activity. Otter hunters were essentially telling broader riverside cultures that the presence of otter hunts, much like the presence of otters, could only be to their advantage.

Valuing the Unseen Otter

To the dedicated otter hunter the sport was superior to any other. Yet, according to certain authorities, only one-tenth of the hunting fraternity transferred themselves to the sport.[29] This was directly tied to the environment in which the otter lived. The only way to follow hounds through watery terrains was by foot. The absence of horses was an unattractive prospect to anyone who hunted to ride. Foxhunter

---

24. Cameron, *Otters and Otter Hunting*, pp. 16–21.

25. Ibid. p. 20

26. L.C.R. Cameron, *Rod, Pole and Perch. Angling and Otter-hunting Sketches* (London: Martin Hopkinson & Company Ltd, 1928) p. 1.

27. Rawdon B. Lee, ' Otters and Otter Hunting', *The Field* 2 April 1896: 488.

28. Cameron, *Otters and Otter Hunting*, p. 153.

29. Walter Cheesman and Mildred Cheesman, *Diaries of the Crowhurst Otter Hounds, 1904–1906.* East Sussex Record Office, Reference AMS5788/3/1–3 (1904) p. 3.

Sir W. Beach Thomas made this point in *Hunting England*: 'the votaries of otter hunting are relatively few, for the very good reason that in fox- and stag-hunting the horse is at least as important as the hound or the quarry'.[30] The exhilarating speed of riding to hounds was replaced with a moderate to brisk walking pace. Otter hunting offered a day of hard exercise, lasting between five and seven hours and covering distances from three to thirty miles. The pursuit was not confined to the riverbanks: hounds frequently led followers through and across the water. These conditions attracted a certain type of sportsman, hardy individuals with distinctive sporting tastes. As Douglas Macdonald Hastings wrote in the *Picture Post*: 'To qualify as a follower of otter hounds, it is necessary to be blessed with seal-like imperviousness to water; an affection for muddy places; and the urge to out-walk a hiking club.'[31]

The pedestrian nature of the sport meant otter hunting was affordable and inclusive. The kit and equipment required was minimal and relatively inexpensive. The workmanlike clothes consisted of woollen serge and flannel garments: cap, coat, jacket, shirt, knickerbockers and hose. There was no need for extravagant accessories. A 'good pair of legs', 'thick pair of boots'[32] and serviceable pole were the only requirements. Meets were colourful occasions. Packs created their own unique fashions. Mr Collier's OH is a fine example. From as early as 1817 those involved with the pack wore: 'a scarlet coat … with blue and white flannel trousers and waistcoat, the blue lines running around the legs, and a black bowler hat. The kennel huntsman wore an otter-skin cap with the rudder fastened in front with the hunt button.'[33] This combination of colour and carcass was unlike that of any other. Other packs made more subtle references. When the Carlisle OH was established in 1864, for example, the hunt incorporated the working dress of butchers – a blue and white striped waistcoat – into their uniform as some of its co-founders came from that trade. Combinations of blue, white, yellow, grey and green were not out of place along the riverbanks.

Otter hunting was not just an excuse to wear costumes and have a stroll in the country. It was a serious matter. Before an otter could be hunted it had to be found. With no fixed home, their whereabouts were shrouded with mystery. Any sheltered hollow could be a temporary residence. The animal was therefore largely unseen in the landscape. There were visual clues. The five-toed impressions of webbed feet ('spur', 'seal' or 'mark'), the animal's excrement ('spraint', 'wedging' or 'coke') and the remains of partially eaten fish each provided confirmation of a former presence. This did not, however, provide precise locations. The only way

---

30. Sir William Beach Thomas, *Hunting England* (London: B. T. Batsford, 1936) p. 46.

31. Douglas Macdonald Hastings, 'Hunting the Otter', *Picture Post* July 1939: 54.

32. L. Wardell, 'Otter-Hunting', in Frances Elizabeth Slaughter (ed.) *The Sportswoman's Library, Volume II* (London, Archibald Constable & Co, 1898) pp. 171–81, p. 173.

33. Pring, *Records*, p. 21.

an otter could be found was by tracing its enduring trail of scent ('line', 'drag' or 'trail'). As with all forms of hunting, scent was difficult to understand. Its quality was affected by high winds, direct sunlight, high humidity and cold air accounted for bad scent. Olfactory remnants also deteriorated with time. Hunting started early in the morning for this reason. The actual scent of the otter was less mysterious than other hunted animals. Its movement between land and water meant that drops of scent-carrying water were left on the ground. Hounds could trace this with relative ease. The relationship between scent and water was far less reliable. The watery landscape was always in motion, it was always changing. If an otter entered flowing water, the buoyant remnants were by no means coherent or conclusive. Currents and erratic flows carried the scent, providing confirmation of a former presence. The uncontrollable environment undoubtedly confused the noses of hounds, making the process of bringing about the presence of an otter very difficult.[34]

As the otter had the opportunity to disappear back into its watery environment, otter hunting was often likened to 'a glorified game of hide and seek'.[35] When a pack of hounds searched for an otter's trail they were encouraged 'to examine … every likely-looking place … over and over again'.[36] This thorough approach ensured that the followers remained at close proximity to the hounds. Although hound-work was important throughout hunting cultures, it was particularly valued in otter hunting. 'The true otter hunter' wrote Neale in 1950, 'loves to see hounds working out the overnight drag of their quarry, and many a sportsman can derive as much delight and enjoyment from this age-old instance of the mystery of hunting by scent as he may from the pursuit of the otter itself.'[37] Experienced huntsmen interpreted the sounds and movements of the dogs, translating every possible situation. If the trail did not lead to an otter, the hounds might have 'flashed over' or 'passed over' the drag, leaving the otter undisturbed in its holt. This could happen through the pack's eagerness, with hounds overrunning the drag at speed. Alternatively, the quarry could be 'out of mark', that is, residing in a holt with an underwater entrance which concealed its scent from the outer air. Failing this, the otter may have travelled a considerable distance in the water or swum across to the adjacent bank. Hounds could also follow the drag in the reverse direction and be 'hunting the heel'. The perceived complexity of finding the otter helped elevate ideas

34. Daniel Allen. '"A Delightful Sport with Peculiar Claims": the specificities of otter hunting, 1850–1939', in Richard Hoyle (ed.) *Our Hunting Fathers: Field Sports in England after 1850*. Lancaster: Carnegie Publishing, 2007. pp. 143–164. pp. 154–156.

35. Waddy Wadsworth, *Vive La Chasse. A celebration of British field sports past and present* (Kent: Dickson Price, 1989) p. 128.

36. Reverend George Clark Green, *Collections and Recollections of Natural History and Sport. In the life of a country vicar* (London: Reeve & Co. 1886) pp. 143–144.

37. Douglas Neale, *Nearly All Hunting* (London: Vinton & Co. 1950) p. 96.

of the skilled sportsman. It allowed otter hunters to style themselves as perceptive individuals who understood an older more authentic style of hunting.

The unique composition of every pack contributed to this. Different breeds of dog had different qualities, including strength, stamina, speed, voice, marking ability and appearance. Otter hunters became accustomed to the particular attributes of their working pack. As these characteristics directly contributed to both the experience and the aesthetic of otter hunting, opinions on which type of hound was best-suited to hunt the otter were often quite different. There was a distinct regional variation in the selected blend of breeds. William Pook Collier, who was Master of the Culmstock OH from 1837 to 1890, was particularly intrigued by this. Shortly before retiring from his 43-year mastership, he had declared that, 'in all his experience of otter hunting he had never seen an otterhound', but 'hoped to have a day with one of the more northern packs in order to see what they were like.'[38] Arthur Heinemann of the Cheriton OH was also drawn to these regional differences. In 1903, he claimed that: 'North countrymen prefer the rough hound, west countrymen the smooth.'[39]

These preferences primarily reflected ownership and projected self-identity, although the hardiness of different breeds was also important. Advocates of smooth foxhounds argued the watery hunting environment made rough coated otterhounds susceptible to chills, irritability, short temper and fatigue. Despite this, there was a common appreciation of the aesthetic of the otterhound. Trevor-Battye for instance, wrote: 'Every master of Otter-hounds would, no doubt, like to have some of these beautiful hounds in his pack, but the fact is this: the fox-hound does the work better.'[40] Kathleen F. Barker went further, admiring the breed as living relics of the sports romanticised past: 'To me otter-hunting possesses a flavour reminiscent of other older and more gracious days ... particularly ... when the hounds are of the pure, rough-coated variety.'[41]

Followers also played an important role in finding the otter. Everyone was expected to actively assist the hounds. Individuals would spread out along the riverside focusing their eyes on the water. A knowledgeable field knew what signs to look for. If the otter was swimming deep under water, air bubbles from its fur often rose to the surface and produced a 'chain' of bubbles. When swimming closer to the surface, such movements were more likely to cause a wave. It might 'vent'

---

38. Gerald Lascelles, 'Otter', in Hedley Peek and Frederick Aflalo (eds.) *Encyclopaedia of Sport, Volume I* (London: Lawrence & Bullen, 1897) pp. 564–9, p. 564.

39. Arthur Heinemann, 'Otter Hunting', in Frederick Aflalo (ed.) *The Sports of the World* (London: Cassell & Co. 1903) pp. 344–7, p. 346.

40. Aubyn Trevor-Battye, 'July. Otter Hunting', in Oswald Crawford (ed.) *A Year of Sport and Natural History* (London: Chapman & Hall, 1895) pp. 158–63, p. 159

41. Kathleen Frances Barker, *The Young Entry. Fox-Hunting, Beagling and Otter-Hunting for Beginners* (London: A & C Black, 1939) p. 114.

Figure 2. Otter hunters often waded through deep waters to assist the hounds.

Source: Graham Downing, *The Hounds of Spring. The History of the Eastern Counties Otter Hounds* (Powys: Graham Downing in association with *Hounds* magazine, 1988). Thanks to Graham Downing for permission to reproduce.

– that is, take in air – by pushing its snout above the water. It might be viewed in clear water, or even take to the land. Actually knowing whether the otter had really been 'gazed' was often considered as one of most difficult parts of otter hunting. Once the otter had been found there was the distinct possibility it would escape. A device known as the 'stickle' was used to help avoid this. When instructed by the huntsman, men women and children would wade into the river and form a line from one bank to the other. Standing conjoined they would then use their poles to splash the water. This bodily barrier aimed to prevent the animal from going upstream ('top stickle') or downstream ('bottom stickle'). If successful, the otter would change direction and return to the hounds.

These collective practices heightened a sense of belonging. The close proximity also positioned the bodies and prepared the eyes for the kill. Although there were individuals who claimed the quarry 'should always be allowed to escape',[42] killing was the intended conclusion. The spectacle itself was a frenzy of frothing water, barking hounds, excitement, tension, teeth, flesh and blood. As followers watched, hunt-staff would use their hands, knees and poles to retrieve the dead otter. This culminated in a moment of display and symbolism, where the huntsman would ceremoniously raise the otter above his head. The carcass was then weighed, recorded and dismembered. Once removed the head ('mask'), tail ('rudder') and feet ('pads') could be distributed as trophies, visceral reminders of the day. Newcomers would also be initiated with the blooding of forehead, cheeks and chin. Finally,

---

42. J.C. Bristow-Noble, 'Should Otter be Hunted?' *Madame* 9 September 1905: 515.

Figure 3. A mounted otter mask was a highly sought after trophy.

Source: L.C.R. Cameron, *Otters and Otter-Hunting* (London: L. Upcott Gill, 1908).

the body was thrown to the pack and the horn was blown to announce that a kill had been scored.[43]

The unseen nature of the otter meant that this spectacle did not always take place. The chances of seeing one were considerably less than even. If found, roughly half would go on to escape. This uncertainty enhanced ideas of fair play. Blank days were not as favourable. For cynics, hunting without an otter was a sport

---

43. Geoffrey Hill of Hawkstone killed 544 otters between 1870 and 1884 and William Collier of Culmstock accounted for 144 between 1879 and 1884. In the 1932–33 season, the 25 packs in existence found 905 otters and killed 459.

without a purpose. Otter hunters responded by promoting broader aspects of their sport: 'in otter hunting, the hounds, the invigorating air of the early morning, and the superb beauty of England's valleys and dales constitutes the chief attractions … the quarry itself is quite a secondary consideration.'[44] The role of the otter and its death was underplayed. Instead the season, settings, time of meet and pace of pursuit were valued. Otter hunting was styled as a leisurely pastime, which encouraged social intercourse and offered relaxation. An intriguing part of this was the lunchtime interval. After long summer mornings afoot, a short break for food and light refreshments was an eagerly awaited event. Blank mornings, long drags and kills were all suitable circumstances for this unscheduled rest. Although newcomers were often surprised that an otter hunt could resemble a giant picnic, it was by no means a novelty. Food and fraternising had been integral since the 1830s. In July 1835 for instance, a member of the Dartmoor Otter Hounds wrote in his diary: 'found above Plym Bridge and had him up two or three hours, but did not kill, as the pretty girls and the picnic spread engaged the hearts of the gallants and the hungry ones'.[45] Although some felt this leisurely dimension detracted from the sport, others saw it as the main attraction. Jack Ivester Lloyd reflected on this in 1952:

> In the days before 1939, when food was plentiful and in amazing variety, I believe that a few people actually paid their subscriptions, drove many miles to meets, wandering down mill lanes and over hump-backed bridges just because the sport gave them an excuse to picnic by the river with other cheery folk.[46]

The one thing that all otter hunters agreed was that the endless variety and beauty of the river valleys could never disappoint.

The Price of Absent Otters

One of the consequences of organising otter hunts was that otters became a necessity. To put it simply, otter hunts needed otters. After the mid-nineteenth century the majority of people who formed packs did not do so simply to kill otters. Individuals used their personal wealth to gain unlimited access to their preferred hunting experience. It was about sport. Socially, as Master of Otter Hounds, they also positioned themselves at the helm of their newly created group. In this role they were keen to satisfy the sporting needs of friends, family, landowners and the local inhabitants who followed the pack. Without the otter this experience could not happen and this position would not exist.

---

44. Cheesman and Cheesman, *Diaries*, p. 3

45. Geoffrey R. Mott, *Records of the Dartmoor Otter Hounds, 1740–1940* (Dartmoor: Dartmoor Otter Hounds, 1970) p. 6.

46. Jack Ivester Lloyd, *Come Hunting!* (London: A & C Black, 1952) p. 221.

The perceived absence of otters was a recurring problem in the 1890s and 1900s. After experiencing seasons with relatively few finds and kills various Masters had to decide whether the economic cost of maintaining a pack was worth the possibility of future sport. Some decided it was not financially viable. Mr John Benson, for instance, had maintained the West Cumberland OH at his own expense since 1865. When he chose to sell his hounds in 1890, he gave two reasons: 'there are no otters left, and the people about him do not care for the sport as they once did'.[47] The scarcity of otters had caused a lack of interest and rendered the hunt purposeless. Preventative steps were on occasions called into action. These were often desperate and drastic measures. An example of this was observed by Rawdon B. Lee in *The Field* on 5 April 1902: 'some time ago I noticed a novel advertisement in a weekly paper, evidently coming from Cumberland, the advertiser being desirous of purchasing a dozen live otters for the purpose of turning down'.[48] Although we cannot be certain if this advert came from a Master of the West Cumberland OH, or if he received the 'dozen of live otters', it does show just how highly some people valued the sport.

The practice of purchasing live otters was not widely welcomed by otter hunters. Most sportsmen felt the reputation of the sport was more important than the enjoyment of the few. Lee had in fact condemned the practice in his annual report on 'Otters and Otter Hunting' in 1899:

> Sundry complaints have reached me on this score, and that there are grounds for them is in evidence from advertisements which occasionally appear, offering to purchase live otters. It is to be hoped that these enquiries do not emanate from masters of hounds; in any case, such notices are to be condemned, and no hunting man or anyone else should purchase otters under such circumstances. Indeed, there ought to be a similar etiquette here as prevails with regard to foxes, and he would be looked upon as anything but a gentleman who would purchase 'bagmen' which had probably been surreptitiously obtained from a neighbour's country.[49]

Otter hunters from localities teeming with otters, and indeed the more general observer, would have found it easy to condemn this practice. If those involved were not adhering to the broadest codes of sporting 'etiquette' they could not be defined as sportsmen. Questioning the honour of such individuals was a hard-hitting reprimand. It did however serve a more practical purpose. Bagged otters came from areas where the animal was plentiful, presumably hunting districts. Purchasing such animals from bagmen was, therefore, essentially stealing sport from fellow otter hunters. This was not only unsportsmanlike – it was a selfish act that could not be condoned. Where some people went to great lengths to ensure the future

47. Rawdon B. Lee, 'Otters and Otter Hunting', *The Field*, 26 April 1890: 599.
48. Rawdon B. Lee, 'Otters and Otter Hunting', *The Field*, 5 April 1902: 496.
49. Rawdon B. Lee, 'Otters and Otter Hunting', *The Field*, 1 April 1890: 444.

of hunting in their district, others saw the potential cost of an otterless district as an unattractive prospect.

In Hampshire, Mr Courtenay Tracy's devotion to the sport led him to establish his own self-named pack in the region in 1887. Only eight years later (October 1895),

> Tracy offered his resignation on account of expense, shortage of otters and the increase of barbed wire. A general meeting persuaded him to reconsider, and offered to find £250 per annum. The following autumn he again tendered his resignation owing to scarcity of otters.[50]

However, the followers of this Hampshire pack were eager to safeguard the Hunt. On the suggestion of subscriber Mr Edwards, twelve members were elected to form a Committee. On 26 November 1896 the Committee purchased the hounds from Tracy for £100 and the Hunt officially became a subscription pack.

If the 'scarcity of otters' was a contributing factor to the disbandment of private packs, then the same problem presented new pressures for subscription packs. Hunt clubs offered members a service for a fee. Their existence relied on the pockets of subscribers. Economic responsibility had been divided between tens or hundreds of people. Such packs therefore had to satisfy each of these individuals. If subscribers did not get what they paid for, they would not re-subscribe and the organisation would go out of business.[51]

Early Calls for Otter Protection

Otter hunting was not welcomed by everyone. Those opposed to blood sports believed it was cruel and called for its abolition. Otter hunters were described as barbaric and vile. The Humanitarian League initiated the campaign against the sport at the beginning of the twentieth century. This was continued by the League for the Prohibition of Cruel Sports (LPCS) and National Society for the Abolition of Cruel Sports (NSACS) from the 1920s. Their main objective was to raise awareness by exposing the cruelties involved. Each institution produced pamphlets and monthly publications to express their views. Individuals also bombarded newspapers and magazines with letters of protest.

In 1906, League members used a larger institution to elevate their campaign. During the RSPCA's 82nd Anniversary meeting on 21 May, Stephen Coleridge unexpectedly proposed that the committee should prepare a bill to make otter hunting illegal. As the RSPCA did not oppose blood-sports this proposal was a radical move. Coleridge recounted the moment when he first witnessed an otter hunt:

---

50. Mollie Van der Kiste, *Mr Courtenay Tracy and his Hounds, being the history of the C.T.O.H.* (Dorset: C.T.O.H. Club, 1983) p. 5.

51. For examples, see Anonymous, 'East of Scotland. *The Field* 13 October 1906: 620.

> The miserable little animal was pursued by men with large poles with spikes in their heads ... Then the poor creature having found refuge in its hole, twenty men got on to the bank and endeavoured by jumping and other means to force the earth down into the unfortunate animal's hiding place, and this 'sport' was continued, until worn out by fatigue and fright surrounded by men and dogs, without the ghost of a chance of escape, the victim became as easy prey to its enemies.[52]

The audience recoiled in horror, supporting the speaker with shouts of 'shame!' After much perseverance by Coleridge, the chairman eventually agreed to put the resolution to the meeting. The motion was supported and the resolution was carried with acclamation. This approval was a remarkable success. It immediately generated adverse reactions and increased press-coverage. The *Daily Mail*, for instance, received several telegrams from Masters of Otter Hounds opposing Mr Coleridge's criticism and justifying their sport. Mr Rose of the Eastern Counties OH described the proposed Bill as 'most unfair and ridiculous'. He also argued that the description of otter hunting was 'grossly misrepresented'. This opposition to the Bill was surprisingly effective. After only two months the ongoing pressure proved too much and the bill was exposed as an empty promise. In July 1906 the *Animal World* announced that the committee was not prepared to take any action on the motion moved by Stephen Coleridge with regards to otter hunting.

    The perceived cruelty of otter hunting, as with any given blood sport, was directly tied to the physical characteristics of the animal involved, and the environment in which it was pursued and killed. Otter hunting was generally perceived as particularly cruel in both these aspects. Invariably, the features lauded by otter hunters translated into cruelties peculiar to the sport. Where the seasonality of the practice was conducive of leisure for otter hunters, its correspondence with breeding season and the pursuit of pregnant otters was seen as a mark of cowardice. Campaigners repeatedly pointed to this subject as proof of the 'inconsistency and heartlessness'[53] of the hunting fraternity. As this practice was almost exclusively[54] reserved to otter hunting, they also tried to divide the hunting fraternity by distinguishing the sporting conduct of otter-hunters from fox-hunters, stag-hunters and hare-hunters: 'If the sporting set consider it unsporting to hunt some animals in the breeding season, why does this not apply to otters?'[55] For campaigners, the killing of defenceless cubs and protective mothers was the antithesis of fair play, sportsmanship and manliness. Justification for killing was also repeatedly questioned. Bertram Lloyd urged the public to make up their own mind: 'If Otters are really pests, as it is often pretended, to hunt them during the breeding season would surely be an

52. RSPCA, *1906 Annual Report* (London: RSPCA, 1906) p. 127.

53. Joseph Collinson, *The Hunted Otter* (London: Animals' Friend Society, 1911) p. 3.

54. On occasions deer-hunters hunted and killed hinds-in-calf.

55. Anonymous, 'Otter-Hunting', *Cruel Sports* August 1909: 58.

effective way of exterminating the species. If they are not pests, why hunt them at all?'[56] H.E. Bates, the well-known country writer, made up his mind in 1937:

> Otters are hunted and killed in England, at something like the rate of four hundred and fifty a year ... [I]t means this: that in my short life of thirty years ... something like twelve thousand otters have been killed in England for the purpose of fun ... This kind of fun is one of the reasons why it is so difficult for me, and for that matter anybody else, to get a sight of an otter.[57]

The duration of hunts was also identified as a particularly cruel feature. Anti-hunting literature is peppered with articles condemning this. For instance, a subsection in the *Hunted Otter* (1911) titled 'Hunted for Seven Hours' described the lengthy pursuit of a female otter by the Culmstock OH in 1910. The LPCS magazine *Cruel Sports* contained an article detailing an 'otter hunted for nine hours' by the Dumfriesshire OH in 1932. Otter hunters embraced these times as they extended their day's sport. Campaigners, on the other hand, argued that the relentless pursuit of one animal for many hours showed a distinct lack of mercy: 'It is difficult to imagine a more inept word than "merciful" for a kill at the end of a harrying which has lasted for many hours!'[58]

The type of people involved and the kind of behaviour it induced also attracted critical attention. Men women and children could all actively participate in this sport alongside one another. Otter hunters were of course proud of this fact. Opponents were offended by it. Joseph Collinson raised this point in his 1911 pamphlet *The Hunted Otter*:

> A deplorable feature of this sport is that its followers include all sorts and conditions of people: ministers of religion with their wives, young men and young women, sometimes even boys and girls. Not only are they present at these infamous scenes, but, like the huntsmen, are worked up to the wildest pitch of excitement, and join in the final worry and the performance of the obsequies, when the spoils of the chase are distributed.[59]

Unlike other blood sports, the main excitement in otter hunting was seen to derive from the involvement in and visual engagement with the visceral spectacle of the kill. If the active roles played by participants in finding the quarry were publicised as signs of inclusiveness and equality, then those same roles meant everyone involved made a greater contribution to, and was more responsible for, the death of the animal.

56. Bertram Lloyd, *A Vile Sport. Facts About Otterhunting* (Harpenden: National Society for the Abolition of Cruel Sports, 1945) p. 8.

57. Herbert Ernest Bates, *Otters and Men* (London: National Society for the Abolition of Cruel Sports, 1938) p. 1.

58. Lloyd, *A Vile Sport*, p. 9.

59. Collinson, *The Hunted Otter*, p. 20.

Figure 4. 'Otter hunt at Curraghmore, May 14, 1901'.

As a socially and physically inclusive sport women and children could directly contribute to the death of otters. With thanks to National Library of Ireland. NLI Ref: P_WP_0334.

For campaigners the behaviour of otter hunters was uncivilised, unchristian and un-English. Otter hunting was not a sport or even a form of leisure. It was an activity that facilitated blood-lust. It was not glamorous or romantic. It was not a true test of physical endurance. It was not even economic. Otter hunting was the ruthless torture of a sentient creature. There could be only one explanation for its existence: 'Otters are hunted for one reason only – for the pleasure a hunted Otter gives to the hunter.'[60]

Conclusion

This chapter has shown how the identity of hunted otter evolved gradually during the nineteenth century. The secretiveness of the animal was important: otter hunts offered individuals the opportunity to be a part of a community where the otter

---

60. Lloyd, *A Vile Sport*, p. 1.

essentially acted as a guide to explore otherwise unseen parts of the countryside. Otter hunting allowed men, women, the rich and poor, old and young, to work together in bringing about the animals' presence and death. The transformation of otter hunters from expert killers to preservationists in the late nineteenth century undoubtedly maintained a sustainable population in hunting districts. Despite being the idea of a relatively marginal and fragmented community the hunted otter gained acceptance within the more established hunting fraternity and became embedded within the broader rural imagination. Had this identity not been accepted, those with a vested interest in fish would have exterminated the species in all but the wildest parts of Britain. The rise of protectionist attitudes from hunting abolitionists was part of a broader movement to protect sentient creatures from unnecessary cruelty. Despite making moral distinctions between wild, captive and domestic animals, their underlying argument was essentially social. The perceived cruelties of otter hunting focused on inclusiveness and the active involvement in killing which the animal facilitated.

As unsavoury as it may seem, the otter hunting fraternity should be acknowledged, even thanked, for giving the animal cultural value: it was their rhetoric which discouraged lutracide. The difficulty that otter conservationists face today is that traditional attitudes of fishery communities are bubbling to the surface, protectionist rhetoric has been tinged with sentimentality and the once authoritative hunting rhetoric which dissuaded from indiscriminate killing has been lost. The cultural history of the hunted otter and the rhetoric associated with that identity should not be excluded from present day conservationist debates. It is hoped that ideas from this chapter will trickle into broader social imaginations and help strengthen arguments supporting the legal protection of otters in Britain.

REFERENCES

Allen, Daniel. 2006. 'The cultural and historical geographies of otter hunting in Britain, 1830–1939'. Ph.D. University of Nottingham. (AHRC Award No. 02/63215).

Allen, Daniel. 2007. '"A Delightful Sport with Peculiar Claims": the specificities of otter hunting, 1850–1939'. In Richard Hoyle (ed.) *Our Hunting Fathers: Field Sports in England after 1850.* Lancaster: Carnegie Publishing. pp. 143–164

Allen, Daniel. 2010. *Otter.* London: Reaktion Books.

Copping, Jasper and Graham Mole. 2009. 'Anglers Call for Cull of Otters over Fish Havoc'. *The Daily Telegraph*, 7 June.

Hoyle, Richard. (ed.) 2007. *Our Hunting Fathers: Field Sports in England after 1850.* Lancaster: Carnegie.

Marvin, Garry. 2000. 'The Problem of Foxes. Legitimate and illegitimate killing in the English countryside'. In John Knight (ed.) *Natural Enemies. People-Wildlife Conflicts in Anthropological Perspective.* London: Routledge. pp. 189–211.

Marvin, Garry. 2003. 'A Passionate Pursuit: foxhunting as performance'. *Sociological Review* 51/2: 46–60.

Matless, David, Paul Merchant and Charles Watkins. 2005. 'Animal Landscapes: Otters and Wildfowl in England 1945–1970'. *Transactions of the Institute of British Geographers* **30**: 191–205.

Philo, Chris and Chris Wilbert (ed.) 2000. *Animal Spaces, Beastly Places: New Geographies of Human-Animal Relations.* London: Routledge.

Tichelar, Michael. 2006. '"Putting Animals into Politics": The Labour Party and Hunting in the First Half of the Twentieth Century'. *Rural History* 17/2: 213–34.

Primary Sources

Anonymous. 1842. 'Otter-Hunting'. *Illustrated London News* 27 May, no pagination.

Anonymous. 1939. 'Otter-Hunting'. *Cruel Sports* August: 58.

Barker, Kathleen Frances. 1939. *The Young Entry. Fox-Hunting, Beagling and Otter-hunting for Beginners.* London: A & C Black.

Bates, Herbert Ernest. 1938. *Otters and Men.* London: National Society for the Abolition of Cruel Sports.

Beach Thomas, Sir William. 1936. *Hunting England.* London: B.T. Batsford.

Bell-Irving, David Jardine. 1920. *Tally-Ho! Fifty Years of Sporting Reminiscences.* Dumfries: Courier and Herald Press.

Bristow-Noble, J.C. 1905. 'Should Otter be Hunted?' *Madame* 9 September: 515.

Cameron, L.C.R. 1908. *Otters and Otter-Hunting.* London: L. Upcott Gill.

Cameron, L.C.R. 1928. *Rod, Pole and Perch. Angling and Otter-hunting Sketches.* London: Martin Hopkinson & Company Ltd.

Cheesman, Walter and Mildred Cheesman. 1904. 'Diaries of the Crowhurst Otter Hounds, 1904–1906'. East Sussex Record Office, Reference AMS5788/3/1–3.

Collinson, Joseph. 1911. *The Hunted Otter.* London: Animals' Friend Society.

Gelert. 1849. *Fore's Guide to the Foxhounds and Staghounds of England; to which are added, the Otter-Hounds and Harriers of several Counties.* London: Whittaker & Co.

Green, Reverend George Clark. 1886. 'Collections and Recollections of Natural History and Sport'. In *The Life of a Country Vicar.* London: Reeve & Co.

Heinemann, Arthur. 1903. 'Otter Hunting'. In Frederick Aflalo (ed.) *The Sports of the World.* London: Cassell & Co. pp. 344–7.

Lascelles, Gerald. 1897. 'Otter'. In Hedley Peek and Frederick Aflalo (eds.) *Encyclopaedia of Sport*, Volume I. London: Lawrence & Bullen. pp. 564–9.

Lloyd, Bertram. 1945. 'A Vile Sport. Facts About Otterhunting'. Harpenden: National Society for the Abolition of Cruel Sports.

Lloyd, Jack Ivester. 1952. *Come Hunting!* London: A & C Black.

Lomax, James. 1892. *Diary of Otter Hunting.* Liverpool: Henry Young & Sons.

The Hunted Otter in Britain, 1830–1939

Macdonald Hastings, Douglas. 1939. 'Hunting the Otter'. *Picture Post* July: 54.

Mott, Geoffrey R. 1970. *Records of the Dartmoor Otter Hounds, 1740–1940*. Dartmoor: Dartmoor Otter Hounds.

Neale, Douglas. 1950. *Nearly All Hunting*. London: Vinton & Co.

Pring, Geoffrey. 1958. *Records of the Culmstock Otterhounds, c 1790–1957*. Exeter: The Quay Printing Works Ltd.

RSPCA. 1906. '1906 Annual Report'. London: RSPCA.

Trevor-Battye, Aubyn. 1895. 'July. Otter Hunting'. In Oswald Crawford (ed.) *A Year of Sport and Natural History*. London: Chapman & Hall. pp. 158–63.

Turnbull, William. 1896. *Recollections of an Otter Hunter*. Farrow-on-Tyne: Brogdon and Wightman.

Van der Kiste, Mollie. 1983. *Mr Courtenay Tracy and his Hounds, being the history of the C.T.O.H. Club*. Dorset: C.T.O.H. Club.

Wadsworth, Waddy. 1989. *Vive La Chasse. A Celebration of British Field Sports Past and Present*. Kent: Dickson Price.

Walsh, Dr John Henry. 1856. *British Rural Sports*. London: Routledge & Co.

Wardell, L. 1898. 'Otter-Hunting'. In Frances Elizabeth Slaughter (ed.) 1898. *The Sportswoman's Library*, Volume II. London, Archibald Constable & Co. pp. 171–81.

The Field

Anonymous. 1906. 'East of Scotland'. 13 October: 620.

J.D. 1868. 'Otter Preservation'. 9 May: 368.

Lee, Rawdon B. 1890. 'Otters and Otter Hunting'. 26 April: 599.

1896. 'Otters and Otter Hunting'. 2 April: 488.

1899. 'Otters and Otter Hunting'. 1 April: 444.

1901. 'Otters and Otter Hunting'. 30 March: 424.

1902. 'Otters and Otter Hunting'. 5 April: 496.

Piscatoris, Sob Sigillo. 1896. 'Destruction of Otters'. 25 January: 114.

Plunger. 1862. 'Reminiscences of Otter Hunting'. 9 August: 137.

Preston, Robert. 1866. 'Otter Hounds'. 21 April: 327.

Sheppard, Captain T. W. 1906. 'Decadence of Otter Hunting'. 20 October: 658.

Chapter 6

No Tears for the Crocodiles: Representations of Nile Crocodiles, and the Extermination Furore in Zululand, South Africa, from 1956–8

Simon Pooley

In December 1957 in South Africa's Natal Province, strident and widespread calls went up for the extermination of all crocodiles in Zululand. This followed the fatal attack on a white boy (a South African of European origin) at False Bay, on Lake St Lucia, attributed to a crocodile. David Raymond-Jones was swimming unsupervised in the lake, and had ignored official warnings to stay out of the water. Furthermore, this was in a protected area for wildlife, known for its crocodiles, and crocodile attacks were not uncommon in the region – so the extent of the reaction is surprising and disproportionate to the incident.

This chapter begins with an examination of how crocodiles and their relations with humans had been represented to South Africans from the late nineteenth century to 1958. It then explores the social and ecological causes – and the sequence of events – which contributed to this explosive (and unprecedented) demand for the killing of all Nile crocodiles in Zululand. These events provide an instructive case study of how human environmental interventions and activities contributed to a 'crocodile menace'. Prejudice and ignorance about a species were exploited by a variety of interests, ranging from commercial hunters to anglers, farmers and nationalist politicians.

The Union of South Africa's province of Natal (now KwaZulu-Natal) was a former British colony which, from 1897, also incorporated the Zulu kingdom. Many Natalians regarded the province as a last outpost of Britishness, holding out against the rising tide of Afrikaner nationalism in the twentieth century. The Afrikaner National Party came to power in South Africa in 1948 and began to institute its policies of apartheid in the 1950s. Although the designs of Afrikaner politicians on land in the Province fuelled the crocodile controversy of 1957–8, the furore was primarily fought out in the provincial newspapers, in English. The political dominance of the whites meant that Africans were largely excluded from the debates over what to do about crocodiles, despite the fact that most attacks on humans were on rural Africans. This review is thus partial, focusing on representations of crocodiles in southern Africa in English-language books, journal articles, newspapers and films.

Representations of Crocodiles

Hunters' and Explorers' Tales

It is worth noting the contrast between Europeans' almost universal loathing of crocodiles in Africa and the more complicated relationships different African peoples have had with crocodiles.[1] Readers of accounts by European hunters and explorers of their travels in the region would find little variation in attitudes towards crocodiles. In his book on the European exploration of Africa, McLynn comments that:

> it may be an exaggeration to say that every single book of nineteenth-century African exploration featured hair-raising stories about crocodiles, but not by very much. Without question this terrifying saurian was the most feared and detested of all the animals dangerous to man.[2]

The Scottish hunter and traveller Roualeyn Gordon-Cumming wrote in the 1850s that crocodiles were 'terrible animals'. He described 'a huge old sinner' lying on a sandbank, and another 'snapping his horrid jaws' (this in response to being shot in the side) and the corpse of another of his victims as a 'hideous monster of the river'.[3] Other hunters and explorers travelling through the region similarly described crocodiles as 'brutes', 'cowardly', 'cruel', 'loathsome', 'horrible' and 'hideous'.[4]

The 1950s and 1960s were the heyday of crocodile hunting for skins in Africa and there was a brief vogue for accounts of the exploits of these hunters. Two such books were published before 1960, Lawrence Earl's *Crocodile Fever* (1954) and Paul Potous's *No Tears for the Crocodile* (1956). Earl's book recounted the story of South African crocodile hunter Bryan Dempster. Dempster was a curious figure, a loner down on his luck, who was ironically defensive of the crocodiles he shot for a living: 'I like the croc. I shoot him but I admire him. ... you can't blame him for eating humans ... a man is only another animal to him ... if you don't bother him,

---

1. M.C. Musambachime, 'The Fate of the Nile Crocodile in African Waterways', *African Affairs* 86 (343) (1987): 197–207.

2. F. McLynn, *Hearts of Darkness* (London: Hutchinson, 1992) pp. 188–9.

3. R. Gordon-Cumming, *A Hunter's Life among Lions, Elephants, and other Wild Animals of South Africa* (New York: Derby & Jackson, 1857) pp. 202, 136, 273.

4. P. Gillmore, *The Land of the Boer* (London: Cassell, Petter, Galpin & Co. n.d. [c.1880]) pp. 29, 281; A. St H. Gibbons, *Africa from South to North through Marotseland*, Vol.1 (London: The Bodley Head, 1904) p. 64; R.F.C. Maugham, *Portuguese East Africa* (New York: E.P. Dutton and Co. 1906) p. 49; F.C. Selous, *A Hunter's Wanderings in Africa* (Macmillan and Co.: London, 1907) p. 175.

he isn't likely to bother you.'[5] He was however amazed when Rhodesia's Minister of Game and Forests told him crocodile hunting had been banned, exclaiming: 'but surely you consider crocodiles to be vermin!'[6] Potous recounted his experiences hunting crocodiles on Lake Malawi.[7] The key passage in the book comes after a section where Potous confesses he is tiring of 'killing a lovely animal merely to see it cut up and gorged by the natives'. However, he continued,

> No one can be cruel to a crocodile. Repulsive and loathsome, it is held in abject fear by the natives, for it preys on them unceasingly and is responsible for a greater number of human deaths than any wild animal in Africa ... In hunting it, I should still have the excitement of the chase, but at its death there would be no tears for the crocodile.[8]

In practice, this exciting chase came down to blinding a crocodile with a spotlight at night and then blowing its brains out at point-blank range with a high-powered rifle.[9] Potous's book does contain interesting observations of crocodile behaviour and he improves on the conservationist Stevenson-Hamilton (see below) by observing that a mother crocodile releases her young from their underground nest when they are ready to hatch. However, he claimed incorrectly that once she has released them, she abandons them. This observation is delivered in the unusual opening to the book, in which Potous imagined the birth of a crocodile which he named 'Snappy', described as a 'nasty-minded little fellow'. While delivering her brood to the river, the mother crocodile passes her 'mate of that year', a 'lazy, fat, good-for nothing brute' who cares nothing for the safety of his offspring.[10] Potous goes out of his way to contradict the opinions of the British herpetologist Arthur Loveridge that crocodiles are neither voracious eaters nor a threat to fisheries.[11] Crocodile hunters were keen to encourage images of rapacity in order to convince game departments to grant them licences so that they could continue to hunt crocodiles for commercial gain.

Fiction

Leighton and Surridge have discussed the symbolism of crocodiles in nineteenth century British literary and visual culture, arguing that they '[functioned] culturally as a sign of excessive appetite, hypocrisy, violence, and, most predominantly, alter-

5. L. Earl, *Crocodile Fever: A true story of adventure* (London: Collins, 1954) pp. 19–20.
6. Ibid. p. 197.
7. P.L. Potous, *No Tears for the Crocodile* (London: Hutchinson, 1956) pp. 18, 29–33.
8. Ibid. pp. 22–3.
9. Ibid., p. 66.
10. Ibid. pp. 10–12.
11. Ibid. pp. 152–3. On Loveridge, see below.

ity'. Readers of the fictions of Rudyard Kipling, Rider Haggard and G.A. Henty would have become accustomed to the crocodile as narrative cliché, a malevolent presence (often associated with the colonised 'other') to be battled and subjugated by the colonial hero.[12]

Edgar Rice Burroughs's Tarzan has a titanic struggle with a 'monster' crocodile, stabbing its 'slimy carcass' en route to being dragged into 'the creature's horrid den' where the crocodile conveniently expires on its 'slimy, evil-smelling bed'. This account derives from the well-known (and unsubstantiated) story about crocodiles dragging their prey into their underground lairs. Burroughs indulges the common misconception that crocodiles are 'slimy' (also a routine allegation about snakes) and finally departs from all semblance of verisimilitude when he has Tarzan escaping into a tree's overhanging branches from two more crocodiles, whose 'gaping mouths snapped venomously below him' (crocodiles have no venom).[13]

Two very popular novels featuring crocodiles and located in the region were published in this period. In his 'Author's Note' to *The People of the Mist* (1894), Rider Haggard confessed that his decision to make the people of the title worship a gigantic crocodile was prompted by a friend – 'an African explorer of great experience' – who felt that his original idea of a giant snake was beyond the pale. It was only subsequently that Haggard discovered that 'in the course of the recent campaign against Malaboch, a chief living in the north of the Transvaal, his fetish or god was captured, and that [this] god [was] a crocodile fashioned in wood, to which offerings were made'.[14] Haggard's story is thus pure moonshine and not based on any knowledge of the important cultural associations crocodiles have for many local peoples.

James Percy Fitzpatrick (1862–1931) was born to Irish parents in South Africa, and as a young man went to the newly discovered goldfields of the Eastern Transvaal, during which period he also worked as a transport rider between the Transvaal and Lourenço Marques in Portuguese East Africa. He later wrote a fictionalised account of his adventures in his novel *Jock of the Bushveld* (1907), which went on to become a South African classic and has been in print ever since. Crocodiles are prominent in two chapters, 'The First Hunt', and 'The Old Crocodile', in both of which they are depicted as sinister man-killers. In the former chapter, Fitzpatrick writes:

There is nothing that one comes across in hunting more horrible and loathsome

12. M.E. Leighton and L. Surridge, 'The Empire Bites Back', in D.D. Morse and M.A. Danahay (eds.) *Victorian Animal Dreams: Representations of Animals in Victorian Literature and Culture* (Aldershot: Ashgate Publishing Ltd, 2007) pp. 249–70, see pp. 257–8. See R. Kipling, 'The Undertakers', in *The Second Jungle Book* (New York: The Century Co., 1915) pp. 117–54; G.A. Henty, *By Sheer Pluck* (London: Blackie & Son Ltd, n.d. [1880]) pp. 140–1, 315–16.

13. E.R. Burroughs, *The Beasts of Tarzan* (Chicago: A.C. McClurg & Co. 1916) pp. 241–4.

14. H. Rider Haggard, *The People of the Mist* (London: Longmans, Green & Co. 1895 [1894]) p. ii.

Simon Pooley

than the crocodile: nothing that rouses the feeling of horror and hatred as it does ... Many things are hunted in the Bushveld; but only the crocodile is hated. There is always the feeling of horror that this hideous, cowardly, cruel thing ... will mercilessly drag you down – down – down to the bottom of some deep still pool, and hold you there till you drown.[15]

Thus one of the most popular and widely-read fictional works in South Africa to deal with crocodiles comprehensively vilifies them as universally hated, cowardly man-eaters. Leighton and Surridge's judgement that by the turn of the century the crocodile had 'lost its force' as a symbol of moral evil and destruction may apply to literature written in Britain, but does not adequately describe the continuing symbolic potency of crocodiles in South African fiction and many accounts of hunting and travel on the continent.[16]

Natural History

For those seeking reliable, expert information on Nile crocodiles in the period up to 1958, there was surprisingly little available. Aside from a handful of notes from the field, most of the literature consisted of reviews, usually including material going back to classical Greek times and routinely dedicating significant space to sensational stories and myths known to be untrue.

John Anderson (1833–1900), a Scottish zoologist and one of the first to write in a scientific style, was to some extent an exception. He oversaw a large collecting effort in Egypt from 1892, which formed the basis of his *Zoology of Egypt* (1901). 'Volume the First: Reptilia and Batrachia' began with a judicious and often entertaining review of the literature on crocodiles in Egypt from Herodotus until the late nineteenth century.[17] Anderson was nowhere pejorative about crocodiles. He admitted that 'the Nile crocodile has always and justly been credited with much ferocity, but the degree to which it manifests this seems to depend largely on the abundance of its food supply', which he notes is 'principally fish'.[18] Anderson recounted debates over the myth of the 'crocodile bird' believed to clean crocodiles' teeth or pick leeches from inside their mouths (fully six pages) and the ichneumon (Egyptian mongoose) alleged to run down sleeping crocodiles' gullets and kill them by eating its way out from the inside.[19]

Hans Gadow (1855–1928) was a German zoologist who became Lecturer on Advanced Morphology of Vertebrata at Cambridge University. His *Amphibia and*

---

15. P. Fitzpatrick, *Jock of the Bushveld* (London: Longmans, Green & Co. 1909[1907]) pp. 102–3.

16. Leighton and Surridge, pp. 265–7.

17. J. Anderson, *Zoology of Egypt: Volume First: Reptilia and Batrachia* (London: Bernard Quaritch, 1898) pp. 1–27.

18. Anderson, *Zoology*, pp. 17–18.

19. See Anderson, *Zoology*, pp. 11–13, 18–23.

Reptiles (1901) included detailed information on the morphology of crocodilians, along with material on the biology and behaviour of individual species.[20] Like Anderson, Gadow had nothing pejorative to say about crocodilians. He did observe that 'such a conspicuous and dangerous creature has naturally always enjoyed notoriety' and included the description of Leviathan from the Book of Job (historically the Nile crocodile was found in Syria and what was Palestine).[21] This identification of the crocodile with Leviathan has often been made and in the first full translation of the Bible into Afrikaans (1933, revised 1953) this armoured riverine monster is rendered vivid to South Africans as the crocodile.[22]

In *The Alligator and its Allies* (1915) the American zoologist Albert Reese described the Nile crocodile as 'a much feared species' and wrote that 'this man-eating crocodile, according to Ditmars, destroys more human lives than any other wild animal of the dark continent'.[23] Raymond Ditmars, Curator of Reptiles in the New York Zoological Park, expressed this rather more luridly in his *Reptiles of the World* (1910):

> none among the legions of wild brutes of the Dark Continent has caused greater loss of human life than the present terrible creature. And it is consequently no wonder this ponderous, vicious reptile has been notorious from ancient times down to the present.[24]

The most extended treatment of crocodiles in a South African context is in Col. James Stevenson-Hamilton's book *Wild Life in South Africa* (1947).[25] This passionate conservationist and first warden of the Kruger National Park (South Africa's first national park) tells us a great deal about how to kill crocodiles.[26] He also includes interesting observations of their behaviour. With regard to parental behaviour, he maintains that mother crocodiles remain nearby while their eggs hatch, but thereafter take no further notice of them, unless 'it be as article of diet'.[27] This was in keeping with the prevailing prejudice that crocodiles, like all 'cold-blooded' reptiles, do not care for their young (untrue).

20. H.F. Gadow, *Amphibia and Reptiles*, The Cambridge Natural History Vol. 8. (London: Macmillan and Co. 1901). On Gadow's life, see: D.M.S.W. 'Hans Friedrich Gadow', in 'Obituary Notices', *Proceedings of the Royal Society of London*, Series B **107** (754) (1931): i-iii.

21. Gadow, *Amphibia*, p. 461.

22. On the crocodile, see from Job 40: 20, in J.D. du Toit, *et al.* (translators), *Die Bybel* (London: Britse en Buitelandse Bybelgenootskap, 1953 [1933]). Available on: http://www.bybel.co.za Accessed 30 August 2012.

23. A.M. Reese, *The Alligator and its Allies* (Landisville: Arment Biological Press, 2000 [1915]) p. 30.

24. R.L. Ditmars, *The Reptiles of the World* (New York: The Macmillan Co. 1922 [1910]) p. 77.

25. J. Stevenson-Hamilton, *Wild Life in South Africa* (London: Cassell & Co. 1947), pp. 303–15.

26. Ibid. pp. 305–7.

27. Ibid. pp. 308–9, and 315.

Stevenson-Hamilton conjectured that 'the number of natives who through Africa annually fall victims to these sinister brutes must be enormous' and dedicated fully half of his entry on crocodiles to stories of attacks on humans.[28] He also noted crocodiles' alleged partiality to eating dogs, lamenting that 'we have lost many faithful friends through these brutes'.[29] He calls crocodiles 'sinister brutes' and describes them as dangerous, cunning and suspicious.[30]

Walter Rose (1884–1964) was an enthusiastic amateur herpetologist who practised as a dentist in Cape Town. His book *The Reptiles and Amphibians of Southern Africa* (1950) became a popular text for those newly interested in these animals.[31] He freely admitted that his 'personal observations of crocodiles are limited to captive specimens and anatomical preparations' and that his chapter on the subject is largely a literature review.[32] Inevitably, he repeated the charge that 'the Nile Crocodile is a ferocious creature and is responsible for a greater number of human deaths annually than any other African wild animal'. He also related that 'crocodiles are said to have a special taste for dogs' and repeated the tall tale that 'a crocodile killed in Zululand some time ago was found to contain in its stomach … no less than thirty-two aluminium dog licence tags'.[33] (Potous recounted the same anecdote in 1956, but in his version it was 22 name tags.[34]) Rose included several other points based on hearsay and ended with sixteenth-century stories about crocodile tears.[35]

Films

The 1950s were a boom period for feature films set in wild African landscapes (see Beinart and Schafer, this volume) and crocodiles feature as villains in several of these. In a series of Tarzan films from 1934–59 Tarzan was either rescued from a crocodile or had to save others from crocodiles.[36] In the opening scenes (and trailer) of *King Solomon's Mines* (1950), crocodiles rushed into the water the protagonists were trying to cross. Elizabeth Curtis (played by Deborah Kerr) slipped and Alan

---

28. Ibid. pp. 309–14.

29. Ibid. p. 314.

30. Ibid. pp. 311, 314.

31. W. Rose, *The Reptiles and Amphibians of Southern Africa* (Cape Town: Maskew Miller, 1950). On Rose's life, see D.G. Broadley, 'Obituary: Walter Rose'. *Journal of the Herpetological Association of Rhodesia* **23–24**/1 (1965): 58.

32. Rose, *The Reptiles*, pp. 351–8, see p. 351.

33. Ibid. p. 354.

34. Potous, *No Tears*, p. 93.

35. Rose, *The Reptiles*, pp. 354–8.

36. For the period to early 1958, see C. Gibbons (director), *Tarzan and his Mate* (Metro-Goldwyn-Mayer, 1934); B. Haskin (director), *Tarzan's Peril* (RKO Pictures, 1951).

Quatermain (Stewart Granger) was depicted as shooting a crocodile (actually an alligator) in the act of trying to catch her.[37] In the 1955 film *Safari*, directed by Terence Young and starring Janet Leigh (as Linda), Linda was catapulted from her raft into the river where she was chased by a crocodile. The hunter Ken Duffield (played by Victor Mature) shot the crocodile and rescued Linda.[38] In *Dark Venture* (1956), the hero John Kenyon saved a child from a crocodile attack and later the disaffected doctor Cameron committed suicide by letting himself be caught by crocodiles.[39]

An Image Problem

It is clear, then, that anyone seeking entertainment featuring the Nile crocodile, or even education about these animals, would have encountered a farrago of myths and prejudices. On the evidence of the media surveyed here, the major reason for the widespread dislike of the species was the fear of being killed and consumed, but also the manner of this. There was apparently something horrific but also 'unsporting' about being ambushed by these 'stealthy', 'cowardly' killers. Humans and all other mammalian prey were depicted as out of their element in the water, the lakes and waterways in which these reptiles remain the supreme predator. The idea that crocodiles are primitive intruders on the mammalian kingdom was expressed by Maugham, who referred to 'this unnecessary intruder into the wide family of the mammalia', and Fitzpatrick also regarded crocodiles as intruders (a nonsensical idea, considering their antiquity in comparison with mammals).[40]

The association of crocodiles with alterity is bound up with prejudice against reptiles. Gadow theorises that herpetology is unpopular because of 'a prejudice against creatures some of which are clammy and cold to the touch, and some of which may be poisonous'.[41] Add the size and teeth of a crocodile, and this prejudice is easily amplified to hatred: descriptions of crocodiles as 'slimy' and 'venomous' suggest a generic dislike for reptiles. Crocodiles were also a symbol of the otherness and dangers of Africa. The renowned Victorian hunter-naturalist Frederick Courteney Selous described how an idyllic canoe trip in Africa 'recalled many a pleasant day spent in times gone by upon the quiet reaches of my dear old native Thames ... [but] now and then a hideous crocodile, lying like a log upon the sand, broke the association of ideas, and recalled the fact that many a mile of land and water lay between me and the old country'.[42]

37. C. Bennett and A. Marton (directors), *King Solomon's Mines* (Metro-Goldwyn-Mayer, 1950).
38. T. Young (director), *Safari* (London: Warwick Films, 1955).
39. J. Calvert (director), *Dark Venture* (DreamQuest Productions, 1956).
40. Maugham, *Portuguese East Africa*, p. 50; Fitzpatrick, *Jock*, p. 375.
41. Gadow, *Amphibia*, p. v.
42. Selous, *A Hunter's Wanderings*, p. 175.

Simon Pooley

The Zululand Crocodile Furore

In the mid-nineteenth century the Nile crocodile was found as far south as South Africa's Eastern Cape Province. By the 1950s, reports of crocodiles south of the Tugela River (the border of Natal and Zululand) were rare. There had been extensive agricultural development, particularly the planting of wattles and sugarcane along the coastal strip of Natal, and settlements had grown up whose inhabitants were not prepared to co-exist with crocodiles. In Natal, legislation from 1866 offered rewards for dead crocodiles and their eggs and this remained the case until 1933. From the 1930s, crocodiles were shot in northern Zululand for their belly hides and this persisted until some measure of protection was put in place for all crocodiles within and outside of game reserves in 1969.[43]

Lake St Lucia is the largest estuarine lake system in Africa, with a total surface area of approximately 300 square km (or 116 square miles). It comprises three main compartments, linked to the sea by a narrow channel and estuary some 12 km (7.5 miles) long. The hydrology is complex, reliant on rainfall in the catchment regions of its feeder rivers and seepage from vegetated dunes and wetlands along its eastern shores, as well as sea-water intake shaped by tidal rhythms and the condition of the estuary mouth, which links the lake to the Indian Ocean.[44]

The area was a favoured hunting ground for Europeans from the 1850s and a small settlement sprung up near the estuary mouth in the mid-1880s, by which time most of the big game had been shot out. In 1897, the Natal government proclaimed the water surface a game reserve, making it one of the oldest in Africa. It had, and still has, one of the largest, and certainly the southernmost, wild breeding populations of the Nile crocodile in Africa.[45]

Hydrological Engineering

The Mfolozi River provided more fresh water to the Lake system than all of the other rivers and streams which feed the Lake put together.[46] From 1911, land was granted for growing sugar cane on the fertile alluvial Mfolozi Flats southwest of St Lucia Estuary. In 1932 the combined mouth was closed off behind a sand berm,

43. A.C. Pooley, 'The Ecology of the Nile Crocodile (*Crocodylus niloticus*) in Zululand' (MSc Thesis: University of Natal, Pietermaritzburg, 1982) pp. 1–2, 297–8.

44. Pooley, 'The Ecology', pp. 48–9, 54.

45. A.C. Pooley and I. Player, I. *KwaZulu-Natal Wildlife Destinations* (Johannesburg: Southern Book Publishers, 1995), p. 145.

46. My hydrological history is based on R. Taylor, 'The St Lucia-Mfolozi Connection: An Historical Perspective', and 'The Mfolozi Floodplain: Water and Sediment Processes', in G.C. Bate, A.K. Whitfield and A.T. Forbes, 'A Review of Studies on the Mfolozi Estuary and Associated Flood Plain, with Emphasis on Information Required by Management for Future Reconnection of the River to the St Lucia System', WRC Report No. KV 255/10, 2011, pp.2–21 and 22–44. See also Pooley and Player, *KwaZulu-Natal*, pp. 145–6.

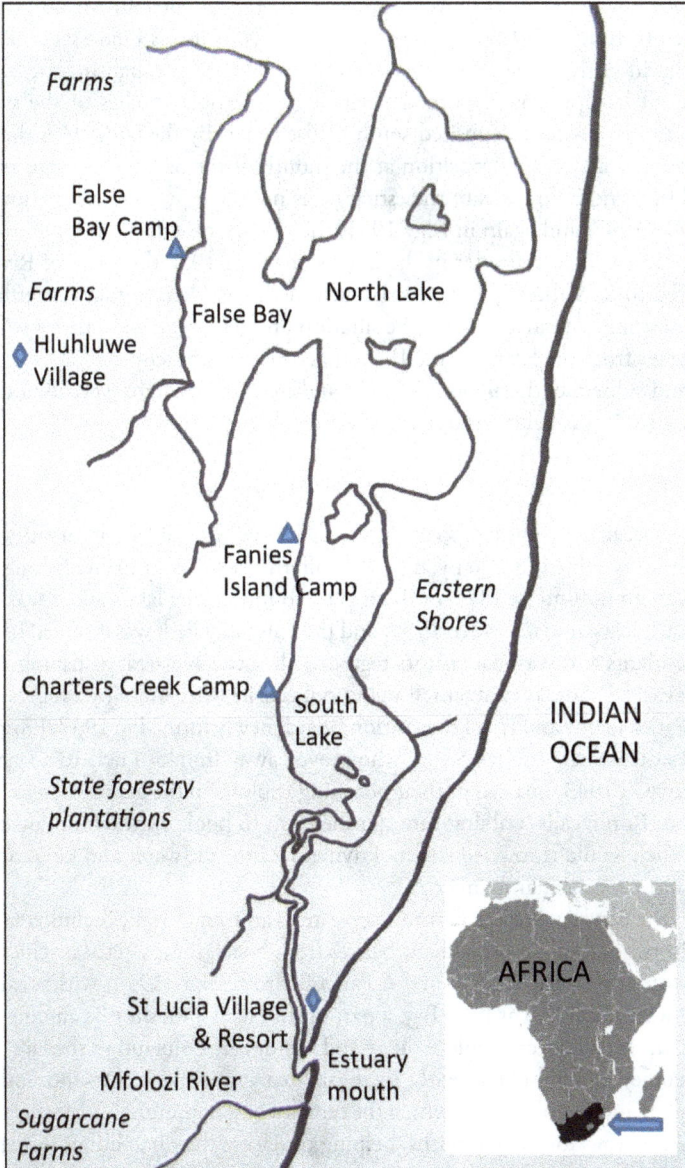

Figure 1. Map of the St Lucia Lake System.

Pyramid icons denote campsites and resorts and diamond icons denote settlements. Drawn by the author.

Simon Pooley

damming up 4.6 m (15 ft) above mean sea level. This flooded the Mfolozi flats and impeded the outflow of drains from the canefields. Wilson's Drain was built and, more significantly, Warner's Drain was completed in 1936, canalising the Mfolozi. Where silt had previously been deposited in the upper reaches of the swampy floodplain, it was now deposited south of the canal. By the late 1930s there was concern over major silt deposition at the mouth of the St Lucia system: reduced tidal action and inflow meant the estuary was no longer scoured out naturally.

In 1947, and again in May 1951, the estuary mouth silted up entirely. To prevent an ecological disaster in the Lake system, in 1952 the Mfolozi River was re-routed to flow directly out to sea south of the St Lucia Estuary mouth. This re-engineering, intended to solve the siltation problem, removed a major source of fresh water from the lake system. The estuary mouth was reopened at St Lucia by 1956 and subsequently suction dredgers and mechanical grabs were used to keep a lifeline (so it was believed) open to the sea.

A Contested Space

The lake became a contested space in the 1940s: celebrated by conservationists as a haven for wildlife but also by anglers as offering a string of prime fishing spots. Although an 800-metre (874-yard) strip surrounding the lake's shore was added to the St Lucia game reserve in 1939, and the False Bay Park was reserved in 1944, local residents and seasonal visitors regarded all accessible areas as fishing resorts. By the early 1950s, they resented being policed in these areas by rangers of the Natal Parks, Game and Fish Preservation Board, newly formed in 1947. Prominent local residents such as Nick Selley, who moved away from St Lucia to a farm near Hluhluwe in 1943, boasted of their poaching exploits in the game reserves. Nick's grandson Ron recalls 'walking through the bush to pools on the Hluhluwe River where Nick would throw red sticks of dynamite into the water and kill crocodiles in the most spectacular manner'.[47]

The newly protected nature reserve areas around the lake included facilities for visitors, resulting in novel disturbances from boats, camps, jetties, vehicles and anglers on or near the lake's shore. A Parks Board reserve (1944) with a campsite (1949) was established at False Bay, a part of the lake famous for its angling.[48] Little was known about crocodile ecology and biology in Zululand in the late 1950s. Tony Pooley would subsequently establish that crocodiles court and couple in September and October, after which the females nest communally. Mothers guard their buried eggs for three months, helping to release their hatchlings in February or March. They ferry them to a nursery area, and keep watch over them for several

47. Pooley and Player, *KwaZulu-Natal*, p. 145; R. Selley, *West of the Moon* (Johannesburg: 30° South Publishers, 2009) p. 112.

48. Pooley and Player, *KwaZulu-Natal*, pp. 145, 153.

No Tears for the Crocodiles

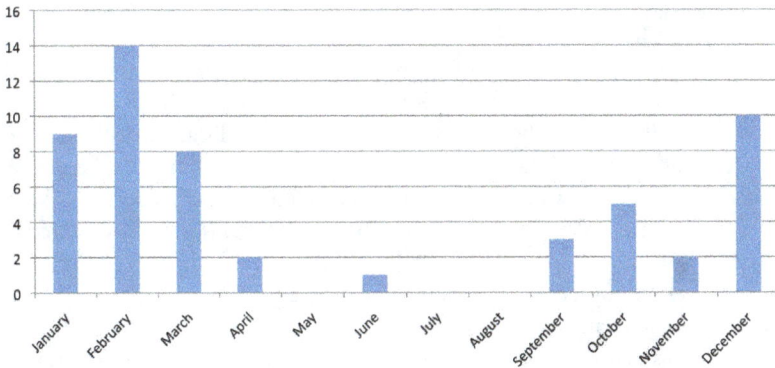

Figure 2. Seasonality of crocodile attacks in Zululand, 1949–69.

Compiled from newspaper reports in the *Natal Mercury, Daily News, Natal Witness* and *Sunday Tribune*. N = 54.

weeks after hatching.[49] It is notable that, for Zululand, most attacks on humans occurred from December to March. This is the hottest time of year, when water levels are high, and crocodiles are most widely dispersed. They are also most active at this time and this includes aggressive territorial defence by males and the defence of nests, and later hatchlings, by females.

For Africans living in this rural region, rivers, streams, pans and the Lake often provided the only source of fresh water for themselves and their livestock. They washed themselves and their clothes in these waters and fished. Children played in the water during the hot summer and when the waters were high they often had no option but to cross bodies of water. All of this exposed them to attacks from crocodiles and by far the most victims of crocodiles were Africans.

Roots of the Furore

In 1956, the Estuary mouth was reopened, allowing an influx of marine fishes. Combined with the disruption of engineering works on the Umfolozi flats, this resulted in a migration of crocodiles to near the estuary mouth. In January 1956 the *Natal Mercury* newspaper ran a story entitled 'Crocodile Lake'.[50] It was illustrated with an aerial photograph of crocodiles basking on a sandbank. The paper complained that visitors to St Lucia were unaware of the danger of crocodiles,

49. Pooley, 'The Ecology', pp. 160–215.
50. 'Crocodile Lake', *Natal Mercury* 27 January 1956.

swimming happily in the estuary. The lack of control of crocodiles was lamented. Colonel Jack Vincent, director of the Natal Parks Board, replied promptly that St Lucia was a game reserve, not a holiday resort. (The aerial photo used in the article was later identified as having been taken on the lake but nearly 40 km north of the estuary.[51]) Provoked, the *Mercury* then championed local residents annoyed they were not allowed to shoot the crocodiles. It was alleged that the estuary was infested with crocodiles and it was a miracle that no human had yet been attacked.[52]

The anticipated tragedy came, not in the estuary, but in a man-made waterway named Wilson's Drain on the Umfolozi Flats, where an African man (unnamed in reports) was killed by a crocodile while swimming on 2 February 1956.[53] This was within a so-called native reserve. As noted, most attacks around the lake occurred in or near areas that were densely populated by Africans. The Wilson's Drain attack sparked a controversy which raged in the Natal newspapers into March. The Zulu-land Chamber of Commerce, local farmers and sundry letter writers demanded that all crocodiles at St Lucia Estuary be 'exterminated' (no-one mentioned the African reserves).[54] In mid-February the Natal Administration buckled under the pressure and instructed Natal Parks Board rangers to shoot all crocodiles seen between the St Lucia bridge and the estuary mouth.[55]

Public feeling against crocodiles was running high in the country. In March 1956, ten crocodile hatchlings were displayed at the Rand Easter Show in Johannesburg. There were chaotic scenes where visitors teased, jeered and prodded the hatchlings; some picked them up and dropped them or threw stones, cigarette ash and ink into their water. The exhibitor called the police, disgusted that 'people could behave in such an uncivilized, inhuman manner', then withdrew the crocodiles from the show.[56] In the same month the *Natal Mercury* newspaper printed a prominent review of crocodile hunter Paul Potous's book *No Tears for the Crocodile*.[57]

Crocodile Hunters

From the 1930s crocodile skins were being used not only for luxury watchstraps and shoes, but increasingly for mass-produced goods. International trade boomed between 1945 and 1960, with an estimated six million skins sold each year in the

51. D.E. Mitchell, 'Crocodiles', 'Letter to the Editor', *Natal Mercury* 8 February 1956.
52. 'Crocodiles at St Lucia defended' *Natal Mercury* 28 January 1956; 'St Lucia residents resent hungry crocs on doorstep', *Natal Mercury* 31 January 1956.
53. 'Crocodile takes boy near St Lucia' *Natal Mercury* 3 February 1956.
54. See, for example, 'Farmers want crocodiles shot' *Natal Mercury* 7 February 1956; 'Zululand request on crocodiles', *Natal Mercury* 27 February 1956.
55. 'All crocodiles in St Lucia Estuary to be shot', *Daily News* 16 February 1956.
56. 'Crowds ill-treat ten baby crocodiles', *Sunday Times* 25 March 1956.
57. 'Thrill and dangers of "croc" hunting', *Natal Mercury* 23 March 1956.

period.[58] Hunters were amongst the few to engage regularly with crocodiles and they became a major source of information in the press. They eagerly provided their views for the media and several were profiled in the Natal newspapers in the 1950s. Their self-publicity had three common strands – they maintained that:

1. crocodiles were malicious, cowardly killers unworthy of conservation;

2. they were notorious man-eaters which killed and maimed countless Africans, and these Africans were deeply grateful when 'great white hunters' shot these crocodiles;

3. crocodile numbers were out of control and the services of professional crocodile hunters were urgently required to rein them in.

Hunters did not emphasise that they were hunting for skins, rather posing as altruistic crusaders for humans in the face of this deadly enemy. Playing on the impact of crocodiles on Africans was important because the hunters sought concessions to shoot in the rural native reserves.[59]

The Furore Ratchets up

On 21 December 1956 an African man, unnamed in the press, was killed by a crocodile in the St Lucia estuary. He was working in the water on the reclamation scheme despite the sighting of numerous crocodiles around the dredger – they were known to move into the estuary from the Mfolozi following summer floods.[60] A week later a large crocodile was alleged to have made a 'vicious attack on a 20ft motorboat', and in February/March 1957 four Africans were attacked by crocodiles in Zululand, one fatally (Alice Msomi, who was pregnant). Local residents demanded that crocs be shot out in their areas. Once again, crocodile hunters' tales were recounted in the media, one exhibiting 'grim relics of croc's victims' displayed on the skull of an alleged man-eater he had shot.[61]

Up to this time, the reported victims of crocodile attacks in Natal were all Africans. The white-owned provincial newspapers and related public opinion went into overdrive when David Raymond-Jones was killed by a crocodile at False Bay

58. J. MacGregor, 'The Call of the Wild: captive crocodilian production and the shaping of conservation incentives, TRAFFIC online report series, 12. (Cambridge: TRAFFIC International, 2006) p. 2.

59. See A. Hunter, 'Humans or Crocodiles – which should have protection?' *Natal Mercury* 9 February 1956; *Natal Mercury*, 'Thrills and dangers'; 'Hunter calls for blitz on crocodiles', *Natal Mercury* 18 January 1957; 'Pro hunter offers to kill crocodiles', *Natal Mercury* 20 December 1957.

60. 'Native killed by crocodile in Estuary terror', *Daily News* 21 December 1956.

61. 'More crocodile victims', *Natal Mercury* 25 February 1957; 'Large crocodile attacks boat at St Lucia', *Daily News* 29 December 1956; 'Hunter calls for blitz on crocodiles', *Natal Mercury* 18 January 1957.

Figure 3. Crocodile hunter H. Hearder displaying 'grim relics of croc's victims'.
From 'Hunter calls for blitz on crocodiles', *Natal Mercury* 18 January 1957.

on 18 December 1957. Local farmers demanded the immediate extermination of all crocodiles in Zululand.[62] Hearder, a self-proclaimed professional crocodile hunter who claimed 4,000 kills, offered to 'eradicate every one of these reptiles from Zululand'.[63]

The Chairman of the Natal Parks Board, Jim Grantham, responded by arguing that shooting crocodiles in game reserves would disperse them into waterways in adjoining areas, thus increasing the risk to the public. Further, he noted that the public was routinely warned about the danger of entering the water in game reserves and that only four attacks had occurred within reserves over the ten years of the Parks Board's existence. Most had occurred outside game reserves, where

62. 'Zululand crocodiles kill two people in one week', *Natal Mercury* 19 December 1957; 'Kill all Zululand crocs cry', *Natal Mercury* 19 December 1957.

63. 'Pro hunter offers to kill crocodiles', *Natal Mercury* 20 December 1957.

shooting crocodiles was legal.[64] However, Grantham had misjudged the mood and his comments infuriated the public and the media. At a public meeting near False Bay on 21 December 1957, local residents and regional politicians called for the extermination of all crocodiles and deproclamation of game reserves around the lake, to be replaced with holiday resorts. Farmers threatened to take the law into their own hands if the Parks Board failed to act.[65]

Clearly, there was more at stake than crocodiles. The idea that Natal had too many game reserves was debated nationally.[66] United Party politicians alleged in the press that the National Party was using the crocodile scare to get game reserves deproclaimed in order to settle their supporters on this land. This would threaten Natal as the last outpost of English-speaking resistance to the transformation of the country into an Afrikaner-dominated republic (South Africa would become a republic in 1961).[67]

Political and public pressure on the Natal Parks Board was intense. At an emergency meeting on 30 December 1957, the Board agreed to instruct rangers to shoot crocodiles on sight. However, over the following weeks details of how many crocodiles had been shot were not forthcoming, and by early 1958 the public and the newspapers suspected that the Parks Board had little intention of carrying out a sustained campaign.

It is true that the Parks Board's heart was not in the shooting campaign. At first they assured the public that they were in earnest, and hired crocodile hunter Jack Barnett to shoot crocodiles on Lake St Lucia, starting at False Bay. However they subsequently clarified that this applied only to any crocodile found near a settlement or area used by the public. They denied that it was possible to exterminate all crocodiles from such a large body of water and argued that this would compromise angling, as the resulting increase in barbel (catfish) would reduce numbers of desirable fish species. In an interview with the author, Ian Player, then conservator for Zululand, maintained that he went out of his way to make Barnett's life difficult and the hunter soon resigned. He and other members of staff had shot 67 crocodiles, but he was not replaced.[68] No one knows whether the crocodile which killed (but did not consume) Raymond Jones (he probably stood on it) and those which

64. 'Public warned to stay away from croc waters', *Natal Mercury* 20 December 1957.

65. '"Exterminate crocs or we'll do it ourselves" farmers warn', *Sunday Tribune* 22 December 1957.

66. R. Bigalke, 'Natal Natuurreservate nie te veel nie', *Die Transvaler* 31 December 1957.

67. 'Political capital over crocs deplored', *Natal Mercury* 15 January 1958. '"Answer this" challenge to Nationalist M.P.C.', *Sunday Tribune* 26 January 1958.

68. 'War declared on crocodiles by Parks Board', *Natal Mercury* 31 December 1957; 'Croc killing cloaked in secrecy', *Natal Mercury* 8 January 1958; 'All crocodiles in Zululand not to be shot', *Natal Mercury* 5 February 1958; Author's interview with Ian Player, Puza Moya, KwaZulu-Natal, 6 May 2011; Pooley, 'The Ecology', p. 300.

Figure 4. Cartoon depicting the National Party leader C.R. Swart using crocodiles for political ends.

By 'Robin', *Sunday Tribune*, January 1958; reproduced with permission.

attacked other humans in the run-up to the Parks Boards' directive were among those killed. Most of the crocodiles killed would never have attacked a human.

Conclusion

The chief lesson for the conservation authorities from this affair was that widely reinforced popular and scientific myths, prejudices and ignorance about crocodiles had proved a liability. Clearly individual crocodiles had become dangerous or potentially dangerous to humans and had to be destroyed (no facility yet existed for removing them to a safe place of captivity). The potential for crocodile attacks had been exacerbated by human interventions in the crocodiles' habitat, increasing recreational use of the lake system and popular and scientific ignorance of the behaviour of crocodiles. However, the negative social constructions of crocodiles in folktales, fiction, films, natural science books and the memoirs of hunters, explorers and conservationists had enabled a wide range of interest groups to stoke the 'crocodile furore' of 1956–8 in order to advance their diverse interests.

The many ways in which crocodiles had been imagined were almost all detrimental to the survival of this species. The primary dynamic of this imagined relationship was adversarial, with crocodiles represented as murderous intruders into human space and a deadly threat to human society. Such a monster apparently deserved none of the consideration accorded by the conservation-minded to other occasional man-killers like lions, leopards and elephants and it was frequently repeated that 'no one can be cruel to the crocodile'.[69] There was no place in a settled, developed Zululand for 'marauding crocodiles'. The public responses to the killing of David Raymond-Jones clearly demonstrated how this imagined relationship directly influenced calls to exterminate crocodiles in Zululand. An editorial in the *Natal Mercury* newspaper noted that 'the depredations of crocodiles have made an all-out offensive necessary in the interest of human life and safety'.[70]

Acknowledgements

I am grateful to St Antony's College, Oxford, and the John Fell OUP Research Fund for support while researching this project. I am indebted to my late father Tony, pioneer crocodile conservationist and ecologist, for more than I can express here.

REFERENCES

Anderson, J. 1898. *Zoology of Egypt: Volume First: Reptilia and Batrachia*. London: Bernard Quaritch.

Broadley, D.G. 1965. 'Obituary: Walter Rose'. *Journal of the Herpetological Association of Rhodesia* 23–4/1: 58.

Burroughs, Edgar Rice. 1916. *The Beasts of Tarzan*. Chicago: A.C. McClurg & Co.

Cott, H.B. 1961. 'Scientific results of an inquiry into the ecology and economic status of the Nile Crocodile (*Crocodilus niloticus*) in Uganda and Northern Rhodesia'. *Transactions of the Zoological Society of London* 29/4.

Ditmars, R.L. 1922 [1910]. *The Reptiles of the World*. New York: The Macmillan Co.

D.M.S.W. 1931. 'Hans Friedrich Gadow'. In 'Obituary Notices', *Proceedings of the Royal Society of London*, Series B **107** (754): i–iii.

Du Toit, J.D., E.E. Van Rooyen, J.D. Kestell, H.C.M. Fourie and B.B. Keet (translators). 1953 [1933]. *Die Bybel*. London: Britse en Buitelandse Bybelgenootskap.

Earl, L. 1954. *Crocodile Fever: A True Story of Adventure*. London: Collins.

Fitzpatrick, P. 1909 [1907]. *Jock of the Bushveld*. London: Longmans, Green & Co.

---

69. 'The Crocodile – an Increasing Menace', letter to the editor from L.B. Anderson, *Natal Mercury* 15 Feb 1958.

70. 'A menace under control', editorial, *Natal Mercury* 1 March 1958.

Gadow, H.F. 1901. *Amphibia and Reptiles.* The Cambridge Natural History Vol. 8. London: Macmillan and Co.

Gordon-Cumming, R. 1857. *A Hunter's Life among Lions, Elephants, and other Wild Animals of South Africa.* New York: Derby & Jackson.

Gibbons, A. St H. 1904. *Africa from South to North through Marotseland.* Vol.1. London: The Bodley Head.

Gillmore, P. n.d. [c.1880]. *The Land of the Boer: Adventures in Natal, the Transvaal, Basutoland, and Zululand.* London: Cassell, Petter, Galpin & Co.

Haggard, H.R. 1895 [1894]. *The People of the Mist.* London: Longmans, Green & Co.

Henty, G.A. n.d. [1880]. *By Sheer Pluck: a tale of the Ashanti War.* London: Blackie & Son Ltd.

Hubbard, W.D. 1927. 'Crocodiles'. *Copeia* 165: 115–16.

Kipling, R. 1915. 'The Undertakers'. In *The Second Jungle Book.* New York: The Century Co. pp. 117–54.

Leighton, M.E. and L. Surridge. 2007. 'The Empire Bites Back: the Racialized Crocodile of the Nineteenth Century'. In D.D. Morse and M.A. Danahay (eds.) *Victorian Animal Dreams: Representations of Animals in Victorian Literature and Culture.* Aldershot: Ashgate Publishing Ltd.

Loveridge, A. 1928. 'The Nilotic Crocodile'. *Copeia* 168: 74–6.

Maugham, R.F.C. 1906. *Portuguese East Africa: The History, Scenery, & Great Game of Manica and Sofala.* New York: E.P. Dutton and Co.

McLynn, F. 1992. *Hearts of Darkness: the European Exploration of Africa.* London: Hutchinson.

Miller, W.T. 1958. *Wild Life of Southern Africa.* Pietermaritzburg: Shuter and Shooter.

Musambachime, M.C. 1987. 'The Fate of the Nile Crocodile in African Waterways'. *African Affairs* 86/343: 197–207.

Pooley, A.C. and I. Player. 1995. *KwaZulu-Natal Wildlife Destinations.* Johannesburg: Southern Book Publishers.

Pooley, A.C. 1982a. 'The Ecology of the Nile Crocodile (*Crocodylus niloticus*) in Zululand'. MSc Thesis: University of Natal, Pietermaritzburg.

Pooley, A.C. 1982b. *Discoveries of a Crocodile Man.* Johannesburg: Collins.

Potous, P.L. 1956. *No Tears for the Crocodile.* London: Hutchinson.

Reese, A.M. 2000 [1915]. *The Alligator and its Allies.* Landisville: Arment Biological Press.

Rose, W. 1950. *The Reptiles and Amphibians of Southern Africa.* Cape Town: Maskew Miller.

Selley, R. 2009. *West of the Moon: a Game Ranger at War.* Johannesburg: 30° South Publishers.

Selous, F.C. 1907. *A Hunter's Wanderings in Africa: being a Narrative of Nine Years Spent amongst the Game of the Far Interior of South Africa.* London: Macmillan and Co.

Stevenson-Hamilton, J. 1947. *Wild Life in South Africa.* London: Cassell & Co.

No Tears for the Crocodiles

Reports

MacGregor, J. 2006. 'The Call of the Wild: captive crocodilian production and the shaping of conservation incentives, TRAFFIC online report series, 12. Cambridge: TRAFFIC International.

Taylor, R. 2011. 'The St Lucia-Mfolozi Connection: An Historical Perspective', and 'The Mfolozi floodplain: water and sediment processes'. In G.C. Bate, A.K. Whitfield and A.T. Forbes (eds.) 'A Review of studies on the Mfolozi Estuary and associated flood plain, with emphasis on information required by management for future reconnection of the river to the St Lucia System', South African Water Research Commission (WRC) Report KV 255/10.

Newspapers

[in chronological order]

Natal Mercury. 1956. 'Crocodile Lake'. 27 January.

Natal Mercury. 1956. 'Crocodiles at St Lucia defended'. 28 January.

Natal Mercury. 1956. 'St Lucia residents resent hungry crocs on doorstep'. 31 January.

Natal Mercury. 1956. 'Crocodile takes boy near St Lucia'. 3 February.

Natal Mercury. 1956. 'Farmers want crocodiles shot'. 7 February.

Mitchell, D.E. 1956. 'Crocodiles', 'Letter to the Editor'. *Natal Mercury*. 8 February.

Hunter, A. 1956. 'Humans or Crocodiles – which should have protection?' *Natal Mercury*. 9 February.

Daily News. 1956. 'All crocodiles in St Lucia Estuary to be shot'. 16 February.

Natal Mercury. 1956. 'Zululand request on crocodiles'. 27 February.

Natal Mercury. 1956. 'Thrill and dangers of "croc" hunting'. 23 March.

Sunday Times. 1956. 'Crowds ill-treat ten baby crocodiles'. 25 March.

Daily News. 1956. 'Native killed by crocodile in Estuary terror'. 21 December.

Daily News. 1956. 'Large crocodile attacks boat at St Lucia'. 29 December.

Natal Mercury. 1957. 'Hunter calls for blitz on crocodiles'. 18 January.

Natal Mercury. 1957. 'More crocodile victims'. 25 February.

Natal Mercury. 1957. 'Zululand crocodiles kill two people in one week'. 19 December.

Natal Mercury. 1957. 'Kill all Zululand crocs cry'. 19 December.

Natal Mercury. 1957. 'Pro hunter offers to kill crocodiles'. 20 December.

Natal Mercury. 1957. 'Public warned to stay away from croc waters'. 20 December.

Sunday Tribune. 1957. "Exterminate crocs or we'll do it ourselves' farmers warn'. 22 December.

Natal Mercury. 1957. 'War declared on crocodiles by Parks Board'. 31 December.

Bigalke, R. 1957. 'Natal Natuurreservate nie te veel nie'. *Die Transvaler*. 31 December.

Natal Mercury. 1958. 'Croc killing cloaked in secrecy'. 8 January.

Natal Mercury. 1958. 'Political capital over crocs deplored'. 15 January.
Sunday Tribune. 1958. "Answer this' challenge to Nationalist M.P.C.'. 26 January.
Natal Mercury. 1958. 'All crocodiles in Zululand not to be shot'. 5 February.

Films

Bennett, C. and A. Marton (directors). 1950. *King Solomon's Mines* (Metro-Goldwyn-Mayer).
Calvert, J. (director). 1956. *Dark Venture* (DreamQuest Productions).
Gibbons, C. (director). 1934. *Tarzan and his Mate* (Metro-Goldwyn-Mayer).
Haskin, B. (director). 1951. *Tarzan's Peril* (RKO Pictures).
Young, T. (director). 1955. *Safari* (London: Warwick Films).

Chapter 7

Science, 'Stars' and Sustenance: The Acquisition and Display of Animals at the Bristol Zoological Gardens, 1836–c. 1970

Andrew J.P. Flack

When the Bristol, Clifton and West of England Zoological Society formed in late summer of 1835, plans were laid for 'zoological subjects' to be purchased to populate the zoo in Bristol's prosperous suburb of Clifton. This article builds on the recognition that animals were commodified through this extractive and translocatory process. Between the opening of the Gardens in 1836 and the beginning of the period in which zoo practices significantly transformed, c. 1970, the Zoo's animal acquisition policy was motivated by a range of requirements to possess particular animals at particular times, for particular purposes. Whilst all animals were considered valuable, not all animals were valued equally. Some species were sought for their scientific value whilst other particularly spectacular attractions were desired for their commercial potential and the associated prestige they might bestow on the Society. Moreover, the manner in which these animals were displayed further exemplifies this binary. The dual motives of science and commerce were, however, complicated by variables such as age, sex and aesthetic perfection. To further complicate matters, an array of animals, both exotic and domestic, were valued not for wholly scientific or spectacular purposes, but for the nutritional value latent in their fleshy forms. The formation and display of the collection thus disclose a diversity of ways of perceiving animal bodies, illuminating their fluctuating and uncertain presence in the social imagination.

Acquisitions

By 1843 the Zoo was in possession of creatures drawn from environments the world over. The core of the collection was of sub-Saharan African origin but early exhibits included gold and silver pheasants from China, primates and cats from India and South East Asia, a range of marsupials from New South Wales and New Holland

Figure 1. Camel at the Bristol Zoo. c. 1955.

Bristol and Aberdeen: Harvey Barton & Son. Roy Vaughan Collection, BCWEZS Archive.

and birds and boas, moose and Labrador dogs from the Americas.[1] This extensive collection was acquired through the Society's immersion in a vibrant market in wild animals, a trade which contributed to significant, and increasingly apparent, damage to the biosphere.[2] Extracted from every continent, except Antarctica, the geographical scope of the Zoo's collection remained truly global throughout the period under discussion in this chapter.[3]

Just as in other zoos, once animals had arrived at Bristol there was no guarantee they would survive.[4] The records of the Zoo exhibit a 'natural wastage'

---

1. *Catalogue of the Animals, Birds &c in the Bristol and Clifton Zoological Gardens, with short descriptive notices of their organisation and habits, as well as in a state of nature as in captivity* (Bristol: BCWEZS, 1843).

2. William Beinart, 'Empire, Hunting and Ecological Change in Southern and Central Africa', *Past and Present* **128** (2002): 163–66.

3. See, for instance, J. Le H. Phillips, *The Gardens and Menagerie of the BCWEZS* (Bristol: BCWEZS, c. 1882). Fred W. Knocker, *Illustrated Official Guide to the Gardens of the BCWEZS* (Bristol: BCWEZS, 1904). *Illustrated Official Guide to the Gardens of the BCWEZS* (Bristol: BCWEZS, c.1924–5); *98th Annual Report of the BCWEZS* (henceforth AR/BCWEZS). 11 Apr. 1934; *118th AR/BCWEZS*. 18 Mar. 1954; *The 128th AR/BCWEZS*. 29 Apr. 1974; (BCWEZS/BZG/6/1/Z).

4. Eric Baratay and Elisabeth Hardouin-Fugier, *Zoo: A History of Zoological Gardens in the West* (London: Reaktion, 2002) p. 124.

of exotic animals maintained in captivity in cold climes. The period 1854–5, for instance, saw the 'less numerous than usual' number of 23 deaths and there were 66 fatalities during the winter of 1855–6.[5] The maintenance of primates was a particular concern, with the 1843 guide acknowledging that very few survived longer than a few months.[6] It was reported in 1881 that three-quarters of the monkey collection had expired during a particularly severe winter and similarly destructive conditions prevailed once more in 1940.[7] Indeed, the successful maintenance of animals in captivity throughout an entire winter was often a great challenge, 'a great experiment', particularly in the early years.[8] Consequently, the Society cultivated reliable supply lines from its inception to ensure that there were always animals available to replace the expired. Indeed, Baratay and Hardouin-Fugier argue that the wild animal trade was itself driven by such high levels of animal mortality.[9]

The Society's records show that there was no preferred supplier; instead, there were numerous individuals and organisations able to produce animals for purchase. Indeed, Nigel Rothfels has illustrated how an array of individuals sourced animals to satiate demand in Europe during the nineteenth century.[10] Early on, animals were procured from professional animal dealers such as Charles Jamrach, J.D. Hamlyn and Charles Rice and throughout the period purchases were made from other zoos, circuses and travelling menageries. Animals were also extensively sourced through donations from other zoos and individuals in a variety of contexts. Annually, around sixty animals were donated to the Society between 1847 and 1970.[11]

Scientific Commodities

When it was conceptualised, the Zoo was foremost a locus of science. Although there is a scarcity of evidence of research focused on animals at the Zoo in the early years, the maintenance of 'wild' animals, particularly through the British winter, was an experiment in itself. Moreover, the displays provisioned for the rational amusement and instruction of paying visitors and members of the Society. Animals were categorised as specimens, representative of their species, to be collected and catalogued, stationed in an anthropocentrically determined natural order and holding in their forms and behaviours secrets which might be extracted through

5.   *19th AR/BCWEZS.* 11 Apr. 1855. p. 12; *20th AR/BCWEZS.* 9 Apr 1856. pp. 13–14.

6.   *Catalogue of Animals,* p. 5.

7.   'Bad weather monkey deaths', *The York Herald,* 21 January 1881; *104th AR/BCWEZS.* 10 Apr. 1940. p. 7.

8.   'Meeting, 20 Oct 1841' (BCWEZS/BZG/1/1/1), p. 264.

9.   Baratay and Hardouin-Fugier, *Zoo,* p. 124.

10. Nigel Rothfels, 'Catching Animals', in Mary J. Henninger-Voss (ed.) *Animals in Human Histories: the Mirror of Nature and Culture* (Rochester, N.Y: University of Rochester Press, 2002) p. 197.

11. *12th AR/BCWEZS.* 8 Apr, 1847. – *134th AR/BCWEZS.* 15 Apr. 1970.

learning. Just as at London Zoo, and in museums more generally (Sir Richard Owen aspired to 'lodge the samples of the Works of Creation of every class, of all time, and from the whole World' in his new natural history collection at South Kensington[12]), it was desirable that Bristol held as complete and as extensive a collection as possible in its presentation of a mastered animate natural world, ripe for curious consideration.[13]

Totality meant that gaps in the exhibited animal catalogue were conspicuous. In 1854 it was stated that 'your Committee ... lost no time in filling up the blanks in your Menagerie as they occurred, adding more specimens where possible'.[14] The inclusion of native fauna in the collection bears witness to the desire to possess a total world in a single space, not just unseen denizens of exotic climes. An aviary for English birds formed part of the exhibition from 1863 and by 1899 there were specimens of chaffinch, siskin, brambling and hedge sparrow. Moreover, a number of English foxes and squirrels were included around this time while badgers could be observed in the collection during the first half of the twentieth century.[15]

Efforts were made throughout the period, despite the lack of space afforded by a twelve-acre site and wartime embargoes, to work toward totality in the zoological collection. It was recorded in 1930, for instance, that 'during the year £1,113 was spent on new animals ... the collection is now as complete as accommodation allows'.[16] And, in 1943, despite the difficulties in obtaining animals presented by the economic limitations of war, the Zoo was still able to boast, with some palpable relief, that it had 'a large and representative collection'.[17]

The display of many and varied strange and exotic creatures alongside native fauna was necessary to the Zoo's substantiation of its claim to possession of an animate wholeness rather than merely an array of curiosities akin to the travelling menageries of the early part of the period. This way of perceiving animals was central to the Zoo's mission, reflecting a scientific valuation of animal bodies that is further in evidence in the manner of the Society's display of its collection.

---

12. Richard Owens, 'On the Extent and aims of a National Museum of Natural History (Excerpt)' [1862] in Jonah Siegel (ed.) *The Emergence of the Modern Museum: An Anthology of Nineteenth Century Sources* (Oxford: Oxford University Press, 2008) p. 236.

13. Harriet Ritvo, 'The Order of Nature: Constructing the Collections of Victorian Zoos', in R. J. Hoage and William. A. Deiss (eds.) *New Worlds, New Animals, From Menagerie to Zoological Park in the Nineteenth Century* (London: John Hopkins University Press, 1996) p. 46.

14. *18th AR/BCWEZS*. 12 Apr. 1854. p. 7.

15. 'Meeting, 8 Jun. 1863', (BCWEZS/BZG/1/1/4), p. 111; 'Meeting, 3 Aug. 1864', (BCWEZS/BZG/1/1/4), p. 159; 'Meeting, 7 Feb. 1872', (BCWEZS/BZG/1/1/5), p. 172; Fred W. Knocker, *Illustrated Official Guide to the Gardens of the BCWEZS* (Bristol: BCWEZS, 1899) p. 19; Phillips, *The Gardens and Menagerie*, p. 24; *Bristol Zoo Book and Official Guide* (Bristol: BCWEZS, 1948).

16. *94th AR/BCWEZS*. 9 Apr. 1930. p. 7.

17. *107th AR/BCWEZS*. 14 Apr. 1943. p. 4.

Science, 'Stars' and Sustenance

The 1843 catalogue shows that animals were presented separately in taxo-nomic arrangement, including animal groups explicitly presented as carnivorous, quadruped, ruminant and gallinaceous. The arbitrary separation of animals from each other and in such order remains fundamentally unchanged in the 1899 guide-book to the zoo. Exhibits included an aviary for owls, an enclosure for jackals and a large series of cages for individual species of big cat. Small, separate compartments contained foxes, cats, ocelots, lemurs, opossum, coati and mongoose, whilst later aviaries housed pheasants and parrots separately. By this time a purpose-built reptile house had been erected which exhibited only specimens of that class.[18] This manner of display continued until the erection of the 1954 Nocturnal House which rejected overt taxonomic classification in favour of presentation by habitat and reveals the sustained importance attached to the overtly scientific display of animal specimens into the latter half of the twentieth century.[19]

The provision of scientific instruction alone, however, was not enough to sustain the Zoo's activities and thus was not the only influence on acquisition and exhibition. Animals needed to be acquired which could attract and amuse paying visitors. Scientific and commercial ways of viewing animals thus often interacted and complemented each other in the Zoo's acquisition policy.

Animal Spectacular

The Zoo was an arena of entertainment as much as it was one of scientific endeavour and instruction. Enclosure prior to the advent of immersive exhibits in the last decades of the twentieth century dominantly privileged sight and movement, allow-ing for maximum visibility and animal animation. Bob Mullan and Garry Marvin argue that 'in the earliest zoos the physical presence of the living animal was the only important factor'.[20] Yet the privileging of visibility remained dominant into the twentieth century. Small cages in which animals had no place to hide defined enclosure style in most zoos throughout the period.[21] Enclosures like the polar bear court (Figure 2) were small and bare, thrusting the animal into the visitors' line of sight, whilst later barless, more naturalistic, enclosures such as the 1935 Volcanic Coast exhibit (Figure 3) similarly allowed for better observation whilst catering to changing sensibilities about animal incarceration.[22]

---

18. *Catalogue of Animals*; Knocker (1899), *Illustrated Official Guide*; *Bristol Zoo Book and Official Guide* (Bristol: BCWEZS, 1957).

19. For a description the Nocturnal House, see *Bristol Zoo Book*, 1957, p. 11.

20. Bob Mullan and Garry Marvin, *Zoo Culture* (Urbana: University of Illinois Press, 1999) pp. 31–2.

21. Baratay and Hardouin-Fugier, *Zoo*, p. 149.

22. Ibid. pp. 194–7.

Figure 2. 'Jenny', Clifton Zoo. c. 1904.

Bristol and Aberdeen: Harvey Barton & Son, 1904. Roy Vaughan Collection, BCWEZS Archive.

Figure 3. 'Penguins – Volcanic Coast'. c. 1962.

In *Photographs of Penguins* (BCWEZS/BZG/9/3/12).

Later innovations such as glass barriers, employed in the display of big cats from 1959, further enhanced visibility whilst obscuring the mechanisms of captivity.[23] Other animal exhibits, such as the bear pit (Figure 4), operational at the Zoo into the late 1960s, privileged movement and activity. As Jonathan Burt has argued, the zoo animal 'was not simply an object but also an event. From an entertainment point of view, the more dynamic the event, the greater the interest.'[24] Through enticing the animal up its pole to receive buns and biscuits, the entertainment of the exhibit was enhanced. Privileging visibility and movement, these enclosures reflect the valuation of zoo animals as objects of amusement.

Some species, however, were more central to the exhibition than others, reflecting a far from homogenous valuation of species by the Zoo and its visitors. During the period, the 'star' animals at the Zoo were usually the charismatic megafauna, capable of satiating popular tastes for the wild and physically imposing. Just like London Zoo during the period, Bristol kept its collection well stocked with these popular attractions.[25] Part of the appeal of these animals may have been their centrality as characters in popular culture. Lions, tigers, elephants, zebras and giraffes were the animals which visitors might have associated with places where 'wild' things lurked. Indeed, there are a number of instances in which it is recognised that visitors arrived with some expectation based on exposure to animals in literature. For instance, the 1894 guide to the collection suggests that the sight of big cats stimulates memories 'so that the exciting stories read, years ago, come back again to the mind'.[26]

Sitting centrally in the collection for much of the period were the big cats. Harriet Ritvo has pointed to their significance in the collections of nineteenth-century zoos, whilst John MacKenzie has examined their allure to imperial hunters in Africa and Asia, who often saw them as mighty adversaries whose destruction in intimate combat testified to the complete mastery of Europeans of the rest of the natural world.[27]

The display of big cats in zoos might be read as a comparable expression of western human mastery of 'wild' nature in the domestic spaces of the British

23. 'Meeting, 14 Nov. 1949, (BCWEZS/BZG/1/1/10)', p. 160; 'Meeting, 10 Jul. 1950', (BCWEZS/BZG/1/1/10), p. 182; 'Meeting 11 Dec. 1950', (BCWEZS/BZG/1/1/10), p. 195; *Bristol Zoo Book*, 1954. p. 8.

24. Jonathan Burt, 'The Illumination of the Animal Kingdom: the Role of Light and Electricity in Animal Representation', *Society and Animals* 9/3 (2001): 213.

25. Robert W. Jones, 'The Sight of Creatures Strange to our Clime: London Zoo and the Consumption of the Exotic', *Journal of Victorian Culture* 2/1 (1997): 14.

26. *Illustrated Official Guide to the Clifton Zoological Gardens* (Bristol: BCWEZS, 1894) p. 23.

27. Harriet Ritvo, *The Animal Estate: The English and other Creatures in the Victorian Age* (Cambridge, Mass. Harvard University Press, 1987) p. 47; John M. MacKenzie, *The Empire of Nature: Hunting, Conservation and British Imperialism* (Manchester: Manchester University Press, 1988) p. 47; see also Susie Green, *Tiger* (London: Reaktion, 2008) esp. pp. 68–150.

Figure 4. Russian Bear, 'Jack', Clifton Zoo. c. 1916.

Viner and Co. Publishers, c. 1916. Roy Vaughan Collection, BCWEZS Archive.

Empire.[28] The c. 1882 guidebook to the zoo relates at length the history of lion and tiger hunting in the Empire, emphasising the instinctual violence of these predators, as if to illustrate the triumph of the Society in rendering them submissive in its ordered, controlled collection.[29] The importance attached to the display of big cats can best be seen in a number of specific instances. In 1838 the Zoo secured a bank loan of £150 specifically for the purchase of a lion and intended to contribute to the overall cost of acquisition which, it was stipulated, was to be no more than £210. In any event, the final purchase price was £250; the Zoological Society of London (ZSL) would not accept a penny less.[30] The price demanded by ZSL reflects awareness of the desirability of lions for display, and the price Bristol eventually paid points to the importance the Society placed on the acquisition of this species. A similar transaction took place in 1853.[31] Lions were thus critical assets and their presentation throughout the nineteenth and early twentieth centuries made it quite clear to visitors that they were at the apex of the exhibition. Frequently situated toward the front of guidebooks (as well as among the first exhibits to be encountered upon entering the Zoo Gardens), they were commonly described in terms of 'prowess' and 'prominence'. Indeed, the 1937 guide stated that lions were the 'finest and most majestic of all animals'.[32]

By the end of the nineteenth century, the Zoo had earned a national reputation for possessing 'superior' (by which they meant larger, especially aesthetically pleasing) lions, tigers and other big cats.[33] Local newspapers regularly reported the arrival of animals of this family, reflecting the newsworthy nature of such acquisitions and disclosing an element of a broader civic pride in their possession by a Bristol institution. In 1890 the *Bristol Mercury and Daily Post* proclaimed that the recent acquisition of two tigers served to render the collection of carnivora held one of the finest in the Kingdom, if not in Europe.[34] Florence Grinfield's 1894 unofficial guide to the Gardens, *Our Clifton Zoo*, noted that the admission price of 6d would be worthwhile if nothing but lions were on display. Lions were, according to Grinfield, ever an institution at the Clifton Zoo.[35] These cats were thus afforded

---

28. Ritvo, *The Animal Estate*, p. 223.

29. Phillips, *The Gardens and Menagerie*, pp. 10–13.

30. 'Meeting, 6 Jul. 1838', (BCWEZS/BZG/1/1/1), p. 171; 'Meeting, 9 Jul. 1838', (BCWEZS/BZG/1/1/1), p. 172.

31. 'Meeting, 27 May 1853', (BCWEZS/BZG/1/1/2), p. 142.

32. See, for instance, *Illustrated Official Guide*, 1894, p. 7, 23; Knocker (1899), *Illustrated Official Guide*, p. 19; F.L. Vanderplank, *Official Guide to the Gardens and Aquarium of the BCWEZS* (Bristol: BCWEZS, 1937) p. 12.

33. 'Reputation for Having Big Cats', *The Bristol Mercury and Daily Post*, 30 Jul. 1894.

34. 'This Morning's News', *The Bristol Mercury and Daily Post*, 25 Jul. 1890.

35. Florence G. Grinfield, *Our Clifton Zoo, and the Folks we Meet there. A Semi-Comic Description in Prose and Verse* (Weston Super Mare: J. R. Walters & Co. 'Gazette' Office, 1894) pp. 5–6, 28.

special status as animal assets hoisted above the rest of the Zoo's 'representative' collection in the provision of exciting spectacle.

For much of the Zoo's history, the larger charismatic animals appear to have been considered to be more intrinsic to the collection than smaller species. Guidebooks during the period devote relatively more space and attention to the larger mammals. The cats, bears, elephants and large apes and monkeys were the core foci of these publications, reflecting their perceived centrality in the collection.[36]

The Zoo's procurement of polar bears, for instance, reflects the preeminent status of this particular species. A newspaper reported in 1881, following the death of one individual, that this species was one of the Zoo's 'most popular' animals.[37] Such was the reputation of this species, the arrival of another bear in 1894 from North Sea shipping agents in Dundee generated press interest and when the Society found itself without a polar bear once more in 1905, it issued an urgent call to friends who might wield influence with the North Sea fisheries or whaling companies, asking for a specimen to be procured for immediate display.[38]

The necessity of acquiring large mammals was consistent throughout the period. Particularly popular animals stimulated especially energetic activity in the Zoo's acquisition networks. In 1926, for instance, the Zoo, in its desperation to secure a new resident elephant after the demise of the popular Rajah created an 'Elephant Fund' to raise money and the Sixth Battalion of the Gloucester Regiment held a military Tattoo to support the cause.[39] The quest for a new elephant to walk in the Society's Gardens was a civic exercise and is reflective of the ways in which the public and the Zoo interacted in the acquisition of a particular species which both parties considered to be of special import in their Zoo. Later, in 1966, Superintendent Reginald Greed enquired regarding the availability of a pair of sea lions and asked for their quick delivery since he had 'hoped to get them for Easter'. [40] Sea lions, evidently, formed an integral element in the complete Zoo attraction during holiday seasons. Animals were often acquired, therefore, to cater to public interests and enthusiasms.

The worth attached to animals with proven commercial power illustrates that the value of the Zoo's animal commodities was diverse and was frequently

---

36. See, for instance, *Catalogue of Animals*; Phillips, *The Gardens and Menagerie*; Knocker (1904), *Illustrated Official Guide*; Vanderplank, *Official Guide*; *Bristol Zoo Book and Official Guide* (Bristol: BCWEZS, 1954).

37. 'Death of Polar Bear', *The Bristol Mercury and Daily Post*, 2 Jul. 1881.

38. 'New Polar Bear from Dundee Shipping Agents', *The Bristol Mercury and Daily Post*, 26 Oct. 1894; *69th AR/BCWEZS*. 12 Apr. 1905. p. 12.

39. 'Meeting, 1 Sept. 1926', (BCWEZS/BZG/1/1/8), p. 201; 'Meeting, 13 Sept. 1926', (BCWEZS/BZG/1/1/8), p. 203.

40. 'Correspondence from the Director of BCWEZS to Mr B M Williams, Tyseley Pet Stores Ltd, Birmingham'. 6 Apr. 1966. In (BCWEZS/BZG/6/4/I).

Science, 'Stars' and Sustenance

Figure 5. 'Judy' at Clifton Zoo. c. 1927.
Roy Vaughan Collection, BZG Archive.

determined by factors beyond the scientific, a dynamic which is further exemplified in the acquisition of animals which, through the direct deployment of their muscular bodies, generated revenue. Throughout the history of the Zoo, replacement elephants were sourced almost immediately upon the expiration of the Gardens' pachyderm resident. They were especially valuable to the Society as beasts of burden, physically active participants in the visitor experience (Figure 5).

Whilst the elephant Zebi began to be walked around the Gardens daily from 1869, it is unclear whether she also gave children rides.[41] Certainly in 1915, however, the Society recorded that 'elephant rides, although tabulated as 16s 6d only, have a promising prospect to come'.[42] It was not only the elephant, though, that was able to provide a service to visitors and thus generate additional revenue. Throughout the period goats, ponies, camels and llamas were all either ridden or compelled to pull carts and carriages which visitors paid for the privilege of riding in.[43] By 1950, revenue generated by elephant and llama rides totalled £552, a not insignificant proportion of the Society's total revenue of £8,616 for that year.[44]

---

41. 'Meeting 2 Jun. 1869' (BCWEZS/BZG/1/1/5), p. 96.

42. *The 79th Annual Report to the BCWEZS*. 14 Apr. 1915. p. 10.

43. See, for instance, *Bristol Zoo Book,* 1948. p. 31.

44. 'BCWEZS Accounts for the year ended 30 September 1950', in (BCWEZS/BZG/2/1/a).

Thus, the zoo's animals could be commercially lucrative in a variety of ways. Analysis of prices between the 1860s and the 1880s, and early in the twentieth century, for instance, illustrates this diversity in animal valuations.[45] In the nineteenth century, big cats usually fetched upwards of £50 (though the famous lion Hannibal II was allegedly valued at £400–500 in 1893),[46] whilst a polar bear usually cost about £30. In comparison, most animals bought were valued at a maximum of £5 and monkeys and many small birds, in particular, would usually be bought for much less and often in bulk.[47] As well as reflecting levels of supply, prices are indicative of exhibition value, the most expensive animals, such as lions, being those which were more central to the display.

In 1935 the Zoo issued an estimate on the respective values of the animals in its collection. One of the highest prices (£700) was attached to the extremely popular riding elephant, Judy. The big cats (£70–150), zebra (£50) and Oryx (£60) were the next most expensive, closely followed by the polar bear (£40). At the lower end of the scale were Java monkeys, badgers and eagle owls, all of which were usually valued at just £1 per specimen.[48] The prices attached to the larger fauna are not surprising, but the disparity between the prices for big cats and the elephant might be. The gulf between them reflects both the extra commercial power of the elephant, her popularity as an exhibit, and the obvious additional challenge involved in moving elephants around the trading arena.

Animal Curiosities

Alongside essential components of the collection, especially novel creatures were particularly sought after. Crucial to the scientific aims of the Society, and central to the realisation of commercial objectives, the possession and display of rare specimens was most desirable. Such novelty creatures were not simply components of a vast collection, nor simply among the mainstays of the exhibition; they were of intense and especial interest, distinctly valuable compared to the rest of the collection.[49]

Frequently, the possession of rarely seen and studied creatures was deemed to be a higher priority than the retention of other species in the collection. In 1864, for instance, the Society explicitly stated that it was seeking to improve accommodation which should be used in the housing of any 'rare and valuable' beasts,

---

45.   Nigel Rothfels, *Savages and Beasts: The Birth of the Modern Zoo* (London: John Hopkins University Press, 2002) p. 178.

46.   'The Talk of Bristol', *The Bristol Mercury and Daily Post*, 5 Jun. 1893.

47.   (BCWEZS/BZG/1/1/5).

48.   'BCWEZS Valuation of Livestock as at 30 September 1935', in (BCWEZS/BZG/2/2/a).

49.   Ritvo, *The Animal Estate*, p. 216.

the implication being that such animals were demarcated as significant specimens, requiring special provision to ensure longevity in the collection.[50]

The value frequently attached to the possession of lesser-seen animals led the Zoo to continue to publicise its exhibition of chimpanzees and an Ungka-puti (agile gibbon), both 'very rare and interesting creatures' in its 1843 *Catalogue of Animals*, despite the fact that both had since died and no replacements successfully acquired.[51] In 1838 the Zoo charged one penny additional to the one shilling entrance fee to those who wished to view their first chimpanzee, such was the excitement surrounding such a rarely seen animal,[52] whilst their gibbon was displayed at the Egyptian Hall, Piccadilly, in 1940, such was its novelty.[53]

The popularity of zoological curiosities engendered a steady stream of novelties flowing into the Gardens. The first two-toed sloth ever displayed in the country was received to great acclaim in 1850[54] and, in 1858, the General Committee stated that it 'will lose no opportunity of adding to it any novelty the funds at their disposal will enable them to acquire'.[55] Two years later the Society entered into discussions to acquire a hippopotamus for exhibition, possibly influenced by the popularity of the famous hippopotamus, Obaysch, at the London Zoo in the early 1850s. Whilst the logistics of its accommodation were discussed, however, no hippopotamus ever arrived.[56]

Values attached to such novel and especially popular 'star' creatures frequently far surpassed those ascribed to other members of the collection. The wartime plight of the Zoo's popular gorilla, Alfred, for instance, illustrates this point. Acquired from the Belgian Congo in 1930, Alfred spent eighteen years at the Zoo. At the outbreak of World War Two, the Society's polar bears were shot and the big cats and an elephant deposited with other collections in order to preserve public safety.[57] The exhibition of Alfred, however, despite the equal danger he might pose in the event of escape, was maintained and it was decided that he should not 'under any circumstances' be shot, unless he became an *imminent* danger to the public.[58] In

---

50. 'Meeting, 2 Nov. 1864', (BCWEZS/BZG/1/1/4), p. 167.

51. *Catalogue of Animals*, pp. 33–4.

52. 'Meeting, 18 Jul. 1838', (BCWEZS/BZG/1/1/1), p. 173.

53. 'The Ungka Puti', *The Standard*, 27 Jul. 1840.

54. 'Zoological Curiosity', *The Bradford Observer*, 10 Oct. 1850.

55. *The 22nd Report of the BCWEZS*, 14 Apr. 1858, p. 8.

56. 'Meeting, 2 May 1860', (BCWEZS/BZG/1/1/3), p. 165.

57. 'Meeting, 20 Sept. 1939', (BCWEZS/BZG/1/1/9), p. 271; 'Meeting, 17 Jul. 1940', (BCWEZS/BZG/1/1/9), p. 303–4; 'Meeting, 22 Feb. 1941', (BCWEZS/BZG/1/1/9), p. 320.

58. 'Meeting, 17 Jul. 1940', (BCWEZS/BZG/1/1/9), p. 302.

176

Andrew J.P. Flack

1935 he was prized as the most valuable animal in the collection at £1,000, reflecting his popularity and the scarcity of the species in zoological collections at the time.[59]

During the 1960s the Zoo had its greatest success in the procurement of novel and commercially lucrative species. The 1961 arrival of okapi, followed by the widely acclaimed acquisition of white tigers, were both major coups for the Zoo, both species rarely seen in European zoos at the time. The pair of tigers, descended from an individual known as Mohan (caught in Govindgarh jungle at Rewa, Madhya Pradesh, India, in 1951) and acquired from the Maharaja of Rewa in 1963 for the significant sum of £6,400 (compared to £1,200 the same year for a normal-coloured Bengal tigress),[60] elicited great enthusiasm and the exceptional nature of the animals was accentuated.[61] The *Bristol Evening Post* contained an advert that year which proclaimed: 'let's go to Bristol Zoo to see the white tigers: the only pair in any zoo in Europe!'[62] Such was the commercial potential of these rarities, considerable efforts were made to advertise their presence in the collection; they were even used to illustrate the Society's 1963 Christmas cards, pointing to their place as the sight of the season.[63]

The exhibition of white tigers boosted visitor numbers from 796,437 in 1962 to 874,263 in 1963 and a record-breaking 894,055 in 1964[64] and they were valued at c. £16,400 per specimen less than a decade later, evidencing the massive commercial viability of the creatures.[65] Indeed, their popularity drove the Zoo to seek to preserve 'the white strain' through managed breeding, securing a self-propagating supply.[66] The Zoo and the public, through commercial interaction, perpetuated the high value assigned to these unusual animals.

The extreme popularity of novel creatures was often fleeting, however, and so 'new' specimens were sought regularly to fuel the appetite for the strange. Animals once deemed to be exotic curios often lost their novelty as they emerged from the shadows and were culturally assimilated through prolonged exposure. The oft-neglected history of dogs at the Zoo illustrates this phenomenon of increasing familiarity and fading 'otherness'. From the Zoo's early years, Labradors, St Ber-

---

59. 'BCWEZS Valuation of Livestock as at 30 September 1935', in (BCWEZS/BZG/2/2/a).
60. 'Meeting, 8 Apr. 1963', (BCWEZS/BZG/1/1/11), p. 249.
61. 'Correspondence from J S. Young, President of BCWEZS to the Duke of Beaufort', 1 Jul. 1963. In (BCWEZS/BZG/1/13/J).
62. 'Advert: Bristol Zoo', *Bristol Evening Post*, 2 April 1964.
63. 'Meeting, 8 Jul. 1963', (BCWEZS/BZG/1/1/11), p. 260; 'Meeting, 9 Sept. 1963', (BCWEZS/BZG/1/1/11), p. 265; 'White Tiger Christmas card', 1963, in (BCWEZS/BZG/9/6/19).
64. *127th AR/BCWEZS*, 27 Apr. 1963, p. 4; *128th AR/BCWEZS*, 26 Apr. 1964. p. 4; *129th AR/BCWEZS*, 7 Apr. 1965, p. 4.
65. 'Meeting, 28 Apr. 1971', (BCWEZS/BZG/1/3/A), p. 65; 'The Defeat of the White Tiger Hunters', *Western Daily Press*, 1 Jul. 1971; 'Meeting, 30 Jun. 1971', (BCWEZS/BZG/1/3/A), p. 68.
66. *136th AR/BCWEZS*, 19 Apr. l 1972. p. 5.

nards and Alaskan hunting dogs (Huskies), considered in the twenty-first century to be familiar domesticated animals, were kept as part of the Zoo's exhibition of the world's wildlife. By the twentieth century, however, they had been largely integrated into British culture and in 1950 the last dogs (other than grey wolves) to be held at the Zoo, a number of huskies, were removed. [67] Their otherness had faded, they were exotic novelties no longer and so they disappeared even from the Zoo's representative collection of wildlife. The fading of exotic allure is also evident in the plight of Obaysch at the London Zoo between 1850 and 1878 who, after a year or so, lost his elevated attraction value as visitors ceased to be especially amused by him. [68] The exotic essence of some of these star animals was thus often impermanent. For their initial popularity, however, they were placed momentarily on pedestals in the collection.

Variations: Age, Sex, Perfection

Diverse animal values, however, were not simply influenced by species. They were often complicated by age, sex and aesthetic perfection, which could greatly affect commercial appeal. Young animals were especially popular with the Zoo's visitors and so the Society went to great lengths to acquire animals that could whet this appetite. In 1854 it was reported that:

> the public will learn with interest that the attractions to these gardens are considerably increased, from the circumstance that the young lion cubs, with which Madam Juno lately presented her liege lord, are now on view every day between the hours of 3 & 4 o'clock. The exhibition of these graceful creatures will doubtless largely increase the numbers of visitors. [69]

So great was the Zoo's experience of public excitement upon the event of a new birth that in 1904 the Society explicitly stated that 'we are hoping, of course, for favours to come, and if they should assume the shape of young tigers, a baby elephant or a polar bear cub, they will prove very especially acceptable'. [70]

In 1934, 10,000 visitors came to the public debut of Adam, the first chimpanzee to be born in captivity in the United Kingdom. [71] Indeed, visitor attendance frequently spiked when there were young animals on view in the Gardens. A record 891,953 people came to see the new polar bear cub, Sebastian, when he was born in 1959 (up from 708,448 in 1957) and 937,150 made it to the Zoo during 1971

---

67. *Catalogue of Animals*, p. 20; 'Meeting, 5 Jun. 1867', (BCWEZS/BZG/1/1/5), p. 23; 'Meeting, 13 Mar. 1950', (BCWEZS/BZG/1/1/10), p. 172.
68. Nina J. Root, 'Victorian England's Hippomania', *Natural History* 2 (1993): 34–9.
69. 'Zoological Gardens', *Clifton Chronicle and Directory*, 15 Mar. 1854.
70. *68th AR/BCWEZS*, 13 Apr. 1904. p. 4.
71. 'Thousands call on Adam the chimp – he fascinates women', *News Chronicle*, 7 Aug.1934.

(8.9 per cent higher than the previous year) when young polar bears and great apes were on show, a figure which fell by 50,000 the following year when there were no new-borns on show.[72] Incidentally, the highest attendance coinciding with a new birth was in 1966. A polar bear cub attracted over 1,100,000 visitors to the Zoo that year. However, this was also the year of the opening of the first Severn crossing, allowing increased visitation from those living in South Wales. The high attendance figure is thus likely to have been influenced by both changes in the infrastructure of visitation and the enhanced nature of the collection.[73]

The animals situated at the very top of the Zoo's most-wanted list were young versions of the Zoo's most commercially lucrative animals. Such was the potential commercial power of creatures both young *and* rare that £500 was spent on materials advertising the display of white tiger cubs in 1968.[74] The essence the Zoo favoured in young animals was that infantile appearance which Constance L. Russell argues humans are innately attracted to in animals.[75] Successful breeding of popular animals meant that the Society could equally ensure the continued supply of young animals to encourage visitors to pay their entrance feels, as well as to fill vacancies in the collection as they arose without the need to part with too much money. Moreover, successful breeding created duplicate stock which might then be sold into the wild animal trade for profit. Indeed, the minute books of the Society contain records of a vast number of financial exchanges, many of which feature the sale of young animals to other zoos, circuses and private individuals.

The central position of young animals in the Zoo's commercial activities necessarily attached high value to animals that would be most likely to produce offspring. Fertile females were high on the Zoo's shopping list. In 1859 a 'fresh' lioness, a jaguar and leopards were sought to replace the old specimens. It was hoped that these newer individuals would have a better chance of producing cubs.[76] Later, a female polar bear was specifically requested from animal dealer George Chapman when he offered to procure a twelve-month-old specimen for £75 in 1927.[77] On this occasion, the age and sex of the animal made for an especially lucrative animal asset: a creature ripe for breeding and the production of cute and cuddly commodities for display. The desirability of young animals, however, was dependent on species. Nowhere prior to the 1980s and the advent of a committed

---

72. *123rd Annual Report of BCWEZS*, 17 Mar. 1959. p. 4; *135th AR/BCWEZS*, 19 Apr. 1971. p. 4; *136th AR/BCWEZS*, 19 Apr. 1972. p. 4; *137th AR/BCWEZS*, 30 Apr. 1973. p. 4.
73. 'Attendances and Corresponding Animal Events, 1954–72', in (BCWEZS/BZG/3/4/J).
74. 'Meeting, 8 Jul. 1968', (BCWEZS/BZG/1/1/13), p. 21.
75. Constance L. Russell, 'The Social Construction of Orangutans: An Ecotourist Experience', *Society and Animals* (1995) **3**/2 (1995): 163.
76. 'Meeting, 10 Oct. 1859', (BCWEZS/BZG/1/1/3), pp. 132–3.
77. 'Meeting, 7 Dec. 1927', (BCWEZS/BZG/1/1/8), p. 241.

conservation policy do we find a commercial determination to produce offspring of the less popular animals.

The worth of these variously valued commodities, however, relied, for much of the period, on aesthetic perfection. The Zoo's collection was supposed to contain textbook species representatives. Florence Grinfield recounts how people arriving at the Zoo in the late nineteenth century were expecting to encounter fleshy manifestations of creatures directly identifiable from the two-dimensional images they had devoured in books.[78] Indeed, a representative collection of specimens implied the presence of animals which best epitomised their species. This, combined with some concern for animal welfare, led to the slaughter or sale of animals which deviated from the expected aesthetic form.

Throughout the period, animals born with significant deformity or older, diseased creatures were sometimes killed but more frequently sold or exchanged. In 1870, a litter of tiger cubs were born with deformities and it was stated that if at all possible, rather than being kept, these creatures ought to be sold rather than killed.[79] A litter of tiger cubs, as we have seen, is a valuable commodity when in a state of 'perfection' and the Zoo clearly sought to cash in some of that latent value even if in the form of physically damaged specimens. Instances of the receipt of damaged animals, too, reveal the import of aesthetic perfection. In 1961 a clouded leopard was provided by the Dutch dealer, Frans van den Brink. Zoo Superintendent Reginald Greed stated that the leopard was 'not a good specimen' since it had a bald patch on its head and was infested with parasites. The animate asset was defective and it was agreed that a new animal would be supplied. [80]

Thus, the Zoo was no sanctuary where animals could reside regardless of their physical state. They were required to be perfect specimens representative of their species from a scientific perspective and capable of providing exquisite spectacle. The diverse valuations attached to exotic animals during the period are reflective of imperatives rooted in science and the provision of entertainment sufficiently engaging repeatedly to draw the paying public to the Gardens.

Nutritional Value

The acquisition of animals for display, however, was not the sole commodity dynamic at work within the Zoo. The conversion of display animals into animals of sustenance and the fleeting appearance of domestic beasts destined for carnivorous consump-

78. Grinfield, *Our Clifton Zoo*, p. 15.

79. 'Meeting, 7 Dec. 1870', (BCWEZS/BZG/1/1/5), p. 137.

80. 'Meeting, 9 Jan. 1961', (BCWEZS/BZG/1/1/11), p. 171; 'Meeting, 13 Feb. 1961', (BCWEZS/BZG/1/1/11), p. 173.

tion rather than display deserves attention that scholarship has thus far denied. Very few zoo histories relate this aspect of the operation of zoological gardens.[81]

Aged animals, as well as some in duplicate, were sometimes sacrificed for the benefit of the more exotic creatures in the collection, their values transferred. In 1839, for instance, the 'little old' Zebu was butchered and fed to the carnivores[82] and in 1851 the Society, being overstocked with African sheep, slaughtered one to serve up as dinner.[83] In 1860, extra nourishment was required for the Zoo's newly acquired polar bear, necessitating the killing of two or three animals not good enough to sell.[84] The most recent example of such feeding practices was in July 1940 when two Barbary sheep were fed to the young tigers and pumas.[85] Old animals could be disposed of because, like diseased or deformed creatures, they were not pristine specimens. In their imperfect condition they could more easily be sacrificed for the preservation of creatures more valuable in terms of science and spectacle, whilst duplicates could equally be disposed of because the Society did not *need* to have multiples of the same species in their 'representative' collection. Transformed from creatures of science and spectacle into animals of sustenance, these animals were of distinct, sometimes implicitly less, value compared to in the collection.

Exploiting local networks, the Zoo was also able to acquire domestic animals in order to sustain its core collection. Whole animal commodities flowed into the Zoo, not for display, but for dismemberment. In 1853, the first mention of a 'fat horse' donated for this precise purpose can be found in the minute books.[86] By 1859 the Society appears to have been in possession of a purpose-built slaughter yard to the west of the main entrance lodges; a building presumably used for the relatively large-scale slaughter of animals such as horses and cattle: essential commodities in the operation of the Zoo and the continued vitality of the Society's prized animal possessions.[87] The 1896 Annual Report refers to a good supply of 'excellent horse meat' whilst later documents show that horses, in particular, were being collected from localities surrounding Bristol: a 1910 letter suggests that the Zoo had an agreement with a Tom Adams in which they paid to take his horses once they had ceased to serve his purpose as beasts of burden.[88] They were then butchered and fed to the collection's carnivores.

81. See, for instance, Mayumi Itoh, *Japanese Wartime Zoo Policy: The Silent Victims of World War II* (New York: Palgrave Macmillan, 2010) p. 38.

82. 'Meeting, 30 Oct. 1839', (BCWEZS/BZG/1/1/1), p. 221.

83. 'Meeting, 4 Dec. 1851', (BCWEZS/BZG/1/1/2), p. 79.

84. 'Meeting, 5 Oct. 1860', (BCWEZS/BZG/1/1/3), p. 186.

85. 'Meeting, 17 Jul. 1940', (BCWEZS/BZG/1/1/9), p. 302.

86. 'Meeting, 2 Mar. 1853', (BCWEZS/BZG/1/1/2), p. 127.

87. 'Meeting, 10 Mar. 1859', (BCWEZS/BZG/1/1/3), p. 95.

88. *60th Report of the BCWEZS*. 8 Apr. 1896. p. 6; 'Correspondence from Mr Williams to the Zoological Society'. 24 Oct. 1910, in (BCWEZS/BZG/3/2/l).

Science, 'Stars' and Sustenance

Correspondence from the late 1960s and early 1970s shows the expansive nature of these connections and the way in which dead animal commodities flowed into the Zoo for the benefit of the still-living. Mice, chicks, cattle, horses, ponies, cows and goats were secured by the Zoo, from both private individuals and meat wholesalers, so that the collection might have a regular supply of sustenance.[89]

In this way value was assigned to animals, not for any overtly scientific or spectacular purpose, but for the practical supply of foodstuffs in order to preserve the lives and wellbeing of creatures that served a higher anthropocentric purpose: instruction and amusement. Their value, imbued in the nutritional content of their muscular forms, was stripped from their bones and utilised. Only in death, only in the nutrients embedded deeply within their bodies, were they perceived to have value to the Society.

Conclusion

Acquisition at the Zoo was thus no simple affair. Animals as resources were extracted from environments throughout the world and moved through space to the Zoo in order to fulfil diverse commercial and scientific imperatives. Fundamentally these were scientific commodities, received to populate an exhibition that was designed to be instructive. Some animals, however, were clearly valued more than others, because of their species, age, sex or aesthetic appeal, whilst others had nutritional value inherent in their bodies or which was conferred on them in the event of aging or duplication. As objects of desire, animals taking their places at the Zoo, in the small, naked enclosures or on the bloodied floor of the slaughter yard, were not stable signifiers, their value not rooted in a single set of motives. Instead, they were vulnerable to classification and reclassification as objects of value serving diverse anthropocentric ends and revealing much about the place of exotic and domestic animals in the social imagination.

Acknowledgements

This research was supported by the Bristol Conservation and Science Foundation.

REFERENCES

Secondary Sources

Baratay, Eric and Elisabeth Hardouin-Fugier. 2002. *Zoo: A History of Zoological Gardens in the West*. London: Reaktion.

---

89. (BCWEZS/BZG/2/3/G).

Beinart, William. 1990. 'Empire, Hunting and Ecological Change in Southern and Central Africa'. *Past and Present* **128**: 162–86.

Burt, Jonathan. 2001. 'The Illumination of the Animal Kingdom: the Role of Light and Electricity in Animal Representation'. *Society and Animals* **9**/3: 203–28.

Green, Susie. 2008. *Tiger*. London: Reaktion.

Itoh, Mayumi. 2010. *Japanese Wartime Zoo Policy: The Silent Victims of World War II*. New York: Palgrave Macmillan.

Jones, Robert W. 1997. 'The Sight of Creatures Strange to our Clime: London Zoo and the Consumption of the Exotic'. *Journal of Victorian Culture*. **2**/1: 1–26.

MacKenzie, John M. 1988. *The Empire of Nature: Hunting, Conservation and British Imperialism*. Manchester: Manchester University Press.

Mullan, Bob and Garry Marvin. 1999. *Zoo Culture*. Urbana: University of Illinois Press.

Ritvo, Harriet. 1987. *The Animal Estate: The English and other Creatures in the Victorian Age*. Cambridge, Mass.: Harvard University Press.

Ritvo, Harriet. 1996. 'The Order of Nature: Constructing the Collections of Victorian Zoos'. In R. J. Hoage and William. A. Deiss (eds.) *New Worlds, New Animals, From Menagerie to Zoological Park in the Nineteenth Century*. London: John Hopkins University Press. pp. 43–50.

Robbins, Louise. 2002. *Elephant Slaves and Pampered Parrots: Exotic Animals in Eighteenth Century Paris*. London: John Hopkins University Press.

Root, Nina J. 1993. 'Victorian England's Hippomania'. *Natural History*. **2**: 34–9.

Rothfels, Nigel. 2002a. 'Catching Animals'. In Mary J. Henninger-Voss (ed.) *Animals in Human Histories: the Mirror of Nature and Culture*. Rochester, N.Y: University of Rochester Press. pp. 182–228

Rothfels, Nigel. 2002b. *Savages and Beasts: The Birth of the Modern Zoo*. London: John Hopkins University Press.

Russell, Constance L. 1995. 'The Social Construction of Orangutans: An Ecotourist Experience'. *Society and Animals*. **3**/2: 151–70.

Published Primary Sources

'Advert: Bristol Zoo'. *Bristol Evening Post*. 2 April 1964.

'Bad weather monkey deaths'. *The York Herald*. 21 January 1881.

Bristol Zoo Book and Official Guide. 1948, 1954, 1957. Bristol: BCWEZS

Catalogue of the Animals, Birds &c in the Bristol and Clifton Zoological Gardens , with short descriptive notices of their organisation and habits, as well as in a state of nature as in captivity. 1843. Bristol: BCWEZS.

'Death of Polar Bear'. *The Bristol Mercury and Daily Post*. 2 July 1881.

'Defeat of the White Tiger Hunters'. *Western Daily Press*. 1 July 1971.

Grinfield, Florence G. 1894. *Our Clifton Zoo, and the Folks we meet there. A Semi-Comic Description in Prose and Verse*. Weston Super Mare: J. R. Walters & Co., 'Gazette' Office.

Hagenbeck, Carl. 1909. *Beasts and Men: Being Carl Hagenbeck's experiences for half a Century among Wild Animals.* London: Longmans, Green & Co.

Illustrated Official Guide to the Clifton Zoological Gardens. 1894. Bristol: BCWEZS.

Illustrated Official Guide to the Gardens of the BCWEZS. c. 1924–5. Bristol: BCWEZS.

Knocker, Fred W. 1899 and 1904. *Illustrated Official Guide to the Gardens of the BCWEZS.* Bristol: BCWEZS.

'New Polar Bear from Dundee Shipping Agents'. *The Bristol Mercury and Daily Post.* 26 October 1894.

Orwell, George. 1949. *Animal Farm.* London : Secker & Warburg.

Owen, Richard. 1862. 'On the Extent and aims of a National Museum of Natural History (Excerpt)', in Jonah Siegel (ed.) *The Emergence of the Modern Museum: An Anthology of Nineteenth Century Sources.* Oxford: Oxford University Press, 2008. pp. 234–8.

Phillips, J. Le H. 1882. *The Gardens and Menagerie of the BCWEZS.* Bristol: BCWEZS.

'Reputation for Having Big Cats'. *The Bristol Mercury and Daily Post.* 30 July 1894.

'The Talk of Bristol'. *Bristol Mercury and Daily Post.* 5 June 1893.

'The Ungka Puti'. *The Standard.* 27 July1840.

'This Morning's News'. *The Bristol Mercury and Daily Post.* 25 July 1890.

'Thousands call on Adam the chimp – he fascinates women'. *News Chronicle.* 7 August 1934.

Vanderplank, F.L. 1937. *Official Guide to the Gardens and Aquarium of the BCWEZS.* Bristol: BCWEZS.

'Zoological Curiosity'. *The Bradford Observer.* 10 October 1850.

'Zoological Gardens'. *Clifton Chronicle & Directory.* 15 March 1854.

Bristol, Clifton and West of England Zoological Society (BCWEZS) Archive

Proceedings of Meetings of the General Committee (PMGA)

Proceedings of Meetings of the General Committee and the Finance Committee (PMGCFC)

The 1st to 145th Annual Report of the BCWEZS (AR/BCWEZS) (1836–1981). Bristol: BCWEZS.

BCWEZS PMGA (22 July 1835–12 April 1854), (BCWEZS/SOC/3/2/1).

BCWEZS PMGA (13 April 1836–4 October 1848), (BCWEZS/BZG/1/1/1).

BCWEZS Proceedings of Meetings of the Special and later General Committee (7 May 1836–2 April 1856), (BCWEZS/BZG/1/1/2).

BCWEZS PMGA (16 April 1856–5 June 1861), (BCWEZS/BZG/1/1/3).

BCWEZS PMGA (5 June 1861–5 September 1866), (BCWEZS/BZG/1/1/4).

BCWEZS PMGCFC (3 October 1866–8 September 1880), (BCWEZS/BZG/1/1/5).

BCWEZS PMGCFC (10 November 1880–23 March 1893), (BCWEZS/BZG/1/1/6).

BCWEZS PMGA (12 April 1893–6 December 1911), (BCWEZS/BZG/1/1/7).

BCWEZS PMGA (3 January 1912–3 December 1930), (BCWEZS/BZG/1/1/8).

Andrew J.P. Flack

BCWEZS Proceedings of the Meetings of the Animal Sub-committee (27 September 1967–28 December 1977), (BCWEZS/BZG/1/3/A).

BCWEZS Proceedings of the Meetings of the Animal Sub-committee (7 January 1931–25 July 1944), (BCWEZS/BZG/1/1/9).

BCWEZS Proceedings of General Committee and Executive Committee Meetings (29 August 1944–9 January 1956), (BCWEZS/BZG/1/1/10).

BCWEZS Council Minute Book (13 February 1956–14 February 1966*)*, (BCWEZS/BZG/1/1/11).

BCWEZS Council Minute Book (14 March 1966–14 August 1967*)*, (BCWEZS/BZG/1/1/12).

BCWEZS Council Minute Book (11 September 1967–12 December 1983), (BCWEZS/BZG/1/1/13).

J.S. Young, President of the Council, Correspondence (1 July 1963–12 January 1967) (BCWEZS/BZG/1/1/B).

Accounts of the BCWEZS, 1923–50, (BCWEZS/BZG/2/1/a).

Animal Stock List, with purchase price and valuations, 1935–7 (BCWEZS/BZG/2/2/a).

Ledger of accounts with butchers buying horses and cows, 27 July 1967–22 October 1979 (BCWEZS/BZG/2/3/G).

Correspondence about Animals and Offers from the General Public, 29 October 1910–29 December 1912, (BCWEZS/BZG/3/2/l).

Miscellaneous Papers of Reginald Greed, 1954–1973 (BCWEZS/BZG/3/4/J).

BZG Annual Stock Inventory (2010) (BCWEZS/BZG/6/1/Z).

Correspondence relating to acquisition of animals from Tyseley pet stores ltd (11 June 1959–10 October 1978) (BCWEZS/BZG/6/4/I).

BCWEZS Christmas Cards (c. 1963) (BCWEZS/BZG/9/6/19).

Chapter 8

From Poetry to Politics: The Romantic Roots of the 'German Forest'

Johannes Zechner

This chapter explores the interplay between real and imagined landscapes by focusing on German forest imaginations in the first half of the nineteenth century. Against the backdrop of the French Revolution, prominent men of letters inscribed the silvicultural realm with cultural and political meanings based on selective readings of ancient and early modern sources. 'German Forest' and 'German Oak' as organic allegories of collective identity grew to epitomise the imagined nature of the nation versus societal and spatial fragmentation. Following the mostly poetic evocation of *Waldeinsamkeit* by Ludwig Tieck and Joseph von Eichendorff's forests of freedom, the Grimm Brothers' fairy tales glorified the woods as a Germanic treasure of the past. Subsequently, patriotic writers like Ernst Moritz Arndt propagated them as a native symbol of continuity and sovereignty. Sylvan wilderness was thus progressively domesticated to serve as a seemingly natural cipher for national distinctiveness.

Prelude: Romans in the German Forest

Once upon a time, there were unending Germanic forests. Or at least that was the admittedly Mediterranean perspective of the Roman commander, statesman and writer Gaius Julius Caesar (c. 100–44 BCE) when he wrote his famous *De bello Gallico* (c. 52/51 BCE). According to his sources, the 'Hercynian forests'[1] were so large that pedestrians needed nine days of vigorous walking to get across. Another nameless forest on the eastern side of the Rhine river could not be traversed in two months; no one knew where it ended.[2] In these virtually impenetrable dark woodlands, the belligerent Germanic tribes lived an accordingly chaste and frugal life based on hunting in place of organised agriculture.[3] Caesar – or a later inter-

---

1. Gaius Julius Caesar, *De bello Gallico* [c. 51/52 BCE] (Munich and Zurich: Artemis, 1990) 6.25, p. 288.

2. Ibid. 6.25, p. 289.

3. Wolfgang Maria Zeitler, 'Zum Germanenbegriff Caesars: Der Germanenexkurs im sechsten Buch von Caesars "Bellum Gallicum"', in Heinrich Beck (ed.) *Germanenprobleme in heutiger Sicht* (Berlin and New York: Gruyter, 1986) pp. 41–53.

polator – portrayed a mixture of strange wild creatures very different from the more arcadian animals of the Italian peninsula:[4] a kind of unicorn with one large branched horn, an elk-like species without knee joints leaning upright on trees to sleep and a ferocious aurochs about the size of an elephant.[5] Some 150 years later, another Roman statesman and writer returned to the topic in his work *Germania* (c. 98 CE) without ever having been close to the area.[6] Publius Cornelius Tacitus (c. 55–c. 120 CE) nonetheless described the Germanic territories – with far more disgust than awe – as comprising 'either grim forests or hideous morasses', among them once more a Hercynian forest.[7] He deduced the martial appearance and the ethnic homogeneity of the fair-haired and blue-eyed warriors from the rough climate and environment in which they had their indigenous origin.[8] These children of nature were said to be living amid the woods in preference to a metropolitan city like Rome and worshipping their age-old gods within a 'sacred forest' in lieu of a temple built of stone.[9] In another book entitled *Annales* (c. 110–120 CE), Tacitus wrote again about the 'obscure forests' of the North that were so different from the man-made pastoral landscapes of home. More importantly, he relayed the story of the soon-legendary battle of the 'Teutoburg forest' in the year 9 CE, a skirmish of Germanic tribes against Roman troops not familiar with the treacherous woodlands and swamplands of the area. He went on to call the Cheruscan leader Arminius, or Hermann, 'without doubt the liberator of Germania'.[10] Later on this leader came to be better known as Herman the German, the popular paragon of a literary hero.[11]

After the rediscovery of Tacitus' *Germania* in 1455, proto-nationalist humanists like Conrad Celtis (1459–1508) began to locate the prehistoric origins of the Germanic-German people in the Hercynian and/or Teutoburg forest.[12] Such an *interpretatio silvana* of Caesar's and Tacitus' works always quoted the same few

---

4. Caesar, *De bello Gallico*, 6.25–8, pp. 289–291.

5. Walter Woodburn Hyde, 'The Curious Animals of the Hercynian Forest'. *The Classical Journal* 13/4 (1918): 231–245.

6. Christopher B. Krebs, *A Most Dangerous Book: Tacitus' 'Germania' from the Roman Empire to the Third Reich* (New York and London: Norton, 2011); Simon Schama, *Landscape and Memory* [1995] (London: Fontana, 1996) pp. 81–91.

7. Publius Cornelius Tacitus. *Germania* [c. 98 CE], in Tacitus, *Agricola–Germania*. (Munich and Zurich: Artemis & Winkler, 1991) pp. 78–135, 5, p. 82; 30, p. 112.

8. Eduard Norden, *Die germanische Urgeschichte in Tacitus 'Germania'* (Berlin and Leipzig: Teubner, 1920).

9. Tacitus, *Germania*, 39, p. 122.

10. Publius Cornelius Tacitus, *Annales* [c. 110–120 CE]. 5th edn. (Düsseldorf: Artemis & Winkler, 2005) 1.50, p. 74; 1.60, p. 86; 2.88, p. 202.

11. Richard Kuehnemund, *Arminius or the Rise of a National Symbol in Literature: From Hutten to Grabbe* [1953] (New York: AMS, 1966).

12. Gernot Michael Müller, *Die 'Germania generalis' des Conrad Celtis: Studien mit Edition, Übersetzung und Kommentar* (Tübingen: Niemeyer, 2001); Schama, *Landscape*, pp. 91–100.

From Poetry to Politics

Figure 1. Return of the Germans from the battle in the Teutoburg Forest.
Paul Thumann, before 1883. Source: Wikicommons. http://commons.wikimedia.org/wiki/
File:Glaspalast_München_1883_085.jpg

passages but did so *ad nauseam* and without questioning their degree of reality. Ironically enough, only Roman sources were available to lay the foundation of German national identity in texts often written in Latin, as the then-language of scholars. About three centuries later, the poet Friedrich Gottlieb Klopstock (1724–1803) added a new layer of sylvan meaning through the veneration of one particular tree species.[13] His odes enthusiastically revered the oak and its leaves, which he claimed to be more authentic for genuinely German poetry than the traditional Greek laurel.[14] In his play *Herman's Battle* (1769), Klopstock described the Cheruscan warriors to be 'enrooted like the oak' and equated the fatherland with 'the tallest, eldest, most sacred oak' of the grove.[15] As a result, several discursive nexuses between natural woodlands, patriotic emancipation and national identity were already in place when

---

13. Harro Zimmermann, *Freiheit und Geschichte: F. G. Klopstock als historischer Dichter und Denker* (Heidelberg: Winter, 1987).

14. Friedrich Gottlieb Klopstock, *Oden. Band 1: Text* (Berlin and New York: Gruyter, 2010).

15. Friedrich Gottlieb Klopstock, 'Hermanns Schlacht: Ein Bardiet für die Schaubühne' [1769], in Gottlieb, *Hermann-Dramen. Band 1: Text* (Berlin and New York: Gruyter, 2009). pp. 1–154, p. 30, p. 80; Cäcilia Friedrich, 'Klopstocks Bardiet "Hermanns Schlacht" und seine Nachgeschichte', in Hans-Georg Werner (ed.) *Friedrich Gottlieb Klopstock: Werk und Wirkung* (Berlin: Akademie, 1978). pp. 237–246.

Johannes Zechner

Figure 2. Friedrich Gottlieb Klopstock.

Carte de visite after an engraving (artist unknown, nineteenth century). Source: Wikicommons. http://commons.wikimedia.org/wiki/File:Friedrich_Gottlieb_Klopstock.jpg

From Poetry to Politics

the writers associated with Romanticism entered the stage. While the woodlands of visual and musical imagination would certainly deserve detailed treatment,[16] the following reflections will concentrate on the contemporaneous literary forests.[17] Those were profoundly shaped by the historical context of the French Revolution and its reverberations on the eastern side of the Rhine: primarily the demise of the Holy Roman Empire of the German Nation in 1806, the French occupation or control of most of its territories and the 'Wars of Liberation' from 1813 to 1815 which reclaimed their sovereignty.

Solitude of the Woods: Tieck's Forests of Longing

The early Romantic Ludwig Tieck (1773–1853) was one of the most widely read German authors of his day, on par with the likes of Goethe or Schiller.[18] After fervently supporting the French Revolution in his youth, he developed into a critic of Napoleon's escalating politics of power and a defender of monarchy, stability and tradition. Whereas the majority of his writing was not overtly political, he however became thoroughly interested in national affairs between 1806 and 1815. During those years of enhanced patriotic feelings, Tieck began to rediscover and soon popularise the all but forgotten world of folk legends, songs and tales from the Middle Ages.[19] In that lore he thought to have found the glorious past of the German people, since divided along the lines of dynastic loyalty, political orientation and religious denomination.

Despite Tieck being a city dweller in Berlin and Dresden for most of his life, or perhaps exactly because of it, a great many of his poems, novels, novellas and fairy tales commemorated the woods as a temporary otherworld. To be sure, this adored nature was little more than an emotional projection, a sensualist literary device.[20] Part of an elaborate reference system, it was neither described with realistic precision nor invested with any intrinsic value. For this reason, Tieck's literary forests are usually dark, mysterious and impassable in an almost stereotypical way. Following the older traditions of German nature poetry and Klopstock's role model,

16. Joseph Leo Koerner, *Caspar David Friedrich and the Subject of Landscape* (London: Reaktion, 1990); Ute Jung-Kaiser (ed.)*Der Wald als romantischer Topos* (Bern et al.: Lang, 2008).

17. Wolfgang Baumgart, *Der Wald in der deutschen Dichtung* (Berlin and Leipzig: Gruyter, 1936); Hilda Fondi, *Der deutsche Wald in der deutschen Lyrik* (Wien: Phil. Diss. 1941).

18. Roger Paulin, *Ludwig Tieck: A Literary Biography* (Oxford: Clarendon, 1986); Edwin Hermann Zeydel, *Ludwig Tieck the German Romanticist: A Critical Study* [1935] (Hildesheim and New York: Olms, 1971).

19. Gisela Brinker-Gabler, *Poetisch-wissenschaftliche Mittelalter-Rezeption: Ludwig Tiecks Erneuerung altdeutscher Literatur* (Stuttgart: Kümmerle, 1980).

20. George Henry Danton, *The Nature Sense in the Writings of Ludwig Tieck* [1907] (New York: AMS, 1966); Walter Donat, *Die Landschaft bei Tieck und ihre historischen Voraussetzungen* [1925] (Hildesheim: Gerstenberg, 1973).

linden and oak trees were the most prominent individual species depicted – in stark contrast to the silvicultural reality on the ground, already dominated by large-scale pine and spruce plantations.

Within Tieck's sizeable œuvre, his poems especially evoked his favourite kind of nature as a landscape of yearning. In the ode 'Forest, Garden and Mountain' (1798), he solemnised communion with the harmonious woodlands to achieve peace of mind and human happiness: 'What with all this trepidation? / Shed your little sorrow / Come, come into our green umbrage / Shed all worries and open up your heart for joyfulness'. On the opposite side of the emotional spectrum, the forest also symbolised the grave longing to be alone and die. The 'Lament of the Girl in the Forest' (1816) thus ends on a note of desperation: 'Gardens, mountains, forests vast / Are my tomb and solitude'.[21] In addition, the 'holy temple' of nature operated as a place of poetic initiation and artistic stimulation, of chaste adoration and vigorous passion – an appropriate interim haven for self-doubting artists and forlorn lovers.[22]

Apart from aesthetic or spiritual stylisations, Tieck's imagined forests were also a convenient cypher for an escapist critique of contemporary society. Much like more current imaginations of natural wilderness, they served as a sanctuary in opposition to the stresses and strains of city, family and job life. Probably the sharpest contrast between urban and sylvan life emerges in his epistolary novel *William Lovell* (1793–1796) where he used London as the epitome of an industrial metropolis. The soulless life of the many is rendered in horrendous terms: 'everything is so narrow and sombre, you do not see any field or tree ... this much moved yet dead chaos'. An alluring counter-image is the dream of a modest solitary living close to and in accordance with nature: 'in a little shed on the edge of a lonely forest, forgetting the whole world and being forgotten by her in perpetuity, only acquainted with the earth as far as my eye can look, not found by any human, just greeted by the morning breeze and by the whisper of the bushes'.[23] During the turbulent 'Wars of Liberation', a number of verses reflected on the political and national value of the forest. In the poem 'To a Lover in the Spring of 1814', German trees celebrate the victory over the French like fellow combatants: 'The trees blossom victory and freedom, / Hail Fatherland! sounds / Jubilantly through the greenscapes / Freedom! roars the wood of oak'.[24] A similar message is conveyed in the novella *Summer Journey* (1834), based on autobiographical elements. Here, one of Tieck's protagonists feels the need to proclaim within eyeshot of the venerable Wartburg, surrounded by wooded hills:

21. Ludwig Tieck, *Gedichte: Neue Ausgabe* (Berlin: Reimer, 1841) p. 52, 405.

22. Ludwig Tieck, *Franz Sternbald's Wanderungen: Eine altdeutsche Geschichte* [1798]. (Berlin: Gruyter, 1966[c]) p. 36.

23. Ludwig Tieck, *William Lovell. Erster Theil* [1793/95] (Berlin: Gruyter, 1966[g]) p. 27, 167.

24. Tieck *Gedichte*, p. 428.

Figure 3. Genoveva in the solitude of the forest.

Adrian Ludwig Richter, 1841. Source: Wikicommons. http://commons.wikimedia.org/wiki/
File:Adrian_Ludwig_Richter_013.jpg

The German ... continues to take his peculiar delight in the splendour of the forests; these vistas so enrapturing for us are horrifying for the Italian and the other nations hardly feel this hallowed dread or that ceremonial devout mood that we are seized with in woody mountains or in the lonely dark forest.[25]

25. Ludwig Tieck, 'Eine Sommerreise' [1834], in Tieck, *Ludwig Tieck's gesammelte Novellen. Siebenter Band* (Berlin: Gruyter, 1966[d]) pp. 3–156, pp. 126–7.

Tieck coined the phrase 'solitude of the woods' in his rendering of the won-derbird's song for the literary fairy tale *Eckbert the Blond* (1796): 'Waldeinsamkeit, / You delight me / Tomorrow as today / For all eternity / O how I am rejoiced / Waldeinsamkeit'.[26]

This expression quickly gathered an immense popularity that persists today and ultimately turned into a mere commonplace employed by mostly epigonic writers.[27] Soon, Tieck modified his invention to include 'green solitude', the 'soli-tude of the mountain', the 'solitude of the firs' or the 'solitude of the vale'.[28] How-ever, the fact that sylvan solitude had initially been dangerous and every so often deadly became more and more lost in these adaptations and transformations. In the original story of *Eckbert*, the female protagonist Bertha falls victim to misdeeds she has committed in the forest and her husband dies there after listening to the bird singing its song for the third and final time.

Eventually, Tieck took it upon himself to satirise this arbitrariness by writ-ing his late novella *Solitude of the Woods* (1841). The main protagonist, evocatively named Ferdinand von Linden, is a professed fancier of lonely nature. Reciting the aforesaid song, he plans to persuade his beloved to move into the wild. Yet after a short imprisonment in a forest cabin designed to thwart his wedding, he is immediately cured of his affection for the 'damned and miserable solitude of the woods'.[29] In the unfolding intellectual history of the German Forest, such a (self-) ironic and playful treatment of symbolic nature remained a rare exception from the earnest rule.

Beautiful Land of Oaks: Eichendorff's Forests of Freedom

Although quite a few German Romantics wrote intensely about the forest, it is Joseph von Eichendorff (1788–1857) who is known to this day as the exemplary bard of the German forest.[30]

---

26. Ludwig Tieck, 'Der blonde Eckbert' [1796], in Tieck, *Phantasus. Erster Theil* (Berlin: Gruyter, 1966[b]). pp. 144–169, p. 152.

27. Michael Paul Hammes, *'Waldeinsamkeit': Eine Motiv- und Stiluntersuchung zur Deutschen Früh-romantik, insbesondere zu Ludwig Tieck* (Frankfurt: Phil. Diss, 1933).

28. Ludwig Tieck, 'Der Blaubart: Ein Mährchen in fünf Akten' [1796], in Tieck, *Phantasus. Zweiter Theil* (Berlin: Gruyter, 1966[a]) pp. 7–152, p. 129; Tieck *Gedichte*, p. 293; Ludwig Tieck, 'Der junge Tischlermeister: Novelle in sieben Abschnitten' [1836], in Tieck, *Ludwig Tieck's gesammelte Novellen. Zwölfter Band* (Berlin: Gruyter, 1966[e]) pp. 3–466, p. 23, p. 99.

29. Ludwig Tieck, 'Waldeinsamkeit' [1841], in Tieck, *Gesammelte Novellen. Zehnter Band* (Berlin: Gruyter, 1966[f]) pp. 473–567, p. 536.

30. Günther Schiwy, *Eichendorff: Der Dichter in seiner Zeit. Eine Biographie* (München: Beck, 2000); Hartwig Schultz, *Joseph von Eichendorff: Eine Biographie* (Frankfurt am Main and Leipzig: Insel, 2007).

From Poetry to Politics

Figure 4. Joseph von Eichendorff.
Etching based on a drawing by Franz Kugler,
1832. Source: Wikicommons.
http://commons.wikimedia.org/wiki/
File:Eichendorff.jpg?uselang=de

The Silesian nobleman, faithful Catholic and Prussian civil servant was born too late to have experienced the French Revolution directly. Nevertheless, he strongly criticised abrupt changes in society and politics while backing reforms within the limits of the venerated tradition.[31] Eichendorff's developing national sentiment was defined by the historical contexts, namely the French control of German-speaking territories and the fragmentation of the former empire into several hundred political entities.[32] In 1810, he began to write a never-finished drama about Herman the German and his wife Thusnelda for which he read comprehensively on Germanic history.[33] Three years later, he volunteered to participate in the fight against Napoleon, but for logistic reasons never saw actual combat.

Having grown up on a rural estate, he found his professional life took him predominantly to cities like Berlin, Breslau and Königsberg. His nature writing might have been a spiritual compensation for a lost childhood as well as an antidote against urban tediousness.[34] These texts deserve special attention less because of

---

31. Peter Krüger, 'Eichendorffs politisches Denken. Teil 1'. *Aurora* **28** (1968): 7–32; Peter Krüger, 'Eichendorffs politisches Denken. Teil 2'. *Aurora* **29** (1969): 50–69.

32. Manfred Häckel, 'Der patriotische Gedanke im Frühwerk Joseph von Eichendorffs', in Heinrich Scheel (ed.) *Das Jahr 1813: Studien zur Geschichte und Wirkung der Befreiungskriege* (Berlin: Akademie, 1963) pp. 177–205.

33. Joseph von Eichendorff, 'Herrmann und Thusnelda' [1811/12], in Eichendorff, *Historische Dramen und Dramenfragmente: Text und Varianten* (Tübingen: Niemeyer, 1996) pp. 39–65.

34. Alexander von Bormann, *Natura loquitur: Naturpoesie und emblematische Formel bei Joseph von Eichendorff* (Tübingen: Niemeyer, 1968); Joachim Heidenreich, *Natura delectat: Zur Tradition des locus amoenus bei Eichendorff* (Konstanz: Hartung-Gorre, 1985).

the well-known multitude of their forest associations than for their little-known diversity. His literary woodlands were codes in a complex system of religious and spiritual symbols that formed an indeterminate landscape of sensibility. Therefore, we do not get any information on the concrete location or the types of trees growing in these German forests. Certain atmospheric adjectives like merry and green or dark and eerie are repeatedly – and all but formulaically – applied to create a moodscape of either enticement or intimidation. And unlike Tieck's forests of poetry, Eichendorff's are imbued with singing wanderers or chirping birds instead of being tranquil echo chambers of the human soul.

Prevailing in the public memory are idylls of joy and delight, eloquently celebrating God's creation and revelation. Eichendorff, as a sensitive artist, saw himself capable of deciphering these meanings and thus praising the forests. Take for example his popular poem 'The Hunters' Farewell' (1810), which – after being set to music in 1841 – quickly became a favourite piece of male choral societies: 'Who has you, you fine forest, / Built there that high up / I will well praise the master / As long as my voice is ringing out / Farewell, farewell, you fine forest!' Besides sylvan harmonies, Eichendorff wrote much less idyllic – and today nearly forgotten – poems which oscillate between sublime shiver and demonic terror. In 'Forest Conversation' (1812), the men-eating Loreley has climbed down from her usual rock overseeing the river Rhine in order to go hunting in the woods. Her sinister last words 'You will nevermore get out of this forest!' elicit precisely the opposite of a cheerful wayfaring experience and characterise Eichendorff as more than just a naive idoliser of nature.[35]

Other poems presented the wild woods as an appealing alternative to the dull order of bourgeois life and the domesticated nature of the garden. The wistful bard of 'Farewell' (1810) seeks to flee to the forests forever, but is sooner or later bound to come back to the modern life with its domestic, familial and occupational duties: 'O vast vales, O hills / O fine, green forest, / For my delights and sorrows / You are the rapt refuge! / Out there, ever scorned, / Whirls the bustling world, / Once more wrap your boughs / Around me, you green tent!' With the semantic juxtaposition of *Wald* for forest versus *Welt* for world, the poeticised nature of the woods became a hoped-for retreat from the impositions of city, society and polity. In a related poem called 'The Renouncing One' (1838), Eichendorff cited Tieck's already well-known neologism: 'Waldeinsamkeit! / You green preserve, / How far away lies / The World from here!'[36] Eichendorff's *Zeitlieder*, or contemporary songs, from the years of the anti-Napoleonic wars were political in the more narrow sense of the word. These verses clearly exceeded mental discontent with the middle class existence of a bureaucrat or diffuse social criticism by a disenchanted nobleman

---

35. Joseph von Eichendorff, *Gedichte. Erster Teil: Text* (Stuttgart et al.: Kohlhammer, 1993) p. 150, p. 367.

36. Ibid. p. 34, p. 314.

forced to earn his living. In those agitated days, the forests stood as a powerful symbol for the reputedly natural characteristics of stability and immutability which were lacking in the German-speaking territories.[37] The shielding collective of trees as a model for the nation becomes manifest in 'The Vigil of the Tyroleans' (1810): 'Just like the trunks in the forest / We want to cohere, / A solid castle, defence against force, / The old ones staunchly endure'.[38] By using the motif of natural cohesion, the poet contrasted the reality of social conflict and political discord with the vision of fraternal community and harmonious concord.

In 'The Hunters' Farewell' already quoted above, Eichendorff also declared the forest to be the 'streaming and rustling German Banner' of a wooden and leafy nation.[39] His late work 'Liberta's Lament' (1850) glorified an immortal 'German forest' of freedom, loyalty and virtue as a potent allegory of resistance and survival. Constructing an emotional and symbolic topography, the same poem then exploited an imagined 'beautiful land of oaks' to advance the unfulfilled unity of the nation.[40] The ode 'To the Most' (1810) called upon the compatriots to refuel their endangered self-assurance by looking for moral advice and assistance from nature: 'And a new generation will be invigorated / By this forest for German deeds'.[41] Along these expressly patriotic and occasionally nationalist lines, the woods were supposed to bridge the levels of the past, the present and the future.

To mark the end of the Napoleonic occupation as the proud reclamation of natural and national sovereignty alike, Eichendorff's poem 'To the Friends' (1814) has the forests, mountains and rivers liberated together with the people: 'God released the roar held back for long / Of the rivers around – and the Rhine is ours! / On free mountains may the German dwell/ And he can anew call his forests his own.'[42] Even though such a pointed instrumentalisation of nature equally contravened biology and history, similar sylvapatriotic efforts would be undertaken by fellow intellectuals evermore.

Old German Woodland Cult: The Grimms' Forests of Yesteryear

Jacob (1785–1863) and Wilhelm Grimm (1786–1859) ranked among the most productive and influential philologists of their generation and helped to establish

37. Klaus Lindemann, '"Deutsch Panier, das rauschend wallt": Der Wald in Eichendorffs patriotischen Gedichten im Kontext der Lyrik der Befreiungskriege', in Hans-Georg Pott (ed.) *Eichendorff und die Spätromantik* (Paderborn et al.: Sch.ningh) pp. 91–130..

38. Eichendorff, *Erster Teil*, p.148.

39. Ibid. p. 151.

40. Joseph von Eichendorff, *Gedichte. Zweiter Teil: Verstreute und nachgelassene Gedichte. Text* (Tübingen: Niemeyer, 1997) p. 4.

41. Eichendorff, *Erster Teil*, p. 150.

42. Eichendorff, *Zweiter Teil*, p. 49.

the discipline of *Germanistik* or German Studies.[43] In their view, language and literature were powerful factors of cultural cohesion in the midst of confessional strife, political upheaval and territorial disintegration.[44] During the French occupation of their homeland Hesse, they took mental and patriotic strength from focusing on the recovery and rescue of medieval and early modern German texts from oblivion. Moreover, the brothers personally supported the Prussian-led 'Wars of Liberation' by donating subscription money from one of their source editions to the needs of military volunteers.[45] They relied on a magnificent Germanic past to overcome a sobering German present by studying prehistoric mythology and its assumed reverberations in more contemporary fables and legends.[46] To aid that cause, Wilhelm visited the presumed site of the Battle of the Teutoburg Forest as recorded by the Roman writers.[47] Jacob re-published what he called Tacitus' 'immortal work on Germany' for the use of his students and the interested public.[48] Later in their careers, both lost their Göttingen professorships for political reasons and Jacob was voted into the first German parliament in 1848 proposing freedom rights and the annulment of nobility.

For the Grimms, who spent most of their adult lives in residential or university cities, abundant forests of fairy tale and legend, of myth and metaphor soon became the central symbol of folk culture, collective character and organic solidity.[49] Faithful to the sylvan epics of the Middle Ages,[50] the enchanted woods were depicted mostly as bleak and gloomy transitional spheres of imminence and defiance as well as numinous spaces opposed to the domain of ordinary life. These

43. Steffen Martus, *Die Brüder Grimm: Eine Biographie* (Berlin: Rowohlt, 2009); Murray B. Peppard, Murray *Paths through the Forest: A Biography of the Brothers Grimm* (New York et al.: Holt, Rinehart and Winston, 1971).

44. Roland Feldmann, *Jacob Grimm und die Politik* (Kassel: Bärenreiter, 1970).

45. Wilhelm Grimm [with Jacob Grimm], 'Vorrede zum "Armen Heinrich"' [1815], in W. Grimm, *Kleinere Schriften. Zweiter Band* (Berlin: Dümmler, 1882) p. 505.

46. Beate Kellner, *Grimms Mythen: Studien zum Mythosbegriff und seiner Anwendung in Jacob Grimms 'Deutscher Mythologie'* (Frankfurt am Main et al.: Lang, 1994).

47. Wilhelm Grimm, 'Teutoberg' [1817], in W. Grimm, *Kleinere Schriften. Erster Band* (Berlin: Dümmler, 1881[a]), p. 559.

48. Jacob Grimm 'Anzeige der "Deutsche Mythologie"' [1835], in J. Grimm, *Kleinere Schriften. Band 5: Recensionen und vermischte Aufsätze. Band 2* (Berlin: Dümmler, 1871) pp. 198–202, p. 199; Jacob Grimm (ed.) *Taciti 'Germania': Edidit et quae ad res Germanorum pertinere videntur e reliquo Tacitino opere excerpsit* (Göttingen: Dieterich, 1835[b]).

49. Robert Pogue Harrison, *Forests: The Shadow of Civilization* [1992] (Chicago and London: University of Chicago Press, 1993) pp. 164–177; Dore Rebholz, *Der Wald im deutschen Märchen: Das Erlebnis als Grundlage für die Auffassung des Waldes, seine Darstellung und Rolle im deutschen Märchen* (Heidelberg: Phil. Diss. 1944); Schama, *Landscape*, pp. 106–7; Jack Zipes, *The Brothers Grimm: From Enchanted Forests to the Modern World* (New York and London: Routledge, 1988).

50. Marianne Stauffer, *Der Wald. Zur Darstellung und Deutung der Natur im Mittelalter* (Zurich: Juris, 1958).

were in no sense empty and lonely; on the contrary, they were populated by a diverse ensemble of talking animals and dangerous bandits, perilous drakes and helpful dwarfs, violent giants and bewitched princes, evil sorceresses and many more figures. Whilst both brothers endeavoured tirelessly to base the Romantic search for the criteria of national identity on more scholarly principles, most of Wilhelm's publications stayed in the boundaries of poetry, compared with the more openly political writings of Jacob.

Most influential within the Grimms' body of work – and a bestseller to this day – are the *Children's and Household Tales*, collected and compiled over a period of four decades in a constant procedure of amending and revising. In his foreword from 1812, Wilhelm mentioned 'forests in their tranquillity' to be some of the last refuges for the 'purely German' tales which were on the brink of extinction by an encroaching modern world. He asserted that this archaic lore had especially survived in 'venerable areas of German liberty' like the Paderborn region close to the Teutoburg forest. Additionally, he praised the sublime 'solitude of the forest' prevalent in the stories supposedly told by charcoal burners, peasants and spinners.[51] The second edition of 1819 contained a scholarly introduction in which Wilhelm marvelled: 'what an enticement resides in this hidden forest life which sure enough every natural human once yearned for!'[52] In the seventh edition of 1857 – the last one during their lifetimes – 96 of the 200 tales incorporated the woods as agent, arena or allusion and at least three of these fairy forests had been inserted later on to dramatise formerly woodless stories.[53] The 1857 version of *Fitcher's Bird* for instance features a murderous master warlock who kidnaps beautiful young women and brings them to his house in the middle of a 'gloomy forest'. These sylvan surroundings of evil had not yet been mentioned in 1812.[54] When Wilhelm took charge of the fairy tales from 1819 onwards, more portentous adjectives like dark, opaque or wild accentuated primordial otherworldliness against an increasingly industrial forestry. Take the famous first tale *The Frog Prince or Iron Henry*, opening with a princess sitting at a well and playing with her gold ball. In the 1812 version, the scene is placed in a non-descript 'forest' which in 1857 had turned 'large and dark'.

51. Wilhelm Grimm, 'Vorrede zu den "Kinder- und Hausmärchen" [1812/1815] in W. Grimm, *Kleinere Schriften. Erster Band* (Berlin: Dümmler, 1881[b]) pp. 320–332, p. 320, p. 332, p. 329, p. 322.

52. Wilhelm Grimm, 'Über das Wesen der Märchen' [1819], in W. Grimm, *Kleinere Schriften. Erster Band* (1881[c]) pp. 333–358, p. 334.

53. Hisako Ono, 'Waldsymbolik bei den Brüdern Grimm', *Fabula* 48/1–2 (2007): 73–84, 75.

54. Jacob and Wilhelm Grimm (eds.) *Kinder- und Hausmärchen gesammelt durch die Brüder Grimm: Große Ausgabe. Erster Band* [1812], 7th edn. (Göttingen: Dieterich, 1857[a]) p. 228; Jacob and Wilhelm Grimm (eds.) *Kinder- und Hausmärchen gesammelt durch die Brüder Grimm: Vergrößerter Nachdruck der Erstausgabe* [1812/15] (Göttingen: Vandenhoeck & Ruprecht, 1986) pp. 200–3.

Johannes Zechner

Figure 5. The Three Little Men in the Wood.

Illustration for an edition of the *Children's and Household Tales* (Hermann Vogel, around 1900). Source: Wikicommons.http://commons.wikimedia.org/wiki/File:Hermann_Vogel-The_Three_Little_Men_in_the_Wood.jpg?uselang=de

Moreover, an 'old linden tree' had been added, a tree of great cultural significance in the German literary tradition.[55]

Three of the tales feature the forest in their title: *The Old Woman in the Wood* tells the story of a witch transforming a handsome king's son into a tree, who is luckily saved by a daring maidservant soon to be his wife. In *The Hut in the Forest* and *The Three Little Men in the Wood*, the attitude and behaviour of young girls is tested by supernatural or spellbound creatures before letting them return from the woods either rewarded or punished.[56]

Generally speaking, the sylvan domain is presented as a transitory residence for human beings in contrast to a permanent one for non-humans. *Hansel and Gretel* are sent away by their parents into an arcane and dangerous 'witch wood', yet the siblings manage to escape the evil hag and come back with a fortune.[57] And *Little Red Riding Hood* imperils her and her grandmother's lives by straying from the right path into the territory of wild nature, but at the happy ending pledges with hindsight: 'as long as you live, you will never again go astray into the woods by yourself'.[58]

Most notably in Jacob's academic publications, expansive woods were said to have covered 'all of Germany' from early antiquity on – including Caesar's and Tacitus' 'Hercynian forest'. He went on to elaborately describe these forests of the past as places of worship and sacrifice: 'therefore *temple* is withal *forest* ... a sacred site unspoiled by the hand of man, nurtured and enclosed by trees growing on their own'. This had purportedly been the state of affairs from times immemorial until the missionaries arrived to destroy or convert the sites of an 'Old German woodland cult'. Repeatedly citing Tacitus, Jacob furthermore invoked various cases of 'sacred forests', 'sacred groves', 'sacred trees' and above all 'sacred oaks'. Designating the Germanic tribes to be direct predecessors of the Germans, he compared these sites of native paganism favourably with the ancient temples and Christian churches built of soulless stone.[59]

55. Ibid. p. 1; J. and W. Grimm (eds.) *Kinder- und Hausmärchen* (1857a) p. 1; Uwe Hentschel, 'Der Lindenbaum in der deutschen Literatur des 18. und 19. Jahrhunderts', *Orbis Litterarum* 60/5 (2005): 357–376.

56. J. and W. Grimm (eds.) *Kinder- und Hausmärchen* (1857b) pp. 181–3, pp. 334–9; J. and W. Grimm (eds.) *Kinder- und Hausmärchen* (1857a) pp. 70–5.

57. J. and W. Grimm (eds.) *Kinder- und Hausmärchen* (1857a) p. 86; Regina Böhm-Korff, *Deutung und Bedeutung von 'Hänsel und Gretel': Eine Fallstudie* (Frankfurt am Main et al.: Lang, 1991).

58. J. and W. Grimm (eds.) *Kinder- und Hausmärchen* (1857a) p. 143; Marianne Rumpf, *Rotkäppchen: Eine vergleichende Märchenuntersuchung* (Frankfurt am Main et al.: Lang, 1989).

59. Jacob Grimm, 'Deutsche Grenzalterthümer' [1843], in J. Grimm, *Kleinere Schriften. Band 2: Abhandlungen zur Mythologie und Sittenkunde* (Berlin: Dümmler, 1865) pp. 30–74, p. 33; Jacob Grimm, *Geschichte der deutschen Sprache. Zweiter Band* (Leipzig: Weidmann, 1848) p. 570; Jacob Grimm, *Deutsche Mythologie* (Göttingen: Dieterich, 1835[a]) p. 41; Jacob Grimm, *Deutsche My-*

Johannes Zechner

Lastly, the Grimms operated extensively with organic metaphors throughout their work. *Altdeutsche Wälder*, or Old German forests, came to stand for a primeval wilderness and a treasure trove from the past. The brothers identified the German language with a 'massive tree', albeit one endangered by the 'vermin' of neglect and the 'weeds' represented by nonessential loanwords. In a similar vein, the legends were for them budding 'green timber' with a strong 'Germanic smell of the forest' and folk poetry was a 'saturating and softening greenery'.[60] Defining culture and history as a quasi-natural process of growth, such imagined woodlands of fairy and trope could serve as the mythical soil and spiritual bedrock for future generations.

Woodlands and Peasants: Arndt's Forests of Fatherland

In the era of the anti-Napoleonic wars, Ernst Moritz Arndt (1769–1860) was one of the most prominent political authors and poets.[61] A professor of history at the University of Greifswald and later in Bonn, he attempted to apply the lessons of (pre-)history – as construed by him – to inform and influence the present. His publications were mainly magazine and newspaper articles, pamphlets and poems intended to incite the fighting spirit of the broad population.[62] The political writings of Arndt became ever more dominated by the idolisation of German culture, language and nation with the reverse side being a strong anti-French, anti-Jewish and anti-Slavic bias, including diatribes warning about the perceived menace of *Verbastardung* or mongrelisation.[63] In doing so, he closely linked ethno-national stereotypes with natural landscapes in the tradition of ancient and early modern

thologie. Erster Band [1835]. 2nd edn. (Göttingen: Dieterich, 1844) p. xliv; J. Grimm, *Deutsche Mythologie* (1835a) p. 43, p. 70, p. 47, p. 45.

60. Jacob Grimm, 'Über die wechselseitigen Beziehungen und die Verbindung der drei in der Versammlung vertretenen Wissenschaften' [1846], in J. Grimm, *Kleinere Schriften. Band 7: Recensionen und vermischte Aufsätze. Band 4* (Berlin: Dümmler, 1884) pp. 556–563, p. 557; Wilhelm Grimm, 'Einleitung zur Vorlesung über Hartmanns "Erek"' [1843], in W. Grimm, *Kleinere Schriften. Vierter Band* (Gütersloh: Bertelsmann, 1887) pp. 577–617, p. 616; Jacob Grimm, *Deutsche Grammatik. Erster Theil* (Göttingen: Dieterich, 1819) p. xiv; Jacob Grimm 'Gedanken wie sich die Sagen zur Poesie und Geschichte verhalten' [1808], in J. Grimm, *Kleinere Schriften. Band 1: Reden und Abhandlungen* (Berlin: Dümmler, 1864) pp. 399–403, p. 402; Jacob Grimm, *Reinhart Fuchs* (Berlin: Reimer, 1834) p. ccxciv; W. Grimm, 'Vorrede zu den "Kinder- und Hausmärchen"', pp. 320–332, p. 330.

61. Ernst Müsebeck, *Ernst Moritz Arndt: Ein Lebensbild. Erstes Buch: Der junge Arndt 1769–1815* (Gotha: Perthes, 1914); Alfred George Pundt, *Arndt and the Nationalist Awakening in Germany* [1935] (New York: AMS, 1968).

62. Karl Heinz Schäfer, *Ernst Moritz Arndt als politischer Publizist: Studien zu Publizistik, Pressepolitik und kollektivem Bewußtsein im frühen 19. Jahrhundert* (Bonn: Röhrscheid, 1974).

63. Hans Kohn, 'Arndt and the Character of German Nationalism', *American Historical Review* 54/4 (1949): 787–803.

Figure 6. Ernst Moritz Arndt.

Lithograph by Carl Wildt after a painting by Julius Roeting, 1855). Source: Wikicommons.
http://de.wikipedia.org/w/index.php?title=Datei:Ernst_Moritz_Arndt_litho.jpg&filetimes
tamp=20090531184857

climate thinking. More than three decades after the wars, the life-long champion
of a free press and a reform of nobility was elected to the 1848 parliament.

While Arndt's dictum about the mighty Rhine being 'Germany's river, not
Germany's border' continues to be part of scholarly knowledge, his numerous references to forests and oaks have attracted less academic attention.[64] For the city resident
Arndt, woodlands firmly rooted in the native soil were stabilising a society that he
saw threatened by sweeping transformations. His predominantly mimetic poems
drew heavily upon familiar literary motifs: the forest being a childhood memory,
an arena for love and God's sacred creation. During the propaganda war against
the French, he generated and refined a radical nationalist imagery of blood, oaks
and corpses – the latter two fittingly rhyming in German as *Eichen* and *Leichen*. In
doing so, he followed in the metaphorical footsteps of Klopstock and of Theodor
Körner (1791–1813), a patriotic poet and war martyr.[65]

These poeticised forests are evidently more interesting for their imaginative
potential than for their literary value. Corresponding with the Romantic tradition
to which he was close, the poems merely projected human emotions like pleasure,
elation or grief onto the trees. In 'Forest Wedding' (1808) the woods were an erotic
and sexual playground; in 'Forest Air' (1841) Arndt proclaimed the desire to become
one with nature; and in 'The Green Forest' (1835) he referred to the mournful
death of his son Willibald in 1834. His solemn 'Forest Greeting' (1846) idolised
a divinely inspired and mythical tree landscape in safe distance from the troubles
of everyday life: 'O book of God! O which sounds / From a solitude most silent
of all! / Escaped from the world's wild hustle / To the communality of a superior
world: / Like from times long bygone, / Like from spiritual eternity / Fables and
legends are whispering herein'.[66]

Other verses attempted to interrelate botany with identity like 'Scharnhorst,
the Herald of Honour' (1813), written during the 'Wars of Liberation'. Here, Arndt
named the deeply divided German-speaking territories his 'fatherland of green
oaks' ready to blossom. In 'Rustle through the Woods' (1853), the poet hoped for
the nation to turn 'green like the forest's greenest oakwood', using an explicitly
organic metaphor for the desired rebirth in unity.[67] One encounters this tree spe-

---

64. Ernst Moritz Arndt, 'Der Rhein Teutschlands Strom, aber nicht Teutschlands Grenze' [1813], in
Arndt, *Kleine Schriften. Band 2* (Berlin et al.: Bong, 1912) pp. 37–82; Caroline Delph, 'Nature and
Nationalism in the Writings of Ernst Moritz Arndt', in Catrin Gersdorf and Sylvia Mayer (eds.)
Nature in Literary and Cultural Studies: Transatlantic Conversations on Ecocriticism (Amsterdam
and New York: Rodopi, 2006) pp. 331–354.

65. Theodor Körner, *Sämmtliche Werke* [1834] 3rd edn. (Berlin: Nicolai, 1838).

66. Ernst Moritz Arndt, *Gedichte. Vollständige Sammlung* (Berlin: Weidmann, 1860) p.134–5, p.
415–16, p. 383, p. 536.

67. Ibid. p. 253, p. 590.

From Poetry to Politics

cies on a number of symbolic occasions, typically described as a 'German' oak[68]: signifying *inter alia* regional recognition in 'Welcome' (1812) and military victory in 'Celebrating the 18th of October' (1814), national despair in 'Reverberation from 1848–9' (1853) and patriotic prophecy in 'Meditation under German Oaks' (1846). According to 'Song of the Free' (1803), trees should be planted on the last resting places of fallen warriors to facilitate the flourishing of new life from death and to ascertain the mutual survival of nature and nation: 'Comrades in heroism are lowering him / Together with his armour / And plant oaks proud and green / As a monument on his grave'.[69]

The political works of Arndt disseminated a deterministic understanding of environmental influences that he thought decisively moulded ethnic groups. Quite naturally, the rural and wooded areas of his beloved homeland had the best influences on his fellow Germans: 'Up here in the lonely mountains and forests, most people have the Old German features of simplicity, honesty, benign good-naturedness and hospitality.' Likewise, Sweden's vast forests and awe-inspiring mountains embodied a Nordic landscape of freedom for a similar people. By contrast, Italy with its southern vegetation and population was defamed as a 'land of lemons and bandits'. This was probably an ironic allusion to Johann Wolfgang von Goethe (1749–1832) and his personal Arcadia 'where lemons blossom and golden oranges glow in the dark foliage'.[70]

Arndt's imagined forests grew most lavishly in a political article on *Woodlands and Peasants* (1815/16) where the son of a freed bondman ideologically conflated two traditional elements of pretended nativeness and rootedness. Referring to Caesar and Tacitus, Arndt first described the territories of the Germanic tribes to have been 'covered by thick and sometimes impenetrable forests', with a populace worshipping in hallowed groves and with wild aurochses roaming. He went on to deplore the progressive deforestation caused by speculative greed and industrial need which in the long run, he claimed, must lead to 'a different, inferior, weaker and less godlike people than the Germans still are'. For him, this would mean the

---

68. Annemarie Hürlimann, 'Die Eiche, heiliger Baum deutscher Nation', in Bernd Weyergraf (ed.) *Waldungen: Die Deutschen und ihr Wald* (Berlin: Nicolai, 1987) pp. 62–8; Klaus Lindemann, '"In den frischen Eichenhainen webt und rauscht der deutsche Gott": Deutschlands poetische Eichwälder', in Josef Semmler (ed.) *Der Wald in Mittelalter und Renaissance* (Düsseldorf: Droste, 1991) pp. 200–239.

69. Arndt, *Gedichte*, p. 187, p. 290, p. 586, pp. 530–1, p. 60.

70. Ernst Moritz Arndt, *Wanderungen rund um Bonn ins rheinische Land* [1830] (Köln: Bachem, 1978) p. 113; Ernst Moritz Arndt, *Reise durch Schweden im Jahr 1804*, 4 vols (Berlin: Lange, 1806); Ernst Moritz Arndt, *Reisen durch einen Theil Teutschlands, Ungarns, Italiens und Frankreichs in den Jahren 1798 und 1799. Erster Theil* [1801] 2nd edn. (Leipzig: Gräff, 1804) p. 390; Johann Wolfgang Goethe, 'Wilhelm Meisters Lehrjahre: Ein Roman' [1795/96], in Goethe, *Wilhelm Meisters theatralische Sendung / Wilhelm Meisters Lehrjahre / Unterhaltungen deutscher Ausgewanderten* (Frankfurt am Main: Klassiker, 1992) pp. 355–992, p. 503.

end of Germany as he knew and cherished it. To cure the ailments of timber and people, he proposed state control of privately owned forests alongside substantial reforestation and protection. Hence, the woods could renew their roles as the 'true front lines of the state ... behind which a brisk and strong people can live in peace and joy'.[71] In 1852, Arndt became, at the age of 83, personally active in trying to save an endangered forest in the southern Rhineland.[72] Although he mentioned arguments of climate and soil fertility, his main concern was the preservation of the people and not of the forest, since 'the axe wielded against the tree often turns into an axe wielded against the people as a whole'.[73] Whereas the earlier forests of imagination had been relatively open to a certain array of cultural and political interpretations, Arndt's were by then closed and strictly nationalist ones. Subsequent writers would utilise the politicised timber even more ruthlessly for their own political ends.[74]

Conclusions

The different forests surveyed in this chapter were not real woodlands but rather ideal versions of and imaginings about nature, in each case vacillating between poetry and politics. This should remind us that nature in general is cultural as well as material, providing a promising topic for the environmental humanities and cultural history. Nevertheless, while nature can only be thought and written about by means of selective abstraction, its representations keep referring to certain elements of reality. In other words, constructions of the mind need suitable – and in this instance natural – canvases to draw from and to be projected upon. When used to influence or to legitimise political decisions, these intellectual concepts based on widely held images can become powerful forces shaping human history.

To frame the complex and ever-changing interplay between real and imagined landscapes, this article puts forward a perspective of reluctant yet assured constructivism. The forests certainly – albeit unwillingly – provided a welcome and sufficiently undefined surface for a variety of cultural, political and social inscriptions.

71. Ernst Moritz Arndt, 'Ein Wort über die Pflegung und Erhaltung der Forsten und der Bauern im Sinne einer höheren, d.h. menschlichen Gesetzgebung', *Der Wächter* 2/4 (1815): 346–408, 371, 381, 397.

72. Ernst Moritz Arndt, 'Der Flamersheimer Erbenwald', *Kölnische Zeitung* 97 (1852): 3.

73. Arndt, 'Ein Wort': 375.

74. Ursula Breymayer and Bernd Ulrich (eds.) *Unter Bäumen: Die Deutschen und der Wald* (Dresden: Sandstein, 2011); Kenneth S. Calhoon and Karla L. Schultz (eds.) *The Idea of the Forest: German and American Perspectives on the Culture and Politics of Trees* (New York et al.: Lang, 1996); Albrecht Lehmann and Klaus Schriewer (eds.) *Der Wald – Ein deutscher Mythos?* (Berlin and Hamburg: Reimer, 2000); Ann-Katrin Thomm (ed.) *Mythos Wald* (Münster: LWL, 2009); Johannes Zechner, 'Politicized Timber: The "German Forest" and the Nature of the Nation 1800–1945', *The Brock Review* 11/2 (2011): 19–32.

Interested parties projected human interests and perspectives onto the treescape, which then corroborated the developing ideals of nature. Meanwhile, those ideals grew ever farther away from the discursive soil they had originally been based upon. Whilst the dense and wild forests of imagination were at least nominally still related to actual woods, their creators increasingly ignored the silvicultural reality, which was rapidly changing to uniform and efficient conifer monocultures.

It is not a historical coincidence that the 'German Forest' and within it especially the 'German Oak' came into intellectual being as a symbol for the solid and rooted nature of the nation around 1800. Those natal years of modern German nationalism were a tumultuous period of French military hegemony that alienated even former advocates of the revolution. During a phase of substantial imponderability and accelerated transition, some urban men of the mighty word began to intertwine nature and nation in a multitude of literary, academic and political texts. In the course of their ardent search for criteria of collective exceptionalism, the poets, philologists and publicists inscribed the natural phenomenon of the woods with markers of ethnicity.

The complexions of Germanness could take on varying forms, ranging from Tieck's patriotic through Eichendorff's and the Grimms' national to Arndt's racial sentiment. Yet despite such variations and differing political opinions, all of them understood imagined sylvan landscapes as conciliative emblems of identity. To counter the French revolutionary values of *liberté, égalité, fraternité*, the alleged German principles of stability, inequality and hierarchy were proposed. Corresponding forests of longing and belonging existed beyond time and history, claiming a static harmony unaffected by the controversial and occasionally violent developments in politics and society.

But despite this ostensible timelessness, German forest thinking was discernibly influenced by the undulations of patriotic consciousness. With the end of the empire in 1806, intellectuals glorified the sylvan nationscape. They hoped that its extensive and encompassing nature would provide an overarching symbol to overcome all denominational, societal and territorial cleavages. In the fight with the French armies 1813–15, the woods were aggressively instrumentalised to fuel hostile emotions by alluding to the historical memory of Herman the German successfully defeating the Romans. After the high hopes for unity had been shattered in the failed revolution of 1848, the forests of the mind were, in conjunction with culture and language, among the few unifying elements remaining.

In the manifold processes of reception, most of the adaptations and transformations were highly selective and performed with little concern for the original historical and political contexts. Whereas time-honoured quotes from Caesar and Tacitus were incorporated into changing sylva-national frameworks, new concepts like Tieck's *Waldeinsamkeit* were reworked and adjusted by subsequent writers. Gradually, a transfer occurred from the metaphor of the individual oak tree to the

Johannes Zechner

collective metaphor of the woods in their entirety. Such ideological aggregation and amalgamation of imagined forest characteristics mostly happened in times of crises and led to a noticeable shift from sylva-poetry to sylva-politics – thus rooting not only the past but also the present and future of the people in the unending German forests.

Acknowledgements

This article is related to the author's doctoral project 'Between Ideal of Nature and Ideology. Imaginations and Constructions of the "German Forest" 1801–1945', supported by Heinrich Böll Stiftung – The Green Political Foundation. All translations from German and Latin were made by the author. I would like to sincerely thank my critical readers, especially my sister Katharina Zechner and my colleagues Aygül Cizmecioglu, Michael Dusche, Katja Kaiser, Bradley Nichols, Wiebke Senff, Albrecht Wolfmeyer and Eva Zimmermann, as well as the editors and the peer reviewer for their many helpful suggestions.

REFERENCES

Arndt, Ernst Moritz. 1804. *Reisen durch einen Theil Teutschlands, Ungarns, Italiens und Frankreichs in den Jahren 1798 und 1799. Erster Theil* [1801]. 2nd edn. Leipzig: Gräff.

Arndt, Ernst Moritz. 1806. *Reise durch Schweden im Jahr 1804.* 4 vols. Berlin: Lange.

Arndt, Ernst Moritz. 1815. 'Ein Wort über die Pflegung und Erhaltung der Forsten und der Bauern im Sinne einer höheren, d.h. menschlichen Gesetzgebung'. *Der Wächter* 2/4: 346–408.

Arndt, Ernst Moritz. 1816. 'Ein Wort über die Pflegung und Erhaltung der Forsten und der Bauern im Sinne einer höheren, d.h. menschlichen Gesetzgebung. Fortsetzung'. *Der Wächter* 3/3–4: 209–289.

Arndt, Ernst Moritz. 1852. 'Der Flamersheimer Erbenwald'. *Kölnische Zeitung* 97: 3.

Arndt, Ernst Moritz. 1860. *Gedichte. Vollständige Sammlung.* Berlin: Weidmann.

Arndt, Ernst Moritz. 1912. 'Der Rhein Teutschlands Strom, aber nicht Teutschlands Grenze' [1813]. In Arndt, *Kleine Schriften. Band 2.* Berlin et al.: Bong. pp. 37–82.

Arndt, Ernst Moritz. 1978. *Wanderungen rund um Bonn ins rheinische Land* [1830]. Köln: Bachem.

Baumgart, Wolfgang. 1936. *Der Wald in der deutschen Dichtung.* Berlin and Leipzig: Gruyter.

Böhm-Korff, Regina. 1991. *Deutung und Bedeutung von 'Hänsel und Gretel': Eine Fallstudie.* Frankfurt am Main et al.: Lang.

Bormann, Alexander von. 1968. *Natura loquitur: Naturpoesie und emblematische Formel bei Joseph von Eichendorff.* Tübingen: Niemeyer.

Breymayer, Ursula and Bernd Ulrich (eds.) 2011. *Unter Bäumen: Die Deutschen und der Wald*. Dresden: Sandstein.

Brinker-Gabler, Gisela. 1980. *Poetisch-wissenschaftliche Mittelalter-Rezeption: Ludwig Tiecks Erneuerung altdeutscher Literatur*. Stuttgart: Kümmerle.

Caesar, Gaius Julius. 1990. *De bello Gallico* [c. 51/52 BCE]. Munich and Zurich: Artemis.

Calhoon, Kenneth S. and Karla L. Schultz (eds.) 1996. *The Idea of the Forest: German and American Perspectives on the Culture and Politics of Trees*. New York et al.: Lang.

Danton, George Henry. 1966. *The Nature Sense in the Writings of Ludwig Tieck* [1907]. New York: AMS.

Delph, Caroline. 2006. 'Nature and Nationalism in the Writings of Ernst Moritz Arndt'. In Catrin Gersdorf and Sylvia Mayer (eds.) *Nature in Literary and Cultural Studies: Transatlantic Conversations on Ecocriticism*. Amsterdam and New York: Rodopi. pp. 331–354.

Donat, Walter. 1973. *Die Landschaft bei Tieck und ihre historischen Voraussetzungen* [1925]. Hildesheim: Gerstenberg.

Eichendorff, Joseph von. 1993. *Gedichte. Erster Teil: Text*. Stuttgart et al.: Kohlhammer.

Eichendorff, Joseph von. 1996. 'Herrmann und Thusnelda' [1811/12]. In Eichendorff, *Historische Dramen und Dramenfragmente: Text und Varianten*. Tübingen: Niemeyer. pp. 39–65.

Eichendorff, Joseph von. 1997. *Gedichte. Zweiter Teil: Verstreute und nachgelassene Gedichte. Text*. Tübingen: Niemeyer.

Feldmann, Roland. 1970. *Jacob Grimm und die Politik*. Kassel: Bärenreiter.

Fondi, Hilda. 1941. *Der deutsche Wald in der deutschen Lyrik*. Wien: Phil. Diss.

Friedrich, Cäcilia. 1978. 'Klopstocks Bardiet "Hermanns Schlacht" und seine Nachgeschichte'. In Hans-Georg Werner (ed.) *Friedrich Gottlieb Klopstock: Werk und Wirkung*. Berlin: Akademie. pp. 237–246.

Goethe, Johann Wolfgang. 1992: 'Wilhelm Meisters Lehrjahre: Ein Roman' [1795/96]. In Goethe, *Wilhelm Meisters theatralische Sendung / Wilhelm Meisters Lehrjahre / Unterhaltungen deutscher Ausgewanderten*. Frankfurt am Main: Klassiker. pp. 355–992.

Grimm, Jacob. 1819. *Deutsche Grammatik. Erster Theil*. Göttingen: Dieterich.

Grimm, Jacob. 1834. *Reinhart Fuchs*. Berlin: Reimer.

Grimm, Jacob. 1835a. *Deutsche Mythologie*. Göttingen: Dieterich.

Grimm, Jacob. (ed.) 1835b. *Taciti 'Germania': Edidit et quae ad res Germanorum pertinere videntur e reliquo Tacitino opere excerpsit*. Göttingen: Dieterich.

Grimm, Jacob. 1844. *Deutsche Mythologie. Erster Band* [1835]. 2nd edn. Göttingen: Dieterich.

Grimm, Jacob. 1848. *Geschichte der deutschen Sprache. Zweiter Band*. Leipzig: Weidmann.

Grimm, Jacob. 1864. 'Gedanken wie sich die Sagen zur Poesie und Geschichte verhalten' [1808]. In J. Grimm, *Kleinere Schriften. Band 1: Reden und Abhandlungen*. Berlin: Dümmler. pp. 399–403.

Grimm, Jacob. 1865. 'Deutsche Grenzalterthümer' [1843]. In J. Grimm, *Kleinere Schriften. Band 2: Abhandlungen zur Mythologie und Sittenkunde*. Berlin: Dümmler. pp. 30–74.

Grimm, Jacob. 1871. 'Anzeige der "Deutschen Mythologie"' [1835]. In J. Grimm, *Kleinere Schriften. Band 5: Recensionen und vermischte Aufsätze. Band 2.* Berlin: Dümmler. pp. 198–202.

Grimm, Jacob. 1884. 'Über die wechselseitigen Beziehungen und die Verbindung der drei in der Versammlung vertretenen Wissenschaften' [1846]. In J. Grimm, *Kleinere Schriften. Band 7: Recensionen und vermischte Aufsätze. Band 4.* Berlin: Dümmler. pp. 556–563.

Grimm, Jacob and Wilhelm Grimm (eds.) 1857a. *Kinder- und Hausmärchen gesammelt durch die Brüder Grimm: Große Ausgabe. Erster Band* [1812]. 7th edn. Göttingen: Dieterich.

Grimm, Jacob and Wilhelm Grimm (eds.) 1857b. *Kinder- und Hausmärchen gesammelt durch die Brüder Grimm: Große Ausgabe. Zweiter Band* [1815]. 7th edn. Göttingen: Dieterich.

Grimm, Jacob and Wilhelm Grimm (eds.) 1986. *Kinder- und Hausmärchen gesammelt durch die Brüder Grimm: Vergrößerter Nachdruck der Erstausgabe* [1812/15]. Göttingen: Vandenhoeck & Ruprecht.

Grimm, Wilhelm. 1881a. 'Teutoberg' [1817]. In W. Grimm, *Kleinere Schriften. Erster Band.* Berlin: Dümmler. p. 559.

Grimm, Wilhelm. 1881b. 'Vorrede zu den "Kinder- und Hausmärchen"' [1812/1815]. In W. Grimm, *Kleinere Schriften. Erster Band.* Berlin: Dümmler. pp. 320–332.

Grimm, Wilhelm. 1881c. 'Über das Wesen der Märchen' [1819]. In W. Grimm, *Kleinere Schriften. Erster Band.* Berlin: Dümmler. pp. 333–358.

Grimm, Wilhelm. [with Jacob Grimm]. 1882. 'Vorrede zum "Armen Heinrich"' [1815]. In W. Grimm, *Kleinere Schriften. Zweiter Band.* Berlin: Dümmler. p. 505.

Grimm, Wilhelm. 1887. 'Einleitung zur Vorlesung über Hartmanns "Erek"' [1843]. In W. Grimm, *Kleinere Schriften. Vierter Band.* Gütersloh: Bertelsmann. pp. 577–617.

Häckel, Manfred. 1963. 'Der patriotische Gedanke im Frühwerk Joseph von Eichendorffs'. In Heinrich Scheel (ed.) *Das Jahr 1813: Studien zur Geschichte und Wirkung der Befreiungskriege.* Berlin: Akademie. pp. 177–205.

Hammes, Michael Paul. 1933. *'Waldeinsamkeit': Eine Motiv- und Stiluntersuchung zur Deutschen Frühromantik, insbesondere zu Ludwig Tieck.* Frankfurt: Phil. Diss.

Harrison, Robert Pogue. 1993. *Forests: The Shadow of Civilization* [1992]. Chicago and London: University of Chicago Press.

Heidenreich, Joachim. 1985. *Natura delectat: Zur Tradition des locus amoenus bei Eichendorff.* Konstanz: Hartung-Gorre.

Hentschel, Uwe. 2005. 'Der Lindenbaum in der deutschen Literatur des 18. und 19. Jahrhunderts'. *Orbis Litterarum* **60**/5: 357–376.

Hürlimann, Annemarie. 1987. 'Die Eiche, heiliger Baum deutscher Nation'. In Bernd Weyergraf (ed.) *Waldungen: Die Deutschen und ihr Wald.* Berlin: Nicolai. pp. 62–8.

Hyde, Walter Woodburn. 1918. 'The Curious Animals of the Hercynian Forest'. *The Classical Journal* 13/4: 231–245.

Jung-Kaiser, Ute (ed.) 2008. *Der Wald als romantischer Topos.* Bern et al.: Lang.

Kellner, Beate. 1994. *Grimms Mythen: Studien zum Mythosbegriff und seiner Anwendung in Jacob Grimms 'Deutscher Mythologie'.* Frankfurt am Main et al.: Lang.

Klopstock, Friedrich Gottlieb. 2009. 'Hermanns Schlacht: Ein Bardiet für die Schaubühne' [1769]. In Klopstock, *Hermann-Dramen. Band 1: Text*. Berlin and New York: Gruyter. pp. 1–154.

Klopstock, Friedrich Gottlieb. 2010. *Oden. Band 1: Text*. Berlin and New York: Gruyter.

Koerner, Joseph Leo. 1990. *Caspar David Friedrich and the Subject of Landscape*. London: Reaktion.

Kohn, Hans. 1949. 'Arndt and the Character of German Nationalism'. *American Historical Review* 54/4: 787–803.

Körner, Theodor. 1838. *Sämmtliche Werke* [1834]. 3rd edn. Berlin: Nicolai.

Krebs, Christopher B. 2011. *A Most Dangerous Book: Tacitus' 'Germania' from the Roman Empire to the Third Reich*. New York and London: Norton.

Krüger, Peter. 1968. 'Eichendorffs politisches Denken. Teil 1'. *Aurora* 28: 7–32.

Krüger, Peter. 1969. 'Eichendorffs politisches Denken. Teil 2'. *Aurora* 29: 50–69.

Kuehnemund, Richard. 1966. *Arminius or the Rise of a National Symbol in Literature: From Hutten to Grabbe* [1953]. New York: AMS.

Lehmann, Albrecht and Klaus Schriewer (eds.) 2000. *Der Wald – Ein deutscher Mythos?*. Berlin and Hamburg: Reimer.

Lindemann, Klaus. 1985. '"Deutsch Panier, das rauschend wallt": Der Wald in Eichendorffs patriotischen Gedichten im Kontext der Lyrik der Befreiungskriege'. In Hans-Georg Pott (ed.) *Eichendorff und die Spätromantik*. Paderborn et al.: Schöningh. pp. 91–130.

Lindemann, Klaus. 1991. '"In den frischen Eichenhainen webt und rauscht der deutsche Gott": Deutschlands poetische Eichwälder'. In Josef Semmler (ed.) *Der Wald in Mittelalter und Renaissance*. Düsseldorf: Droste. pp. 200–239.

Martus, Steffen. 2009. *Die Brüder Grimm: Eine Biographie*. Berlin: Rowohlt.

Müller, Gernot Michael. 2001. *Die 'Germania generalis' des Conrad Celtis: Studien mit Edition, Übersetzung und Kommentar*. Tübingen: Niemeyer.

Müsebeck, Ernst. 1914. *Ernst Moritz Arndt: Ein Lebensbild. Erstes Buch: Der junge Arndt 1769–1815*. Gotha: Perthes.

Norden, Eduard. 1920. *Die germanische Urgeschichte in Tacitus 'Germania'*. Berlin and Leipzig: Teubner.

Ono, Hisako. 2007. 'Waldsymbolik bei den Brüdern Grimm'. *Fabula* 48/1–2: 73–84.

Paulin, Roger. 1986. *Ludwig Tieck: A Literary Biography*. Oxford: Clarendon.

Peppard, Murray B. 1971. *Paths through the Forest: A Biography of the Brothers Grimm*. New York et al.: Holt, Rinehart and Winston.

Pundt, Alfred George. 1968. *Arndt and the Nationalist Awakening in Germany* [1935]. New York: AMS.

Rebholz, Dore. 1944. *Der Wald im deutschen Märchen: Das Erlebnis als Grundlage für die Auffassung des Waldes, seine Darstellung und Rolle im deutschen Märchen*. Heidelberg: Phil. Diss.

Rumpf, Marianne. 1989. *Rotkäppchen: Eine vergleichende Märchenuntersuchung.* Frankfurt am Main et al.: Lang.

Schäfer, Karl Heinz. 1974. *Ernst Moritz Arndt als politischer Publizist: Studien zu Publizistik, Pressepolitik und kollektivem Bewußtsein im frühen 19. Jahrhundert.* Bonn: Röhrscheid.

Schama, Simon. 1996. *Landscape and Memory* [1995]. London: Fontana.

Schiwy, Günther. 2000. *Eichendorff: Der Dichter in seiner Zeit. Eine Biographie.* München: Beck.

Schultz, Hartwig. 2007. *Joseph von Eichendorff: Eine Biographie.* Frankfurt am Main and Leipzig: Insel.

Stauffer, Marianne. 1958. *Der Wald. Zur Darstellung und Deutung der Natur im Mittelalter.* Zurich: Juris.

Tacitus, Publius Cornelius. 1991. Germania [c. 98 CE]. In Tacitus, *Agricola–Germania.* Munich and Zurich: Artemis & Winkler. pp. 78–135.

Tacitus, Publius Cornelius. 2005. *Annales* [c. 110–120 CE]. 5th edn. Düsseldorf: Artemis & Winkler.

Tieck, Ludwig. 1841. *Gedichte: Neue Ausgabe.* Berlin: Reimer.

Tieck, Ludwig. 1966a. 'Der Blaubart: Ein Mährchen in fünf Akten' [1796]. In Tieck, *Phantasus. Zweiter Theil.* Berlin: Gruyter. pp. 7–152.

Tieck, Ludwig. 1966b. 'Der blonde Eckbert' [1796]. In Tieck, *Phantasus. Erster Theil.* Berlin: Gruyter. pp. 144–169.

Tieck, Ludwig. 1966c. *Franz Sternbald's Wanderungen: Eine altdeutsche Geschichte* [1798]. Berlin: Gruyter.

Tieck, Ludwig. 1966d. 'Eine Sommerreise' [1834]. In Tieck, *Ludwig Tieck's gesammelte Novellen. Siebenter Band.* Berlin: Gruyter. pp. 3–156.

Tieck, Ludwig. 1966e. 'Der junge Tischlermeister: Novelle in sieben Abschnitten' [1836]. In Tieck, *Ludwig Tieck's gesammelte Novellen. Zwölfter Band.* Berlin: Gruyter. pp. 3–466.

Tieck, Ludwig. 1966f. 'Waldeinsamkeit' [1841]. In Tieck, *Gesammelte Novellen. Zehnter Band.* Berlin: Gruyter. pp. 473–567.

Tieck, Ludwig. 1966g. *William Lovell. Erster Theil* [1793/95]. Berlin: Gruyter.

Thomm, Ann-Katrin (ed.) 2009. *Mythos Wald.* Münster: LWL.

Zechner, Johannes. 2011. 'Politicized Timber: The "German Forest" and the Nature of the Nation 1800–1945'. *The Brock Review* 11/2: 19–32.

Zeitler, Wolfgang Maria. 1986. 'Zum Germanenbegriff Caesars: Der Germanenexkurs im sechsten Buch von Caesars "Bellum Gallicum"'. In Heinrich Beck (ed.) *Germanenprobleme in heutiger Sicht.* Berlin and New York: Gruyter. pp. 41–53.

Zeydel, Edwin Hermann. 1971. *Ludwig Tieck the German Romanticist: A Critical Study* [1935]. Hildesheim and New York: Olms.

Zimmermann, Harro. 1987. *Freiheit und Geschichte: F. G. Klopstock als historischer Dichter und Denker.* Heidelberg: Winter.

Zipes, Jack. 1988. *The Brothers Grimm: From Enchanted Forests to the Modern World.* New York and London: Routledge.

Chapter 9

Of Trees and the Political Imagination in 'Neo-Colonial' Madagascar

Karen Middleton

On an overcast day in March 1972 a tree festival took place on a small hill in southern Madagascar. The authorities had erected a little village of multicoloured tents, pavilions and sisal-roofed stands especially for the occasion: 'a miniature city with police station, telephone centre, infirmary, water and electricity, refreshment stalls and restaurants'. And for twelve hours, a government bulletin tells us, this 'ephemeral agglomeration' became the 'Capital of Madagascar', its main square thronged by Philibert Tsiranana, President of the Malagasy Republic, every member of his Government, Deputies, officials, soldiers, representatives of United Nations, business and the press, not to mention some 20,000 citizens from the six provinces of this island state. Tsiranana spoke about the vital importance of tree planting, then gave a signal and a short command in Malagasy – 'Plants in place'. And 'in a trice' – we learn –20,000 eucalyptus saplings had been planted on the barren slopes of Beratro hill. Meanwhile, the President and Mme Tsiranana toured the temporary village, inspecting displays of local produce, studying data on regional pluviometry and visiting a photographic exhibition explaining the phenomenon of 'desertification'. Afterwards, Tsiranana convened an 'extraordinary cabinet meeting' at Ambovombe, the so-called 'capital' of Androy, during which he urged every sector of Malagasy society to do its utmost to ensure that 'Operation reforestation Androy' remained a priority (Figure 1).[1]

This festival took place almost a year to the day after what has become variously known as 'the peasant insurrection', 'the revolt of the south' or, more euphemistically, 'troubles in the south'. During the nights of 31 March to 2 April 1971 supporters of MONIMA – the opposition party that was based predominantly in Tuléar Province – attempted localised *coups d'état* in towns across the Malagasy Deep South. In conventional historiography this event and government repression

1. National Archives of Madagascar. VP916 Sauvetage et Développement du Sud 1971–1972. 'Développement et reforestation du Sud'. Notes, Rapport, Correspondance 1971–1972. 27f. *InfoDocuments Madagascar* 18 mars 1972 'La reforestation et le développement du "Grand Sud" Malgache sont possibles'; *Info Madagascar Reflets* 25 mars 1972, 'La Grande Opération, "Reforestation de l'Androy", a demarré'.

Karen Middleton

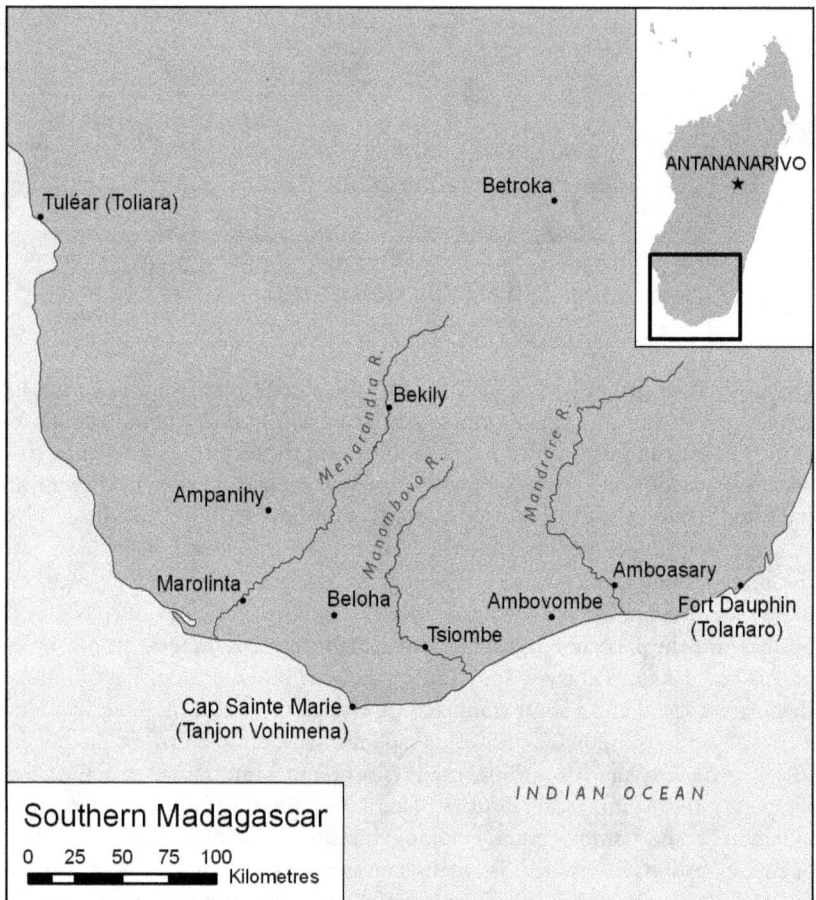

Figure 1. Map of southern Madagascar.

Drawn by Michael Athanson, Map Librarian, Bodleian Library, University of Oxford.

of it are held to be among the factors that, during the following months, fuelled rising discontent throughout the island, culminating in the 'May Revolution' that erupted in Antananarivo, Madagascar's highland capital, the following spring and brought down Madagascar's first post-independence government only weeks after the tree-planting festivities I have described.[2]

---

2. On the 1971 insurrection, see Gérard Althabe, 'Les manifestations paysannes d'avril 1971', *Revue française d'études politiques africaines* 78 (juin 1972): 71–7; Maureen Covell, *Madagascar* (London: Frances Pinter, 1987) pp.43–5; André Saura, *Philibert Tsiranana (1910–1978), Premier*

Of Trees and the Political Imagination

According to the same press release that reported on festivities at Beratro, the President had decided within days of the 'Troubles' in April 1971 to make afforestation of the south a national priority and to stage the next annual Tree Festival there. That an ageing president in a poor state of health, struggling to cope with the most serious political unrest of his eleven years in office, besieged on all fronts with questions about state violence and civil rights abuses, should be thinking about tree festivals is curious. Yet it is plainly on record that, during his tour of Tuléar Province in the wake of the 'Troubles', Tsiranana had preached of peace and reconciliation in every town he visited – *and* had called upon people to plant trees. He began his *tournée* in Betroka on 11 May 1971 by asking the population to plant trees aplenty, if only as wind-breaks. 'Wherever there is forest', he told them, 'there is also rain. It is therefore in your interest to reforest intensively.' 'There was a time', he assured the crowds at Amboasary, 'when the South was verdant and a forest, a time when the waters of the Mandrare [river] ran at the same height 365 days a year. By reforesting, we could restore what existed then and turn the South into a haven of prosperity.'[3]

Why did Tsiranana respond to the most serious political crisis in Madagascar since Independence, and the bloodiest since the anticolonial rebellion of 1947, by urging people to plant trees? Did the President turn to tree planting because he lacked the wherewithal to address the truly intractable problems of the Malagasy Deep South: low rainfall, regular food scarcities and periodic famines, coupled with rising youth unemployment and a lack of investment in viable livelihood alternatives to subsistence agriculture? Did he hope to depoliticise the crisis? Or did tree planting constitute a medium through which the state, in response to manifest public disorder, upped its disciplinary tentacles and sought to reaffirm its control? It is often argued that narratives, or 'myths', about deforestation or soil deterioration were the basis for maladroit state interventions in peasant production. According to this interpretation, forestry projects, especially in the colonial era, were as much about state efforts to territorialise political control over people and resources as they were about soil conservation and protecting trees.[4]

président de la République de Madagascar: Tome 2: Le crépuscule du pouvoir (Paris: L'Harmattan, 2006) pp.121–65; Françoise Raison-Jourde and Gérard Roy, *Paysans, intellectuels et populisme à Madagascar. De Monja Jaona à Ratsimandrava (1960–1975)* (Paris: Editions Karthala, 2010) pp. 229–52.

3. Bibliothèque centrale, Muséum national d'histoire naturelle, Paris, Fonds Decary MS 3042 Troubles en Androy 1971. *Courrier de Madagascar* 2688 12, 13, and 14 mai 1971.

4. For this model of colonial science see eg. Thaddeus Sunseri, *Wielding the Ax: State Forestry and Social Conflict in Tanzania, 1820–2000* (Athens, Ohio: Ohio University Press, 2009); Melissa Leach and Robin Mearns (eds.) *The Lie of the Land: Challenging Received Wisdom on the African Environment* (International African Institute, Oxford; Portsmouth NH; with James Currey/Heinemann, 1996); Philip Stott and Sian Sullivan (eds.) *Political Ecology: Science, Myth and Power* (London: Arnold, 2000); for a critique, William Beinart, Karen Brown and Daniel Gilfoyle, 'Experts and Expertise

Karen Middleton

In this chapter I propose to shift the frame of enquiry by exploring the more symbolic dimensions of tree planting. I am interested in exploring how African politicians in the immediate post-independence period appropriated botany and nature for nation-building projects. Did superficial resemblances of environmental rhetoric and practice to those of the colonial period mask significant reinterpretation, whereby seemingly colonial concerns with deforestation became embedded in rather different political and cultural narratives?

To develop this argument I turn to an essay by anthropologist Gillian Feeley-Harnik on changing representations of *Ravenala Madagascariensis,* the traveller's palm or *ravinala* tree. Feeley-Harnik argues that William Ellis, the nineteenth-century London Missionary Society missionary to Madagascar, 'established the *ravinala* as an icon of Madagascar by using [it] as a graphic statement of the society's purpose "to take possession of [Madagascar] for Christ" ... in circumstances where he could not make that claim openly in words'. She suggests, further, that Malagasy and Europeans alike used plants, especially trees and images of trees, to mark their social-historical places in a common landscape. Botanic imagery, she writes, figured as a kind of *lingua franca* for debating conflicting views of death and regeneration of political groups, as well as creating alternative social geographies.[5]

In her essay Feeley-Harnik is not concerned to explore how trees figured in Tsiranana's political and social geography. But her point about the role of botanic imagery in taking possession of land is certainly worth pursuing in explaining tree festivals in the First Republic. Is it possible, for example, that for Tsiranana public acts of tree planting, far from simply perpetuating colonial practice, symbolised the collective re-appropriation by newly independent Malagasy citizens of their ancestral land? Might replanting have been both metaphor and material action for reclaiming a natural order from foreign influences after colonialism, as well as uniting citizens in a national effort? Were national tree festivals used to make statements about citizenship and regionalism, key dilemmas for many newly independent states? And if so, what light might this cast on Tsiranana's decision to focus the nation's attention on the reforestation of Androy in the wake of the 'Troubles'?

in Colonial Africa Reconsidered: Science and the Interpenetration of Knowledge', *African Affairs* **108** (432)(2009): 413–33. For the depoliticising function of 'development' operations see James Ferguson, *The Anti-politics Machine. 'Development', Depoliticization, and Bureaucratic Power in Lesotho* (Cambridge: Cambridge University Press, 1990). On 'territorialisation', see Peter Vandergeest and Nancy Lee Peluso, 'Territorialization and State Power in Thailand', *Theory and Society* 24 (1995): 385–426.

5.   Gillian Feeley-Harnik, '*Ravenala Madagascariensis* Sonnerat: The Historical Ecology of a "Flagship Species" in Madagascar', *Ethnohistory* 48/1–2 (2001): 31–86, 42.

Of Trees and the Political Imagination

Colonial Tree Festivals

The idea of promoting afforestation in Madagascar through an annual festival was by no means an innovation of the Tsiranana era. The first 'Tree Festival' (*Fête de l'arbre*), or 'Tree Week' (*Semaine de l'Arbre*) in the island was instituted by High Commissioner Robert Bargues in 1951. According to Bargues, the aim had been to nurture a kind of tree worship/devotion (*culte de l'arbre*) among the Malagasy population, and more specifically to use the medium of bodily learning to achieve this aim. By [reinforcing] the facts about tree planting by sensory, indeed even affective habit', Bargues hoped 'to get people fully to grasp the importance of reforestation and to create in this way a kind of mysticism around the tree'.[6]

It goes without saying that Bargues' initiative had deep taproots in western narratives about environmental degradation in Madagascar that dated to the earliest days of the French colonial regime. Sometimes named the 'Perrier/Humbert hypothesis' for its two most influential twentieth-century exponents, this narrative held that in historic times forest had covered almost all the island but had been decimated since man's arrival by bush fire and *tavy* [swidden-fallow agriculture], turning richly biodiverse forest into species-poor prairie and impoverishing the soil. To combat these perceived dangers, the French soon after conquest (1896) had began enacting legislation regulating fires and promoting forest protection that culminated in the forestry code of 1930.[7]

By contrast, the idea of promoting a love of trees and forest in the hearts and minds of a subject people through festivity and cultic practice was novel in the Madagascan context. In the broadest sense the initiative was the product of the so-called 'development decade' in Africa; its emphasis on techniques of the body as opposed to didactic forms of learning was in keeping with a reforming late colonial approach to governance. The fact that the cult was instituted in Madagascar in the wake of the 1947 anti-colonial rebellion is also significant. This rebellion– perhaps the bloodiest postwar anti-colonial rebellion in an African colony – broke out simultaneously in many towns on the East Coast on the night of 29 March 1947. Brutally quashed by the colonial forces, some authorities estimate it may have cost as many as 100,000 Malagasy lives. At a time when memory of the violence

---

6. National Archives Madagascar. Série IV D.73 Archives Provinciales. 6. Province de Tuléar. Service des Eaux et Forêts. Ambovombe Semaine de l'arbre 1951–1954. Chemise 1 Semaine de l'arbre 1951. Folio 12. Service Eaux et Forêts No 2963-SE/EF re Semaine de l'arbre, Tananarive 24 Octobre 1950 Inspecteur général de FOM Haut Commissaire de la République française à Madagascar et dépendances à Msrs les chefs de Province.

7. Henri Perrier de la Bâthie, 'La végétation malgache', *Annales du Musée Colonial de Marseille* 29/3 (1921): 9; Henri Humbert, 'Destruction d'une flore insulaire par le feu. Principaux aspects de la végétation à Madagascar', *Mémoires de l'Académie Malgache* V (1927): 1–80; cf. Christian Kull, 'Deforestation, Erosion, and Fire: Degradation Myths in the Environmental History of Madagascar', *Environment and History* 6/4: 423–50 and Christian Kull, *Isle of Fire. The Political Ecology of Landscape Burning in Madagascar* (Chicago and London: University of Chicago Press, 2004).

was still fresh for both colonisers and subjects, the state sought to discipline the peasant masses by encouraging the internalisation of late colonial values through bodily practice as much as the coercive imposition of norms. More specifically, the cult attempted to re-socialise spaces that during those years of insurrection and repression had become deeply anti-social – to bring forests, so often sites of fear and violence during the rebellion, back within state control.[8]

Bundesarchiv, B 145 Bild-F013783-0025
Foto: Wegmann, Ludwig I 29. August 1962

Figure 2. President and Mme Tsiranana being greeted by Willy Brandt at Tempelhof Airport during a state visit to Berlin in August 1962.

Typical of the genre of image that is regularly reprinted to support the thesis of a 'neo-colonial' regime. Source: Bundesarchiv B 145 Bild- F013783-0025 Berlin, Staatsbesuch aus Madagaskar, 29 August 1962. Wikimedia Commons.

The parallels between the context in which Bargues originally developed the tree festival in Madagascar and the circumstances in which Tsiranana decided to stage its performance in Androy are striking. And yet reiterated recourse to tree planting in the wake of bloody insurgence seems counterintuitive, in that tree-focused rules and regulations in the colonial and postcolonial periods were

---

8.   On the 1947 insurrection see Jacques Tronchon, *L'Insurrection Malgache de 1947: essai d'interprétation historique* (Paris: F. Maspero, 1974); Alain Spacensky, *Madagascar, cinquante ans de vie politique de Ralaimongo à Tsiranana* (Paris: Nouvelles Editions Latines, 1970); Virginia Thompson and Richard Adloff, *The Malagasy Republic. Madagascar Today* (Stanford, Ca.: Stanford University Press, 1965) Chapters 4 & 5. For Foucault's concept of disciplinary power, see Michel Foucault, *Discipline and Punish: the Birth of the Prison,* trans. Alan Sheridan (New York: Vintage, 1979).

among the environmental interventions that are said to have given rise to enduring hostilities between the Malagasy peasantry and the state.[9] The reiteration is likely to appear unproblematic to scholars who take the standard line on Madagascar under the First Republic (1960–1972), namely that it was a 'neocolony' in which an elite selected and groomed by the departing colonial power moved into government positions, 'exchanging its protection of the interests of the former colonial power for that power's protection of its own position'.[10] Environmental regulation had been a key trope in French colonial Madagascar and a nominally independent state, still 'glutted' with French advisors, might only to be expected to continue with the kinds of intervention favoured by the colonial state. Such is the general approach to the Tsiranana period taken by recent overviews of the history of conservation efforts in the island.[11] It is, however, my general contention that the 'neo-colonial' gloss, while capturing certain features of the Tsiranana period, obscures a more complex reality. One problem with an approach that focuses on continuity and persistence is that it leaves too many questions around the rituals of nation-building in the immediate post-independence period unexplored. I argue that, by examining the environmental rhetoric and practice of Africa's first leaders as much from the cultural and philosophical perspective as from the perspective of economic rationality and political control, it becomes possible to develop a more nuanced historiography of the 1960s, one that recognises new, imaginative appropriations of botany and nature framed by popular expectation and nationalist sentiment.

The Symbolism of Trees

The importance of trees in the human imagination has been highlighted for many contexts and from various disciplinary perspectives. Trees and tree planting have provided fundamental political metaphors in human societies from villages to kingdoms, serving to conceptualise genealogy, authority, and community structure, often naturalising political agendas. Royal efforts under Louis XVI to acclimatise foreign trees in the Rambouillet gardens were expressly designed to re-assert the Bourbon monarchy's commitment to agriculture, commerce and science, while signifying the revival of kingly authority and largesse as manifest in the landscape.

---

9. Covell, *Madagascar*; Daniela Raik, 'Forest Management in Madagascar. An Historical Overview', *Madagascar Conservation and Development* 2/1(2007): 5–10.

10. Covell, *Madagascar*, pp.36–8. On the First Republic see Covell *Madagascar*, ch. 3; Thompson and Adloff *The Malagasy Republic*, Chapters 5–9; Spacensky, *Madagascar, cinquante ans*; Robert Archer, *Madagascar depuis 1972: la marche d'une révolution* (Paris: L'Harmattan, 1976)chapters 2–4; Saura, *Philibert Tsirana*, Tome 1 and 2.

11. Sherry Olson, 'The Robe of the Ancestors. Forests in the History of Madagascar', *Journal of Forest History* 28/4 (October 1984): 174–86; Raik, 'Forest Management'; Kull, 'Deforestation, Erosion, and Fire': 54–6; Kull, *Isle of Fire*, pp.230–6 is more measured.

Karen Middleton

In Madagascar itself arboreal imagery has been central to the imagination of locality, kinship relatedness and clientelism, as well as, more pragmatically, rights in land.[12]

A particularly fertile field of enquiry has concerned the political value of trees in nation-building. Ideologies of state-making often have landscape components. Place is typically assumed to have an instrumental value in transforming residents of localities into citizens of a state through common landscape iconographies or, conversely, in thwarting such endeavours by offering alternative, more particularising idioms. As important aspects of place, plants can be critically implicated in these processes. They can be adopted as unifying one-nation symbols or become emblems of a more provincial identity that pulls against the centralising projects of the state.[13]

The importance of trees in project[s] of modern nation-building is well-documented for Europe and North America. In an edited collection focused on 'ecological nationalism' in postcolonial South Asia, Cederlöf and Sivaramakrishnan point to the equally crucial but less studied role of nature as a reference point for national aspirations and abiding concerns of sovereignty and self-determination in various independent Indian sub-continent states. They explore not only the unifying

---

12. Meredith Martin, 'Bourbon Renewal at Rambouillet', in L. Auricchio, E. Heckendorn Cook and G. Pacini (eds.) *Invaluable Trees: Cultures of Nature, 1660–1830* (Oxford: Voltaire Foundation, 2012) pp. 151–69, p.154; Laura Auricchio, Elizabeth Heckendorn Cook and Giulia Pacini, 'Introduction: Invaluable trees', in L. Auricchio et al. (eds.) *Invaluable Trees*, pp.1–26; Filip De Boeck, 'Of Trees and Kings: Politics and Metaphor among the Aluund of Southwestern Zaire'. *American Ethnologist* 21/3 (1994): 451–73; Laura Rival (ed.) *The Social Life of Trees. Anthropological Perspectives on Tree Symbolism* (Oxford: Berg, 1998); Simon Schama, *Landscape and Memory* (London: HarperCollins, 1995); Victor W. Turner, *The Forest of Symbols: Aspects of Ndembu Ritual* [1967] (Ithaca; London: Cornell University Press, 1982); James George Frazer, *The Golden Bough. A Study in Magic and Religion* [1890] Abridged version. (Oxford: Oxford University Press, 2009); Stephen Daniels, 'The Political Iconography of Woodland in Later Georgian England', in D. Cosgrove and S. Daniels (eds.) *The Iconography of Landscape. Essays in the Symbolic Representation, Design, and Use of Past Environments* (Cambridge: Cambridge University Press, 1988) pp.43–82; Douglas Davies, 'The Evocative Symbolism of Trees', in D. Cosgrove and S. Daniels (eds.) *The Iconography of Landscape*, pp.32–42; Jean Comaroff and John Comaroff, 'Naturing the Nation: Aliens, Apocalypse and the Postcolonial State', *Journal of Southern African Studies* 27/3 (2001): 627–51; Gillian Feeley-Harnik, *A Green Estate: Restoring Independence in Madagascar* (Washington, D.C.: Smithsonian Institution Press, 1991); Karen Middleton, 'How Karembola Men Become Mothers', in J. Carsten (ed.) *Cultures of Relatedness: New Approaches to the Study of Kinship.* (Cambridge: Cambridge University Press, 2000) pp. 104–27.

13. See e.g. Stephen Daniels, *Fields of Vision: Landscape Imagery and National Identity in England and the United States* (Princeton: Princeton University Press, 1993); Schama, *Landscape and Memory*; Coates 2006 Peter Coates, *American Perceptions of Immigrant and Invasive Species: Strangers on the Land* (Berkeley, Ca.: University of California Press, 2006); James W. Fernandez, 'Trees of Knowledge of Self and Other in Culture: On Models for the Moral Imagination', in L. Rival ed. *The Social Life of Trees*, pp.81–110.

power of natural symbols but also the way *contested* natures become engaged with conflicting nationalisms and place-based collective identities.[14]

In Africanist scholarship, Binder and Burnett note that nature and landscape figure in postcolonial fiction with some authors registering an alienation from, and nostalgia for, a landscape lost to colonialism and capitalism as well as the possibility of restoring balance and bounty to the land through collective action and social will.[15] If less perhaps has been written on Africa's first post-independence politicians, this is partly because environmental historians of Africa have largely neglected the 1960s. Treating the period as little more than an *intermezzo* between the colonial era and the rise of 1980s neoliberal conservationism, they have relied more on the broad brush concept of 'colonial legacy' than on empirical case studies to characterise state environmental policy and practice in this decade.[16]

The problem with starting with the premise of persistence is that it runs the risk of obscuring sight of what may be different. I argue that, just as Christian iconography of the verdant cross in Europe drew on earlier pagan imagery and in turn fed into American culture,[17] so too, in appropriating the colonial Tree Festival for an independent Madagascar, Tsiranana both remodelled its practice and its justifying discourse. First, and most obviously, Tsiranana not only addressed his compatriots as a native Malagasy speaker but also deployed different terms of address. Tsiranana was acutely sensitive to the status inflections of local kinship vocabulary and throughout his term in office paid careful attention to the language he used. The significance of voice becomes all the more pertinent when we remember that Tsiranana was noted for his consummate mastery of radio. In the era of mass democracy he was quick to spot its potential to reach the largely illiterate rural masses who constituted the bedrock of his support. As a Malagasy, Tsiranana was also – at least in the early years of his Presidency – better placed than High Commissioner Bargues to exploit the symbolism of authority, fertility and blessing of a ceremony essentially modelled on the *hasina* rituals of the nineteenth-century Merina kings and queens. And, where Bargues had sought to 'back up', as he put it, the 'facts' about tree planting by nurturing spiritual values, Tsiranana now attempted to join prohibition, spiritual values and festivity to an active obligation to reforest in the name of national reconstruction. In 1962 tree planting was instituted as a civic duty in Madagascar. All able-bodied males aged between 21 and 55 years were required to participate in the work of national reafforestation (*l'oeuvre nationale de*

---

14. Gunnel Cederlöf and K. Sivaramakrishnan (eds.) *Ecological Nationalisms: Nature, Livelihoods, and Identities in South Asia* (Delhi: Permanent Black, 2005).

15. Renée Binder and G.W. Burnett, 'Ngugi Wa Thiong'o and the Search for a Populist Landscape Aesthetic', *Environmental Values* 3/1 (1994): 47–59.

16. Wapulumuka Oliver Mulwafu, *Conservation Song. A History of Peasant-State Relations and the Environment in Malawi, 1860–2000* (Cambridge: White Horse Press, 2011) is a rare exception.

17. Schama, *Landscape and Memory*, pp.15, 214–25.

Karen Middleton

Figure 3. 20 franc postage stamp commemorating the 1961 Tree Festival.

Note the conjunction of the national motto 'Liberty – Ancestral Land – Development' [*Fahafana – Tanindrazana – Fandrosoana]* with 'National Reforestation Duty' [*Reboiser Devoir National / adidy amin'ny firenena ny fambolen'hazo*].

reboisement) by planting at least fifty forest or fruit trees annually or by contributing to forest protection or soil conservation work. Any man unable to discharge this national duty in person might get it executed by a third party or pay 100 francs in compensation each year.[18]

Links between tree planting and national reconstruction were given resonances in 1960s discourse that went well beyond the economic. 'Land', or more precisely 'soil', was construed as a critical component of 'national patrimony'. Madagascar's motto under the First Republic was Liberty – Ancestral Land – Development [*Fahafana– Tanindrazana – Fandrosoana*; see Figure 3]. The French term *la terre* is of course convergent with both *le sol* [soil] and *la patrie* [country]. The Malagasy term *tàny* has a similar polyvalence ranging from the strictly geological ('land', 'soil', 'the earth') through types of landscape, both physical and spiritual, to political

---

18. *Journal Officiel de la Republique Malgache* 79(329)/38 (décembre 1963): 2808. On the outcomes of this legislation in the Karembola region, see Karen Middleton, 'Land Rights and Alien Plants in Dryland Madagascar', in G. Campbell, S. Evers and M. Lambek (eds.) *The Politics of Marketing Land: Values, Conservation and Development in Madagascar* (Leiden: Brill, in press).

entities (kingdom, region, country).[19] This semantic complexity is accentuated in the concept of Madagascar as the *tanindrazana* [land of ancestors/ancestral land].

On account of deforestation, the argument went, this precious 'heritage' was being carried in vast quantities by swollen rivers from denuded slopes to the ocean. Thus, it became a fundamental duty incumbent upon the citizens of the fledgling state to conserve this actual and symbolic capital by reforestation and soil conservation works. The language was calculated, implicitly, if not consciously, to appeal to the many Malagasy peoples whose cultural practice focused on retaining vital ancestral resources within endogamous kinship groups.[20]

The masses were urged to hold this *soil* in trust for future generations. Explaining in 1968 why tree planting had remained a regular feature of the state calendar and a core theme of National Reconstruction since Independence, the forestry service proclaimed

> Our most certain wealth is agriculture, which is to say: THE EARTH [LA TERRE]! Year on year, Hèlas! This priceless capital of the whole Nation is degrading inexorably.[21]

In particular, the nearly four million citizens under twenty years old, who constituted 55 per cent of the population, were urged

> never [to] forget that Madagascar, their dear HOMELAND, is located in the terrestrial band that economists call: 'The Famine Belt'. This band, which encircles planet Earth between the 25th degree latitude North and the 25th degree parallel South ... [is a] Zone, where powerful natural elements converge to render the physical and biological equilibrium of the land, of the soil, so precarious that a fertile region can turn into desert within three generations ... The 'Law' of the 'Famine Belt' is inexorable and fatal in this region, holding to ransom all mistakes.[22]

Noting that 1968 had seen an 'infernal outbreak of bush fires', it called upon Malagasy youth to 'affirm its faith in the tree cult'. 'It is in this spirit that we shall smash the tragic "Famine Belt", and ensure the future of free and happy descendants in a green country running with milk and honey.'[23]

It is tempting to dismiss this as colonial discourse in so far as it recuperates imagery already found in 1950s discourse. But to do so would be to miss the key point. The pseudo-religious imagery that had characterised Bargues' discourse was given nationalist inflections, linking a love for trees to a love of *patrie*. We can see such ritual as attempting to naturalise Tsiranana's power, to culturalise what was

---

19. Cf. Philippe Beaujard, Philippe, *Dictionnaire malgache (dialectal)-français: dialecte tañala, sud-est de Madagascar, avec recherché étymologiques* (Paris: L'Harmattan, 1998) p. 691.

20. See e.g. Maurice Bloch, *Placing the Dead: Tombs, Ancestral villages, and Kinship Organization in Madagascar* (London: Seminar Press, 1971); Middleton, 'How Karembola Men Become Mothers'.

21. VP 850. Eaux et Forêts. Direction des Eaux et Forêts. Discours [1968] 14 f.

22. Ibid. f. 7

23. Ibid. f.12–3.

essentially onerous duty through celebration and festivity and to re-present external imposition as 'patriotic duty'. Bargues had intended the tree festivals to be apolitical events in a deeply troubled era; he described them 'as something on which all could agree'.[24] Under the *Parti Social-Démocrate* (PSD), Tsiranana's party, they became political rallies. The post-independence government, combining populism and statism, attempted a new 'moral economy of landscape', aimed at restoring and retaining the national patrimony and uniting Malagasy in that work.

Scholars working within narrative generated by the 1972 'May Revolution' regularly point to the problems of legitimacy that Tsiranana faced. My own per- spective is slightly different. The challenge for the Tsiranana government, I suggest, was not so much its own legitimacy – it enjoyed repeated success at the polls – as a corresponding lack of civic identity among the populace. In the late 1950s French advisors had argued that successful outcomes for state initiatives in agriculture, forestry and soil conservation might be secured by appealing to a 'nascent patriot- ism for the infant Malagasy Republic'. In the event, however, the *loi cadre* in 1956 ushered in a fractious, heterovocal popular culture, involving alternative forms of leadership and identity. These included the resurgence of regional monarchies, reconfigurations of the Christian Churches and the democratisation of spirit pos- session cults. Because citizenship and a true nationalism for *patrie* turned out to be less easy to build than had been anticipated, Tsiranana was obliged to burn the candle at both ends. Nature was appropriated to the project of state building, and nationalism to the conservationist cause. Attempts were made to secure popular support for difficult economic policies by drawing on public sentiment for Tsiranana while also building national identity and leadership through the creative medium of the tree cult.

In constituting tree planting as a civic duty, Tsiranana was less concerned with nature preservation (whether at the scale of landscapes or of particular species) than with protecting and improving the conditions of human subsistence. Unlike his contemporary, the Indian prime minister Indira Gandhi, he did not subscribe to the romantic myth of a wild Africa. He was more interested in safeguarding food production and securing timber for Madagascar's population through the protection of watersheds.[25] Tsiranana was heavily influenced by René Dumont's (1959) analysis of the race between agricultural production and the demographic explosion in Madagascar.[26] This had restated the classic arguments about destructive anthropogenic change but made them compelling for nationalists such as Tsiranana

---

24.   Service Eaux et Forêts No 2963-SE/EF re Semaine de l'arbre, Tananarive 24 Octobre 1950.

25.   Mahesh Ranjarajan, 'Striving for a Balance: Nationalism, Power, Science and India's Indira Gan- dhi, 1917–1984', *Conservation and Society* 7/4 (2009): 299–312; Jonathan Adams and Thomas McShane, *The Myth of Wild Africa* (New York: W.W. Norton and Co, 1992).

26.   René Dumont, *Evolution des campagnes malgaches. Quelques problèmes essentiels d'orientation et de modernisation de l'agriculture malgache* (Tananarive: Imprimerie Officielle, 1959).

by emphasising the devastating impact that deteriorating ecological conditions would have on Madagascar's ability to feed itself. In defining the problem with greater emphasis on the implications for food security than for nature conservation, Dumont's analysis pointed to need for anti-erosive actions *within* farming systems rather than to the creation of further nature/forest reserves. 1960s fears of the population time bomb have been challenged from Boserupian and neo-Boserupian perspectives[27] but Tsiranana took them seriously enough to make agriculture, rather than industrialisation, the investment priority under the first Malagasy Plan (1964).

Rethinking Desert Androy

It was reported that Tsiranana decided to make reforestation the first development operation to undertake in the '*Le Grand Sud*' following the 'Troubles' because 'he considers, wherever there are trees, microclimates develop, bringing humidity and water'. And to prove that development of this the most deprived zone of Madagascar was possible, the head of state had chosen the site at Beratro, in the *driest* region of Androy, to launch 'Operation Reafforestation Androy' on 16 March 1972 to coincide with 'National Reforestation Day' (*Journée Nationale de Reboisement*).[28]

Although reforestation had been a key development strategy in Madagascar throughout the sixties, Androy had been largely left out of the national picture. When in 1968, for instance, the forestry official warned of the 'famine belt' that would encircle Madagascar if current rates of deforestation continued, he illustrated his thesis by contrasting the denuded slopes of the Betsiboka river on the west coast, where 'annually 240 million cubic metres of good fertile land were discharged into the sea', with East Coast Madagascar, where 'waters rise but are not coloured with the blood of the earth' and 'where ferocious, violent swellings were unknown' because plant cover remained.[29] He made no reference to the Malagasy Deep South. In practice, too, state environmental ritual throughout the first decade of independence had expressed Androy's perennial marginality. While 'National Reforestation Day', the ceremony which inaugurated the annual tree planting campaign in Madagascar, continued to rotate between the regions in that finely judged balance between *côtiers*

27. Esther Boserup, *The Conditions of Agricultural Growth: the Economics of Agrarian Change under Population Pressure* (London: Allen and Unwin, 1965); Mary Tiffen, Michael Mortimore and Francis Gichuki, *More People, Less Erosion: Environmental Recovery in Kenya* (Chichester: Wiley, 1994); James Fairhead and Melissa Leach, *Misreading the African Landscape. Society and Ecology in a Forest-savanna Mosaic* (Cambridge: Cambridge University Press, 1996).

28. 'La Grande Opération'; 'La Reforestation'. See note 1.

29. Discours f004–5. The Betsiboka in flood, stained red with the 'blood' of Madagascar's soil, became iconic of environmental degradation in the island (see e.g. Jacques Millot, 'In Conclusion', in R. Battistini & G. Richard-Vindard (eds.) *Biogeography and Ecology in Madagascar* (The Hague: W. Junk, 1972), pp.741–56, p. 752). For a cultural symbolist exploration see Feeley-Harnik, '*Ravenala Madagascariensis*'; Kull, *Isle of Fire* provides a more prosaic account.

Karen Middleton

and highlanders (Merina) that characterised the Tsiranana years, it had never been staged in the Malagasy Deep South.

Following the 'Troubles', Tsiranana not only decided to stage 'National Reforestation Day' for the first time in Androy, but technical assistance within the ministries now saw Androy's parched landscapes as a particularly redolent setting in which to enact the national tragedy of desertification and the redemptive power of tree planting. Androy now became a cipher for what could happen to the whole island if degradation went unchecked. Hardly 250 years ago, the nation was told, the South had been covered with an immense forest, with an extraordinarily rich and varied flora. Water scarcity constituted the great challenge in the region, and reforestation was one means of meeting it. The objective was 'ambitious but realistic and attainable'. It was a matter of combating the phenomenon of 'desertification' through persistent tree planting, to moderate the climate and conserve the soil. Preceded by an intense campaign to sensitise the populations, this 'vast, ambitious operation' aimed, in Tsiranana's own words, 'to restore to arid Androy its once legendary forest, such as Robert Drury described'.[30] In turning to *Robert Drury's Journal*, a book which purports to be the narrative of a English boy held captive in early eighteenth-century Androy, to substantiate the claim that '[t]here was a time when the South was verdant and a forest, a time when the waters of the Mandrare ran at the same height 365 days a year', Tsiranana broke with French tradition. Etienne de Flacourt's *Histoire de la grande isle Madagascar*, the seventeenth-century text that had dominated the French imagination in Madagascar for three centuries, is at best equivocal on forest cover and water resources in the Malagasy Deep South.[31]

Tsiranana responded to perceived dystopia in the South by invoking a botanical utopia that might be possible to recover through collaboration between local people and the state. The verdant forest Tsiranana ascribed to historical Androy made it look more or less like the rest of Madagascar. By contrast, the Deputies had drawn on local oral traditions in imagining an ancestral landscape of prickly pear, a culturally emblematic exotic plant. While the Deputies embraced a botany that was specific to, characteristic of, and (so they believed) endemic to Androy, Tsiranana, wishing to avoid the kind of tribal ecology that colonialism had sponsored, espoused a nationalism that sought to integrate particular localities and diverse histories into one storyline. One People, one Party, one President, one Forest, island-wide.[32]

---

30. 'La Reforestation'.

31. Etienne de Flacourt, *Histoire de la grande isle Madagascar* [1658] edited and annotated by Claude Allibert (Paris: INALCO/Éditions Karthala, 1995) pp.137, 140; Robert Drury, *Madagascar: or, Robert Drury's journal, during fifteen years captivity on that island...Written by himself* [1729] (London: J. Brotherton, T. Worrall; and J. Jackson, 1731). Authorship is disputed, sometimes being attributed [in part] to Daniel Defoe: cf. Philip Furbank and W.R. Owens, *Defoe De-Attributions: A Critique of J.R.Moore'S Checklist* (London: Hambledon, 1994).

32. On prickly pear in southern Malagasy cultures see Raymond Decary, 'L'utilisation des Opuntias en Androy (Extrême-Sud de Madagascar)', *Revue de Botanique Appliquée et d'Agriculture Colo-*

Of Trees and the Political Imagination

We can thus detect at least two kinds of botanical nationalism within the ruling party itself. One underscored the exceptionalism of Androy (albeit with reference to a pseudo-indigenous plant) while the other denied it. Both however denied that Androy suffered 'state of nature' destitution. All saw its aridity and its vulnerability to famines as historically produced. For much of the colonial period aridity had been seen as a natural condition of Androy, one of Nature's laws. Androy had been consequently treated as an exception to the narrative of island-wide anthropogenic desertification. Its xerophilous vegetation, it was claimed, ruled out *tavy* (swidden-fallows) and bush fires.[33] In theory, exemption from the declinist narrative ought to have resulted in positive imagery of the environmental consciousness of Southern Malagasy farmers and herders. In practice, it placed them in a state of nature, outside history. Tandroy abstention from the pyrogenic habits of their compatriots was attributed to Nature rather than to any indigenous 'conservation ethos'.

The narrative of the eternal desert had begun to be questioned in the 1930s when a few colonial administrators made tentative suggestions that Androy was becoming progressively drier.[34] It gathered momentum in the late 1940s with the publication of Henri Humbert's essays warning that destruction of its primitive vegetation was transforming the Deep South into a veritable desert.[35] By the late1950s there was emergent consensus within the colonial technical services that aridity, formerly considered a perennial feature of the region, was an accelerating historical trend for which human-induced processes of deforestation were to blame. Tsiranana and the PSD Deputies drew on these late colonial dessicationist narratives but adapted them to new political exigencies. In the immediate optimism of

niale 5/50 (1925): 769-771; Raymond Decary, *L'Androy (L'Extrême Sud de Madagascar)*. Essai de Monographie Régionale (Paris: Société d'Editions Géographiques, Maritimes et Coloniales, 1930) p. 128; Karen Middleton, 'Circumcision, Death and Strangers', *Journal of Religion in Africa* 27/4 (1997): 341–73 and K. Middleton, 'From Ratsiraka to Ravalomanana: Changing Narratives of Prickly Pears in Dryland Madagascar', Études Océan Indien. Plantes et Sociétés *42–43* (Paris: INALCO, 2009) pp. 47–83 For a succinct account of the *politique des races* in Madagascar see Manassé Esoavelomandroso, 'Une arme de domination: le "tribalisme" à Madagascar (XIXᵉ – milieu du XXᵉ siècle)', in J.-P. Chrétien and G. Prunier (eds.) *Les ethnies ont une historie* [1989] 2nd edn (Paris: Karthala, 2003) pp.259–66.

33. Jean Koechlin, 'Flora and Vegetation of Madagascar', in R. Battistini & G. Richard-Vindard (eds.) *Biogeography and Ecology in Madagascar* (The Hague: W. Junk, 1972) pp.145–90, pp.179–80; Jean Koechlin, J.-L. Guillaumet and Philippe Morat, *Flore et végétation de Madagascar* (Vaduz: J. Cramer, 1974) p.312.

34. Decary, *L'Androy*, pp. 13-16; Fonds Decary MS 3088 Ensemble de notes, cartes et croquis sur le Sud de Madagascar. 7. Famines. Extrait du CR de tournée de chef de District d'Ambovombe du mois de septembre 1934.

35. Henri Humbert 1947, 'Changements survenus dans la végétation du Sud de Madagascar', *Revue internationale de botanique appliquée et d'agriculture tropicale* 27 (301–2) (1947): 441–4; H. Humbert, 'Un exemple suggestif de désertification provoquée: les territoires du Sud de Madagascar', *Naturaliste Malgache* 54 (1953): 5–17.

Karen Middleton

independence the Deputies accepted the theses of anthropogenic desertification and erosion as factual statements but shifted the blame onto the French colonisers and called for landscape renaissance based on prickly pear. Ten years later, concerned to achieve national reconciliation at multiple levels (environmental, political, economic, ethnic and sentimental) in the aftermath of bloody insurrection, Tsiranana insisted that Androy shared a common Malagasy history of desertification and that the work of national reconstruction could and should be extended to the South. Given that Androy had long been seen as an economy in which hunger, deprivation and low productivity were primarily a function of climate, there was something radical and much to be admired in Tsiranana's assertion that a dedicated campaign of tree planting could *alter* the climate of Androy, turn drought-adapted flora back into verdant woodland and cheat Nature of the 'severity of her laws'.

Tsiranana's integrationist approach not only sought environmental unity for the nation. It also sought ethnic reconfiguration by confronting the longstanding ambivalence if not disdain of many nationalists for the Tandroy, generally considered 'the most retarded (*arrières*) of the Malgaches'. To be sure, there had been a new inclusiveness in public discourse in the period leading up to and immediately after Independence as nationalists attempted a rhetoric of belonging that was more inclusive of the South. In practice, however, many Malagasy still perceived Tandroy as utterly other, the nation's 'hinterland' or 'bush'. Many nationalists shared Tsiranana's reluctance to play up ecological difference and regional landscapes because French colonialism had harnessed Madagascar's natural diversity to ideas of human diversity through the idea of the island's eighteen 'tribes', each shaped by its environment to a particular degree of civilisation. In the wake of the 'Troubles', however, the temptation to resort to explanations based on atavistic violence by semi-wild people shaped by an inhospitable landscape was strong. While the measured tones of the Catholic weekly *Lumière* set the precedent for much public commentary, Merina intellectual and leader of the AKFM party,[36] Richard Andriamanjato, could not resist observing that the Tandroy were by nature volatile.

Given the deep history of naturalising Androy and its people, Tsiranana could also have responded to the uprising by portraying it as a brute act of Nature, the 'premodern' violence of a people without culture or history. By assimilating them to more 'civilised' Malagasy peoples who had destroyed their primitive Edens, Tsiranana sought to (re)create a common past for Madagascar where Androy, like other parts of the island, had once been forested – and with recognisable woodland too. This memory of a humid, forested Androy had a dimension of possibility: it suggested an Androy that might be 'developed' in the future by recovery of its past. This conjunction of past and future recalls a sense of the future that permeates much postcolonial African literature. Noting that utopianism is often supposed to have

---

36. Antokon'ny Kongresy ho an'ny Fahaleovantenan'i Madagasikara.

died with post-independence disillusionment, Bill Ashcroft argues that a vision of the future grounded in a resurgent memory of the past was in fact an essential feature of African literature. He suggests that the function of memory in African post-colonial utopianism 'is not about recovering a past but about the production of possibility'. 'In such transformative conceptions of utopian hope', he writes, 'the In-Front-Of-Us is always a possibility emerging from the past'.[37] The case of Tsiranana and the PSD Deputies suggests that some of the African politicians who came to office with independence – the very men who were sometimes subjected to the fictional critiques–were also capable of envisioning a 'cyclic "return" to the future'. They articulated a vision of a resurgent Madagascar that would restore an ancient verdancy to its drylands through collective social will.

Tsiranana's attempt to expand the parameters of possibility by drawing creatively on colonial narrative was, however, out of step with emergent expatriate scientific expertise. Under the influence of the globally ascendant science of ecology, a number of French technicians in Madagascar had begun to question the hypothesis of the island-wide forest in favour of models that recognised a historical mosaic of diverse ecologies and to reject the narrative of human-induced aridification in Madagascar for one that attributed aridification at least partly to climatic fluctuations.[38] This theoretical revision was at odds with Tsiranana's insistence on man's role in creating the desert and on man's ability to regreen the world. Although these new French positions *partly* absolved their former subjects of responsibility for desertification, they also put Malagasy destinies back in nature, beyond Malagasy control. To attribute aridification to long-term cycles of climate change rather than to man-made deforestation defined it as a problem which National Reconstruction could not tackle through patriotic tree planting.

Multiple Botanies

How did botanic discourse on Androy's deep past relate to nation-building? A salient feature of the botanic idiom in Malagasy politics, writes Feeley-Harnik, is precisely its sensitivity to place, conveyed in the very rootedness of trees in specific habitats.

---

37. Bill Ashcroft, 'Remembering the Future: Utopianism in African Literature', *Textual Practice* 23/5 (2009): 703–22; Cf. Ralph Pordzik, *The Quest for Postcolonial Utopia. A Comparative Introduction to the Utopian Novel in New English Literatures* (New York: Peter Lang, 2001).

38. F. Bourgeat, 'Contribution à l'étude des sols sur socle ancien à Madagascar. Types de différenciation et intepretation chronologique au cours du Quaternaire'. Mém. ORSTOM 57, 1972; René Battistini, 'L'homme et l'équilibre de la nature à Madagascar', in *Comptes Rendus de la Conférence internationale sur la conservation de la Nature et des ses ressources à Madagascar, Tananarive 7–11 October 1970* (Morges, Switzerland: IUCN, 1972) pp.91–4; René Battistini and Pierre Vérin, 'Man and the Environment in Madagascar; past problems and problems of today', in Battistini and Richard-Vindard (eds) *Biogeography and Ecology*, pp. 311–35, p. 324; Koechlin, 'Flora and Vegetation'; Koechlin et al. *Flore et végétation*.

Karen Middleton

Yet its potential for broader application is derived from the generic attributes of trees which lend themselves to human efforts to grasp the more general political, economic, and ecological dimensions of 'environments'. Clearly one possibility in a country as ecologically diverse as Madagascar is that native or naturalised species can easily become regional symbols, contenders for more particularistic 'ecological nationalisms'.[39] The Tsiranana government is often portrayed as pursuing an identity based on nation and national territory and suppressing alternative identities and celebrations of local belonging. Feeley-Harnik claims that Tsiranana followed French colonial officials in curtailing or outlawing practices in which Malagasy sought to restore dead or exiled rulers of regional polities to political life. In the Analalava (west coast) region she studied such rituals focused on the 'tree-body' of a dead king. From this she elaborates the more general thesis that in Madagascar struggles between state and local communities over land, labour and political loyalty often took the form of struggles over trees.[40] One might suppose therefore that a marked regional endemism in Malagasy flora had the potential to subvert Tsiranana's centralising project. Sensitive to locality, rooted in specific places, Malagasy trees ran counter to a citizenship based on identity and unity.

In fact struggles began early in the 1960s within the ruling party itself to develop an ecological nationalism that allowed for regional diversity and particular histories. In 1963 five PSD Deputies, representing constituencies in the south, petitioned the National Assembly for the national development plan to include a programme to restore Malagasy Cactus to the region. This plant had been an important source of fruit, water and livestock fodder in the Malagasy Deep South; the Deputies argued that its eradication in the 1920s by a French-introduced cochineal insect had ruptured the environmental equilibrium, and destroyed the natural windbreaks, causing soil erosion to escalate. But, although they made their argument chiefly on economic grounds, the Deputies had in mind a broader project of political and cultural renaissance. They intended the replanting to be 'an act of restitution' for 'the most deprived zone of the national territory', an atonement for the particular injury it had suffered at the hands of the colonial regime.[41] This is not a narrative about the feckless native (restyled 'peasantry' since the late

---

39. Feeley-Harnik, '*Ravenala Madagascariensis*': 35–6. Cf Owain Jones and Paul Cloke, *Tree Cultures: the Place of Trees and Trees in their Place* (Oxford: Berg, 2002). On the endemism of Madagascar's flora, Perrier de la Bâthie, 'La végétation malgache' and H. Perrier de la Bâthie, *Biogéographie des plantes de Madagascar* (Paris: Société d'Éditions Géographiques, Maritimes et Coloniales, Challamel, 1936); Humbert, 'Destruction d'une flore' and H. Humbert, 'Origines présumées et affinités de la Flore de Madagascar', *Mémoires de l'Institut Scientifique de Madagascar* Series B, IX (1959): 149–87; Koechlin et al. *Flore et végétation*.

40. Feeley-Harnik, *A Green Estate*. For an alternative view see Suzanne Chazan-Gillig, *La société sakalave: Le Menabe dans la construction nationale malgache, 1947–1972* (Paris: Éditions de l'Orstom, 1991).

41. Cf. Karen Middleton, 'Who killed "Malagasy Cactus"? Science, Environment and Colonialism in Southern Madagascar (1924–1930)', *Journal of Southern African Studies* 25 (1999): 215–48.

1950s) who deforested the landscape through bush fires and tavy. The argument was subtly but profoundly anti-colonial. It accepted deforestation and desertification of the Malagasy Deep South were real observable processes but put the blame on the French. Again, there are analogies with postcolonial African fiction in the reconfiguration, sometimes ironically, of western forms.[42]

In calling for Malagasy Cactus restoration, these PSD loyalists were hoping to recuperate an *authentic* regional ecology. Theirs was a subnationalist discourse, one that chimed with local narrative about forest loss.[43] The Forestry Service in Tananarive objected, pointing out that these traditional landscapes had in fact involved an introduced species, but nevertheless agreed two concessions. First, the 1962 legislation, which had instituted tree planting as a statutory duty in Madagascar, was amended to allow southern Malagasy to meet their annual quotas by planting prickly pear. Second, the forestry service agreed to support this peasant effort by propagating the more popular spiny forms of the plant.

In 1972 the mass Eucalyptus plantings at Beratro prompted Pascal Andriampaniry Ratsimba, an ethnic Merina resident in Ambovombe, to articulate yet another regional botanical nationalism, again figuring Malagasy Cactus but in an interestingly different way. He wrote to the Forestry Service rehearsing familiar criticisms of planting schemes based on this Australian plant family, which was habitually used for state reforestation in Madagascar and which in critical scholarship is typically associated with maladroit western forestry interventions in African colonies. Claiming that Eucalypts had already had deleterious effects on ricefields in the Highlands, he predicted that these plants in Androy would 'empty' the water table and dry up wells. In fact he objected to the use of alien trees in Androy in principle. It was better to reconstitute plant cover with xerophilous species, above all cactus, which he believed was indigenous. Although he expected the task ahead to be arduous, he could already imagine local people praising the President: 'the colonialists killed our grand-fathers' *raketa*, but President Philibert Tsiranana has resuscitated them!'[44]

Like Tsiranana, Ratsimba refused to accept that *la patrie* harboured desert corners by design. But, unlike Tsiranana, Ratsimba believed that reafforestation

42. Pordzik, *The Quest*, p. 29; cf. Elleke Boehmer, *Colonial and Postcolonial Literature. Migrant Metaphors* [1995] 2nd edn (Oxford: Oxford University Press, 2005); Bill Ashcroft, Gareth Griffiths and Helen Tiffen (eds.) *The Empire Writes Back: Theory and Practice in Post-Colonial Literatures.* [1989] 2nd edn (London: Routledge, 2002).

43. Manassé Esoavelomandroso, 'La forêt dans le Mahafale aux XIXᵉ et XXᵉ siècles', *Aombe* 3 (1991): 97–102; Middleton, 'Circumcision, Death and Strangers'.

44. VP916 Sauvetage et Développement du Sud. 1971–1972. 'Développement et reforestation du Sud. Notes, Rapport, Correspondance 1971–1972. Suggestions pour la réalisation de la décision de M. le Président de la République Malagasy sur le reboisement du Sud de Madagascar par M. Pascal Andriampaniry Ratsimba [n.d.]. Forwarded to Secretaire d'Etat à l'hydraulique agricole et aux Eaux et Forêts 22 mars 1972.

Karen Middleton

Figure 4. Alluaudia procera, or fantiolotse.

A member of the *Didiereaceae family*, the most remarkable of plant families endemic to Madagascar, and one of the characteristic species of the xerophilous thickets of the Malagasy Deep South, considered by many botanists to be the most original of Malagasy floral domains. Photograph: Karen Middleton, Tranovaho, south of Beloha, 2003.

efforts in the region should focus on recovering its original drought-adapted plant cover, of which he believed Malagasy Cactus to have been a key species. 'With its cover of xerophilous plants typical of semi-desertic or semi-arid zones, such as the *raketa*', he declared, 'the region never knew the degree of drought it has experienced every year since man destroyed the *raketa* [prickly pear].' Whereas the Deputies nine years earlier had advocated reforestation with one core species, Ratsimba hoped to recover an holistic ecological complex, based on Malagasy Cactus but comprising the full range of species endemic to the South.

These various reimaginings of Androy's floral history were at odds with growing western interest in its actual indigenous flora. For decades French colonial foresters had been reluctant to accept the region's 'dwarf' or 'stunted' flora into the ranks of 'proper', or *beau forêt* ('fine forest'), a term with both aesthetic and utilitarian connotations. New forms of travel writing in the 1950s began to transform botanical curiosity into tourist spectacle; but it was above all during the First

Republic that expatriate scientific interest in the south's curious drought-adapted flora grew. Such interest, among plant collectors who began visiting in increasing numbers but more significantly among French botanists attached to ORSTOM, was driven by consciousness of its extreme particularity [Figure 4].[45] The botanical nationalisms espoused by Tsiranana and the PSD Deputies were either unaware of such developments or ignored them. The Deputies bestowed on Androy a singular past based on prickly pear cactus, an exotic to which they misascribed autochthonous status. Tsiranana espoused an equally mythical vision of a verdant Eden. Ratsimba's vision of its historical plant formation went furthest in recognising the indigenous flora but was still anchored to local oral traditions by making Malagasy Cactus the key species.

World as Picture

It might be argued that, in including the south in an environmental history shared by all Malagasy peoples, Tsiranana sidestepped the specific and critical issues of political economy that had fuelled the 'Troubles': issues of equity and investment. Already marginalised in the colonial period, the drylands of Madagascar had subsequently been excluded from the clientelist–populist relationships that developed during the First Republic, becoming critical to processes of wealth accumulation in the immediate post-Independence period and to new power relations between locality and the state.[46]

It is tempting to regard Tsiranana's initiative with cynicism and to conclude that he turned to tree planting because he lacked the wherewithal to address the truly intractable problems of the Malagasy Deep South. 'If the government intends to carry through this ambitious action', Minister Emile Ramarosaona had told the press beforehand, 'it is not in the least with political designs, that is to say, in order to "pretend to be doing something", but rather to show its firm intention to turn this denuded zone, poor by nature, into a prosperous country like other parts of the island.'[47] Artifice and spectacle were indeed integral to the day's festivities. The ephemeral village at Beratro was suggestive of an earlier tradition of colonial expositions, except that, rather than install a Tandroy village beside ersatz Moorish palace and Angkor Wat temple in the Bois de Vincennes, a modern village, epitomising if not the European then at least the Madagascar 'metropolitan', was imagined on the periphery.

---

45. Perrier de la Bâthie *Biogéographie des plantes*; cf. Humbert 'Origines présumées'; Werner Rauh, *Succulent and Xerophytic Plants of Madagascar* (Mill Valley, Ca.: Strawberry Press, 1995, 1998).

46. The best study of these processes is Chazan-Gillig, *La société sakalave,* for the Morondava region (West Coast) from where many of Madagascar's new statesmen came.

47. 'La Reforestation'.

Karen Middleton

But before we dismiss the event as solely concerned with the creation of 'the world as picture', we should note two important points. First, as far as it is possible to tell from his recorded statements, it appears that Tsiranana genuinely subscribed to the view that by planting trees it was possible to create 'microclimates bringing humidity and fertility to the pre-desertic regions of the Great South'. Such a conviction was in keeping with his faith in redemptive transformation, both biblical and modern. He subscribed to the same postwar possibilism that had been greening the deserts of Israel and Egypt while, as a practicing Roman Catholic, his ecologism drew on Christianity – a religion of utopia *par excellence* – combining this with references to the ancestors. A reading of *Le cahier bleu*– the diary Tsiranana kept during the months he spent in Paris recovering from the stroke he suffered in January 1970 – suggests that he was also drawing on the therapeutic effects of aesthetic engagement with nature he had experienced in his extended convalescence.[48]

Second, and more importantly, in the wake of the 'Troubles' Tsiranana ordered the Second Five Year Malagasy Plan to be redrafted so as to prioritise development operations in *le Grand Sud*. Tsiranana may have turned to environmental discourse as a way of depoliticising the crisis or mystifying its causes. But his socialism led him back to a materialist history that recognised the roots of poverty in disinvestment. Greening Androy was envisioned as part of a broader well-funded rescue operation. Indeed I argue elsewhere that Tsiranana's determination to divert an unprecedented percentage of the national budget to this stricken region alarmed those who benefited from existing patronage networks and was a critical but hitherto unacknowledged factor in his downfall the following year.

In Conclusion

In this essay I have examined some of the conflicting ideas about the native flora of the Malagasy Deep South that circulated within the Tsiranana government, from the anglicised woodland that figured in Tsiranana's Drurian re-imagining, through the functional but no less mythical prickly pear-dominated floral patrimony envisioned by PSD Deputies, to the growing fascination of French technical assistance with the region's indigenous plants. Just as the 1960s saw experimentation with alternative forms of political and cultural expression, so too this was a period of recuperation, innovation and improvisation in the way people thought about trees. Competing nationalisms spilled over into competing botanical imaginations. Seemingly familiar narratives about nature, and about human beings in nature, were being combined with nationalist iconographies of landscape and history. At the same time the

---

48. Philibert Tsiranana, *Le Cahier bleu: pensées et souvenirs* (Tananarive: L'imprimerie officielle, 1971). On the restorative value of nature for human well-being, see Emily Brady, 'Aesthetics in Practice: Valuing the Natural World', *Environmental Values* 15/3 (2005): 277–91; Kay Milton, *Loving Nature: Towards an Ecology of Emotion* (London: Routledge, 2002).

need to address multiple political constituencies and rising popular expectations grounded in nationalist politics led to new inflections of colonial environmental narrative and creative uses of 'mythic time'. The plurality of arboreal values and landscape constructions within the government itself challenges any uncomplicated understandings of the Tsiranana period.

I have suggested that in Tsiranana's discourse on the Malagasy Deep South in the wake of the 1971 insurrection, botanical metaphors and acts of tree planting served to express environmental hopes about the region and its development, to describe the body politic of Madagascar, to reinscribe insurgents in ordered relations and to reclaim the land. If Tsiranana took up many of the rhetorical elements and tropes of colonial discourse, he did so creatively. Like other postcolonial leaders, he had to reach constituencies for which colonial forms of governance provided no models. He reinvented the colonial narrative of an (almost) island-wide original forest by linking it to his long cherished ideal of a Malagasy patriotism based on the sentiment of belonging to one moral community.

More generally, I hope to have shown in a preliminary way the value of looking at early postcolonial environmental discourse as a culturally autonomous phenomenon, shaped by colonial legacy certainly but also distinct from it. In Madagascar, rather than acting as a deadweight on social and environmental imaginations, colonial legacies were reworked. French knowledge producers remained vocal but were often new voices producing new knowledge. Malagasy politicians had their own, innovative, agendas and spoke from positions of authority for the first time. PSD Deputies, mindful of their constituencies, called for planting schemes they believed would lead to the renaissance of native flora. Malagasy politicians also reworked desertification narratives to fit their understanding of colonial history.

Secondly, I hope to have pointed to the value of writing histories that allow for African appropriation and reinvention of western environmental discourse. Readily identifiable resonances with what are identified as longstanding, dominant colonial narratives should not be allowed to obscure the possibility of significant shifts in script. The case study presented here suggests that, just as post-colonial novelists have re-imagined the world by invading the discursive and material structures of English literature, so too the strategy of interpolation may be, if not pervasive, then at least present in African politicians' environmental discourse.

Acknowledgements

I thank participants of the Madagascar Workshop, Toronto, 30–31 March 2012 for comments, particularly Jennifer Cole who also located a copy of *Le Cahier bleu*.

References

Adams, Jonathan and Thomas McShane. 1992. *The Myth of Wild Africa*. New York: W.W. Norton and Co.

Althabe, Gérard. 1972. 'Les manifestations paysannes d'avril 1971', *Revue française d'études politiques africaines* **78** (juin): 71–7.

Archer, Robert. 1976. *Madagascar depuis 1972: la marche d'une révolution*. Paris: L'Harmattan.

Ashcroft, Bill, Gareth Griffiths and Helen Tiffen (eds.) 2002[1989]. *The Empire Writes Back: Theory and Practice in Post-Colonial Literatures*. 2nd edn. London: Routledge.

Ashcroft, Bill. 2009. 'Remembering the Future: Utopianism in African Literature'. *Textual Practice* **23**/5: 703–22.

Auricchio, Laura, Elizabeth Heckendorn Cook and Giulia Pacini. 2012. 'Introduction: Invaluable Trees'. In L. Auricchio, E. Heckendorn Cook and G. Pacini (eds.) *Invaluable Trees: Cultures of Nature, 1660–1830*. Oxford: Voltaire Foundation. pp.1–26.

Battistini, René. 1972. 'L'homme et l'équilibre de la nature à Madagascar', in *Comptes Rendus de la Conférence internationale sur la conservation de la Nature et des ses ressources à Madagascar, Tananarive 7–11 October 1970*. Morges, Switzerland: IUCN. pp.91–4.

Battistini, René and Pierre Vérin. 1972. 'Man and the Environment in Madagascar; past problems and problems of today', in R. Battistini and G. Richard-Vindard (eds.) *Biogeography and Ecology in Madagascar*. The Hague: W. Junk. pp. 311–35.

Beaujard, Philippe. 1998. *Dictionnaire malgache (dialectal)-français: dialecte tañala, sud-est de Madagascar, avec recherché étymologiques*. Paris: L'Harmattan.

Beinart, William, Karen Brown and Daniel Gilfoyle. 2009. 'Experts and Expertise in Colonial Africa Reconsidered: Science and the Interpenetration of Knowledge'. *African Affairs* **108** (432): 413–33.

Binder, Renée and G. W. Burnett. 1994. 'Ngugi Wa Thiong'o and the Search for a Populist Landscape Aesthetic'. *Environmental Values* **3**/1: 47–59.

Bloch, Maurice. 1971. *Placing the Dead: Tombs, Ancestral Villages, and Kinship Organization in Madagascar*. London: Seminar Press.

Boehmer, Elleke. 2005[1995]. *Colonial and Postcolonial Literature. Migrant Metaphors*. 2nd edition. Oxford: Oxford University Press.

Boserup, Esther. 1965. *The Conditions of Agricultural Growth: the Economics of Agrarian Change under Population Pressure*. London: Allen and Unwin.

Bourgeat, F. 1972. 'Contribution à l'étude des sols sur socle ancien à Madagascar. Types de différenciation et intepretation chronologique au cours du Quaternaire'. Mém. ORSTOM 57.

Brady, Emily. 2005. 'Aesthetics in Practice: Valuing the Natural World'. *Environmental Values* **15**/3: 277–91.

Cederlöf, Gunnel and K. Sivaramakrishnan (eds.) 2005. *Ecological Nationalisms: Nature, Livelihoods, and Identities in South Asia*. Delhi: Permanent Black.

Chazan-Gillig, Suzanne. 1991. *La société sakalave: Le Menabe dans la construction nationale malgache, 1947–1972*. Paris: Éditions de l'Orstom.

Coates, Peter. 2006. *American Perceptions of Immigrant and Invasive Species: Strangers on the Land*. Berkeley, Ca.: University of California Press.

Comaroff, Jean and John Comaroff. 2001. 'Naturing the Nation: Aliens, Apocalypse and the Postcolonial State', *Journal of Southern African Studies* 27/3: 627–51.

Covell, Maureen. 1987. *Madagascar*. London: Frances Pinter.

Daniels, Stephen. 1988. 'The Political Iconography of Woodland in Later Georgian England'. In D. Cosgrove and S. Daniels (eds.) *The Iconography of Landscape. Essays in the Symbolic Representation, Design, and Use of Past Environments*. Cambridge: Cambridge University Press. pp.43–82.

Daniels, Stephen. 1993. *Fields of Vision: Landscape Imagery and National Identity in England and the United States*. Princeton: Princeton University Press.

Davies, Douglas. 1988. 'The Evocative Symbolism of Trees'. In D. Cosgrove and S. Daniels (eds.) *The Iconography of Landscape. Essays in the Symbolic Representation, Design, and Use of Past Environments*. Cambridge: Cambridge University Press. pp.32–42.

Decary, Raymond. 1925. 'L'utilisation des Opuntias en Androy (Extrême-Sud de Madagascar)'. *Revue de Botanique Appliquée et d'Agriculture Coloniale* 5/50: 769-771.

Decary, Raymond. 1930. *L'Androy (L'Extrême Sud de Madagascar)*. Essai de Monographie Régionale. Paris: Société d'Editions Géographiques, Maritimes et Coloniales.

De Boeck, Filip. 1994. 'Of Trees and Kings: Politics and Metaphor among the Aluund of Southwestern Zaire'. *American Ethnologist* 21/3: 451–73.

Drury, Robert. 1731[1729]. *Madagascar: or, Robert Drury's journal, during fifteen years captivity on that island... Written by himself.* London: J. Brotherton, T. Worrall; and J. Jackson.

Dumont, René. 1959. *Evolution des campagnes malgaches. Quelques problèmes essentiels d'orientation et de modernisation de l'agriculture malgache*. Tananarive: Imprimerie Officielle.

Esoavelomandroso, Manassé. 1991. 'La forêt dans le Mahafale aux XIXᵉ et XXᵉ siècles', *Aombe* 3:97–102.

Esoavelomandroso, Manassé. 2003[1989]. 'Une arme de domination: le 'tribalisme' à Madagascar (XIXᵉ – milieu du XXᵉ siècle)', in J.-P. Chrétien and G. Prunier (eds.) *Les ethnies ont une historie*. 2nd edition Paris: Karthala. pp.259–66.

Fairhead, James and Melissa Leach. 1996. *Misreading the African Landscape. Society and Ecology in a Forest-savanna Mosaic*. Cambridge: Cambridge University Press.

Feeley-Harnik, Gillian. 1991. *A Green Estate: Restoring Independence in Madagascar*. Washington, D.C.: Smithsonian Institution Press.

Feeley-Harnik, Gillian. 2001. '*Ravenala Madagascariensis* Sonnerat: The Historical Ecology of a "Flagship Species" in Madagascar', *Ethnohistory* 48/1–2: 31–86.

Ferguson, James. 1990. *The Anti-politics Machine. 'Development', Depoliticization, and Bureaucratic Power in Lesotho*. Cambridge: Cambridge University Press.

Karen Middleton

Fernandez, James W. 1998. 'Trees of Knowledge of Self and Other in Culture: On Models for the Moral Imagination' in L. Rival (ed.) *The Social Life of Trees: Anthropological Perspectives on Tree Symbolism.* Oxford: Berg. pp.81–110.

Flacourt, Etienne de. 1995[1658]. *Histoire de la grande isle Madagascar.* Edited and annotated Claude Allibert. Paris: INALCO/Éditions Karthala.

Foucault, Michel. 1979. *Discipline and Punish: the Birth of the Prison.* Translated Alan Sheridan. New York: Vintage.

Frazer, James George. 2009[1890]. *The Golden Bough. A Study in Magic and Religion.* Abridged version. Oxford: Oxford University Press.

Furbank, Philip and W.R. Owens. 1994. *Defoe de-attributions: a Critique of J.R.Moore's Checklist.* London: Hambledon.

Humbert, Henri. 1927. 'Destruction d'une flore insulaire par le feu. Principaux aspects de la végétation à Madagascar'. *Mémoires de l'Académie Malgache* V: 1–80.

Humbert, Henri. 1947. 'Changements survenus dans la végétation du Sud de Madagascar'. *Revue internationale de botanique appliquée et d'agriculture tropicale* 27, (301–2): 441–4.

Humbert, Henri. 1953. 'Un exemple suggestif de désertification provoquée: les territoires du Sud de Madagascar'. *Naturaliste Malgache* 54: 5–17.

Humbert, Henri. 1959. 'Origines présumées et affinities de la Flore de Madagascar'. *Mémoires de l'Institut Scientifique de Madagascar* Series B, IX: 149–87.

Jones, Owain and Paul Cloke. 2002. *Tree Cultures: the Place of Trees and Trees in their Place.* Oxford: Berg.

Koechlin, Jean. 1972. 'Flora and Vegetation of Madagascar'. In R. Battistini and G. Richard-Vindard (eds.) *Biogeography and Ecology in Madagascar.* The Hague: W. Junk. pp.145–90.

Koechlin, Jean, J.-L. Guillaumet and Philippe Morat. 1974. *Flore et végétation de Madagascar.* Vaduz: J. Cramer.

Kull, Christian. 1996. 'The Evolution of Conservation Efforts in Madagascar'. *International Environmental Affairs* 8/1 (Winter): 50–86.

Kull, Christian. 2000. 'Deforestation, Erosion, and Fire: Degradation Myths in the Environmental History of Madagascar'. *Environment and History* 6/4: 423–50.

Kull, Christian. 2004. *Isle of Fire. The Political Ecology of Landscape Burning in Madagascar.* Chicago and London: University of Chicago Press.

Leach, Melissa and Robin Mearns (eds.) 1996. *The Lie of the Land: Challenging Received Wisdom on the African Environment.* International African Institute, Oxford; Portsmouth NH; with James Currey/Heinemann.

Martin, Meredith. 2012. 'Bourbon Renewal at Rambouillet', in L. Auricchio, E. Heckendorn Cook and G. Pacini (eds.) *Invaluable Trees: Cultures of Nature, 1660–1830.* Oxford: Voltaire Foundation. pp. 151–69.

Middleton, Karen. 1997. 'Circumcision, Death and Strangers'. *Journal of Religion in Africa* 27/4: 341–73.

Middleton, Karen. 1999. 'Who killed "Malagasy Cactus"? Science, Environment and Colonialism in Southern Madagascar (1924–1930)'. *Journal of Southern African Studies* 25: 215–48.

Middleton, Karen. 2000. 'How Karembola Men Become Mothers'. In J. Carsten (ed.) *Cultures of Relatedness: New Approaches to the Study of Kinship.* Cambridge: Cambridge University Press. pp. 104–27.

Middleton, Karen. 2009. 'From Ratsiraka to Ravalomanana: Changing Narratives of Prickly Pears in Dryland Madagascar'. Études Océan Indien. Plantes et Sociétés *42–43.* Paris: INALCO. pp. 47–83.

Middleton, Karen. In press. 'Land Rights and Alien Plants in Dryland Madagascar'. In G. Campbell, S. Evers and M. Lambek (eds.) *The Politics of Marketing Land: Values, Conservation and Development in Madagascar.* Leiden: Brill.

Millot, Jacques. 1972. 'In Conclusion', in R. Battistini and G. Richard-Vindard (eds.) *Biogeography and Ecology in Madagascar.* The Hague: W. Junk. pp.741–56.

Milton, Kay. 2002. *Loving Nature: Towards an Ecology of Emotion.* London: Routledge.

Mulwafu, Wapulumuka Oliver. 2011. *Conservation Song. A History of Peasant-State Relations and the Environment in Malawi, 1860–2000.* Cambridge: White Horse Press.

Olson, Sherry. 1984. 'The Robe of the Ancestors. Forests in the History of Madagascar'. *Journal of Forest History* 28/4 (October): 174–86.

Perrier de la Bâthie, Henri. 1921. 'La végétation malgache'. *Annales du Musée Colonial de Marseille* 29/3: 9.

Perrier de la Bâthie, Henri. 1936. *Biogéographie des plantes de Madagascar.* Paris: Société d'Éditions Géographiques, Maritimes et Coloniales, Challamel.

Pordzik, Ralph. 2001. *The Quest for Postcolonial Utopia. A Comparative Introduction to the Utopian Novel in New English Literatures.* New York: Peter Lang.

Raik, Daniela. 2007. 'Forest Management in Madagascar. An Historical Overview'. *Madagascar Conservation and Development* 2/1: 5–10.

Raison-Jourde, Françoise and Gérard Roy. 2010. *Paysans, intellectuels et populisme à Madagascar. De Monja Jaona à Ratsimandrava (1960–1975).* Paris: Editions Karthala.

Ranjarajan, Mahesh. 2009. 'Striving for a Balance: Nationalism, Power, Science and India's Indira Gandhi, 1917–1984'. *Conservation and Society* 7/4: 299–312.

Rauh, Werner. 1995 and 1998. *Succulent and Xerophytic Plants of Madagascar.* Mill Valley, Ca.: Strawberry Press.

Rival, Laura (ed.) 1998. *The Social Life of Trees. Anthropological Perspectives on Tree Symbolism.* Oxford: Berg.

Saura, André. 2006a and b. *Philibert Tsiranana (1910–1978), Premier président de la République de Madagascar: Tome 1:À l'ombre de de Gaulle. Tome 2: Le crépuscule du pouvoir.* Paris: L'Harmattan.

Schama, Simon. 1995. *Landscape and Memory.* London: HarperCollins.

Sivaramakrishnan, K. and Gunnel Cederlöf. 2005. 'Introduction. Claiming Nature for Making History'. In G. Cederlöf and K. Sivaramakrishnan (eds.) *Ecological Nationalisms: Nature, Livelihoods, and Identities in South Asia*. Delhi: Permanent Black. pp. 1–40.

Songster, Elena E. 2004. *A Natural Place for Nationalism: The Wanglang Nature Reserve and the Emergence of the Giant Panda as a National Icon,* Thesis Ph.D. University of California, San Diego.

Spacensky, Alain. 1970. *Madagascar, cinquante ans de vie politique de Ralaimongo à Tsiranana.* Paris: Nouvelles Editions Latines.

Stott, Philip and Sian Sullivan (eds.) 2000. *Political Ecology: Science, Myth and Power.* London: Arnold.

Sunseri, Thaddeus. 2009. *Wielding the Ax: State Forestry and Social Conflict in Tanzania, 1820–2000.* Athens, Ohio: Ohio University Press.

Thompson, Virginia and Richard Adloff. 1965. *The Malagasy Republic. Madagascar Today.* Stanford, Ca.: Stanford University Press.

Tiffen, Mary, Michael Mortimore and Francis Gichuki. 1994. *More People, Less Erosion: Environmental Recovery in Kenya.* Chichester: Wiley.

Tronchon, Jacques. 1974. *L'Insurrection Malgache de 1947: essai d'interprétation historique.* Paris: F. Maspero.

Tsiranana, Philibert. 1971. *Le Cahier bleu: pensées et souvenirs.* Tananarive: L'imprimerie officielle.

Turner, Victor W. 1982 [1967]. *The Forest of Symbols: Aspects of Ndembu Ritual.* Ithaca; London: Cornell University Press.

Vandergeest, Peter and Nancy Lee Peluso. 1995. 'Territorialization and State Power in Thailand'. *Theory and Society* 24: 385–426.

Primary Sources

National Archives of Madagascar. Séries VP916 Sauvetage et Développement du Sud. 343f. 1971–1972; Série IV D.73 Archives Provinciales. 6. Province de Tuléar. Service des Eaux et Forêts; Monographie.

Bibliothèque centrale, Muséum National d'Histoire Naturelle, Paris. Fonds Decary, MS 3042. Troubles en Androy 1971.

British Library, *Journal officiel de la république malgache,* 1957–1972.

Chapter 10

On Revolutionary Dirt in Haiti

Lauren Derby

There are, the muse hath oft abhorrent seen,
Who swallow dirt; (so the chlorotic fair
Oft chalk prefer to the most poignant cates:)
Such, dropsy bloats, and to sure death consigns;
Unless restrain'd from this unwholesome food,
By soothing words, by menaces, by blows:
Nor yet will threats, or blows, or soothing words,
Perfect their cure; unless thou, Pæan, deign'st
By medicine's power their cravings to subdue.

James Grainger, from *The Sugar Cane* (1765), Book IV

In 2008, as the rising cost of petroleum sent food prices soaring worldwide, the story broke that Haitians had resorted to eating dirt since they were no longer able to afford basic commodities such as rice, beans and cooking oil. The UN Food and Agriculture Agency declared a state of emergency in Haiti as prices rose nearly fifty per cent, forcing parents to ration spoonfuls of rice to their children and even eat mud cakes to stave off hunger.[1] The food story became a major topic among international aid agencies and organisations such as the World Bank grew especially concerned as riots broke out in Haiti, where mobs attempted to loot stores and government warehouses. The government of René Preval was a prime target due to the fact that it had given a three-year tax break to the business class, while hacking the minimum legal wage of $1.60 per day in half.[2] The mud pie story circulated among relief agencies, which used it to fund raise, and this in turn catapulted it throughout the global news media. There it retained a half life until the 2010 earthquake, when it resurfaced as concrete evidence of Haiti's status as poorest nation in the western hemisphere.[3]

---

1. Marc Lacey, 'Across Globe, Empty Bellies Bring Rising Anger', *New York Times*, 18 Apr. 2008; The World Bank, *Food Price Inflation and its Effects on Latin America and the Caribbean* (Washington, D.C.: World Bank, 2008); Jonathan M. Katz, 'Poor Haitians Resort to Eating Dirt', *National Geographic News*, 30 Jan. 2008.

2. Saeed Shabazz, 'Rising Food Prices Increase Haiti's Agony', Call.com News, 23 April 2008.

3. See the photo montage at http://www.cncworld.tv/photos/show/344.shtml

Lauren Derby

As a mark of abjection, there is not much worse than eating dirt. As Mary Douglas has taught us, pollution taboos provide the elementary building blocks of culture and eating soil is about as debased as one can get.[4] Indeed, it is an image that renders Haitians virtually animals, since, like goats or pigs, they apparently do not live by elementary food taboos and rules of hygiene; which accounts for the fact that these practices have become the 'locus of fear, disgust and fascination' for the international press.[5]

This essay considers the meaning of earth eating in Haiti, its history and significance. I locate the mud cake phenomenon within several contexts which date from slavery, including the cultural significance of clay as a means of ritual adornment, gendered concepts of personhood – since mud cakes are first and foremost a women's product and food – and finally I consider its articulation with environmental degradation. I also situate Haitian mud pies within Pierre Nora's concept of '*lieu de memoire*', since the earth used to fabricate the patties is culled from the central plateau around Hinche, which, as a central theatre of the Haitian revolution, was a key site of emergent nationhood. I propose that the oft-cited mud cake phenomenon is not a food substitute or sign of abjection but, among other things, a form of gustatory nationalism since the recipe calls for soil taken from the Haitian revolutionary battlegrounds. I make the case for considering how popular nationalism can be embodied in material culture and the environment, what Levi Strauss might call 'the science of the concrete'; yet also argue that we must be attuned to local forms of knowledge in order to decipher the deeper meanings of practices of this kind.[6]

Cookies or Patties?

Poor urban Haitians turned to mud cakes as a food substitute in 2008 during a moment of profound crisis, yet not all Haitians would consider eating them if they did not have to. As I walked around the Marché du Fer – the central market in downtown Port-au-Prince – a year ago with Georges René looking for mud cake vendors to speak with, he was horrified at the thought of eating them. Georges said in disgust that eating mud cakes was akin to consuming cement; he worried that it could harden in the gut, becoming a solid mass, and that one might pass bricks as a result. A person's attitude towards the pies is conveyed in the very terms he or she uses to refer to them. They are called *bonbons terres* (earth candies) or *pain biscuit* (bread biscuit) – terms which connote prepared cuisine – by those who eat them

---

4. Mary Douglas, *Purity and Danger: An Analysis of the Concepts of Pollution and Taboo* (London: Ark Paperbacks, 1988).

5. Peter Stallybrass and Allon White, *The Poetics and Politics of Transgression* (Ithaca, N. Y.: Cornell University Press, 1986), p. 125.

6. Claude Lévi-Strauss, *The Savage Mind* (Chicago: University of Chicago Press, 1966), p. 16.

Figure 1. Eve Pierre Jean Louis with her children preparing mud patties in Sapater, just outside of Hinche, Haiti.

Photograph 2012. Thanks to Jared Heins (from *Pica Haiti*, dir. Edwina Orelus).

and *te-a* (dirt) by those who do not. The fact that eating these cakes is a stigmatised act became apparent during my first interview in the Haitian area across from the *Mercado Modelo* in downtown Santo Domingo, Dominican Republic when the market vendor selling the cakes first turned away and then crossed the street in a resolute refusal to speak with me when I inquired about the patties, leaving me to converse with her daughter, a student. Yet mud cakes are clearly consumed by many, since they are prepared and sold across Haiti, and even exported to the neighbouring Dominican Republic; a fact which renders Haitian dirt one of the nation's most important export commodities after labour.

Food is one of the most important ethnic and class markers and Haitians are not surprisingly loath to be reduced to a nation of mud eaters; moreover, even those who enjoy them consider that mud cakes should be a snack and not a meal.[7] Due to their portrayal in the press as a foodstuff for the hopelessly impoverished, these mud patties are highly tainted in public discourse, their consumption rendering a person less than human, and those who like to eat them tend to keep that fact to themselves.[8] As such, mud pies are the antithesis of *diri* (rice), the quintessential high status white food, which is imported from either the U.S. or the Dominican Republic and today conjures up an 'unattainable life of prosperity' for the majority of Haitians (even if this is ironic, given that rice was originally brought to the New World and grown by slaves).[9] The mud patty may also be disparaged in the New World due to its association with slavery, as we shall see.

In trolling the markets looking for pain biscuit vendors I discovered my first fact about the mud cakes. Haitians clearly do not consider them a central meal component since they are not sold in the meat and poultry area, or even the vegetable or fruit portions, of the market. In Santo Domingo, the capital of the Dominican Republic, they are sold on the periphery of the central market, the Mercado Modelo, next to the flowers, adjacent to where snack items such as candies are sold to pedestrians, across from 'little Haiti', where the transitory Haitian traders temporarily reside. In the Marché du Fer in downtown Port-au-Prince, they are sold with raw condiments and seasonings, such as cinnamon, nutmeg and star anise. Thus in both these contexts they are cast as natural products, akin to spices,

---

7. Mary J. Weismantel, *Food, Gender and Poverty in the Ecuadorian Andes* (Long Grove IL: Waveland Press, 1988), p. 9; Mary Douglas, 'Deciphering a Meal', *Daedalus* **101**/1 (Winter, 1972): 61–81.

8. Young also discusses dirt eating as a marker of poverty: see Sera L. Young, *Craving Earth: Understanding Pica – The Urge to Eat Clay, Starch, Ice and Chalk* (Columbia University Press, 2011) p. 84; Erving Goffman, *Stigma: Notes on the Management of Spoiled Identity* (Englewood Cliffs, NJ: Prentice-Hall, 1963).

9. Weismantel, *Food, Gender and Poverty*, p. 147. For more on slaves and rice, see Judith Carney, *Black Rice: The African Origins of Rice Cultivation in the Americas* (Cambridge, MA: Harvard University Press, 2001). Evidence that earth eating is broadly disparaged is that the definition of geophagy by the World English Dictionary is 'the practice of eating earth, clay, chalk found in some primitive tribes'.

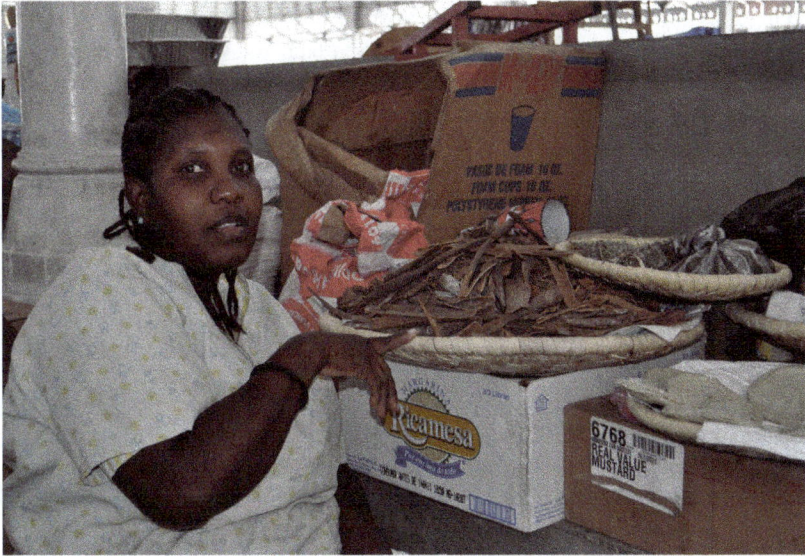

Figure 2. A mud patty vendor in Port-au-Prince, Haiti.

Pain biscuit for sale can be seen on the right, next to the cinnamon and oregano. Photograph 2012 by Lauren Derby.

which complement a meal rather than constitute food on their own. Yet when I spoke to a Haitian woman who eats mud patties regularly and enjoys them, she stressed that they were not raw but rather prepared and thus were indeed food, since they are made according to a recipe which includes salt, butter and Maggi stock flavouring, or chicken bouillon, for taste. In this view, they are not mere earth and water like the mud cakes made by children at play, but rather a foodstuff that, if not cooked, at least involves preparation and a recipe with additional selected ingredients to enhance their taste. In Mary Weismantel's terms, they were thus cast as cuisine, rather than mere diet.[10]

Notwithstanding the purported uniqueness of this trope of barbarism, geophagy or soil eating did not commence in 2008. Nor is it unique to Haiti. During the French colonial period (1697–1804) many Haitian slaves supplemented their diet with earth. Some scholars have taken this to be a form of resistance to slavery,

---

10. Weismantel, *Food, Gender and Poverty*, p. 87.

seeing it as an intentionally suicidal behaviour.[11] In the colonial period, dirt eating was considered extremely harmful and even fatal and was 'the dread of every planter ... and noticed all over the south'.[12] Indeed, consuming 'a particular form of loomy marl' was pathologised as a named disease and considered as serious as tuberculosis, since many planters assumed it was a form of attempted suicide via poisoning.[13] Eating dirt so as to vomit it up and thus appear deathly ill was also used as a stratagem to avoid being sold into slavery, as the emission could be mistaken for the dreaded black vomit of yellow fever.[14] *The London Gazette* recounted the story of a slave who was alternately whipped and fed plenty of wholesome soup, but nothing short of bodily confinement would stop him from regularly sweeping up the dust around the slave abodes and forming it into a heap, whereupon he would lie down and 'put his mouth to it, licking it up as if it had been the greatest delicacy'.[15] Such reports are uncommon, however, since this 'horribly disgusting' practice was generally performed clandestinely.[16] Called 'cachexia Africana', 'black tongue' or 'mal del estomago', dirt eating came to be seen as the root of many diseases, including yaws and food and lead poisoning, and was viewed with extreme contempt and presumed to be contagious.[17] It was taken so seriously that, in 1790, it even became the subject of British parliamentary inquiry.

In an effort to curtail the practice, planters tried various antidotes, including administering roasted bat and purgatives and even iron masks and muzzles.[18] In Dominica, which was populated by poor white small-holders and where slaves were in short supply, this practice was perceived to be so dangerous that one plantation

---

11. Robinson Millwood, *European Christianity and the Atlantic Slave Trade: A Black Hermeneutical Study* (Bloomington, IN: AuthorHouse, 2007), p. 195; Éric Doumerc, *Caribbean Civilization: The English Speaking Caribbean since Independence* (Toulouse: Presses Universitaire du Mirail, 2003), p. 28.

12. Leslie Howard Owens, *The Species of Property: Slave Life and Culture in the Old South* (Oxford: Oxford University Press, 1976), p. 64.

13. Great Britain, Parliament, *Minutes of the Evidence Taken at the Bar of the House of Lords*, 1792, p. 140. For more on slave self-poisoning, see Bernard Moitt, *Women and Slavery in the French Antilles 1635–1848* (Bloomington: Indiana University Press, 2001), pp.144–45.

14. Starkey, *Striving to Make My Way Home*, pp. 56–7, cited in Patricia Yaeger, *Dirt and Desire: Reconstructing Southern Women's Writing, 1930–1990* (Chicago: University of Chicago Press, 2000), p. x; John McNeill, *Mosquito Empires: Ecology and War in the Greater Caribbean, 1620–1914* (New York: Cambridge University Press, 2010), p. 33.

15. Mary Carmichael, *Domestic Manners and Social Condition of the White, Coloured and Negro Population of the West Indies*, Vol. I. (London: Whittaker, Treacher and Co., 1833), p. 215.

16. Kenneth Kiple and Virginia Himmelsteib King, *Another Dimension to the Black Diaspora: Diet, Disease and Racism* (Cambridge: Cambridge University Press, 1981), p. 99.

17. Kiple and King, *Another Dimension*, p. 100.

18. Herbert C. Covey and Dwight Eisnach, *What the Slaves Ate: Recollections of African American Foods and Foodways* (Santa Barbara: Greenwood Press, 2009), p. 17.

manager resorted to smearing the slaves with a mixture of excrement and ashes, even forcing this mixture down their throats as a punishment.[19]

In medical literature, eating earth is cast as an aberrant form of behaviour called pica, defined as a craving among those with dietary deficiencies to eat non-nutritive substances, ice and dirt being prime culprits.[20] Given that the slave diet lacked protein and minerals, since slaves were allocated bones, lard and only rarely 'flesh meat', iron deficiency may have driven women, especially in pregnancy, to eat dirt as a mineral supplement. While planter meals were veritable feasts, with elaborate spreads of several varieties of meat, slave weekly provisions consisted of a couple of mackerel, bones, plantains and, if they were lucky, organs, skins and the head of cattle which had succumbed to disease.[21]

Along these lines, a less punitive approach to the problem of dirt eating was taken by Dr. Collins in his 1803 handbook on the management of negro slaves, in which he argued against whipping or stocks to cure geophagy, stating that strengthening the stomach was a superior method for curing the 'love of dirt' and 'will be found to give way to the more rational desire of something that is better'.[22] Of course, nutritional deficiencies such as a lack of thiamine rendered Beriberi – which was caused by insufficient protein – common among slaves and the presence of parasites such as hookworm was similarly debilitating.[23] Pregnant and lactating women in particular needed to supplement their diet and found that soil could provide the iron, magnesia and calcium they needed.[24] This practice may have originated in African folk medicine. For instance, clay is used widely for therapeutic purposes in Central Africa, where sixty per cent of the late eighteenth century slave imports to Haiti originated.[25] Clay consumption is a highly effective folk remedy for diarrhoea; indeed, the key ingredient in the medicine Kaopectate is kaolin, derived from mineral-rich soil.

---

19. B.W. Higman, *Slave Populations of the British Caribbean, 1807–1834* (Baltimore: Johns Hopkins University Press, 1984), p. 297.

20. Catherine Reef, *Poverty in America* (New York: Infobase Publishing, 2007), p. 53.

21. I am not aware of treatments of the slave diet of Saint Domingue, but a detailed account for Barbados is Richard Ligon, *A True and Exact History of the Island of Barbados Illustrated with a Map of the Island...* (London: Peter Parker, 1673), p. 38.

22. Dr. Collins, *Practical Rules for the Management and Medical Treatment of Negro Slaves, in the Sugar Colonies* (London: Printed by J. Barfield for Vernor and Hood, 1803), p. 347.

23. Kenneth F. Kiple, *The Caribbean Slave: A Biological History* (Cambridge: Cambridge University Press, 1984), p. 99.

24. Eugene Genovese, *Roll, Jordan, Roll: The World the Slaves Made* (New York: Pantheon Books, 1974); Kiple and King, *Another Dimension*.

25. John K. Thornton, '"I Am the Subject of the King of Congo": African Political Ideology and the Haitian Revolution', *Journal of World History* 4/2 (Fall, 1993): 185.

Lauren Derby

The Powers of Clay

But there are more than merely utilitarian explanations for the use of clay in Central Africa; there are also expressive and even ritual dimensions to soil which indicate another layer of significance besides the simply nutritional. The Nsundi of Central Africa have a proclivity for whitened chalk, earth and the clay of ant mounds that form on tree trunks, which are both eaten and mixed with medicines in magical power objects such as *minkisi* ('things which do things') to fatten children; and pregnant women are said to love to eat the red earth of ants' nests.[26] The link between clay and *nkisi* (singular) is significant and indicates that clay is not an everyday substance, since minkisi are a form of Central African sacred amulet that made its way to the New World during the slave trade. Minkisi are bundles containing medicines and spirit-embodying materials, such as cemetery dirt or equivalents like white clay from riverbeds or such red items as powdered camwood or anthill soil. These substances imbue the charm with life force or power and are accompanied by 'spirit-directing medicines', which provide instructions to the nkisi spirit, including stones, seeds or sticks.[27] Minkisi are used to divine the cause of, and rout out, afflictions that may result from ancestral spirits, malevolent acquaintances, witches or other minkisi. Some scholars say that these amulets actually embody the ancestral spirit.[28] Robert Farris Thompson describes them as 'strategic objects in Black Atlantic art', endowed with a mystical agency to heal or protect, though they clearly hover on the boundary of life and death: Wyatt MacGaffey defines them as 'a personalized force from the invisible land of the dead'.[29]

Kaolin or white clay is a key ingredient in these power-assemblages; it is the central ingredient in the spell itself, the blood or connective tissue for the spirit-embedding medicines, which are activated by the spirit-admonishing objects. The Congo priest also rubs his face with chalk, forming broad bands emanating down his arms and chest when performing ceremonies and incantations, in addition to clothing himself with skins and feathers to connote his abilities to channel invisible powers and engage in a form of what Marcy Norton has termed 'regenerative

---

26. Maureen Warner Lewis, *Central Africa in the Caribbean: Transcending Time, Transforming Cultures* (Kingston, Jamaica: University of the West Indies Press, 2003), p. 102. The Minkisi definition is from '13 Things', The Joukowsky Institute for Archeology Classroom, Brown University, see http://proteus.brown.edu/13things/7393

27. Robert Farris Thompson, *Flash of the Spirit: African and Afro-American Art and Philosophy* (New York: Vintage Books, 1984), p. 117.

28. Kajsa Ekholm Friedman, *Catastrophe and Creation: The Transformation of an African Culture* (Pennsylvania, PA: Harwood Academic Publishers, 1991), p. 135.

29. Wyatt MacGaffey, *Art and Healing of the Bakongo* (Stockholm: Folkens Museum-Etnografiska, 1991), p. 4.

Figure 3. Nkisi power figure. Yombe Peoples, Democratic Republic of the Congo, nineteenth century.

Wood, camwood, pigment, mirror, fibre, metal, chain. H. 26.5 cm x 67.879 cm. Gift of the Wellcome Trust. Copyright Fowler Museum at UCLA. Photograph 2010 by Don Cole.

death'.[30] A nineteenth-century traveller to the Congo described the powdered chalk as akin to 'brain matter, that gives intelligence to the whole mass' which also includes fragments of skins of powerful and cunning animals.[31] In this case we see that dirt is not merely what Mary Douglas terms 'matter out of place'; it is a medium linking the living and the dead and one that conveys the (often aggressive) powers of the ancestral spirits.[32] Thompson says, 'the earths embed the spirit in a miniature *mpemba* (the white clay world of the dead), and the objects resting on the earth, or clay, tell the spirit what to do'.[33] White clay painted on the upper body and red camwood to beautify the visage were also deployed in Congo secret societies in which initiates 'die' and are resurrected in the country of the dead.[34] Kindunga societies which announce and perform for the burial of a queen or a chief also wear chalk on their bodies; and, as the colour of death and mourning, white chalk adorns the wooden figurines placed on the burial mound.[35] In Kikongo culture, further evidence that earth is socially significant is the fact that when children are given some of the mourning cloth used to bind their father's corpse it is called 'dirt for the father'.[36] Just as chalk is linked to the powers of the dead, soil from beneath the tombstone is an active substance in spells throughout the Black Atlantic.[37]

So just as kaolin channels the activating spirit in an nkisi spell, white clay is also used by the ritual priest to forge a path between the visible and invisible worlds. As Thompson states, 'the cemetery is not a final resting-place, in Congo terms, but a door between two worlds, a "threshold" marking the line between the two worlds, of the living and the dead, circumscribed by the cosmic journey of

---

30. John H. Weeks, *Among the Primitive Bakongo: A Record of Thirty Years Close Intercourse with the Bakongo and other Tribes of Equatorial Africa, with a Description of their Habits, Customs & Religious Beliefs* (London: Seeley, Service and Co., 1914), pp. 216, 277; Marcy Norton, 'Predation and Adoption: Humans and Animals in the Native Caribbean and South America', unpublished manuscript, 2012.

31. John H. Weeks, *Among Kongo Cannibals. Experiences, Impressions and Adventures during a Thirty Years' Sojourn amongst the Boloki and other Congo Tribes, with a Description of their Curious Habits, Customs, Religion and Laws* (Philadelphia, PA: J.P. Lippincott, 1913), pp. 255–56.

32. MacGaffey, *Art and Healing*, p. 4.

33. Robert Farris Thompson and Joseph Cornet, *The Four Moments of the Sun: Kongo Art in Two Worlds* (Washington: National Gallery of Art, 1981), p. 37.

34. Weeks, *Among the Primitive Bakongo*, p. 171. MacGaffey argues that white chalk is the male element, which pairs with the female red clay in certain assemblages (*Art and Healing*, p. 27).

35. K.E. Laman, *The Kongo*. Vol. II (Uppsala: Studia Etnographica Upsaliensia, 1957), pp. 79–80, 96. White chalk is used on the figurines but a black pomade made from burnt peanuts, charcoal and palm oil is also used on the mourners, depending on the degree of grief.

36. Weeks, *Among the Primitive Bakongo*, p. 270.

37. Harry Middleton Hyatt, '*Hoodoo – Conjuration – Rootwork*', Memoirs of the Alma Egan Hyatt Foundation (Hannibal, MO: Western Publishing, Vol. I, 1970), p. 222. Thanks to Patrick Polk for this citation. Grave dirt is also an ingredient in certain minkisi (MacGaffey, *Art and Healing*, p. 25).

Figure 4. Members of the Nkimba Secret Society adorned with white clay.
From John Weeks, *Among the Primitive Bakongo*, 1914.

the sun'.[38] A paste of finely ground kaolin is painted around the eyes of the priest to grant him mystic vision, enabling him to see from this world to the next.[39] At times, minkisi are housed in clay pots, and smeared with white clay to represent and invoke the other world.

Africans sold into slavery took many of these associations to the New World. For example, in Cuba, minkisi figurines were used for mystical reconnaissance and to attack slave owners and enemies. Similar talismans are also found in Haiti, where they are tellingly called *paket-congo* (sorcery bundles) and are presided over by the Simbi spirits of the dead. The world of the dead in Haiti as in Central Africa is thus glossed as 'the white realm' and, just as graves are white washed, white fowl is their sacrifice of choice.[40] In Haiti the mystical significance of white clay continues

38. Thompson and Cornet, *The Four Moments*, p. 27.

39. Thompson makes this argument but the use of clay around the eyes is also noted in Weeks, *Among the Primitive Bakongo*, p. 217.

40. Thompson, *Flash of the Spirit*, pp. 118–121, 125–127.

to this day. The trickster Gede spirits who come out in force on the Haitian Day of the Dead (All Souls, 1 November) smear white clay on their faces to mark their status as trickster entities which traverse the boundary between humans and spirits. White chalk is also used in *vodou* ceremonies to draw the signs of the gods on the ground in mystical designs called *vèvè*, inviting them to join the festivity. And clay vessels serve as receptacles for the food offerings to certain *lwa* or deities such as the sacred twins (*marassa*) or saints (as opposed to a divinity such as Legba whose food should be served in a basket hanging from a tree).[41] Ritual mud baths are also an important component of *Saut d'Eau* pilgrimage as well as the St. Jacques rites at Plaine-du-Nord where a bull is sacrificed for Ogou, the senior military spirit, and the pilgrims bath in mud and anoint themselves with the sacrificial blood. St. Jacques is one of the earliest devotions in West and Central Africa where it was brought by the Portuguese in the fifteenth century. And the mud baths interestingly take place where the Haitian revolution commenced, in the northern plains near Cap Haïtien in the shadow of the Citadel fortress which is an important icon of Haitian nationality, built after the revolution to protect the new republic from further foreign incursions.[42]

If dirt is matter out of place, then it is a short step to the accoutrements that help keep it at bay.[43] While brooms appear in medieval magic, often powered by gnomes, to protect from sent magic or sorcery, in other contexts there are prohibitions on sweeping dirt out of the house, which indicates that it can also have a protective presence.[44] Among the Yoruba of Nigeria, brooms charged with incantations are commonly deployed as material spells to protect the house from intruders and thieves; a tiny used broom is hidden above the door frame or otherwise hidden from view (as opposed to other ààlè amulets which are publicly displayed as a visible warning, for example, to protect crops.[45] Here the broom, depleted after years of cleaning dust, is charged with keeping out spiritual contamination and evil. In the U.S. south, brooms were also affixed above doors to stop witches and

41. Elsie Clews Parsons, 'Spirit Cult in Hayti', *Journal de la Société des Américanistes* 20/20 (1928): 165.

42. Donald J. Cosentino, 'It's All for You, Sen Jak!', in Donald Cosentino (ed.) *Sacred Arts of Haitian Vodou* (Los Angeles: Fowler Museum, 1995), pp. 243–63. St. Jacques is also treated in Kate Ramsey, *The Spirits and the Law: Vodou and Power in Haiti* (Chicago: University of Chicago Press, 2011) ch. 2.

43. Douglas, *Purity and Danger*, p. 36.

44. Hyatt, *Hoodoo*, p. 1135.

45. See the chapter on brooms in David T. Doris, *Vigilant Things: On Thieves, Yoruba Anti-Aesthetics and the Strange Fates of Ordinary Objects in Nigeria* (Seattle: University of Washington Press, 2011).

Figure 5. Women possessed by Gede Spirits, Day of the Dead, Port-au-Prince, Haiti.
Photograph 2010 by Lauren Derby.

Figure 6. Man drawing a sacred Vèvè design with corn meal, Day of the Dead, Port-au-Prince, Haiti.

Photograph 2010 by Lauren Derby.

illness from entering a room.[46] And in Haiti, brooms are used in Champwel secret society rites as 'spiritual cleansers, chasing away negative spirits and magic traps'.[47]

Sites of Memory

But the question remains: why must the dirt used in the manufacture of mud cakes emanate from Hinche, said to be the sole source of production for the pies? Since the clay of Hinche is also the source for local ceramics and contains accumulated limestone from the stream beds of the Artibonite River, it seems likely that earth from this region has a high mineral content. But I propose that there may also be deeper meanings to this landscape of memory, given the uniquely ferocious reverence for nation that Haitians harbour in their hearts. Haiti has arguably the most passionate nationalist culture of Latin America and the Caribbean.[48] Not only was the colony of Saint Domingue (colonial Haiti) the richest French possession in the eighteenth century, producing more wealth for France than all her other colonies combined, but Haiti is the only nation in the western hemisphere born of a slave revolution (1791–1804) mounted by a largely African army that succeeded in defeating the French, British and Spanish militaries, the strongest in Europe at that time. As the theatre of three of the most important nationalist battles – the Haitian revolution, the defeat of the military occupation of neighbouring Santo Domingo (1822–44) and later the Caco guerilla resistance war during the U.S. Marine occupation of Haiti (1915–34), Hinche is also a zone of extraordinary nationalist resonance.

During the Haitian revolution, Hinche became a military theatre in the closing phase of the war when, after Toussaint Louverture had unified the various revolutionary armies, the Haitians finally defeated the French troops. Revolutionary leader Jean-Jacques Dessalines was commander-in chief when Spain launched an expeditionary force from the east across Spanish territory in a rearguard effort to retake the former jewel in the French crown. In 1802, Dessalines commandeered 30,000 men in two columns to attack the French forces sent by Napoleon Bonaparte at Hinche. This was the final phase of the war, and the one waged in fury, when the greatest violence was unleashed by raging troops intent on holding on to their newly secured freedom.

Yet Hinche's significance as a landscape of revolutionary memory does not end there. In 1844, Hinche once again became a theatre of nationalist warfare

---

46. Newbell Niles Puckett, *Folk Beliefs of the Southern Negro* (Montclair, NJ: Patterson Smith, 1968), passim. Thanks to Katherine Smith for this citation.

47. Elizabeth McAlister, *Rara! Vodou, Power, and Performance in Haiti and its Diaspora*, (Berkeley: University of California Press, 2002), p. 100.

48. Haitian nationalism in the diaspora is treated in Nina Glick-Schiller and Georges Eugene Fouron, *Georges Woke Up Laughing: Long-Distance Nationalism and the Search for Home* (Durham: Duke University Press, 2001).

when, during the Dominican military effort to rout the Haitians after 22 years of occupation, the town was burned and sacked.[49] The Hinche region was later the staging ground for the largest assault by U.S. Marines on the heroic peasant-patriot Caco guerilla force which had risen up to resist American rule in 1917. Caco leader Charlemagne Péralte was closely associated with Hinche, since he was born and owned a parcel of land there and became its mayor. Péralte had been a military chief in the Haitian army but decamped to the field to lead the peasant rebels who had taken up arms when the marines ordered the recruitment of *corvée* and prisoner labour to cut roads. In Hinche the corvée had been suppressed but it was said that the marines endeavoured to keep this decree under wraps. Péralte was arrested on conspiracy charges but when he somehow miraculously escaped from jail, the marines embarked on a bloody campaign to kill him and his 1,200 followers, eventually resulting in his death and that of scores of others throughout the region in 1919.

Long a symbol of resistance to foreign aggression, Charlemagne Péralte was resurrected as an anti-imperialist icon in the popular nationalist fervour following the fall of the Jean-Claude Duvalier regime in 1986. His image was minted into currency and stamps.[50] A martyr who for Haitians belongs in the national pantheon next to revolutionary general Toussaint Louverture, Péralte has been described as one of Haiti's greatest heroes; the inscription on his gravestone goes so far as to compare him to Jesus Christ.[51]

Given this succession of historic battles, the soils of Hinche contain more than just minerals; they have absorbed the blood of many Haitian soldiers spilled in multiple valiant efforts to drive out foreigners seeking to compromise Haitian sovereignty. Built in 1959 in front of the national palace, there is a monument to the Haitian revolution called *le marron inconnu* (the unknown runaway slave), which celebrates the innumerable slaves who fought and died for their freedom and for the idea of an independent Haiti. Could it be, therefore, that the mud cakes are also signs of the 'profoundly self sacrificing love' shown by the thousands of slaves who made the ultimate sacrifice for the nation?[52] Could it be that the urge to nib-

---

49. For more on the Haitian revolutionary war, see Laurent Dubois, *Avengers of the New World: The Story of the Haitian Revolution* (Cambridge, MA: Belnap Press of Harvard University Press, 2004); and C.L.R. James, *The Black Jacobins: Toussaint L'Ouverture and the San Domingo Revolution* (New York: Vintage Books, 1963[1938]).

50. Cécile Accilien, Jessica Adams, and Elmide Méléance (eds.) *Revolutionary Freedoms: A History of Survival, Strength and Imagination in Haiti* (Coconut Creek FL: Caribbean Studies Press, 2006), p. 69.

51. Georges Michel. *Charlemagne Péralte: Un Centenaire 1885–1985* (Port-au-Prince, Haiti: G. Michel, 1989), p. 19. For more on Péralte, see Roger Gaillard, *Charlemagne Péralte: Le Caco* (Port-au-Prince: L'Imprimerie le Natal, 1982).

52. Benedict Anderson, *Imagined Communities: Reflections on the Origin and Spread of Nationalism* (London: Verso, 2006), pp. 129–32.

Lauren Derby

ble a pain biscuit is also a kind of gustatory nationalism? If, as Benedict Anderson has said, it is the 'magic of nationalism to turn chance into destiny', could it be powerful enough to turn dirt into food?

> Mapiange oh! Mapiange oh!
> Mapiange eats what he wants
> Mapiange transforms into what he wants
> Mapiange does not eat people
> Mapiange turns into any animal
> Mapiange turns into snake
> Turns into lizard
> Mapiange does what he wants[53]

Women and Nature

In her classic article 'Is Female to Male as Nature is to Culture?', anthropologist Sherry Ortner argued that women are devalued due to their associations with menstrual defilement and reproduction; their lack of bodily control thus associates them with nature.[54] In Africa and elsewhere, women are often perceived as wild and untamed, their powers potentially regenerative or destructive.[55] Evidence that in Haitian culture women's bodies are similarly held to be more unruly than those of men includes the fact that women are thought to be able to shape-shift into creatures such as bees and snakes, shedding their skin, flying from rooftops, their spirits appearing willy-nilly, like the spirit demon Maloulou who appears in chains with a pack of bull mastiffs and bloodhounds lurking behind her in the shadows.[56] Women's bodies are also linked to the spirit domain; for example in an analogy to sacrificial blood-letting, women's menstrual cycles can be controlled by the *mistère* (spirit) Legba.[57]

---

53. Parsons, 'Spirit Cult in Hayti': 668.

54. Sherry Ortner, 'Is Female to Male as Nature is to Culture?' *Feminist Studies* 1/2 (Autumn 1972): 5–31. For a critical view, see Carol P. MacCormick, 'Nature, Culture and Gender: A Critique', in Carol MacCormick and Marilyn Strathern (eds.) *Nature, Culture and Gender* (New York: Cambridge University Press, 1980) pp. 1–24. For an introduction to the vast literature on nature, culture and gender, see Sherry Ortner and Harriet Whitehead (eds.) *Sexual Meanings: The Cultural Construction of Gender and Sexuality* (New York: Cambridge University Press, 1981); and Jane Fishburn Collier and Sylvia Yanagisako (eds.) *Gender and Kinship: Essays Toward a Unified Analysis* (Stanford: Stanford University Press, 1987).

55. Michael Jackson, *Allegories of the Wilderness: Ethics and Ambiguity in Kuranko Narratives* (Bloomington, IN: Indiana University Press, 1982), p. 21.

56. As reported on Haitian television; see 'Haiti Rumors Woman Transforming into Snake', YouTube: Valabab (http://www.youtube.com/watch?v=R0AP2242tJY), 1 Sept. 2006; and George Eaton Simpson, 'Loup Garou and Loa Tales from Northern Haiti', *Journal of American Folklore* 55/218 (Oct.-Dec., 1942): 220–21.

57. Milo Rigaud, *Secrets of Voodoo* (New York: Arco Publishing, 1985), p. 161.

Moreover, women's bodies are deemed to channel emotions into bodily malaise in ways that men's do not. Women are subject to disorders such as *move san/lèt gate* in which bad blood and spoiled milk result from emotional distress. Paul Farmer interprets this as a result of somaticisation – the 'making corporal of nonbodily experience', in particular that caused by malignant emotions.[58] As in Sigmund Freud's classic notion of hysteria, *move san* thus is a 'protolanguage, communicating through the body messages that cannot be verbalized'.[59] In *let gate*, breast milk can enter the head and make a woman crazy or kill her. In one case, a thunderbolt hit a woman's house while she was sleeping causing her such a fright (*seziman*) that it dried up her breast milk.[60] This is evidence of a highly tangible notion of evil, one that renders it a force so palpable it can make a person ill. But the fact that a husband's beatings or a thunderbolt can eviscerate a woman's breast milk also indicates that in Haitian culture women's bodies are held to channel emotions and even the climate in ways that men's do not; they are perceived as porous and thus at one with nature in a way that is palpably different from men. And given the fact that rape is the single most prevalent form of violence in the tent camps that still house one million people, women in post-earthquake Haiti have plenty of reason to get sick.[61]

Ortner's argument may help us uncover the gendered aspect of the mud-cake phenomenon, since it is in essence a female commodity chain from production to consumption. Women prepare the cakes, distribute and sell them but, most importantly, it is principally women who eat them. Many Haitians and Dominicans I spoke to said that women eat them especially when pregnant; and that they can thus become an addiction, another motif of women out of control. But I also met women who told me they like them just because they taste good. This might make sense according to Ortner's logic. It could be argued that, since Haitian women's bodies are perceived to be polluting, with porous boundaries, they extend into the environment. Viewed in this way, it might therefore seem perfectly appropriate that they should want to eat dirt, because women in this view are one with the landscape in a way in which men are not.

But women in Haiti have a particular relationship to nature that extends into the supernatural domain. If men can become lesser demonic spirits which appear as *galipotes* and *bakas* in the form of dwarves, dogs and cows, only women can become

---

58. Paul Farmer, 'Bad Blood, Spoiled Milk: Bodily Fluids as Moral Barometers in Rural Haiti', *American Ethnologist* 15/1 (2009): 62.

59. Elaine Showalter, 'Four: Hysteria, Feminism and Gender', in Sander Gilman (ed.) *Hysteria Beyond Freud* (Berkeley: University of California Press, 1993), p. 286.

60. Farmer 2009, p. 67.

61. Interview with Los Angeles policemen on patrol in the tent camps of Port-au-Prince, August 2011.

the more diabolical *lougarou*.[62] In this context of female-headed households, it is typically women who care for the most important patio livestock, pigs and turkeys, but they can also become pigs and turkeys and fly around at night, searching for babies whose blood they suck. Lougarou have been described as 'werewolves that turned skin inside out and jumped about loudly on tin ceilings, eyeing little children for future repasts'.[63] Shape-shifting is among the mysteries women harbour, a secret that is mysterious and *puissant* (powerful), as well as potentially threatening.[64]

Haitian lougarou tales are a subset of the devil pact narrative form that is pan-Latin American in scope, although in the Hispanic world these are frequently stories told by men and those accused are usually male.[65] The protagonist secures the assistance of a sorcerer who provides him or her with the secret of shape-shifting and this in turn enables a person to acquire wealth. In Haiti, as throughout the Caribbean, women play an important role as traders and entrepreneurs. Since they tend to be more capitalised than men, lougarou stories aim in part to explain how it is that women have been able to achieve economic success.

What constitutes evidence of a shape-shifter? A pig with human fingernails. A cow that cries. A child that vanishes. A turkey with red eyes. In these lougarou tales, the women conspire in occult and probably malicious acts. For example, in one tale a woman who needed to provide a yearly human sacrifice to retain her shape-shifter powers planned to become a bee so as to kill her husband. In another, a man, who suspected his wife was a lougarou, stayed awake one night observing how, by deploying a potion, she was able to shed her skin and leave through the roof. While she was gone, her husband spiced this skin with red pepper and lemons; upon returning, she died, as she was unable to put it back on.[66] Given the fact that in these stories women have a particularly intimate and even coterminous relationship with the animal world it should not be a surprise that barren women are called 'mules' and adulteresses and prostitutes in rural areas are mocked as 'scabby sheep'.[67]

Lougarou narratives are not the only popular Haitian idiom that presumes that women at times harbour covert and often malevolent designs. Women are

62. Also spelled as Lougawou or Loup Garou. This gendered split was confirmed by Elizabeth McAlister (personal communication).

63. Marie Lily Cerat, 'Maloulou', in Edwidge Danticat (ed.) *Haiti Noir* (New York: Akashic Books, 2011), pp. 179–91.

64. Evelyn Fox Keller, 'Making Gender Visible in the Pursuit of Nature's Secrets', in Teresa de Lauretis (ed.) *Feminist Studies: Critical Studies* (Bloomington, IN: Indiana University Press, 1986), p. 69.

65. Michael Taussig, *Devil and Commodity Fetishism in South America* (Chapel Hill: University of North Carolina Press, 1980); Marc Edelman, 'Landlords and the Devil: Class, Ethnic, and Gender Dimensions of Central American Peasant Narratives', *Cultural Anthropology* 9/1 (Feb. 1994): 58–93.

66. Simpson 'Loup Garou and Loa Tales': 220–21.

67. George Eaton Simpson, 'Sexual and Familial Institutions in Northern Haiti'. *American Anthropologist* 44/4 (Oct.-Dec. 1942): 672.

often presumed to have special powers. For instance, they can enter the world of the *zanges* (a class of ancestral spirits) through a pond or other body of water in which others drown.[68] The wily siren or mermaid spirit can be prone to fits of rage and acts of betrayal, as can *ezili dantor*, the black vodou goddess. And girls who die before having intercourse are reincarnated as *djables* who remain in the woods for years before going to heaven. They lurk on country roads where they attack men; if someone follows a *djables* she turns into a frightening mixture of bones and mud or disappears. They appear as tall women with baskets on their arms and, like miraculous folk Catholic apparitions, affix to particular places such as hills or trees.[69] Lesbians are blamed for misfortunes such as crop failure, droughts and epidemics. Worse yet, women are said to cause natural disasters such as earthquakes and floods. After the 2010 earthquake, rumours attributed the disappearance of infants (who had died, been adopted or had landed in hospitals elsewhere) to women who had snatched them to suck their blood in the dead of night, creating a rash of vengeance killings in Port-au-Prince. Moreover, some said that the earthquake itself, as well as the cholera epidemic, had been caused by a lougarou.

If lougarou tales about women turning into turkeys are male stories and *seziman* (frights) which can cause *lèt move* (bad milk) are women's expressions of bereavement, they nonetheless share something in common: they both assume femaleness to be coterminous with the environment, as women's bodies not only channel natural forces such as lightning but extend into the dirt – and even become mud. They indicate that Haitian mud-cake making is ultimately a story about a vernacular understanding of the landscape in which nature is gendered. This may well have parallels elsewhere, and not only with slave societies. For instance, it is reported that Nahua women ate dirt as their nation and their natural resources were consumed by Spaniards and their cattle.[70] Haiti – the nation that is often indexed as the ground zero of environmental degradation in the Americas – thus reveals the value of Mark Carey's observation that environments are ultimately hybrid landscapes where nature and culture blur indecipherably.[71]

And of course the natural environment of Haiti has been ravaged like nowhere else in the Americas. Tree felling, which gained momentum in Haiti during the eighteenth-century sugar boom, continued into the twentieth century as logging was encouraged as a viable cash crop during the U.S. Occupation; lack of investment in the energy sector under the Duvalier regimes (1957–86) further expanded the use of charcoal in industrial establishments in addition to household food preparation. Today less than four per cent of the original forest cover remains

68. Simpson, 'Loup Garou and Loa Tales': 226.

69. Simpson, 'Sexual and Familial Institutions': 668–9.

70. Marcy Norton, personal communication, 19 Sept. 2011.

71. Mark Carey, 'Latin American Environmental History: Current Trends, Interdisciplinary Insights, and Future Directions', *Environmental History* 14/2 (2009): 239.

in Haiti and this, combined with the fact that most land in Haiti is sloped at an angle of over 30 degrees, renders the land highly prone to desertification. The ecological crisis came to a crescendo during the 1980s, when USAID determined that smallholder subsistence production was inefficient and reoriented the agricultural economy toward exports, notwithstanding the fully anticipated income loss, nutritional decline and massive displacement of farmers to Port-au-Prince as the plantation and assembling economies expanded at the expense of smallholders.[72] The free market policies of the Clinton administration deepened the crisis, as the country was flooded with 'Miami rice', which, due to its artificially low price buoyed by agricultural state subsidies, quickly replaced the nutritious tuber crops that had been dietary staples, destroying local rice production, ruining the domestic food economy and making Haiti the largest net food importer in Latin America. When Clinton was named special envoy to Haiti after the devastating 2010 earthquake, he apologised publicly for spearheading policies that had contributed to food insecurity and hunger – yet this was far too little too late.[73] Hunger is certainly part of the reason why the mud cake shifted from an occasional snack item to a foodstuff in 2008 when ravenousness in Haiti was said to burn stomachs like Clorox and battery acid; and the situation has only worsened since the price of rice and oil has shot up by fifty per cent since August 2011.[74]

It has been argued that the environment is such a powerful form of structuration that it is of an entirely different order from gender, but the Haitian case reminds us that this very splitting of gender and landscape is peculiar to our own cultural lens.[75] (This may be harder to forget in French since *la terre* is feminine.) Adopting this insight requires an approach that not only recognises nature as an historical force, but also considers how modes of interaction between people and the natural world create implicit meanings.[76] This requires a model that moves beyond

---

72. Josh DeWind and David H. Kinley, 'Export-Led Development', in James Ridgeway (ed.) *The Haiti Files: Decoding the Crisis*, (Washington, DC: Essential Books, 1994), p. 125.

73. Jonathan M. Katz, 'With Cheap Food Imports, Haiti Can't Feed Itself', *The Huffington Post* (24 Aug. 2012). For more on the food crisis and the earthquake in Haiti, see Mark Schuller and Pablo Morales, *Tectonic Shifts: Haiti Since the Earthquake* (Sterling VA: Kumarian Press, 2012); and Mark Schuller and Paul Farmer, *Killing with Kindness: Haiti, International Aid, and NGOs* (Piscataway, N.J: Rutgers University Press, 2012).

74. Katherine Smith, 'Dancing in Salon Pep La', *E-Misférica* 7/1 (2010) Unsettling Visuality; Mark Schuller, 'Haiti's Second Goudougoudou: The Global Food Crisis', *Huffington Post*, 2 Oct. 2012.

75. Ellen Stroud, 'Does Nature always Matter? Following Dirt through History', *History and Theory* 42 (Dec. 2003): 75–81.

76. Mary Douglas, *Implicit Meanings: Essays in Anthropology* (Boston and London: Routledge and Kegan Paul, 1975).

an objectified view of nature to attend to the materiality of interactive practice, in this case the desire to eat something forbidden.[77]

The case of the Haitian mud pies reminds us that, in order to decipher other cultural understandings of the nature/culture divide, historians need to step outside some of their most basic assumptions about raw and cooked, nature and culture, femininity and masculinity. If the interpretations offered in this essay are correct, Haitian reverence for dirt is not only about the indignities of poverty; it also tells a story about the sacredness of the nation state. It expresses a passion for a republic which was forged through the ultimate sacrifice as well as constituting an emblem of a particular understanding of female power that defines Haitian culture. The implicit root metaphor is blood, since it was the blood sacrificed that created the nation, that is regenerated through women's reproduction.[78] Such an approach places the humble Haitian mud patty – as an object embodying popular veneration of the land – on a par with Yosemite National Park in northern California and other better-known nationalist monuments of wilderness and history.[79] But these layers of meaning could not be elicited directly via oral testimony, since they are secrets embedded within the cakes and the landscape. They offer us a glimpse of subaltern female nationalism, a love of nationhood that is material rather than discursive.[80] And as Ellen Stroud concludes from her study of dirt through history, 'if other historians would join us in our attention to the physical, biological and ecological nature of dirt, water, air, trees and animals (including humans), they would find themselves led to new questions and new answers about the past'.[81]

Acknowledgments

Research for this essay was supported by grants from UCLA International Studies and the Academic Senate COR Faculty Program, the Center for the Study of Women, UCLA, and a Burkhardt fellowship from the ACLS at the Huntington Library, for which I am most grateful. Thanks to Abercio Alcántara, Don Cosentino, Georges René, Katherine Smith and Frank Polyak who assisted me in my research in Santo Domingo, Dominican Republic and Port-au-Prince, Haiti, in field trips

77. Mark Carey, 'The Nature of Place: Recent Research on Environment and Society in Latin America', *Latin American Research Review* 42/3 (October 2007): 253.

78. Louis Herns Marcelin, 'In the Name of the Nation: Blood Symbolism and the Political Habitus of Violence in Haiti', *American Anthropologist* 114/2 (2012): 253–66. Many thanks to Elizabeth McAlister for bringing this piece to my attention.

79. Simon Schama, *Landscape and Memory* (New York: Vintage, 1996). Of course, *terroir* in French indicates a cult of the earth as well.

80. Contrast with Kamala Visweswaran, 'Small Speeches, Subaltern Gender: Nationalist Ideology and Its Historiography', in Shahid Amin and Dipesh Chakrabarty (eds.) *Subaltern Studies, IX: Writings on South Asian History and Society* (New Delhi: Oxford University Press, 1996), pp. 83–125.

81. Stroud 2003, p. 75.

260

Lauren Derby

between 2008 and 2012; Karen Middleton, Katherine Smith, Judith Bettelheim, Sarah Johnson and Elizabeth McAlister for critical feedback on this essay; Judith Bettelheim and Andrew Apter who provided some crucial leads on African source materials; and Elizabeth Deloughrey, Russell Stockard and Mikael Wolfe for citations, clarification and encouragement. Earlier versions of the essay were presented at the Latin American Studies Association section conference on Ethnicity, Race and Indigenous Peoples at University of California at San Diego on 4 November 2012; the Caribbean Crossroads conference at the University of California at Santa Barbara, 22 February 2012; and the 'Aesthetics, Ecologies and Politics' conference at Warwick University, 24ᵗʰ September 2011, and benefited greatly from the many insights provided at these events, especially those of Claudine Michel and Jean Rahier. Thanks as well to the Fowler Museum for permission to use the Nkisi image and to Jared Heins and Edwina Orelus for permission to use their photo from Hinche.

References

Accilien, Cécile, Jessica Adams and Elmide Méléance (eds.) 2006. *Revolutionary Freedoms: A History of Survival, Strength and Imagination in Haiti.* Coconut Creek FL: Caribbean Studies Press.

Anderson, Benedict. 2006. *Imagined Communities: Reflections on the Origin and Spread of Nationalism.* London: Verso.

Carey, Mark. 2009. 'Latin American Environmental History: Current Trends, Interdisciplinary Insights, and Future Directions'. *Environmental History* 14/2: 221–52.

Carey, Mark. 2007. 'The Nature of Place: Recent Research on Environment and Society in Latin America'. *Latin American Research Review* 42/3 (October 2007): 251–64.

Carney, Judith A. 2011. *Black Rice: The African Origins of Rice Cultivation in the Americas.* Cambridge, MA: Harvard University Press.

Cerat, Marie Lily. 2011. 'Maloulou'. In Edwige Danticat (ed.) *Haiti Noir.* New York: Akashic Books. pp. 179–91.

Collier, Jane Fishburn and Sylvia Yanagisako (eds.) 1987. *Gender and Kinship: Essays Toward a Unified Analysis.* Stanford: Stanford University Press.

Cosentino, Donald J. 1995. 'It's All for You, Sen Jak!' In Donald Cosentino (ed.) *Sacred Arts of Haitian Vodou.* Los Angeles: Fowler Museum. pp. 243–63.

Covey, Herbert C. and Dwight Eisnach. 2009. *What the Slaves Ate: Recollections of African American Foods and Foodways.* Santa Barbara: Greenwood Press.

Deloughrey, Elizabeth, Renée K. Gossen and George B. Handley (eds.) 2005. *Caribbean Literature and the Environment: Between Nature and Culture.* Charlottesville: University of Virginia Press.

Deloughrey, Elizabeth and George B. Handley (eds.) 2011. *Postcolonial Ecologies: Literatures of the Environment.* New York: Oxford University Press.

On Revolutionary Dirt in Haiti

DeWind, Josh and David H. Kinley. 1994. 'Export-Led Development'. In James Ridgeway (ed.) *The Haiti Files: Decoding the Crisis*. Washington, D.C.: Essential Books. pp. 123–9.

Doris, David T. 2011. *Vigilant Things: On Thieves, Yoruba Anti-Aesthetics and the Strange Fates of Ordinary Objects in Nigeria*. Seattle: University of Washington Press.

Douglas, Mary. 1988. *Purity and Danger: An Analysis of the Concepts of Pollution and Taboo*. London: Ark Paperbacks.

Douglas, Mary. 1972. 'Deciphering a Meal'. *Daedalus*. 101/1 (Winter): 61–81.

Douglas, Mary. 1975. *Implicit Meanings: Essays in Anthropology*. Boston and London: Routledge and Kegan Paul.

Doumerc, Éric. 2003. *Caribbean Civilization: The English Speaking Caribbean since Independence*. Toulouse: Presses Universitaire du Mirail.

Edelman, Marc. 1994. 'Landlords and the Devil: Class, Ethnic, and Gender Dimensions of Central American Peasant Narratives'. *Cultural Anthropology* 9/1 (Feb.): 58–93.

Farmer, Paul. 2009. 'Bad Blood, Spoiled Milk: Bodily Fluids as Moral Barometers in Rural Haiti'. *American Ethnologist* 15/1: 62–83.

Friedman, Kajsa Ekholm. 1991. *Catastrophe and Creation: The Transformation of an African Culture*. Pennsylvania, PA: Harwood Academic Publishers.

Gaillard, Roger. 1982. *Charlemagne Péralte: Le Caco*. Port-au-Prince: L'Imprimerie le Natal.

Gaillard, Roger. 1982. *Hinche mise en croix*. Port-au-Prince: L'Imprimerie le Natal.

Genovese, Eugene. 1974. *Roll, Jordan, Roll: The World the Slaves Made*. New York: Pantheon Books.

Glick-Schiller, Nina and Georges Eugene Fouron. 2001. *Georges Woke Up Laughing: Long-Distance Nationalism and the Search for Home*. Durham: Duke University Press.

Goffman, Erving. 1963. *Stigma: Notes on the Management of Spoiled Identity*. Englewood Cliffs, NJ: Prentice-Hall.

Higman, B.W. 1984. *Slave Populations of the British Caribbean, 1807–1834*. Baltimore: Johns Hopkins University Press.

Jackson, Michael. 1982. *Allegories of the Wilderness: Ethics and Ambiguity in Kuranko Narratives*. Bloomington, IN: Indiana University Press.

James, C.L.R. 1963[1938]. *The Black Jacobins: Toussaint L'Ouverture and the San Domingo Revolution*. New York: Vintage Books.

Katz, Jonathan M. 2008. 'Poor Haitians Resort to Eating Dirt'. *National Geographic News*. 30 Jan.

Katz, Jonathan M. 2012. 'With Cheap Food Imports, Haiti Can't Feed Itself'. *The Huffington Post*. 24 Aug.

Keller, Evelyn Fox. 1986. 'Making Gender Visible in the Pursuit of Nature's Secrets'. In Teresa de Lauretis (ed.) *Feminist Studies: Critical Studies*. Bloomington, IN: Indiana University Press. pp. 67–77.

Kiple, Kenneth F. 1984. *The Caribbean Slave: A Biological History*. Cambridge: Cambridge University Press.

262

Lauren Derby

Kiple, Kenneth and Virginia Himmelsteib King. 1981. *Another Dimension to the Black Diaspora: Diet, Disease and Racism.* Cambridge: Cambridge University Press.

Lacey, Marc. 2008. 'Across Globe, Empty Bellies Bring Rising Anger'. *New York Times.* 18 Apr.

Lewis, Maureen Warner. 2003. *Central Africa in the Caribbean: Transcending Time, Transforming Cultures.* Kingston, Jamaica: University of the West Indies Press.

Lévi-Strauss, Claude. 1966. *The Savage Mind.* Chicago: University of Chicago Press.

MacCormick, Carol P. 1980. 'Nature, Culture and Gender: A Critique'. In Carol MacCormick and Marilyn Strathern (eds.) *Nature, Culture and Gender.* New York: Cambridge University Press. pp. 1–24.

MacGaffey, Wyatt. 1991. *Art and Healing of the Bakongo.* Stockholm: Folkens Museum-Etnografiska.

Marcelin, Louis Herns. 2012. 'In the Name of the Nation: Blood Symbolism and the Political Habitus of Violence in Haiti'. *American Anthropologist.* 114/2: 253–66.

McAlister, Elizabeth. 2002. *Rara! Vodou, Power, and Performance in Haiti and its Diaspora,* Berkeley: University of California Press.

McNeill, John. 2010. *Mosquito Empires: Ecology and War in the Greater Caribbean, 1620–1914.* New York: Cambridge University Press.

Michel, Georges. 1989. *Charlemagne Péralte: Un Centenaire 1885–1985.* Port-au-Prince, Haiti: G. Michel.

Millwood, Robinson. 2007. *European Christianity and the Atlantic Slave Trade: A Black Hermeneutical Study.* Bloomington, IN: AuthorHouse.

Minn, Pierre. 2001. 'Water on their Eyes, Dust on Their Land'. *Journal of Haitian Studies* 7/1 (Spring): 4–25.

Moitt, Bernard. 2001. *Women and Slavery in the French Antilles 1635–1848.* Bloomington: Indiana University Press.

Ortner, Sherry. 1972. 'Is Female to Male as Nature is to Culture?' *Feminist Studies* 1/2 (Autumn): 5–31.

Ortner, Sherry and Harriet Whitehead (eds.) 1981. *Sexual Meanings: The Cultural Construction of Gender and Sexuality.* New York: Cambridge University Press.

Owens, Leslie Howard. 1976. *The Species of Property: Slave Life and Culture in the Old South.* Oxford: Oxford University Press.

Parsons, Elsie Clews. 1928. 'Spirit Cult in Hayti'. *Journal de la Société des Américanistes* 20/20: 157–79.

Puckett, Newbell Niles. 1968. *Folk Beliefs of the Southern Negro.* Montclair, NJ: Patterson Smith.

Ramsey, Kate. 2011. *The Spirits and the Law: Vodou and Power in Haiti.* Chicago: University of Chicago Press.

Reef, Catherine. 2007. *Poverty In America.* New York: Infobase Publishing.

Rigaud, Milo. 1985. *Secrets of Voodoo.* New York: Arco Publishing.

Schama, Simon. 1996. *Landscape and Memory.* New York: Vintage.

Schuller, Mark. 2012. 'Haiti's Second Goudougoudou: The Global Food Crisis'. *Huffington Post*. 2 Oct.

Schuller, Mark and Pablo Morales. 2012. *Tectonic Shifts: Haiti Since the Earthquake*. Sterling, VA: Kumarian Press.

Schuller, Mark and Paul Farmer. 2012. *Killing with Kindness: Haiti, International Aid, and NGOs*. Piscataway, N.J: Rutgers University Press.

Shabazz, Saeed. 2008. 'Rising Food Prices Increase Haiti's Agony'. Call.com News. 23 April.

Simpson, George Eaton. 1942. 'Loup Garou and Loa Tales from Northern Haiti'. *The Journal of American Folklore* 55/218 (Oct.-Dec.): 219–27.

Simpson, George Eaton. 1942. 'Sexual and Familial Institutions in Northern Haiti'. *American Anthropologist* 44/4 (Oct.–Dec.): 655–74.

Smith, Katherine. 2010. 'Dancing in Salon Pep La', *E-Misférica* 7/1, Unsettling Visuality.

Showalter, Elaine. 1993. 'Four: Hysteria, Feminism and Gender'. In Sander Gilman (ed.) *Hysteria Beyond Freud*. Berkeley: University of California Press. pp. 286–336.

Stallybrass, Peter and Allon White. 1986. *The Poetics and Politics of Transgression*. Ithaca: N.Y.: Cornell University Press.

Stroud, Ellen. 2003. 'Does Nature always Matter? Following Dirt through History'. *History and Theory* 42 (Dec.): 75–81.

Taussig, Michael. 1980. *Devil and Commodity Fetishism in South America*. Chapel Hill: University of North Carolina Press.

Thompson, Robert Farris. 1984. *Flash of the Spirit: African and Afro-American Art and Philosophy*. New York: Vintage Books.

Thompson, Robert Farris and Joseph Cornet. 1981. *The Four Moments of the Sun: Kongo Art in Two Worlds*. Washington: National Gallery of Art.

Thornton, John K. 1993. '"I Am the Subject of the King of Congo": African Political Ideology and the Haitian Revolution'. *Journal of World History* 4/2 (Fall, 1993): 181–214.

Visweswaran, Kamala. 1996. 'Small Speeches, Subaltern Gender: Nationalist Ideology and Its Historiography'. In Shahid Amin and Dipesh Chakrabarty (eds.) *Subaltern Studies, IX: Writings on South Asian History and Society*. New Delhi: Oxford University Press. pp. 83–125.

Weismantel, Mary J. 1988. *Food, Gender and Poverty in the Ecuadorian Andes*. Long Grove IL: Waveland Press.

World Bank, The. 2008. *Food Price Inflation and its Effects on Latin America and the Caribbean*. Washington, D.C.: World Bank.

Yaeger, Patricia. 2000. *Dirt and Desire: Reconstructing Southern Women's Writing, 1930–1990*. Chicago: University of Chicago Press.

Young, Sera L. 2011. *Craving Earth: Understanding Pica – The Urge to Eat Clay, Starch, Ice and Chalk*. New York: Columbia University Press.

Lauren Derby

Primary Sources

Carmichael, Mary. 1833. *Domestic Manners and Social Condition of the White, Coloured and Negro Population of the West Indies*, Vol. I. London: Whittaker, Treacher and Co.

Collins, Dr. 1803. *Practical Rules for the Management and Medical Treatment of Negro Slaves, in the Sugar Colonies*. London: Printed by J. Barfield for Vernor and Hood.

Grainger, James. 1764. *The Sugar Cane: A Poem*. London: R. and J. Dodsley.

Great Britain. Parliament. 1792. *Minutes of the Evidence Taken at the Bar of the House of Lords.*

Hyatt, Harry Middleton. 1970. '*Hoodoo – Conjuration – Rootwork*', Memoirs of the Alma Egan Hyattt Foundation. Hannibal, MO: Western Publishing, Vol. I.

Laman, K.E. 1957. *The Kongo*. Vol. II. Uppsala: Studia Etnographica Upsaliensia.

Ligon, Richard. 1673. *A True and Exact History of the Island of Barbados Illustrated with a Map of the Island...* London: Peter Parker.

Weeks, John H. 1913. *Among Kongo Cannibals. Experiences, Impressions and Adventures during a Thirty Years' Sojourn amongst the Boloki and other Congo Tribes, with a Description of their Curious Habits, Customs, Religion and Laws*. Philadelphia, PA: J.P. Lippincott.

Weeks, John H. 1914. *Among the Primitive Bakongo: A Record of Thirty Years Close Intercourse with the Bakongo and other Tribes of Equatorial Africa, with a Description of their Habits, Customs & Religious Beliefs*. London: Seeley, Service and Co.

Chapter 11

Reshaping Nature: Underwater Laboratories, Ecology, and Outer Space in West Germany and the United States

Sven Asim Mesinovic

Underwater laboratories were, at a certain period of time, not as unusual as one might think. The idea of the oceans as the new seventh continent became popular in the mid-1960s, and underwater laboratories were part of this conquering-the-seabed discourse. Between 1965 and 1980 more than 65 of these habitats were built around the world by industrialised states. This chapter examines the entangled history of two such laboratories: one placed by the United States of America in the shallow waters of the Caribbean (Tektite), the other deployed by West Germany in the cold waters of the North Sea (Helgoland). Both were experiments in new living spaces

Figure 1. Aquanauts excurt (saturation dive) from Tektite I.

Location St John, USVI, 1969. Credit: OAR/National Undersea Research Program (NURP). Credit: National Oceanic and Atmospheric Administration/Department of Commerce. http://www.photolib.noaa.gov/htmls/nur08039.htm

at the time of outer space exploration and the so-called limits-to-growth debates of the late 1960s. Significantly, the scientists who spent time living in these underwater laboratories were called 'aquanauts', linking them purposefully to the astronauts.

The aim of these underwater houses was twofold. Most obviously, they provided tightly controlled artificial atmospheres from which scientists could safely carry out research in marine environments for varying periods of time of between a few days to several months. At the same time, however, the scientists themselves became 'guinea pigs', observed by other scientists on the surface who were researching either the adaptation of the human body to high atmospheric pressure (Helgoland) or the criteria for the selection of crew-members for future space missions and the specifications for space station design (Tektite I and II). Used as tools in the context of space science, one of their main aims was to find out how man functions in a hostile environment. Their common history of adapting humans to new atmospheres challenged accepted understandings of human nature as circumscribed by its customary biological, chemical and physical habitats. As experiments in the simulation of life and spatial reconceptualisation, these projects were profoundly shaped by the modern ecological movement as well as by the politics of the time.

Living in a Hostile Environment: Tektite I

The first civilian underwater laboratory in the United States was established in 1969 on the seafloor off St. John (American Virgin Islands). Named for a stone 'formed from the melting and rapid cooling of terrestrial rocks that have been vaporized by the high-energy impacts of large meteorites, comets, or asteroids upon the surface of the Earth',[1] Tektite drew an explicit link with the outer space programme. If the expanse beyond earth's atmosphere was 'outer space', the ocean was seen as 'inner space', and 'Tektite' became an ideal name for a project connecting the two.

Starting on 15 February 1969, four scientists in their early to mid-thirties – physical oceanographers Richard A. Waller and Conrad V.W Mahnken, geologist H. Edward Clifton from the US Geological Survey, and John G. Van Derwalker from the US Bureau of Commercial Fisheries – spent sixty days living in the laboratory.[2] Submerged 49 feet deep in Greater Lamashur Bay, on the south side of St. John, the laboratory consisted of two connected vertical cylinders. One cylinder contained the bridge (upper deck) and crew quarters (lower deck) while the other housed the wet room and equipment store (see Figure 2). Close circuit television

---

1.   http://www.britannica.com/eb/article-9071569/tektite

2.   National Archive and Records Administration, College Park, Maryland, USA. RG 303, Records of the National Council on Marine Resources and Engineering Development. Records Relating to Man in the Sea, Box 3. Department of the Interior Office of the Secretary For immediate Release 15 April 1969. Secretary Hickel hails success of 'Tektite' Aquanauts.

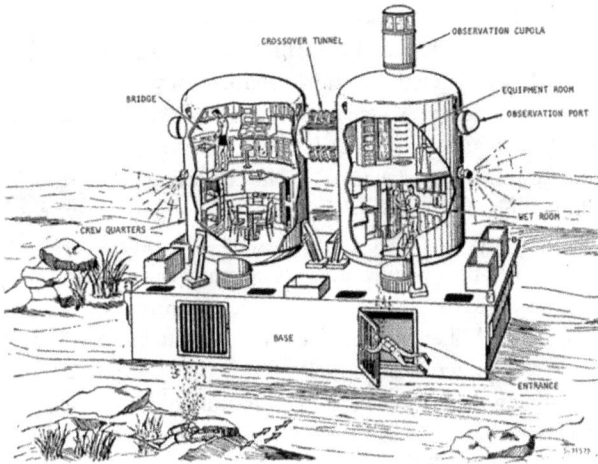

Figure 2. Tektite II Habitat interior arrangement.

D. Nowlis, D.E.C. Wortz, and H. Watters, *Tektite II Habitability Research Program* (Los Angeles: AiResearch Manufacturing Co, 1972), Figure 2–7.

cameras and microphones were installed in every compartment so that officers on the surface could observe everything that happened inside the underwater house.[3]

The atmospheric pressure inside the laboratory was maintained at a level equivalent to that of the surrounding ocean. The idea was to extend the periods spent diving in the sea by keeping the resident scientists in saturation-diving mode. This meant that, unlike conventional divers who have to acclimate to a different pressure before and after every dive, the aquanauts' bodies were required to adapt only at the beginning of their mission and then to re-adapt to normal pressure at its end. During the mission they could dive for as long as they wanted because the dissolved gases in the body were at equilibrium with the pressure in the ambient atmosphere. Furthermore, the atmosphere inside the laboratory consisted of nitrogen-oxygen composition.[4]

---

3. W.L. High, 'Evaluation of the Undersea Habitats – Tektite II, Hydro-Lab, and Edalhab – for Scientific Saturation Diving Programs', in H.P. Pulnheim and Otto Kinne (eds.) *Man in the Sea. In Situ Studies on Life in Oceans and Coastal Waters* (Hamburg: Biologische Anstalt Helgoland, 1973), p. 20.

4. James A. Vorosmarty, 'A Very Short History of Saturation Diving', *Historical Diving Times* **20** (1997): 1–2.

The project was funded by private companies as well as by the state agencies involved in outer space exploration. Of a total budget of over $2 million, General Electric contributed $600,000, as much as the United States Office of Naval Research, the American Space Agency the National Aeronautics and Space Administration (NASA) and the United States Department of the Interior combined.[5] Not everybody supported such a costly project, however. Marine biologist Walter A. Starck II wrote to the editors of the magazine *Science* criticising the expenditure. Insisting that 'No serious biomedical problems have been encountered in other shallow-water habitats and there was no reason to expect any in Tektite I', he argued that the research programme's only justification was to study the behaviour of an 'isolated' group of men subject to the 'stress' of an 'hostile' environment.[6] Responding in the same issue, James W. Miller, aquanaut and participant in the Tektite programme, defended the project in terms of the general benefits of scientific programmes and the value of studying the behaviour of humans undertaking real tasks in field conditions. He argued that this was essential in order to select crews for future space flights and deep sea missions.[7]

Miller's response highlights the fact that, while Tektite I was used as a marine biology research station – the St John location had been chosen for its clear waters and biologically diverse coral reef, its primary function was to study human survival in a hostile milieu. The laboratory was not simply about enabling biologists to conduct fieldwork in the sea; it was also, as four of the aquanauts themselves noted, about testing the capabilities of a team of scientists to carry out research under nitrogen-saturated conditions in a self-contained habitat for sixty days.[8]

Adapting humans to an artificial environment was critical to manned space flight and to the planning of an inhabited orbital space station. Observing the scientists in the closed environment of an underwater laboratory was expected to provide crucial biomedical and psychological data on living in an artificial habitat and important insights into how humans utilise and cope with a confined space.[9] The overall aim was to minimise the risks of manned space flights. Their value to the American Space Agency is evident in an Office of Naval Research (ONR) report on Tektite I. The authors stress the similarity 'between (the) crew behavioral aspect of

5.   National Archive and Records Administration, College Park, Maryland, USA. RG 303, Records of the National Council on Marine Resources and Engineering Development. Records Relating to Man in the Sea, Box 3.

6.   Walter A. Starck II and James W. Miller, '*Tektite*: Expectations and Costs', *Science* N.S. **169** (3952) 25 Sept. 1970: 1264.

7.   Ibid. p. 1265.

8.   H.E. Clifton, C.V.W. Mahnken, J.G. Van Derwalker and R.A. Waller, 'Tektite I, Man in-the-Sea Project: Marine Science Program', *Science* N.S. **168** (3932) 8 May 1970: 659–63.

9.   James W. Miller and Ian G. Koblick, *Living and Working in the Sea* (New York: Van Nostrand Reinhold, 1984).

a long-duration operational saturation dive and a space mission', and the relevance of 'behavioral, habitability and crew effectiveness data obtained in observations of undersea teams' to understanding problems involving 'space teams'.[10] Analogies between inner space and outer space had been discussed by the ONR and NASA psychologists at a NASA Symposium on Isolation and Confinement in November 1966. Further meetings on the value of behavioural studies in underwater habitats for space science had followed in 1967. Comparisons between the conquest of outer and inner space were regularly drawn during this period, including by the pioneers of inner space themselves. In the heyday of the underwater habitats, the popular West German diving magazine *Delphin* published a short article titled (in translation): 'Astro- and Aquanauts have much in common'. Written by Hans Heinrich Vogt, an author of popular science books, it featured a photograph of the aqua- and astronaut Scott Carpenter together with Wernher von Braun, one of the most famous scientists of the Space Age.[11]

Saturation Diving Tests in the Underwater Laboratory Helgoland

Testing the ability of the human organism to adapt to life in a non-natural environment was also the major motivation behind an underwater laboratory established in the Federal Republic of Germany the same year (1969). Located in the North Sea, 3.2 kilometres northeast of Heligoland Island, the German laboratory consisted of a steel construction, nine metres long and two metres wide, submerged to a depth of 23 metres (see Figure 3). At this depth four young scientists carried out biological research on marine life, notably on the ethology of the Heligoland lobster.[12] At the same time, they were themselves observed by other scientists located outside the laboratory, interested in what happens to the human body when it is exposed to high pressure.

The first mission ran from late August to mid-September. The crew consisted of F. Jatzke, a professional diver, Dr. Heinz Oser a physician from the German Space Agency DFVLR, and Drs. Gotram Uhlig and Roland von Hentig, biologists at the *Biologische Anstalt Helgoland*/Heligoland Biological Research Institute [BAH]. As in

10. D. C. Pauli and H. A. Cole, 'Project Tektite I. A Multi-Agency 60-Day Saturated Dive Conducted by the United States Navy, the National Aeronautics and Space Administration, the Department of the Interior, and the General Electric Company, Ocean Technology Branch, Ocean Science and Technology Division', *Office of Naval Research Report* 153 (16 January 1970): 2.

11. H-H. Vogt, 'Astro-und Aquanauten haben vieles gemeinsam'. D*elphin. Offizielle Mitteilungsblatt des Verbandes Deutscher Sporttaucher und des Tauchsportverbandes Österreichs* 6 (June 1969): 4–5.

12. Otto Kinne, 'Erste Erfahrungen mit dem Unterwasserlaboratorium "Helgoland" (Zweiter Teil)', in Karl Steinbuch (ed.) *Systems 69. Internationales Symposium über Zukunftsfragen* (Stuttgart: Stuttgarter Verlagsanstalt, 1970) pp. 293–94.

Figure 3. Underwater laboratory Helgoland

Photo: Klugschnacker. http://upload.wikimedia.org/wikipedia/commons/7/72/UWL_Hel-goland_im_Nautineum_Dänholm%2C_Stralsund%2C_Ansicht_%282008-05-10%29.JPG

Tektite I, the idea was to keep the scientists in saturation-diving mode. Helium was added to the atmosphere in the underwater housing in order to prevent the already known negative effects of excess oxygen in the lungs under high pressure. The addition of helium to the divers' bottles allowed the divers to tolerate greater depths.

Two scientists had planned the 'Helgoland' underwater laboratory together: Professor Siegfried Ruff, director of the Institute for flight medicine at the German Space Agency DFVLR, and Professor Otto Kinne of the BAH. As a marine biologist, Kinne's primary interest was in facilitating 'fieldwork' in the marine environment, whereas Ruff as a physiologist was more concerned with testing the reactions of BAH scientists to hyperbaric pressure. Siegfried Ruff had been a leading German flight physician during the Second World War. Tried at Nuremberg for complicity in inhumane experiments on inmates of Dachau concentration camp, he had been acquitted and allowed to continue his aviation research.[13] In the early 1960s, however, aviation medicine ceased to be a priority for the German Research Foundation. In addition, the leading German political magazine *Der Spiegel,* together with newspapers like *Die Zeit,* published articles about Ruff's war crimes.[14] Perhaps for these reasons, Ruff's research interests turned from experiments on the effects of low pressure to experiments on the effects of high pressure and to the construction of an underwater laboratory. Marine engineering and diving medicine were promising new fields in which he might apply his knowledge. His research on the effects of hyperbaric compression on the human body received widespread attention in October 1963 when miners, rescued from a tunnel in which they had been trapped, were put into a hyperbaric chamber to recover. The media depicted the event as the 'Wonder of Lengede'. Siegfried Ruff finally received German Research Foundation funding for the underwater laboratory project in 1966.[15] The research proposal Ruff and his colleague Karl Gerhard Müller had submitted, to test their theory of how the human body reacts to external 'inputs', notably higher atmospheric pressure, had been critical in securing the funds.[16]

Reading the sources it becomes clear that environmental conditions in Helgoland underwater laboratory proved more difficult to manage than anticipated. A minute written by Gotram Uhlig for a BAH meeting in October 1969 reveals some of the challenges.[17] High humidity (ninety per cent) in the laboratory caused regular ear infections and meant that skin wounds took longer to heal. Attempts to reduce the humidity with silica gel were not altogether successful. Water temperatures of 13.5°C during the dives were challenging.[18] Technical problems occurred in heating the living spaces and drying the diving suits. A great deal of the scientists' time in the underwater laboratory was spent on routine tasks such as changing the granulate to help reduce the humidity, refilling the soda lime which absorbed their carbon dioxide and changing the water tanks. In fact, due to the technical difficulties, only three days per week were dedicated to marine biology, despite the undeniable research advantages offered by the laboratory (for instance, probes were easier to store because the atmospheric pressure was identical to that

---

13. Karl Heinz Roth, 'Flying bodies-enforcing states', in Wolfgang U. Eckart (ed.) *Man, Medicine, and the State. The Human Body as an Object of Government Sponsored Medical Research in the 20th Century,* vol 2 (Stuttgart, Franz Steiner Verlag, 2006) pp. 134–37.

14. 'Menschenversuche. Ruff unter Druck. Ärzte', *Der Spiegel* 42 (12 Oct. 1960): 52; 'Ruff. Tadel verpflichtet. Affären', *Der Spiegel* 48 (24 Nov.1965): 76.

15. Siegfried Ruff, H.D. Fust, Heinz Oser and Anthony F. Low, 'Underwasser Laboratorium Helgoland', *Forschungsbericht Deutsche Luft- und Raumfahrt* 63 (1971).

16. Otto Kinne, 'International Symposium "Man in the Sea – In Situ Studies on Life in Oceans and Coastal Waters": Opening Address', *Helgoland Marine Research* 24 (1973): 1–6.

17. Bundesarchiv der Bundesrepublik Deutschland. Koblenz B 196–7299.

18. Kinne, 'Erste Erfahrungen', pp. 296–97.

of the surrounding sea). As in Tektite I, though for partly different reasons, study of the way the human organism functions in a new environment –Ruff's interest – became the main research activity carried out at the German underwater laboratory.

Behavioural Studies in Tektite II

The German and American underwater laboratories were used for different tasks. The Germans were primarily interested in physiological research (how the human body adapts to hyperbaric pressure), whereas the Americans were more interested in behavioural science (how humans react in confined and alien environments). With its highly developed outer space industry, research on human adaptation to encapsulated space had become a practical matter in the United States: an orbital space station, finally realised as Skylab 1973–74, had been in planning since 1965.[19]

Nonetheless, the German and American underwater laboratory projects were deeply entangled on a personal level. Otto Kinne, the marine biologist who initiated the German laboratory, had worked at the prestigious Woods Hole Oceanographic Institute in Massachusetts, where he continued to lecture after returning to West Germany. Siegfried Ruff, co-founder of the Helgoland underwater laboratory, had been associated with Hubertus Strughold, the German physiologist whose experiments with human beings in pressure chambers in wartime Germany had enabled pilots to survive at heights of 12,000 m and who subsequently went to work for NASA, where he became known as the father of space medicine in the United States. Aquanaut Roland von Hentig had studied biology in the US before joining the BAH in 1966, the German aquanauts had undergone a habitability study in Tektite and in 1974 the German underwater laboratory itself was shipped to the Pacific for a joint German-American fishery project on herring spawning in the Gulf of Main.

Tektite II, successor to Tektite I, 1970 was explicitly designed as an international mission. Its 37 participants included Dr. Merrill A. True of Bio-Oceanic Research, Inc., Mr. Brooks Tenney of the General Electric Company, Dr. Jean-George Harmelin of the Faculté des Sciences de Marseilles and Hickel and von Hentig, two of the German scientists who had been members of the German underwater project Helgoland.

Tektite II's first mission ran from 15 to 29 October 1970 and was dedicated to behavioural research in the context of space flight. Reviewing the Tektite programme in 1969, A.B. Joseph of the National Council on Marine Resources and Engineering Development had noted that 'data were needed on effects of long periods of weightlessness and isolation (from Earth and Society) on the psyche, physiology and productive working ability of scientists-astronauts in cramped,

---

19. Robert D. Launius, *Space Stations. Base Camps to The Stars* (New York: Smithsonian Books, 2003), p. 71.

spaceship conditions'.[20] Thus, research scientists examined the reactions of the men in the closed environment of the underwater laboratory, using surveillance cameras. Psychologists used a system of punch cards to record the men's 'spatial' behaviours, noting the specific action performed. Different physical activities (sitting up, sitting forward, reclining, lying, standing, moving around, etc.) consumed oxygen at varying rates and the aim was partly to define the oxygen requirements associated with different types of work. According to one ONR report (1970), this meta-level research was carried out unbeknownst to the scientists conducting the marine biology research. The marine biologists are described in the report as 'subjects' whose reactions in 'true locked-in isolation' were recorded by 'systematic observation'.[21]

Researcher D. Nowlis and his colleagues used the expression 'fit to live in' to describe these behavioural studies.[22] This expression encapsulates the fact that observations of the scientists living in Tektite II were made with a view not only to establishing criteria for selecting crews for manned space flights, but also to determining spatial measurements for space station design. Paradoxically, the larger the area explored (deep sea, outer space) became, the smaller the explorer's living space became. By using the underwater laboratories (which were generally designed for no more than three to five persons) to determine how man uses limited space in a simulated habitat, NASA scientists hoped to discover a perfect equilibrium between the human being and space, in other words to determine the minimum space required for human life. In the event, humans proved to be highly adaptable, and it was impossible to define a 'perfect', 'natural' human space.[23]

Underwater laboratories shared a number of similarities with space stations/manned space flights. Both were simulated habitats surrounded by hostile environments (hostile in the sense that it was not safe for the individual to leave the artificial habitat for the surrounding environment without life-supporting technology). Both involved humans living in confined spaces. Both were 'habitats' with the ecology of nearly closed systems yet offering their occupants the possibility of bridging the distinction between the inside and the outside. Finally, conditions in the underwater environment were closer to zero gravity than was the surface of the Earth. As 'tools' for future space missions, real-time experiments in underwater laboratories were dangerous enough to simulate life within a closed space in a hostile

20. National Archive and Records Administration, College Park, Maryland, USA.: *RG 303 Records of the National Council on Marine Resources and Engineering Development,* Records Relating to Council Program, Records Relating to Man-in-the-Sea, Records of the President. A.B. Joseph, Executive Office of the President, National Council on Marine Resources and Engineering Development, Review of the Tektite Program, 4 Apr. 1969.

21. Pauli and Cole, 'Project Tektite'.

22. D. Nowlis, D.E.C. Wortz and H. Watters. *Tektite II Habitability Research Program* (Los Angeles: AiResearch Manufacturing Co, 1972), p. 8.

23. James W. Miller and Ian G. Koblick, *Living and Working in the Sea* (New York: Van Nostrand Reinhold, 1984).

environment, but far cheaper and less risky than outer space research. (NASA still uses a 1:1 model of the *International Space Station* in an indoor pool to test gear and instruments for space missions.) Furthermore, on account of their lower cost and more limited risk, underwater laboratories made it possible to send more than a select few researchers to hostile environments.

It was necessary to manned space flight to delve deeper into the relationship between man and environment. Such questions were not just of academic interest. They were crucial to the astronauts' survival. Constructing artificial habitats in places beyond the surface of the earth required identifying all the features an environment required in order to sustain human life. Although the dynamics of sending a space ship into outer space turned out to be much more difficult and expensive than expected, observations in underwater houses could be used to investigate many of the practical questions: questions that ranged from how humans use limited space and how living in such a space affects their work to which particular composition of gases constitutes a good habitat and how much oxygen people within a closed habitat consume depending on physical activity they take.

Ecology, Outer Space and the Concept of Habitat

Establishing an artificial environment that guaranteed living conditions for humans was inseparable from questions about the interdependence of man and his natural environment. Was it possible to adapt the human body to survival in other environments? What kind of atmosphere is needed to enable human life in locations beyond the earth? To what extent is human nature circumscribed by man's habitual biological, chemical and physical habitats? NASA scientists began tackling these questions in the mid-1960s when work started on the construction of portable life support systems, technologies which entailed precise definitions of the life enabling system(s) of the earth.

The challenges raised and explored by scientists involved in the underwater laboratories went beyond addressing the practical and technological issues involved in adapting astronauts to outer space. As environmental experiments in habitat and habitability, underwater laboratories and space missions were based on new understandings of human-space relations. Both were 'technologies' for experimenting with relationship between man and environment, with the former being less expensive of the two.[24] Writing in 1962, Orr E. Reynolds, director of NASA's bioscience department, had explicitly promoted the exploration of outer space as a way of exploring the relationship between man and his biological environment: he saw

24.   Christina Vagt, 'Umzu wohnen. Umwelt und Maschine bei Heidegger und Uexküll', in Thomas Brandstetter (ed.) *Ambiente das Leben und seine Räume*. (Wien: Turia + Kant, 2010), pp. 91–108.

the 'space environment' as offering 'tools for analyzing the organism-environment relationship'.[25]

This imaginative project, with its 'post-human' view of human nature, was partly the culmination of a historical process that had begun in the 1940s, when war made research on human pilot survival at high altitudes important, and continued in the Cold War period, when the need to monitor enemy rocket launch sites led to the idea of sending humans into orbit. This, together with concerns about nuclear fall-out 'poisoning' the atmosphere, made testing human bodily reactions in new environments a key political issue.

At the same time, the idea of adapting human nature to new worlds evolved in close relationship with developments in the biological sciences in the 1960s, in particular the emergence of ecology. Ecology marked a shift of focus within biology from the study of the individual organism to the study of the relation between individual organisms, and from the study of an organism to the study of organism and its environment.[26] This kind of holistic approach first emerged in limnology, botany and cell biology, where it was not possible to study the individual unit alone. In his pioneering study, *The Trophic Dynamic Aspect of Ecology*, which appeared in 1942, American biologist Raymond Lindemann had pointed to the need to treat units in landscape holistically and to focus on relations between organisms and their surrounding environment rather than on relations within single autonomous units (organisms).[27] As for the term 'ecology', it had been used by R.H. Yapp in a 1922 article entitled 'The Concept of Habitat',[28] and to describe biological communities by the British botanist Sir Alfred Tansley in 1927. Initially used by botanists and limnologists, ecology subsequently developed into a scientific discipline with multiple sub-disciplines including 'ecosystem ecology', 'population ecology' and 'system ecology'. The ability of ecology to bring a range of concepts to bear on the task of modelling relationships within larger and ever more complex units partly accounts for its great popularity in the 1960s, while the arrival of computers also contributed by making it possible to work with the voluminous data this approach entailed.

This paradigmatic shift went hand in hand with new understandings of the man–environment relationship and greater consciousness of potentiality and adaptability. System theory paved the way for an approach that overturned the longstanding human sense of superiority to nature and reconceptualised man and nature as distinct and equal autonomous agents. This kind of re-evaluation of relations between man and environment became evident in James Lovelock's GAIA

25.　Orr E. Reynolds, 'Space Biosciences', *AIBS BULLETIN* 12/5 (Oct. 1962): 49–53.

26.　On the history of ecology and its various sub-disciplines ('ecosystem ecology', 'population ecology', 'systems ecology', etc.), see Robert McIntosh, *The Background of Ecology. Concept and Theory* (Cambridge: Cambridge University Press, 1985).

27.　Raymond L. Lindeman, 'The Trophic-Dynamic Aspect of Ecology', *Ecology* 23 (1942): 399–417.

28.　R.H. Yapp, 'The Concept of Habitat', *Journal of Ecology* 10/1 (1922): 1–17.

theory, which portrays the Earth as a purposefully acting living organism with a 'built-in', 'teleological' programme.

By challenging the conventional hierarchy between man and environment, a theoretical approach based on system ecology paved the way for experiments that probed the plasticity of human nature and explored the possibility of creating artificial habitat(s) in which human beings could survive. 'Habitat', as the basic spatial unit sustaining life, was no longer treated as a given, but instead became something that man could change and perhaps even improve.[29] With models of a habitat now becoming almost as complex as the habitat itself, holistic simulation(s) of the world seemed to be possible for the first time. Influencing the way the world was itself perceived, ecosystem theory laid the basis for the exploration of inner and outer space. If it were possible to understand how conditions on Earth make human life possible, it ought also to be possible to re-create life-enabling habitats for human beings beyond the Earth.

The 1960s were the heyday of human adaptability studies, as the establishment of the *International Biological Program* (IBP) in 1965 showed. Planned through the International Council of Scientific Unions and the International Union of Biological Science,[30] and supported in the United States by the National Science Foundation to the tune of $47 million between 1965 and 1974, the IBP was similar in conception to the *International Geophysical Year* (IYG) initiated in 1957 to provide an international research effort to examine the stratosphere. The IBP served as an umbrella organisation for a range of research projects, loosely bound together through the concept of 'habitat'. IBP projects aimed not only at developing large-scale mathematical models of entire ecological systems such as tundra, desert and forests.[31] They also explored interactions between historical human societies and their environments. Under the 'Human Adaptability Project', researchers sought to establish the potential of human groups to adapt to difficult environments, including extremes of cold or heat. Significantly, in 1969, Gabriel W. Lasker described the Human Adaptation Projects as being about 'man's survival in a changing world'.

Was it possible to adapt human beings to life in the oceans? This specific question led to a meeting, in Washington, D.C. on 15 and 16 July 1969, where oceanographers, politicians and engineers discussed the present and future status of a national Man-in-the-Sea programme and its technical requirements. The minutes of the meeting show two things. First, that the experts genuinely saw the oceans as a future living space for *homo sapiens* and, second, that they compared exploration

---

29. Stephen Bocking, 'Ecosystems, Ecologists, and the Atom: Environmental Research at Oak Ridge National Laboratory', *Journal of the History of Biology* 28/1 (Spring 1995): 2.

30. McIntosh, *The Background of Ecology*, p. 196.

31. Philip M. Boffey, 'International Biological Program: Was it worth the cost and effort?' *Science* 193/4256 (3 Sept. 1976): 866.

of the oceans to the exploration of outer space. Participants discussed the problems of oxygen poisoning, decompression sickness and inert gases and ventured often deeply divergent estimations of the depths at which humans might ultimately be able to live and work in the sea and of the timescales over which they expected the associated practical issues to be resolved, if at all.[32] Significantly, space scientists such as John Billingham collaborated with the National Council for Marine Science and Engineering Development and contributed to the 'Study of the Present and Future Aspects of Man-in-Sea', which proposed to adapt humans to a life in the sea.

Ecology was thus more than a sub-discipline of biology; it also shaped a specific anthropological definition of life. This double sense of ecology as both a sub-discipline of biology and an anthropological concept is evident in the dual function of the underwater laboratories. Scientists used the laboratories for *in-situ* field research on the marine environment, while they themselves became the subjects of psychological and physiological research. This duplication arose partly because the marine biologists depended on a well-functioning laboratory in order to be able to carry out their ecological research. In contrast to the assurances given in official statements and research proposals, life in a house on the seafloor was risky. Thus, investigation of the researcher's fragile human body under unfamiliar environmental conditions formed an essential part of *in situ* marine ecology research.[33] However, interest in the technological challenges of adapting the human body to life on the seabed was driven by more than the need to address practical or functional issues. The desire to make human life possible beyond the earth, be this expressed as the idea of conquering the seabed or the idea of sending humans into orbit, coincided with and expressed new understandings of the man–environment relation, which was in turn shaped by this.

Planning a Space Station: Using System Ecology as a Manual

The mid-1960s had marked a shift in NASA policy concerning outer space exploration from survival to permanent stay. The prospect of maintaining a manned space station in orbit had been entertained since the beginning of the space age but was made more realistic in 1968 by the successful landing on the moon. At the same time NASA engineers abandoned the idea of constructing a space station with artificial gravity, and decided to design directly for zero-gravity. (The original

---

32. National Archive and Records Administration, College Park, Maryland, USA. RG 303 Records of the National Council on Marine Resources and Engineering Development. Records Relating to Man-in-the-Sea: MAN-IN-THE-SEA Consultant Panel Meeting, 15 July 1969.

33. Bruno Latour has of course questioned the boundaries between field research and laboratory research in science, noting that developments in climate research raise the question of whether the world itself should be considered a 'laboratory' (Bruno Latour, 'Ein Experiment von uns und mit uns allen', *Die Gesellschaft im 21 Jahrhundert: Perspektiven auf Arbeit, Leben, Politik* (Frankfurt am Main: Campus, 2004), pp. 186–87).

idea, based on a suggestion by von Braun, had been to reproduce Earth's gravity by means of a rotating wheel but this was abandoned on the grounds of weight and prohibitive expense.)[34] With the question of adapting the human body to living and working in zero-gravity now a key issue for the space programme, underwater laboratories offered NASA the facilities to test crews and material in an environment similar to zero-gravity. Carrying out scientific tasks in orbit required many specific adaptations to zero-gravity, such as fixed tools and instruments and a careful use of liquids. The buoyant force of water gave a proxy of weightlessness. As Vogt noted in his article for the popular diving magazine, the underwater environment enabled weightlessness training for the astronauts. They could test space walks in the sea, connected to their safe habitat by little more than a thin cable.[35]

The effects of zero-gravity on the human body were not the only challenge. Other risks attached to constructing an artificial habitat with atmospheres different from that on the surface of the earth were highlighted in January 1967 when three astronauts in the high-pressured GEMINI capsule died in a fire, sparked by a circuit in an atmosphere of pure oxygen, while conducting a simulation safety test to find potential leaks.[36] The tragic incident not only led to the use of non-flammable materials and improved safety measures. It also stimulated further NASA research on the composition of gases in artificial habitats and their effects on humans under different pressures, with the underwater laboratories seemingly the perfect venue for these experiments in controlling atmospheres.

Another challenge lay in reducing the weight of a space station in order to reduce fuel and costs. This led to the idea of creating a sustainable habitat incorporating recycling. The theme of the spaceship as a fully self-sufficient living system became iconic. The artist and visionary Buckminster Fuller applied the idea to the Earth itself: Planet Earth became a Spaceship and human beings became its passengers riding through time. Fred S. Singer, Deputy Assistant Secretary at the US Department of the Interior, elaborated the analogy in a 1968 NASA publication on bioengineering and the space cabin. Singer recommended that ecologists and space cabin engineers should work closely together to create a perfect habitat.[37]

It is important to note that Systems Ecology, which had its heyday in academic biology in the 1960s, is primarily a spatial conceptualisation of life systems, in that it seeks to determine the functional interrelations of organisms in a specific

34. Launius, *Space Stations*, p. 71.

35. Vogt, 'Astro-und Aquanauten': 4–5.

36. Andrew Chaikin, *A Man on the Moon: The Voyages of the Apollo Astronauts* (New York: Viking, 1994), pp. 22–5.

37. Fred S. Singer, 'Spaceship Earth – A Global View of Ecology', in W.B. Cassidy (ed.) *Bioengineering and Cabin Ecology: proceedings of a symposium sponsored by the American Astronautical Society and American Association for the Advancement of Science held Dec. 30, 1968, Dallas, Texas* (Washington D.C.: American Astronautical Society, 1969), pp. 1–9.

geographical unit.[38] With its focus on feedback interactions between elements in closed units, the systems ecological approach was thus an eminently suitable tool – a 'manual' as it were – for the spatial planning of created environments such as space stations.

In addition, along with paving the way for a new view of man and nature that stressed their parity as purposeful actors, a system-theoretical approach to the world also led scientists to contemplate the possibility of restructuring the man-environment relation through technology. NASA consistently prioritised the smooth interaction between man and machine and the feasibility of merging humans and technology became a prominent theme in the 'Human Ecology in Space Flight' workshops it ran between 1963 and 1965.[39]

Thus, during one Symposium, held in Princeton, New Jersey in October 1964, Robert B. Livingstone of the US National Institute of Health emphasised the contribution cybernetics – an approach that no longer differentiates between humans and technology – could make to the organisation of manned space exploration.[40] Cybernetic perceptions of nature as a unit with a foreseeable programme played a major role in the conceptualisation of an Earth-like habitat in Outer Space.[41] The assumption that data obtained by observing the behaviour of 'subjects' in one closed system – the underwater habitat – could be applied to another system – the space station – itself shows the close connection with the cybernetic psychology and anthropology that typified outer space research in the late 1960s.[42] Debates about adapting man to live in the deep oceans were thus simultaneously debates about the possibility of new human–technology relations and the 1960s boom in oceanography was part of a paradigmatic revolution whereby life systems were reconceptualised.

The challenge of developing a space station turned on 'habitat' and 'habit-ability', and the artificial habitat of the underwater laboratory provided a close proxy

---

38. Cf. Ludwig von Bertalanffy, *General System Theory: Foundations, Development, Applications* (New York: Braziller, 1968).

39. Peder Anker, 'The Ecological Colonization of Space', *Environmental History* 10/2 (2005): 239–68. Cf. Doris Calloway and American Institute of Biological Sciences, *Human Ecology in Space Flight. Proceedings of the First International Interdisciplinary Conference* (New York: New York Academy of Sciences Interdisciplinary Communications Program, 1966); Doris Calloway, *Human Ecology in Space Flight II. Proceedings of the Second International Interdisciplinary Conference* (New York: New York Academy of Sciences Interdisciplinary Communications Program, 1967); Doris Calloway, *Human Ecology in Space Flight III. Proceedings of the Third International Interdisciplinary Conference* (New York: New York Academy of Sciences Interdisciplinary Communications Program, 1968).

40. Calloway, *Human Ecology in Space Flight II*, p. 27.

41. Chunglin Kwa, 'Representations of Nature Mediating between Ecology and Science Policy: the case of the International Biological Programme', *Social Studies of Science* 17/3 (Aug. 1987): 43.

42. See e.g., Stanley Deutsch, 'A Man–Systems Integration Study of the Behaviour of Crews and Habitability in Small Spaces', Report for the US Space Science and Technology Panel of the President's Science Advisory Committee, 1971.

for the earth environment. Autarchy and recycling became important issues, and underwater laboratories were valuable experimental sites. However, the American Space Agency had its own indoor pools to conduct zero-gravity simulation studies,[43] and underwater laboratories also had functions unrelated to the outer space industry. There were many underwater laboratories that were not connected to a national space flight programme.

Aquanauts and the Cold War

Neither the American nor the German underwater laboratory can be understood apart from their contemporary political contexts. To begin with, the idea of creating artificial habitats on the seafloor was deeply entangled with Cold War debates about the militarisation of the seabed. A scientific symposium on the challenges of underwater physiology held in Washington D.C. in 1955 had already underscored the value of diving research in the post-war military context.[44] With the growing fear that the USA and the Soviet Union might place nuclear weapons on the seabed, keeping divers in the sea became a matter of military deterrence in the late 1960s and extending the period humans could stay on the seabed a research priority.

The threat of militarisation of the seabed came to an end on 11 February, 1971, when the Soviet Union, the USA and Great Britain signed a treaty prohibiting the placement of nuclear weapons on the seafloor.[45] However, technological advances since the 1950s had made questions of the ownership of the international seabed and its resources more pressing. Arvid Pardo, the Maltese delegate to the United Nations, raised the issue in 1968.[46] At a symposium in Rome the following year (1969), experts in international law debated the judicial consequences of allowing nations to appropriate and exploit parts of the seabed beyond territorial waters.[47] Claiming proprietary rights in such a hostile environment was a difficult undertaking, however. A temporarily inhabited research facility the context of global debate, underwater laboratories became tools for colonising the seabed. In West Germany, a highly industrialised country with a short coastline, their establishment

---

43. Ruth H. Fry, 'GE Underwater Test Facility Studies in Zero G. Simulation'. *Space Simulation. Proceedings of a Symposium held May 1–3, 1972* (New York: Scientific and Technical Information Office, 1972).

44. Loyal G. Goff, *Proceedings of the Underwater Physiology Symposium: January 10–11, 1955, Washington, D.C.* (Washington: National Academy of Sciences, 1955), pp. 1–142.

45. The *Treaty on the Prohibition of the Emplacement of Nuclear Weapons and other Weapons of Mass Destruction on the Seabed and the Ocean Floor and in the Subsoil Thereof* was ratified by twenty-five nations on 18 May 1972.

46. Arvid Pardo, 'Who will control the seabed?' *Foreign Affairs; an American Quarterly Review* 47 (1968): 123.

47. Jerzy Sztucki, *Symposium on the International Regime of the Sea-Bed Proceedings* (Rome, Accademia Nazionale dei Lincei, 1970), p. 698.

partly anticipated calls for upcoming international controls on the exploitation of seabed in international waters in the context of a new world order. This highlights significant differences between the German and American projects, which resulted partly from different national situations *vis-à-vis* cold war geopolitics. In the USA the idea of establishing underwater houses was linked directly to the military's strategic interest in controlling territory, whereas the German Federal Government provided state support for ocean research, partly in the hope of extracting mineral resources from the seabed and to keep pace with the cutting edge 'men-in-the-sea' marine technology being developed by the United States and France. Significantly, Vogt opened his article in *Delphin* by asserting that 'billions' of dollars were to be found in the sea-bed, available to whoever could get their hands on them. He expected this 'treasure' to be so critical in the future that oceanography would ultimately replace astronautics in importance.[48]

The popularity of oceanography and ideas of adapting humans to a life in the sea were also related to ongoing global debates around sustainable futures in the context of predicted population growth. In an age when fears about the population bomb and the shrinking planet dominated public discourse – it was during this period that the Club of Rome presented its scenario of a globe with finite resources – only two spaces seemed to be left for future living space: the deep oceans and outer space. In the context of a postmodern discourse of 'man and the biosphere', the project of colonising the seabed, as of conquering other planets, was entangled with the question of achieving sustainability for human beings, and technology was the key to both.

It would be mistaken to think that the project to conquer the inner space was driven solely by Cold War military interests and the desire to expand new frontiers in the postcolonial era. Although many underwater laboratory projects built during this era were partly or wholly funded by the military, including one in the German Democratic Republic in 1969,[49] underwater habitats were also financed by individuals and by private corporations. Enthusiast divers helped to establish an underwater village in Lago dei Tre Communi in northern Italy. When it became apparent that human life was not bound by its traditional parameters, the idea of substituting artificial worlds for the real world and of creating new civilisations beyond the Earth proved to be attractive to many people. In 1964, a special exhibition called *Futurama* at the New York World Fair had displayed a model of a possible future civilization on the sea-floor as well as proposals for settlements in the Antarctic, and between 1969 and 1971, the heyday of underwater laboratories, the benefits of submarine habitats were widely discussed in popular literature.[50] In

48. Vogt, 'Astro-und Aquanauten': 5.

49. Manfred Börner, 'Malter 1. 1 Tauchstation der DDR', *Jugend und Technik (Hrsg. Zentralrat der FDJ)* **17**/5 (May 1969): 408–11.

50. Miller and Koblick, *Living and Working*, p 383.

the popular imagination, the world had become mutable, and the Earth replaceable: the spaceship became the new Earth and Earth itself turned into a spaceship.

Conclusion: The Spatiality of Life and the Limits to Growth

It is not by coincidence that system theory, space stations and underwater laboratories emerged together. Life-support technologies such as astronaut suits and space stations, which provided humans with living systems independent from life on the surface of the earth, were stimulated by ecological research and in turn impacted on ecological discussion, triggering attempts to improve not only the human being but also the environment. Exploration of inner and outer space stimulated discussion of autarchy (life independent of the earth environment), which in turn became a reality through experimentation with created environment(s). Ultimately, underwater laboratories and outer space stations were 'experiments' in the possibility of reshaping human-environment relations. By adapting human beings to unfamiliar atmospheres in which human survival was only possible with a highly technological habitat, these projects reinvented human nature and its relation to the environment.

Debates on the possibility of constructing artificial environments far beyond the earth were part of a broader postmodern discourse of 'man and the biosphere'. To construct an artificial environmental system meant identifying the features an environment required to maintain basic human functions. These questions emerged at a time when the relation between man and environment was being debated in a new way. As Sheila Jasanoff has emphasised in a seminal article, a new environmental consciousness based on a broader conception of the place of man in the biosphere figured prominently as a rationale for outer space exploration.[51]

While it would be too simple to suggest that the rise of ecology led to the conquest of inner and outer space, these developments were certainly interconnected: on 20 July 1969 the Americans landed the first humans on the Moon; three years later the *United Nations Conference on Human Environment* (5–16 June 1972) put environmental consciousness on the international agenda. Outer space and inner space exploration were both embedded in an evolving discourse on the biosphere focused on two paired issues: that of defining the man-environment relation on Earth and that of reconstructing it in environments beyond the Earth. 'Space' became the core research topic in the sense not only that new space would be discovered beyond earth in outer space or on the sea floor but also that 'space' itself would be reinvented as human–environment relations were reformulated under conditions very different from those governing life on earth.

51. Sheila Jasanoff, 'Image and Imagination: The Formation of Global Environmental Consciousness', in Clark A. Miller and Paul N. Edwards (eds.) *Changing the Atmosphere: Expert Knowledge and Environmental Governance* (Cambridge, Mass.: MIT Press, 2001) pp. 309–37.

Reshaping Nature

The created environments of the underwater laboratories and space stations thus both reflected and helped to develop an ecological approach to the world. The idea of duplicating man–environment relation in artificial worlds was itself an ecological idea and underwater laboratories and space stations were its technological expressions. By studying life as system in this manner, the concept of ecology became more tightly defined. Exploration of inner and outer inner space led to better understandings of earth ecology: scientists learned more about how the earth 'works' by developing technologies for sending humans into orbit or to the ocean floor.

The concept of 'habitat' – which in ecological analysis denotes a (nearly) closed system where ecological interactions between organisms take place – was applied interchangeably between real and artificial domains. The marine environments at St John and at Heligoland were researched as 'habitats'. But so too were the artificial houses on the seabed. In this sense the underwater laboratories of the late 1960s and early 1970s could be seen as technological embodiments of key ecological concepts such as 'habitat' that had emerged in the previous decade, concepts which they, together with the space missions, in turn helped to shape. As such, their study provides an invaluable perspective on the twentieth-century history of ecology as a discipline.

References

Anker, Peder. 2005. 'The Ecological Colonization of Space'. *Environmental History* 10/2: 239–68.

Bocking, S. 1995. 'Ecosystems, Ecologists, and the Atom: Environmental Research at Oak Ridge National Laboratory'. *Journal of the History of Biology* 28/1: 1–47.

Boffey, P.M. 1976. 'International Biological Program: Was It Worth the Cost and Effort?' *Science* 193 (4256): 866–68.

Börner, Manfred. 1969. 'Malter 1. 1 Tauchstation der DDR', *Jugend und Technik (Hrsg. Zentralrat der FDJ)* 5: 408–11.

Calloway, Doris H. 1966. *Human Ecology in Space Flight; Proceedings of the First International Interdisciplinary Conference.* New York: New York Academy of Sciences, Interdisciplinary Communication Program.

1967. *Human Ecology in Space Flight II: Proceedings of the Second International Interdisciplinary Conference.* New York: New York Academy of Sciences, Interdisciplinary Communications Program.

Chaikin, A. 1994. *A Man On The Moon: The Voyages Of The Apollo Astronauts.* New York: Viking.

Chunglin Kwa 1987. 'Representations of Nature Mediating between Ecology and Science Policy: the case of the International Biological Programme'. *Social Studies of Science* 17/3 (August): 43.

284

Sven Asim Mesinovic

Clifton, H.E., C.V.W. Mahnken, J.G. Van Derwalker and R.A. Waller. 1970. 'Tektite I, Man-in-the-Sea Project: Marine Science Program'. *Science N.S.* **168** (3932), 8 May: 659–63.

Deutsch, S. 1971. 'A Man-Systems Integration Study of the Behavior of Crews and Habit-ability in Small Spaces'. In United States Interior Department (ed.) *Scientists in the Sea* (Washington, D.C.: US Government Printing Office): VII 1–48.

Fry, Ruth H. 1972. 'GE Underwater Test Facility Studies in Zero G. Simulation'. In Goddard Space Flight Center (ed.) *Space Simulation. Proceedings of a Symposium held May 1–3, 1972.* New York: Scientific and Technical Information Office. pp. 89–102.

Goff, Loyal G. 1955. *Proceedings of the Underwater Physiology Symposium: January 10–11, 1955, Washington, D.C.* Washington: National Academy of Sciences. pp.1–142.

High, W.L. 1973. 'Evaluation of the Undersea Habitats – Tektite II, Hydro-Lab, and Edalhab – for Scientific Saturation Diving Programs'. In H.P. Pulnheim and O. Kinne (eds.) *Man in the Sea. In Situ Studies on Life in Oceans and Coastal Waters.* Hamburg: Biologische Anstalt Helgoland. pp. 16–44.

Jasanoff, Sheila. 2001. 'Image and Imagination: The Formation of Global Environmental Consciousness'. In Clark A. Miller and Paul N. Edwards (eds.) *Changing the Atmosphere: Expert Knowledge and Environmental Governance.* Cambridge, Mass.: MIT Press. pp. 309–37.

Kinne, Otto. 1970. 'Erste Erfahrungen mit dem Unterwasserlaboratorium *'Helgoland'* (Zweiter Teil)'. In Karl Steinbuch (ed.) *Systems 69. Internationales Symposium über Zukunftsfragen.* Stuttgart: Stuttgarter Verlagsanstalt. pp. 296–329.

Kinne, Otto. 1973. 'International Symposium "Man in the Sea – in Situ Studies on Life in Oceans and Coastal Waters: Opening Address"'. *Helgoland Marine Research* **24**: 1–6.

Latour, Bruno. 2004. 'Ein Experiment von uns und mit uns allen'. In Gerhard Gamm, Andreas Hetzel and Markus Lilienthal (eds.) *Die Gesellschaft im 21 Jahrhundert: Perspektiven auf Arbeit, Leben, Politik.* Frankfurt am Main: Campus. pp. 185–96.

Launius, Robert D. 2003. *Space Stations. Base Camps To The Stars.* New York: Smithsonian Books.

Lindeman, Raymond L. 1942. 'The Trophic-Dynamic Aspect of Ecology'. *Ecology* **23** (1942): 399–417.

McIntosh, Robert P. 1985. *The Background of Ecology. Concept and Theory.* Cambridge: Cambridge University Press.

Miller, James W. and Ian G. Koblick. 1984. *Living and Working in the Sea.* New York: Van Nostrand Reinhold.

Nowlis, D., D.E.C. Wortz and H. Watters. 1972. *Tektite II Habitability Research Program.* Los Angeles: Air Research Manufacturing Co.

Pardo, Arvid. 1968. 'Who will control the seabed?' *Foreign Affairs; American Quarterly Review* **47**:123–38.

Pauli, D.C. and H.A. Cole. 1970. *Project Tektite I: A Multiagency 60-Day Saturated Dive Conducted by the United States Navy, the National Aeronautics and Space Administration, the Department of the Interior, and the General Electric Company, Ocean Technology Branch, Ocean Science and Technology Division.* Washington, D.C.: ONR Report DR 153.

Reynolds, Orr E. 1962. 'Space Biosciences'. *AIBS BULLETIN* 12/5: 49–53.

Roth, Karl Heinz. 2006. 'Flying bodies – enforcing states'. In W.U. Eckart (ed.) *Man, Medicine, and the State. The Human Body as an Object of Government Sponsored Medical Research in the 20th Century*, vol. 2. Stuttgart, Franz Steiner Verlag. pp. 108–37.

Ruff, Siegfried, H.D. Fust, Heinz Oser and Anthony A. Low. 1971. 'Underwater Laboratory Heligoland'. *Forschungsbericht Deutsche Luft- und Raumfahrt 63*.

Sandal, G.M. 2001. 'Psychosocial Issues in Space: Future Challenges'. *Gravitational and Space Biology Bulletin* 14/2: 47–54.

Singer, Fred S. 1969. 'Spaceship Earth- A Global View of Ecology'. In W.B. Cassidy (ed.) *Bioengineering and Cabin Ecology: Proceedings of a Symposium Sponsored by the American Astronautical Society and American Association for the Advancement of Science held Dec. 30, 1968, Dallas, Texas.* Washington D.C.: American Astronautical Society. pp. 1–9.

Starck II, Walter A. and James W. Miller. 1970. '*Tektite*: Expectations and Costs'. *Science N.S.* 169 (3952): 1264–5.

Sztucki, Jerzy. 1970. *Symposium on the International Regime of the Sea-Bed Proceedings*. Rome: Accademia Nazionale dei Lincei.

Vagt, Christina. 2010. 'Umzu wohnen. Umwelt und Maschine bei Heidegger und Uexküll'. In Thomas Brandstetter (ed.) *Ambiente: Das Leben und seine Räume*. Wien: Turia + Kant. pp. 91–108.

Vogt, H.-H. 1969. 'Astro-und Aquanauten haben vieles gemeinsam'. *Delphin. Offizielles Mitteilungsblatt des Verbandes Deutscher Sporttaucher und des Tauchsportverbandes Österreichs* 6: 4–5.

von Bertalanffy, Ludwig. *1968. General System Theory: Foundations, Development, Applications*. New York: Braziller.

Vorosmarty, James A. 1997. 'A Very Short History of Saturation Diving'. *Historical Diving Times* 20: 1–2.

Yapp, R.H. 1922. 'The Concept of Habitat'. *Journal of Ecology* 10/1: 1–17.

Archives

Bundesarchiv der Bundesrepublik Deutschland. Koblenz B 196–7299.

National Archive and Records Administration, College Park, Maryland, USA, RG 303, Records of the National Council on Marine Resources and Engineering Development. Records Relating to Man in the Sea, Box 3.

National Archive and Records Administration, College Park, Maryland, USA.: *RG 303 Records of the National Council on Marine Resources and Engineering Development,* Records Relating to Council Program, Records of the President. A. B. Joseph, Executive Office of the President, National Council on Marine Resources and Engineering Development, Review of the Tektite Program, 4 April 1969.

Author Biographies

DANIEL ALLEN is an independent scholar and Fellow of the Royal Geographical Society. After completing his doctoral research on the cultural and historical geographies of otter hunting in Britain (University of Nottingham, 2006), he became an Affiliate Member of the IUCN SSC Otter Specialist Group. His first book, *Otter* (Reaktion Books, 2010), explores the cultural history of otters, providing a new way of thinking about the animal. As a regular wildlife speaker, his public talks continue to raise awareness for the species. Daniel is also the editor of the *Earth* series (Reaktion Books, 2012), a magazine columnist for *Small Furry Pets* and *Practical Reptile Keeping* and author of *The Nature Magpie* (Icon Books, 2013).

WILLIAM BEINART is Rhodes Professor of Race Relations at the University of Oxford. In recent years he has focused on environmental history, publishing the *Rise of Conservation in South Africa* (2003), *Social History and African Environments* (ed. with JoAnn McGregor, 2003) and, with Lotte Hughes, *Environment and Empire* (2007). He co-authored *Prickly Pear: the Social History of a Plant in the Eastern Cape* (2011) with Luvuyo Wotshela and is working more generally on the history of plant transfers, invasive species and biodiversity. William is currently involved in a British Academy funded project on the history of wildlife film and photography on Africa and is working with Karen Brown on local knowledge about livestock management and veterinary ideas in rural South Africa.

TYLER CORNELIUS earned his Ph.D. from the University of Michigan's Program in American Culture in 2010. His doctoral dissertation, 'A River Imaginary: Nature and Narrative in the Columbia River Gorge', was awarded 'Honourable Mention' in the 2011 Ralph Henry Gabriel Dissertation Prize, awarded annually by the American Studies Association for the best dissertation in the field. Dr Cornelius's current research project focuses on the mid-century hydroelectric development of the Columbia River, and the social, cultural, and economic changes that the hydroelectric dams brought to the region. He is Visiting Assistant Professor of History at Western Washington University, in Bellingham, Washington, USA, where he teaches courses relating to American Indian History, environmental history and the history of the North American West.

LAUREN DERBY is Associate Professor in the Department of History at the University of California at Los Angeles. She has worked on issues of memory, violence and rumour in the Dominican Republic and Haiti for two decades. Her publications include *The Dictator's Seduction: Politics and the Popular Imagination in the Era of Trujillo* (2009), which won the Gordon K. and Sybil Lewis award from the Carib-

Author Biographies

bean Studies Association and the Bolton-Johnson Prize from the Council on Latin American History, American Historical Association. She was co-editor of *Activating the Past: History and Memory in the Black Atlantic World* (2010). She is currently writing a book on demonic animal narratives in Haiti and the Dominican Republic.

ANDREW FLACK is based at the University of Bristol, working on an AHRC-funded collaborative doctoral award on the animal histories of the Bristol Zoological Gardens from 1835–c. 2000. His interest in animal histories stems from immersion in environmental histories more broadly, particularly those of the Anglo-settler colonies, and histories and theories of colonialisms. He will shortly be publishing work relating to the imagining of famous captive animals in Victorian London.

AMY HALLIDAY studied Visual and Art History at the University of Cape Town, before moving to Siena, Italy, where she taught Art History in Florence. She completed a Masters in the History of Art at University College London, was research assistant for the exhibition *Figures & Fictions: Contemporary South African Photography* at the Victoria & Albert Museum (2011) and worked in the South African art department at Bonhams' auctioneers (2102–2013). A long-standing editor of the online South African art platform *ArtThrob*, she continues to write about contemporary South African art and photography for various publications.

KAREN JONES is Senior Lecturer at the University of Kent and a specialist in American and environmental history. She is the author of *Wolf Mountains: A History of Wolves along the Great Divide* (2002); *The Invention of the Park* (2005); and *The American West: Competing Visions* (2009). Particularly interested in animals, nature and visual culture, she is currently working on projects related to hunting and taxidermy in a trans-national context.

SVEN MESINOVIC is a historian who wrote his dissertation thesis about the history of the underwater laboratories 'Helgoland' (1969) and 'Tektite' (1969) at the European University Institute in Florence (Italy). During his work, he discovered how important it is to see Outer Space and ecology as related topics. In his writing and ongoing research, he continues to explore the topic of biospace and the close links between the rise of ecology and the outer space programmes of the 1960s.

KAREN MIDDLETON is an independent researcher with expertise on Madagascar. She has published analyses of kinship and ritual in the island's deep south, where she lived for several years. A Nuffield Foundation research fellowship enabled her to train in environmental history, since when she has drawn on archival research, oral history and continuing ethnographic fieldwork to explore the historical ecology of southern Madagascar, focusing on the cultural and economic dimensions of plant transfer.

SIMON POOLEY is a Junior Research Fellow (JRF) in Conservation Science at Imperial College, working on an environmental history of the conservation of crocodilians, c.1950–2010. He completed his Arts and Humanities Research Council (AHRC) funded doctorate on the history of wild fire in South Africa at the University of Oxford in 2010, before taking up a JRF at St Antony's College, Oxford. He has presented his research on wild fire, and invasive species, in Europe, South Africa and Australia and published it in *Environment and History* and *Environmental History*. In 2012, he was the researcher on an AHRC Science and Culture exploratory award for multiple disciplinary research on problems of the environment.

DOMINIQUE SCHAFER completed her MSc in African Studies at Oxford in 2009. Thereafter she worked in the UK and the Caribbean, for Save the Children International, the Bianca Jagger Human Rights Foundation and researching wildlife film in Africa at the University of Oxford. She is a consultant at RB Africa, in South Africa.

JOHANNES ZECHNER is currently a doctoral candidate at the history department of Freie Universität Berlin. After his studies had taken him from Berlin to Tel Aviv and Washington, DC, he worked at the German Historical Museum as a research fellow and curator specialising in the twentieth century. His research interests include contemporary intellectual, environmental and film history. In addition to papers on anti-Semitism and resistance against National Socialism, he has published a monograph and several articles investigating forest imaginations in German political thought.

Index

Index

Index

Index

Index

Index

Index

Index

Index

Index

Index

www.ingramcontent.com/pod-product-compliance
Lightning Source LLC
Chambersburg PA
CBHW050629280326
41932CB00015B/2576